ATHLETIC INSIGHT'S WRITINGS OF 2012

SPORTS AND ATHLETICS PREPARATION, PERFORMANCE, AND PSYCHOLOGY

Additional books in this series can be found on Nova's website
under the Series tab.

Additional e-books in this series can be found on Nova's website
under the e-book tab.

PSYCHOLOGY RESEARCH PROGRESS

Additional books in this series can be found on Nova's website
under the Series tab.

Additional e-books in this series can be found on Nova's website
under the e-book tab.

SPORTS AND ATHLETICS PREPARATION, PERFORMANCE, AND PSYCHOLOGY

ATHLETIC INSIGHT'S WRITINGS OF 2012

ROBERT SCHINKE
EDITOR

nova
publishers
New York

For permission to use material from this book please contact us:
Telephone 631-231-7269; Fax 631-231-8175
Web Site: http://www.novapublishers.com

NOTICE TO THE READER

The Publisher has taken reasonable care in the preparation of this book, but makes no expressed or implied warranty of any kind and assumes no responsibility for any errors or omissions. No liability is assumed for incidental or consequential damages in connection with or arising out of information contained in this book. The Publisher shall not be liable for any special, consequential, or exemplary damages resulting, in whole or in part, from the readers' use of, or reliance upon, this material. Any parts of this book based on government reports are so indicated and copyright is claimed for those parts to the extent applicable to compilations of such works.

Independent verification should be sought for any data, advice or recommendations contained in this book. In addition, no responsibility is assumed by the publisher for any injury and/or damage to persons or property arising from any methods, products, instructions, ideas or otherwise contained in this publication.

This publication is designed to provide accurate and authoritative information with regard to the subject matter covered herein. It is sold with the clear understanding that the Publisher is not engaged in rendering legal or any other professional services. If legal or any other expert assistance is required, the services of a competent person should be sought. FROM A DECLARATION OF PARTICIPANTS JOINTLY ADOPTED BY A COMMITTEE OF THE AMERICAN BAR ASSOCIATION AND A COMMITTEE OF PUBLISHERS.

Additional color graphics may be available in the e-book version of this book.

Library of Congress Cataloging-in-Publication Data

ISBN: 978-1-62618-120-5

Athletic insight's writings of 2012 / Robert Schinke, editor .
    pages cm.
  Includes index.
  ISBN: 978-1-62618-120-5 (hardcover)
  1. Sports journalism. I. Schinke, Robert J.
  PN4784.S6A75 2013
  796.01'9--dc23
                        2013004728

Published by Nova Science Publishers, Inc. † New York

CONTENTS

EDITORIAL

Athletic Insight has now completed its fourth year of collaborations with Nova Science Publishers. As the journal's editor and co-proprietor, I have been mindful of how the journal is advancing as an emerging journal in the field of sport and exercise psychology. Slowly but steadily, the journal is gaining in reputation. The contributing authors in Athletic Insight are often well-established researchers and practitioners, from the global landscape. In addition, the submission rates are increasing with each year. In the present year we have already gained 70 submissions, of which approximately 25% have been accepted. With increasing submission numbers, acceptance rates will decrease, positioning Athletic Insight as a select referee journal in the sport science realm.

The diversity of authors is an additional indicator of Athletic Insight's advancement in the field, as an emerging leader of innovative work. When one combs through the accepted manuscripts from 2012, the contributing authors are from the following countries: Canada, United Stated, United Kingdom, Sweden, Australia, Israel, Norway, and Korea. Hence, the 21 papers that follow feature authors from eight countries. In addition, submissions have been made to Athletic Insight, this year, from five continents. We hope this trend of internationalization in the journal will continue to advance. Athletic Insight's editorial board continues to encourage prospective authors from countries often not featured in sport and exercise psychology to submit their work to our journal.

Athletic Insight also seeks to provide a venue for innovative thinking. Topics that might not be considered in more conventional journals will be considered in Athletic Insight. I encourage prospective authors immersed in new – uncharted topic areas and emerging methodologies to consider Athletic Insight as a potential outlet for their work. This journal is positioned to encourage innovative work, and also, controversial thinking. In the next few years, Athletic Insight will expand its reputation as an outlet for unconventional thought and how such work might then bridge with effective practice. For now, the reader will find, as previously stated, 21 accepted submissions. Eighteen of these papers were accepted through our peer reviewing process, thanks to the hard work of our editorial board. Three additional invited – featured submissions are also found at the very end of the book. These invited pieces were solicited by the Athletic Insight Editor, and each features a unique perspective. What follows below are the abstracts from each accepted writing.

CHAPTER 1

Scientific progress requires a commitment to theory development, empirical examination, and assimilation and accommodation of empirical findings. With growing professional acceptance worldwide, the acceptance-based behavioral movement that began within clinical psychology represents a potential paradigm shift within sport psychology as well. This article proposes how sport psychology can shift from a paradigm maintained by insufficient evidence to a new paradigm that demonstrates empirical efficacy as a performance enhancement intervention. We present (a) a discussion of the historical development of the traditional psychological skills training approach and compare its development to that of the cognitive behavioral model from which it arose, (b) a discussion of the basic theory of and empirical status for acceptance-based approaches to performance enhancement, (c) an appreciation for how the acceptance-based movement represents a paradigm shift within sport psychology, and (d) a presentation of challenges and opportunities in developing an acceptance-based practice for the enhancement of athletic performance.

CHAPTER 2

The purpose of this article was to review peer review procedures and related research in order to offer potential implications for sport and exercise psychology. Publication procedures and evaluation criteria from four sport and exercise psychology journals are reviewed. Drawing upon a limited number of studies and editorials in the sport and exercise psychology literature and a much larger body of research in the biomedical and mainstream psychology literatures, a critique of the peer review process is presented. Issues addressed include determinants of publication decisions, evaluations of the effects of peer review, and characteristics of high quality reviews.

Suggestions for preparing a review, reviewer training, editors, and publishers are presented.

CHAPTER 3

Scholars in sport psychology have begun to create intellectual spaces for the exploration of the self as dynamic fluid and multiple, using autoethnography whereby researchers tell stories about their own experiences. These reflexive "narratives of self" display multiple layers of consciousness, which are intertwined with the socio-cultural realm. Autoethnography is a useful methodological tool to explore the contradictory and complex interrelationships between society, the body, sport, physical activity and the self. However, these forms of research are on the fringes of sport psychology. This paper extends self-reflexive writing in sport psychology into new theoretical territory by exploring two aspects of Foucault's (1988) technologies of the self: critical self-awareness and aesthetic self-stylization. Autoethnography and creative non-fiction are combined to produce a self-reflexive story about exercise self-identity and embodied running. Facets of the story are discussed within the context of Foucault's concepts of critical self-awareness and aesthetic self-stylization, illuminating running and embodied experiences as transformational practices of freedom, which allow for challenging and changing the limits of exerciser self-identities. The paper concludes with a discussion of the implications of exploring self-reflexive knowledge from a Foucauldian perspective for understanding the self and physical activity participation.

CHAPTER 4

Changes that occur in technology and the internet have a strong influence upon the provision of teaching, research and practice within the field of sport and exercise psychology (SEP) and other mental health fields. These influences upon SEP are made even more dramatic given the rate of change in these evolving technologies. The purpose of the current research project was to better understand how SEP practitioners (members of the Association for Applied Sport Psychology) utilize the internet in their teaching, research and practice. Participants (N=292) completed an online survey which assessed demographics, time spent using the internet, proficiency, and importance of the internet in one's professional endeavors. Further questions relate to ethical concerns related to the use of the internet in the practice of SEP. Analyses of the data revealed significant differences between students and professionals, certified/licensed and non-certified/non-licensed practitioners, and psychology and physical education professionals with regard to their use of, perceived competence with, and ethical concern for using the internet in teaching research and service.

CHAPTER 5

Athletes have suggested they use a variety of mental training and preparation techniques in their quest for Olympic glory, including: goal-setting (Weinberg, Burton, Yukelson, & Weigand, 2000), pre-performance routines (Gould, Eklund, & Jackson, 1992a), attentional focus and performance imagery (Orlick & Partington, 1988). However, few studies to date have retrospectively asked Olympic champions what they did to prepare for Olympic gold. The purpose of this study was to gain a better understanding of Olympic gold medalists' use of psychological skills during preparation for their Olympic gold medal performance. Both team and individual Olympic gold medal winners participated in semi-structured interview sessions. Analyses revealed that all athletes in the current study utilized strategies and techniques previously identified in the literature. Specifically, analyses revealed four major themes: process focus, imagery, self-talk, and goal-setting.

CHAPTER 6

Current expertise theory suggests that while variables such as genetics and environmental factors are likely to play a role in the development of an expert, other mediators such as deliberate practice and an adaptation to task constraints lead to expertise. However, empirical research describing the underlying mechanisms responsible for expertise in sport is limited. Therefore, the purpose of this study was to gain an understanding of the psychological components of elite cycling. Five cyclists (4 male, 1 female) from the British national and junior cycling squads were interviewed to determine expertise from a psychological perspective. Interviews revealed that both deliberate physiological training and overcoming psychological obstacles were of particular importance. Specifically, the interpretation of anxiety and pain as being debilitative or facilitative as well as social support concerns were found to effect performance. Implications for expertise development and future psychological intervention protocols in cycling are discussed.

CHAPTER 7

The aim of this study was to examine the perceptions of within-career transition, as experienced by student-athletes striving to reach the international level. Interviews were used to examine the perceptions of 26 Swedish student-athletes with a mean age of 22.5 years practicing individual sports at the national elite level, involved in a career assistance program. Categories identified through thematic content analysis were changes experienced in the transition, the career assistance program, resources to adjust to the new level in sport, satisfaction with their current situation, and strategies to adjust to the new level in sport. The athletes highlighted the value of interpersonal support and commitment, and recognized the need to develop further coping strategies, such as stress and time management. Practical implications for promoting successful within-career transitions are discussed.

CHAPTER 8

Superstitious behavior and beliefs are evident in all sports. The present study examines the self-report of superstitious behavior among 120 male professional footballers in Ghana. The Superstitious Ritual Questionnaire and Sport Attributional Style Scale were the instruments used to measured superstitious behavior and attributional styles of elite Ghanaian footballers. Significant negative correlations ($p<.05$) were found between number of rituals and scores for positive-internality (-0.27) and negative-internality (-0.17). A significant positive correlation was found between superstitious behaviour and positive-controllability (0.20). Simple correlations and multiple regression showed that scores for attributional styles significantly but weakly predicted scores on the Superstition Ritual Questionnaire, accounting for 11% of the variance with the latter measured. This is important in understanding professional footballers' usage of superstitious rituals. Follow up work needs to address cross-cultural differences among Africans and Western professional athletes.

CHAPTER 9

Biofeedback training prepares athletes for activities requiring concentration and motor coordination. It assists in controlling competition anxiety, which is necessary for quality performance (Rozman & Rosch, 2004). The purpose of this research was to investigate the effects of heart rhythm variability (HRV) biofeedback training with emotional regulation on the athletic performance of women collegiate volleyball players. Individual biofeedback training using Heart Math's emWave® PC (1.0) was provided to 13 student-athletes during six weekly sessions. The emWave® PSR, a portable biofeedback device, was given to each player for independent self-regulation rehearsal. The quantitative results suggested the athletes recruited for this study were of high athletic caliber, but it did not support that the intervention improved performance. However, the qualitative analysis revealed numerous benefits of the intervention including a reduction of physical and mental stress, and an enhancement of physical and mental states improving academic and athletic performance.

CHAPTER 10

This study was designed to validate a new instrument created to measure motives for physical activity (PA) – the PALMS (Physical Activity and Leisure Motivation Scale), which was found to yield sound psychometric properties. Regular exercisers, ages 9 – 89 (M = 28.65; SD = 16.48), from over 30 different fitness and recreational facilities in Israel were invited to participate in this study. A total of 678 completed the PALMS questionnaire consisting of 40 items rated on a 5-point Likert scale from 1 (*strongly disagree*) to 5 (*strongly agree*). Exploratory factor analysis yielded nine factors that explained 73.29% of the variance: mastery, physical condition, affiliation, psychological condition, appearance, family and friends' expectations, health professionals' and employers' expectations, enjoyment, and competition/ego. We propose the PALMS as a comprehensive and reliable measure of participation motivation in PA.

CHAPTER 11

Studies on childhood sexual abuse often represent perpetrators and survivors as faceless "them" with brief excerpts from interviews, removed from the person who lived the experience. This study provides an in-depth, first-person narrative from a survivor of sexual exploitation in sport. Inspired by autoethnography, the narrative draws on personal memories to illustrate the profile of the groomer/seducer and his target. The text discusses the processes of gaining access, grooming, seducing, resisting, doubting, and distancing, as well as long-term effects. The paper is aimed to help raise awareness about the significance of sexual exploitation in youth sport for sport psychology professionals. Whereas previous research has mostly provided "snippet" accounts across cases, this narrative allows the reader to follow the development of an abusive coach-athlete relationship from beginning to end. The author calls practitioners to action and for further research to examine how the culture of sport contributes to sexual exploitation.

CHAPTER 12

Research on flow (Csikszentmihalyi, 1975) has traditionally focused on reactive, externally-paced sports (e.g., tennis) without exploring those that are self-paced and stop-start in nature. This study investigated the occurrence of flow in a sample of thirteen elite golfers by conducting semi-structured interviews discussing: (i) their experiences of flow, (ii) factors that influenced flow occurrence, and (iii) the controllability of these experiences. Results shared similarity with existing research in terms of the majority of influencing factors reported, including motivation, preparation, focus, psychological state, environmental and situational conditions, and arousal, and that flow was reported to be at least potentially controllable. Golf-specific influences were also noted, including pre-shot routines, use of psychological interventions, standard of performance, and maintenance of physical state, suggesting that flow may have occurred differently for this sample. Findings are discussed and applied recommendations are made that may help golfers put relevant factors in place to increase the likelihood of experiencing flow.

CHAPTER 13

Evidence suggests athletes will try to regulate pre-competition emotions to a state that helps goal pursuit (Hanin, 2003) and supposedly unpleasant emotions such as anger and tension have been found to associate with successful performance. The present study focused on emotional states associated with optimal performance. Male athletes (N = 222) were asked to recall an optimal sport performance and then completed the Brunel Mood Scale (Terry, Lane, & Fogarty, 2003) to assess pre-competition emotion. Emotion data were dichotomized into either a depression group (that is whether participants reported a score of 1 or more for either confusion or depression on the BRUMS) or no-symptoms of depression group (a score of zero for confusion and depression, see Lane & Terry, 2000). Results indicated participants in the depression group reported high scores of anger and tension and lower scores of pleasant emotions. Among such participants, happiness inversely related to tension. By contrast, among the no symptoms of unpleasant emotions group, participants reported higher scores of calmness, happiness, and vigor along with lower scores of anger and tension. Among such participants, happiness correlated positively with anger and tension, a finding.

CHAPTER 14

Masters athletes are a growing and competitive subsection of the athletic population. The purpose of this study was to describe competitive masters level cyclists in relation to: (a) basic demographic characteristics, (b) motivation to compete, and (c) life balance and personal satisfaction issues associated with training and competition. A total of 397 masters cyclists responded to a survey investigating these factors. The results of this study indicate that fun, personal achievement and fitness/health are the main reasons these athletes compete. Further, the majority of participants indicated that their lives, and the life roles they held, were "somewhat balanced". The authors have provided a discussion and application of the findings that may help coaches and sport psychology consultants work more effectively with this population.

CHAPTER 15

This article studies subjective beliefs about relational issues between coaches and athletes in sport, and how they affect the achievement process seen from the coaches' point of view. Relationship dimensions such as dependency, independency and mutuality are discussed from the viewpoint of how they affect intrinsic motivation, the ability for athletes to take responsibility in the achievement process and achieve better performances. A concourse of 36 different opinions on how relational issues affect motivation, responsibility and development was presented to 18 different Norwegian coaches who are working with talented Norwegian athletes at the late junior and early senior age. The analysis show that the coaches have congruence views about what they believe are the most ideal relationship between them self and their athletes in sport. The dominant view was that the relationship between the coach and the athlete should be built on mutuality. The author will discuss this one factor that emerged from their analysis and behavioural consequences for coaches.

CHAPTER 16

Obesity in our nation has reached epidemic levels. Contributing to the problem is people's inaccuracies when accounting for caloric expenditure. For the purpose of this article, the researchers used the planning fallacy to explain why people may misestimate caloric expenditure. Nine men and women ages 17-34 participated in this study. Actual caloric expenditure was assessed through the use of the bodybugg™ armband apparatus. It was hypothesized that individuals would underestimate calories burned in an entire day, while overestimating caloric expenditure during exercise. Results indicated that individuals underestimated caloric expenditure both throughout the entire day and during exercise. With the proper tools and education, including an accurate perception of caloric expenditure and the ability to engage in a weight loss and/or healthy living program, healthy and maintainable results are possible.

CHAPTER 17

The purpose of the study was to examine coaching behaviors based on youth sport context and coaching certification. Sixty-three coaches, equally divided among three coaching contexts in Canada, and with varying degrees of certification, each completed the Revised Leadership Scale for Sport (Zhang, Jensen, & Mann, 1997). Results showed no significant interactions or main effects for context or possession of certification, which suggested that Canadian youth sport coaches exhibited similar perceived coaching behaviors. These perceived behaviors were mostly positive, with high occurrences of training and instruction, positive feedback, and consideration behaviors. The perceived focus on positive and supportive coaching behaviors, regardless of the contextual stream or formal coaching education may help create environments that foster positive psychosocial development of youth sport athletes in Canada.

CHAPTER 18

This analysis reevaluated the existence of home advantage (HA) within English professional soccer using a point-based calculation that included drawn matches. The analysis also examined whether the magnitude of HA is influenced by the crowd size or the relative importance of the match. Thirty seasons of archival data (1978/79-2007/08) regarding home results, away results and corresponding crowd attendance was gathered for every club in the top four English professional football leagues. HA was calculated as the number of home points gained throughout the season expressed as a percentage of all points gained whether home and away. Therefore a HA value of greater than 50% would indicate a more points gained at home whereas a HA value of less than 50% would indicate more points gained away. HA was confirmed for all four divisions (mean 61.7, $s=0.3\%$) but there was no difference between the divisions in the magnitude of HA ($F_{3,116}=0.3$, $P>0.05$) despite differences in crowd size ($F_{3,87}=226$, $P<0.0001$). The magnitude of HA was no different between high-stake large-crowd play-offs matches and corresponding league fixtures ($t_{21}=-0.3$, $P>0.05$). Home advantage is evident in English professional soccer but the apparently complex underlying causes are not very well understood. The magnitude of HA does not appear to be influenced by crowd size or match importance.

FEATURE CHAPTER 19

The purpose of this article was to review a series of studies ($n = 34$) on psychological preparation in free-throw (FT) shots in basketball. The main finding of this review was that FT performances can be enhanced by the use of psychological techniques, such as quite eye (QE), focusing attention, pre-performance routines, verbal feedback, and modeling. However, prior to the implementation of these interventions, sport psychology consultants (SPCs) should be aware of a number of research limitations and methodological concerns associated with the reviewed studies, among them the lack of data on the effectiveness of interventional techniques in achieving FT success in actual games, the lack of authentic practice, and the lack of qualitative data on psychological profiles of FT shooters. In addition, a number of practical implications for SPCs aimed at preparing basketball players for the FT are given.

FEATURE CHAPTER 20

Physical activity has been associated with numerous physical and psychological benefits and exercise has been considered a "medicine" for helping depression and anxiety, and managing stress (Hausenblas, Cook, & Chittester, 2008). However, exercise taken to the extreme can have deleterious effects and can resemble an addiction. Various terms have been used to label this overexercise behavior, including exercise dependence, exercise addiction, and dysfunctional exercise (Calogero & Pedrotty-Stump, 2010). This chapter will focus on identifying unhealthy exercise patterns and symptoms as well as how to address over exercise behaviors. The importance of a mindful and intuitive approach to exercise is covered with an emphasis on promoting diverse activities for enjoyment motives.

FEATURE CHAPTER 21

The purpose of this study was to identify Asian professional tennis players' stress sources and coping strategies to understand its influences on their performance and subjective well-being during the training and competition periods. A qualitative research method was employed, and data were analyzed by thematic analysis. The results indicated that Asian professional tennis players perceived psychological, physiological, social, and environmental stress sources and employed psychological skills, active coping, searching for social support, and avoidance to deal with those stress sources. The findings also revealed influences of culture and sport-specific contexts in athletes' perceived stressors and coping styles.

In: Athletic Insight's Writings of 2012   ISBN: 978-1-62618-120-5
Editor: Robert Schinke   © 2013 Nova Science Publishers, Inc.

Chapter 1

A SCIENTIFIC REVOLUTION IN SPORT PSYCHOLOGY: CHALLENGES AND OPPORTUNITIES IN THE ASSIMILATION AND DELIVERY OF ACCEPTANCE-BASED BEHAVIORAL INTERVENTIONS

Frank L. Gardner[*][1] *and Zella E. Moore*[2]

[1]Department of Doctoral Studies in Psychology, Kean University, NJ, US
[2]Department of Psychology, Manhattan College, NY, US

ABSTRACT

Scientific progress requires a commitment to theory development, empirical examination, and assimilation and accommodation of empirical findings. With growing professional acceptance worldwide, the acceptance-based behavioral movement that began within clinical psychology represents a potential paradigm shift within sport psychology as well. This article proposes how sport psychology can shift from a paradigm maintained by insufficient evidence to a new paradigm that demonstrates empirical efficacy as a performance enhancement intervention. We present (a) a discussion of the historical development of the traditional psychological skills training approach and compare its development to that of the cognitive behavioral model from which it arose, (b) a discussion of the basic theory of and empirical status for acceptance-based approaches to performance enhancement, (c) an appreciation for how the acceptance-based movement represents a paradigm shift within sport psychology, and (d) a presentation of challenges and opportunities in developing an acceptance-based practice for the enhancement of athletic performance.

Keywords: Acceptance, mindfulness, MAC, sport psychology, performance enhancement

---

[*] Correspondence concerning this article should be addressed to Frank L. Gardner, Department of Doctoral Studies in Psychology, Kean University, 215 North Avenue, Hillsdale, New Jersey, 07205. E-mail: fgardner@ kean.edu.

Athlete-clients participate in some of the most fascinating tasks one can imagine, from speed skating to archery, from gymnastics to lacrosse. These same athletes come to us with a vast array of personal and performance needs, from clinical concerns such as depression and anxiety, to performance enhancement aspirations requiring task-focused attention, poise, and commitment to one's goals. These athletes, regardless of their personal and performance issues, place their psychological wellbeing and athletic functioning in our hands. At each precise moment that occurs, these athletes are convinced that we will be providing them with the most cutting-edge interventions based on sound psychological science and empirical evidence. This is precisely what they expect of their personal trainers, nutritionists, and surgeons who care for their physical bodies, so why would they expect anything else from their sport psychologist?

Yet in many training institutes, private practices, athletic departments, and sport organizations worldwide, sport psychologists are providing performance enhancement interventions that dominated the mainstream over 30 years ago, with little adjustment or alteration of services based on newer developments in basic or applied science. To the athlete, the decades-old interventions seem intuitive. Goal setting *should* help athletes reach their aspirations one step at a time; self-talk *should* help athletes maintain rational cognitions, reduce anxiety, and focus attention; and imagery *should* build confidence by giving a sense of mastery and control, and reducing anxiety. Yet such procedures, known as psychological skills training (PST) procedures (Hardy, Jones, and Gould, 1996), have not demonstrated efficacy or effectiveness after more than 30 years of empirical study and direct implementation, and yet still continue to be the standard interventions to enhance performance in North America and many other countries worldwide.

In response to the disconnect between scientific advancements and typical practice strategies (described in more detail below), for the past decade, some researchers and practitioners have been suggesting the need for change and accountability in the predominant sport psychology performance enhancement model (Dishman, 1983; Gardner and Moore, 2006, Greenspan and Feltz, 1989; Hill, 2001; Moore and Gardner, 2001; Moore, 2003; Meyers, Whelan, and Murphy, 1996; Smith, 1989; Strean and Roberts, 1992; Whelan, Mahoney, and Meyers, 1991), and newer developments have challenged the way sport psychologists and athletes approach performance. During the past decade, one particular theoretical and applied movement (acceptance-based behavioral interventions) has gained scientific standing as an effective performance enhancement strategy with athletic clientele and other high performing personnel. With emerging acceptance worldwide, this movement represents a potential paradigm shift within sport psychology. Yet to understand how we might move from a previous paradigm based on insufficient evidence to a new paradigm based on sound scientific developments, we present herein: (a) an understanding of the historical development of traditional PTS methods, (b) a comparison of its development to the model from which it arose (traditional cognitive behavioral therapy), (c) a discussion of the theoretical development and empirical status of acceptance-based approaches to performance enhancement, and (d) an appreciation for the process of scientific advancement and revolutionary change.

HISTORICAL DEVELOPMENT OF
TRADITIONAL PSYCHOLOGICAL SKILLS TRAINING METHODS

The genesis of psychological skills training methods can be traced to the "cognitive revolution" within professional psychology (Bandura, 1969), which moved beyond a focus on overt-behavior change that exemplified the original behavioral tradition (Skinner, 1953), to a model which sought to reduce, eliminate, or control internal processes such as cognitions and emotions in order to enhance psychological well-being (Beck, 1976; Ellis, 1963;Meichenbaum, 1977). As such, traditional psychological skills training (PST) methods were directly influenced and informed by the theoretical models and intervention strategies and procedures that were in vogue during this period of time. Specifically, PST can be seen as a direct descendent of Meichenbaum's stress inoculation training model (1977), which posited that specific psychological interventions can improve human functioning by developing specific skills to aid in the management and/or control of stress (i.e., life challenges). This treatment package generally followed a three-stage model. In stage 1, the education stage, the basics of the model and its uses were explained to the client. In stage 2, the skill acquisition stage, specific skills such as positive self-statements were taught and practiced in-session with the client. Finally in stage 3, the practice stage, the client regularly utilized his or her skills in real life settings, thus allowing for skill refinement and reinforcement of their use. This model was highly influential in its day, and remains the basic strategy underlying the psychological skills training packages utilized in sport psychology today. However, this model was developed in the mid to late 1970s, and since that time, the cognitive behavioral movement in professional psychology from which it arose has dramatically changed following 3 decades of basic and applied science.

HISTORICAL DEVELOPMENT OF COGNITIVE BEHAVIORAL THERAPY
AND ACCEPTANCE-BASED MODELS OF INTERVENTION

The foundation of behavioral psychology, including cognitive behavioral models, has always included a full commitment to an expectation that empirical research would result in the constant evolution of psychological science. Between the late 1970s and mid 1990s, treatment models based upon the work of such notable psychologists as Aaron Beck (1976) and David Barlow (1988) dominated both the research and practice of cognitive behavioral theory and therapy.

During that time, the skills training models best represented by stress inoculation training were surpassed, primarily based upon limited empirical support. By the mid 1990s, few informed professionals in mainstream cognitive behavioral therapy were utilizing stress inoculation training as a first line treatment strategy. While occasionally utilized as a secondary treatment approach, other, more empirically supported interventions were clearly dominating the professional scene.

While the development of cognitive behavioral therapies led to relatively effective, albeit at times imperfect, interventions for a wide range of psychological issues (Nathan and Gorman, 2002), important scientific developments began to reshape cognitive behavioral therapy in the late 1990s (Hayes, Strosahl, and Wilson, 1999), giving rise to a new way of thinking about human behavior and psychological interventions. From the mid 1990s to the present time, a revolution within cognitive behavioral therapy has been well underway, not unlike the significant revolution that occurred from Bandura, Ellis, and Beck's work in the late 1960s through late 1970s.

Based on emerging empirical findings, the theoretical underpinnings of what has been referred to as the *acceptance-based behavioral movement* take a very different perspective on the relationship between cognitions, emotions, and behavior. While a complete description can be found elsewhere (Hayes et al., 1999), by way of summary, the foundation of acceptance-based models has developed from empirical findings suggesting the following: (a) Reviews of the literature indicate that little data has been accumulated over more than 40 years of research to support the position that modification of cognitions is the essential mechanism of change in cognitive behavioral therapy (Jacobson et al., 1996; Longmore and Worrell, 2007); (b) Findings within experimental psychopathology have suggested that constructs such as deficits in emotion regulation, experiential avoidance, and distress intolerance are better predictors of a wide range of psychopathology and behavioral problems, and are more likely mediators of therapeutic change than the modification of specific cognitions (Roemer and Orsillo, 2009); and (c) An ever growing body of evidence suggests that interventions based upon acceptance-based models are both efficacious and work by different mechanisms than more traditional cognitive behavioral interventions (Foreman, Herbert, Moitra, Yeomans, and Geller, 2007).

These empirical findings in turn led to the development of a different, empirically derived theoretical model at the foundation of acceptance-based approaches, which posits that the *avoidance* of internal processes such as cognitions and emotions (i.e., experiential avoidance) leads to a wide array of problematic behaviors, and as such, the presence of experiential avoidance and lack of experiential acceptance largely form the basis of human suffering and dysfunction (Hayes, Wilson, Gifford, Follette, and Strosahl, 1996; Kabat-Zinn, 2005; Roemer and Orsillo, 2009). Rather than seeking to change, reduce, eliminate, or control internal processes such as cognitions and emotions as is typical of traditional cognitive behavioral interventions, the acceptance-based theoretical model has spawned a number of psychological interventions that seek to develop mindful non-judging awareness of internal experiences, acceptance of internal states, and a willingness to experience these states *while* engaging in behaviors that directly pursue one's personal life values. In addition, these approaches have explicitly posited that the goal of intervention is not necessarily the reduction of subjective distress or the increase in constructs such as confidence, but rather, the enhancement of those specific *behaviors* that directly promote the attainment of personal values (Hayes et al., 1999).

It is important to state, however, that the acceptance-based behavioral model *is* cognitive behavioral therapy. It is not a competing movement. Cognitive behavioral therapy has evolved past many of the models that were presented in the 1970s, as it should given the natural evolutionary process of science.

On the other hand, while practice models in empirically based professional psychology have dramatically changed over the last 40 years, the dominant performance enhancement approach in sport psychology has maintained a commitment to the decades-old cognitive behavioral psychological skills training methods. The maintenance of PST research foci and practice methodology has occurred despite the vast evolutions within the cognitive behavioral traditions in clinical and counseling psychology, and despite a lack of consistent evidence for the efficacy of the traditional PST procedures for the enhancement of athletic performance (Dishman, 1983; Gardner and Moore, 2006, Greenspan and Feltz, 1989; Hill, 2001; Moore and Gardner, 2001; Moore, 2003; Meyers et al., 1996; Smith, 1989; Strean and Roberts, 1992; Whelan et al., 1991).

Given the less than stellar empirical support for the efficacy of traditional PST approaches, and given the evolution of the evidence based practice movement in all of the helping professions, including professional psychology (Moore, 2007), it would seem reasonable to assume that sport psychologists would consider utilizing sport adaptations of acceptance-based interventions to enhance athletic performance. Further, as research in sport psychology has consistently demonstrated the importance of a present-moment task oriented focus of attention and full absorption in the competitive task in the development of optimal performance (Crews and Landers, 1993;Csikszentmihalyi, 1990), it is logical that the acceptance-based behavioral movement would have direct theoretical and applied relevance to the practice of sport psychology. Based on this logic, the first and most empirically tested sport adaptedacceptance-based behavioral intervention was the Mindfulness-Acceptance-Commitment (MAC) approach to performance enhancement (Garner and Moore, 2001, 2004, 2006, 2007).

MAC's theoretical model and manualized intervention protocol was essentially developed as a result of the intersection between the new acceptance-related empirical findings within clinical psychology and the lack of empirical support garnered by traditional PST methods in sport psychology (Gardner and Moore, 2006, 2007; Moore, 2003). As is the case with all acceptance-based behavioral interventions, MAC does not promote thinking more positively or less negatively, feeling better, or becoming more confident, less stressed, or more aroused. Rather, MAC seeks to promote the development of those processes necessary to engage in present-moment attention, without becoming entangled in one's internal experience by judging these experiences as good/bad, right/wrong, and/or wishing or attempting to make them different.

The development of the capacity to be mindfully present (i.e., mindfulness) is a core component of all acceptance-based behavioral interventions, including MAC. *Mindfulness* can be defined as "being with" one's internal processes rather than "doing" something with those processes (as is the norm within traditional cognitive behavioral interventions that seek change of internal states).

Thus, the development of mindfulness supports and enhances one's ability to non-judgmentally accept internal experiences, and as such, promotes enhanced present-moment attention and awareness (Gardner and Moore, 2007). In addition, acceptance-based behavioral interventions seek to promote value-driven behaviors such as effective training, self-care, and communication, on a day-to-day basis, regardless of one's internal experience (i.e., anxiety, anger, frustration, thoughts about possible failure).

Rather than engaging in behaviors aimed at in some way reducing the form or frequency of discomfort, which is known as *experiential avoidance*, these approaches instead promote *experiential acceptance*. Experiential acceptance isa willingness to approach (rather than avoid) all aspects of one's life no matter how or what we may feel or think (Gardner and Moore, 2007).

EMPIRICAL STATUS OF ACCEPTANCE-BASED BEHAVIORAL INTERVENTIONS IN SPORT PSYCHOLOGY

Since the first inception of the MAC approach in 2001, and the addition of other acceptance-driven performance enhancement models since that time, there have been a number of empirical advances. These advances include evolutions both within the basic science of psychology, and intervention studies within sport psychology.

Studies in Basic Science

The most significant basic science advancements relating the constructs of mindfulness/acceptance to the practice of sport psychology have come from studies investigating the effects that enhanced mindfulness and experiential acceptance have on physiological systems and executive (cognitive) functions. Recent studies have indicated that regular mindfulness practice results in increased immune functioning (Davidson et al., 2003), enhanced alertness and improved orienting of attention (Jha, Krompinger, and Baime, 2007), and improvements in sustained attention and attention switching. In addition, Brefczynski and colleagues (2007) studied experienced vs. less experienced meditators and found that the automated attentional process found in more experienced meditators allows for more efficient allocation of cognitive resources, and as such, enhanced attentional focus can occur with lower levels of overt effort. The implication of these findings for sport psychology is that by directing attentional resources more consistently, and with less engagement of attention to surrounding cognitive "noise" such as random cognitions and emotions, the elite athlete can maintain full, or even heightened awareness of the environmental cues inherent in the competitive sport, while simultaneously engaging in sustained on-task attention. Findings in studies of the relationship between mindfulness practice and its neural correlates indicate that mindfulness practice facilitates the development of this more economical mode of using and allocating cognitive (in particular) attentional resources. It should be noted that the *automated* attentional processes found in those experienced in mindfulness practice is in marked contrast to the control-based approaches most typically found in traditional PST approaches, in which regular and ongoing cognitive activities are utilized to first notice and then *effortfully* "correct" internal experiences seen as problematic. Finally, a study by Gooding and Gardner (2009) evaluated the relationship between mindfulness, trait arousal, pre-shot routine, and basketball free throw shooting percentage among Division I male basketball players.

Findings demonstrated that free throw skill, basketball experience, and levels of mindfulness each predicted game free throw percentage, while trait arousal and consistency and/or length of pre-shot routine did not.

The data from this study further indicated that a 1 standard deviation increase in mindfulness score resulted in a 5.75% increase in competitive free throw percentage, which strongly suggests the utility and power of an intervention strategy designed to enhance mindfulness and experiential acceptance.

INTERVENTION STUDIES WITHIN SPORT PSYCHOLOGY

Since its inception with the MAC approach in 2001, a number of studies have demonstrated the efficacy of acceptance-based behavioral interventions for the enhancement of athletic performance. These studies have included a series of case studies (Gardner and Moore, 2004) with high-level competitive athletes, which suggested enhancements in both process measures of awareness and attention, and outcome measures of competitive performance following administration of the MAC protocol. In addition, an open trial of MAC demonstrated an increase in self and coach ratings of performance, as well as self and coach ratings of attention and practice intensity as compared to no treatment controls (Wolanin, 2005). Finally, in a randomized controlled trial, MAC resulted in greater increases in measures of attention and flow, as well as coach ratings of performance (Gardner and Moore, 2007; Lutkenhouse, Gardner, and Moore, 2010) when compared to a standard PST package. The combination of these studies suggests the efficacy of MAC for the enhancement of competitive athletic performance.

Further, a number of empirical studies have utilized similar acceptance-based behavioral interventions that are related to MAC both theoretically and procedurally. Somewhat similar to the MAC approach, the noted interventions have been described by the authors as sport modified versions of Acceptance and Commitment Therapy (ACT; Hayes et al., 1999), an acceptance-based behavioral intervention successfully used as a psychological treatment for a vast array of clinical conditions (Hayes et al., 1999). In one study using an adapted version of ACT with elite canoeists, Garcia and colleagues found that the sport modified ACT intervention resulted in greater performance on a canoeing training apparatus than a matched control of participants receiving a more traditional cognitive-behavioral hypnosis intervention (Garcia, Villa, Cepeda, Cueto, and Montes, 2004). In another study, Bernier and colleagues found that an ACT intervention adapted for use with elite golfers at a national training institute resulted in improved golf performance as defined by increases in national ranking, when compared with a control condition receiving a traditional PST intervention (Bernier, Thienot, Codron, and Fournier, 2009). Finally, a modification of MAC for use with an early to mid-adolescent population (MAC-A) was evaluated via case study, with results suggesting that the age-modified MAC protocol may be equally effective with this important age group (Schwanhausser, 2009).

It can be concluded that in the nearly 10 years since MAC's theory and intervention protocol were established, and 6 years since MAC and other acceptance-based behavioral interventions applied to sport have been studied, sufficient and continually growing empirical support for acceptance-based theory and intervention efficacy as a performance enhancement intervention has been accumulated. Importantly, acceptance-based behavioral interventions have been compared to both controls and what would be considered the most standard interventions to date (traditional PST strategies), and in all cases have performed better. Additionally, MAC and related acceptance-based behavioral intervention research has emphasized not only performance outcomes, but mechanisms of change as well, an approach to outcome studies that has been nearly totally absent within sport psychology intervention research (Gardner, 2009; Moore, 2007). While additional studies on acceptance-based behavioral intervention processes and outcomes are needed in order to continue to advance the science and most effectively assist athletic clientele, acceptance-based behavioral interventions should be considered a viable option for performance enhancement efforts with high-level competitive athletes.

Of course, the growing empirical support for acceptance-based behavioral interventions leads to the following question: If the theory, basic science, and outcome research in both the clinical/counseling and sport psychology domains support that acceptance-based behavioral interventions have garnered empirical standing, will the field of sport psychology willingly assimilate these methods into the mainstream?

SCIENTIFIC REVOLUTIONS AND SPORT PSYCHOLOGY

By nature, revolutions seek to change institutions in ways that the institutions themselves never would. Scientific paradigm shifts often have the same general goal, and typically follow the same general path that political revolutions follow (Kuhn, 1962). At its core, the suggestion that acceptance-based models be considered within sport psychology is a major paradigm shift for the field. The dominant paradigm represented by traditional PST methods sees change and/or control of internal processes as absolutely central to the development and enhancement of optimal athletic performance. In contrast, the new paradigm represented by acceptance-based models suggests a vastly different view, and rather than change or control, views mindful non-judging awareness and acceptance of internal processes as central to the development and enhancement of optimal performance states. This difference is striking and calls into question the very core of the current mainstream practice of sport psychology. The new paradigm asserts different predictions about behavior, emphasizes different psychological processes, utilizes different intervention strategies and techniques, and emphasizes different goals and outcomes. Altering the meaning and importance of previously established and accepted concepts is a key component of a scientific revolution (i.e., paradigm shift), yet it is rarely easily accepted by the existing scientific community (Kuhn 1962). New scientific paradigms, however, typically evolve from aspects of older paradigms that were once in vogue, and the new shift may even incorporate offshoots of similar concepts, theories, and terminologies, albeit utilized in very different ways. For example, while the acceptance-based paradigm incorporates the vocabulary of cognitions, emotions, and behavior, as did the prevailing skills-training paradigm and other traditional cognitive behavioral methods, these terms and concepts have a vastly different relationship to one another and thus result in significant differences in the way that athletes, their performance issues, and the strategies/techniques utilized to serve them are conceptualized and delivered.

As the developers of the MAC approach to performance enhancement, we have asserted that the development of acceptance-based theory and technique within sport psychology came about due to what we believe is a scientific crisis, a crisis of empirical evidence. Specifically, it came about as a direct result of the insufficient empirical support for the traditional PST methods that are often utilized without question for the enhancement of athletic performance (Gardner and Moore, 2006; Moore, 2003), coupled with the substantial impact that acceptance-based behavioral interventions were/are having in the clinical and counseling domains. Yet despite the crisis in sport psychology, which can be seen both in research findings and by the lack of growth and public utilization of the field, there has been a 30-year investment in the dominant PST paradigm. Not surprisingly, as is typical of scientific revolutions, the opportunity for assimilation and ultimate accommodation of the new paradigm was first ignored or minimized. Similar to when acceptance-based behavioral interventions were proposed in the clinical domain, many sport psychology researchers and practitioners overlooked the new ideas and related findings, argued against the suggestion that traditional PST approaches lacked evidence of efficacy by reporting meta-analytic findings of PST investigations, or inaccurately suggested that acceptance-based models were simply repackaged traditional PST procedures. While this is to be expected when previous paradigms are challenged, such responses have relied on inaccuracies that deserve attention. First, the meta-analytic approach is well known to be a technique that can present vastly different results by even the slightest of procedural modification, and as such, scholars have suggested that meta-analyses that are performed by those with a vested interest in the results should be interpreted very cautiously (Barlow, 2010).

Second, the idea that acceptance-based models are actually no different than traditional PST techniques and are simply a repackaging of traditional methods is incorrect both theoretically and empirically (Bernier et al., 2009; Foreman et al., 2007; Gardner and Moore, 2007; Lutkenhouse et al., 2010).

Regardless of inevitable reactions to challenges of the dominant paradigm for performance enhancement, attention to sport-focused acceptance-based behavioral interventions is accumulating worldwide. So, what then can be expected next? The answer is slow, but inevitable progress.

The scientific community in any field has shared beliefs, values, and professional activities. While these binding forces within the sport psychology community keep our passions strong and help us form collaborative working relationships among colleagues, these same shared beliefs, values, and activities can foster resistance to new developments that challenge the existing paradigm. However, as new scientific developments emerge and public pressure to provide efficacious and evidence-based services increases, paradigm shift or restructure will be inevitable.

In this regard, Kuhn (1962) suggested that it typically takes longer than one generation to change a dominant paradigm within a field, yet a historical glance at the evolution of any science clearly demonstrates that scientific communities ultimately embrace new paradigms (albeit sometimes following great resistance).

Psychologists witnessed this in the 1960s and 1970s when behavioral psychology experienced the cognitive revolution, which directly led to a major paradigm shift that dramatically altered the face of professional psychology. Psychologists are witnessing it once again in both clinical/counseling and sport psychology as the new acceptance-based scientific revolution has been disseminated. As a discipline, sport psychology now has an opportunity to embrace the changes in mainstream cognitive behavioral psychology along with the sister disciplines of clinical and counseling psychology, and can find itself at the cutting-edge of the scientific revolution.

While all will not embrace this movement, there are many who will be interested in embracing the challenge along with those of us worldwide who are already taking part in the movement.

Such practitioners may be asking what they can do to begin their own individual paradigm shift and consider adopting an acceptance-based model of practice. The remainder of this article addresses this by discussing challenges to and opportunities in embracing the acceptance-based model.

CHALLENGES AND OPPORTUNITIES:
DEVELOPING AN ACCEPTANCE-BASED BEHAVIORAL PRACTICE

Apart from the larger issue of scientific progress, each individual practitioner has an ethical and moral responsibility to provide the best service available to his or her clients, based upon the best available scientific evidence in accord with the carefully determined needs and values of the client (Moore, 2007).

Practitioners who desire to obtain the requisite knowledge and experience to practice within the acceptance-based behavioral framework do in fact face some challenges, especially as sport psychology conferences and journals are still solidly dominated by presentations and publications on traditional PST methodology (Moore, 2007). We therefore provide the following helpful, albeit probably imperfect suggestions, in exact sequence:

1. Begin by engaging in a comprehensive review of the data in support of traditional PST procedures. The focus should not simply be of the reviews previously described and presented by others, but rather, the practitioner should personally seek out and closely examine the actual studies, noting (a) how infrequently statistically significant results are obtained, (b) how frequently non-significant results and trends are over-reported and exaggerated, (c) the populations studied (often analogue), and (d) the final, exaggerated claims and dismissal of the lack of evidence for the strategies and techniques. The practitioner will then consider whether there is any evidence that the traditional PST procedures effectively and consistently enhance competitive athletic performance.

2. Engage in a thorough reading of the basic theory of acceptance-based models, not from the standpoint of sport psychology, but from the original developers within empirical clinical psychology (e.g., Hayes et al., 1999; Kabat-Zinn, 2005). This is essential, as these readings provide the theoretical base from which to move forward.

3. Read about the variety of clinical treatments that have been spawned by this model, their strategies and techniques, the mechanisms of change that they promote, and the outcomes to which they lead (e.g., Roemer and Orsillo, 2009). These readings are recommended even if the practitioner has no interest in clinical phenomena, as much is to be learned from how these models have faired in clinical trials.

4. Read about the development of acceptance-based behavioral interventions within sport psychology, including the theory, the basic science, the relationship to athletic performance, and the empirical evidence for their efficacy alone and compared to traditional PST approaches (Gardner and Moore, 2004, 2006, 2007; Kee and Wang, 2008; Mindfulness- and Acceptance-based Approaches, 2009). The MAC approach, for example, is a formal, step-by-step, manualized protocol that has been published in a way that walks the practitioner through every step of the intervention process, including challenging client situations (Gardner and Moore, 2007).

5. Read about and personally practice (on oneself) the techniques of mindfulness meditation and cognitive defusion, distress tolerance exercises, emotion-focused/exposure exercises, values identification, and behavior activation and commitment that are core to acceptance-based behavioral interventions.

6. If available, when beginning to utilize these strategies with clients, seek out consultation and supervision. While it is likely to be somewhat difficult at this time to find a local sport psychology practitioner to provide effective consultation, it should be fairly easy to find a local clinical or counseling psychologist that has developed competence in this approach. This individual does not need to have a sport specialty, as the consultation-seeking practitioner already holds this specialty. If consultation/supervision is not readily available, the practitioner can tape sessions and compare these session tapes to the presentations of acceptance-based sessions transcribed in books and presented at national and international clinical and counseling psychology conferences. The consultation/supervision step should only be undertaken once the practitioner has personally gained a full understanding of acceptance-based behavioral theory and interventions. Otherwise, the practitioner will be unaware of whether the consultant/supervisor actually maintains competence in the acceptance-based model.

CHALLENGES AND OPPORTUNITIES TO THE PRACTICE OF THE ACCEPTANCE-BASED MODEL

Given the lack of significant scientific and applied developments in sport psychology performance enhancement practice over the last 3 decades, and given the ever-present desire of athletes of all ages and skill levels to enhance and maintain their athletic performance, we believe there are ample opportunities for practitioners to enhance their own practices by using acceptance-based behavioral interventions. That said, the practitioner may find a number of personal challenges in attempting to deliver acceptance-based strategies to their athlete-clients.

Unlike other approaches to athletic performance enhancement that attempt to help the client think and feel *better* as a means of creating an optimal performance state, acceptance-based behavioral interventions are best described as a means of helping the client maintain attention and respond to the stress and challenge of athletic performance with poise and consistency, *without* the need to reduce, limit, or control internal experiences(Gardner and Moore, 2007). Clients are helped to view their cognitions, emotions, and physiological sensations as transitory experiences that naturally come and go. It is essential that this point be made early and often, as it is the foundation of acceptance-based models. As we have found during the nearly 10 years since we developed the MAC approach, the challenge for the practitioner is typically threefold:

1. It is not uncommon (but is certainly problematic) for practitioners to maintain their own pre-existing attitudes about "negative" thoughts, "negative" emotions, and similar constructs. If practitioners do not fully understand and personally adopt the core assumptions inherent in the acceptance-based behavioral model (that non-judging acceptance of internal experiences results in less need to avoid or control such experiences, which in turn promotes task-focused attention and task-appropriate behavior), they have little chance of effectively training their clients in these core concepts. While theoretically it is relatively easy to comprehend, and is based on

sound and consistent empirical findings, humans often grow up and function in a feel-good culture that actively promotes the idea that thinking "right" and feeling "good" are necessary and sufficient for life success. In our experience (a) utilizing the acceptance-based clinical model with therapy clients and the MAC approach with athletes, business professionals, artists, physicians, and others who must consistently reach and maintain high-level performance, and (b) training clinical psychologists in the acceptance-based clinical model and sport psychologists in the MAC approach to performance enhancement, we have found that the biggest challenge for practitioners is their own struggle with these concepts. In essence, practitioners must first understand the distinction between the change- and acceptance-based models and then personally commit to the model before attempting to utilize it in their work.

2. Similar to the above difficulty often faced by the practitioner, the client may initially have a difficult time accepting the concept of acceptance (see Gardner and Moore, 2007, for a full description of addressing such client difficulties). The very same reasoning noted above holds for the client as well. Humans are conditioned throughout life to believe that "anything is possible" if we only hold the right attitude (cognitions) and feel the right way (i.e., the absence of sadness, anxiety, anger, over-/under-arousal). This is especially the case with athletes who are taught that they must feel little or no anxiety, must maintain positive cognitions, and must feel confident in order to perform adequately. The fact that other than post-hoc correlational data, there is no empirical evidence to support these assumptions does not seem to matter, and it does in fact seem to make intuitive sense. As such, when presented with an idea (such as that one can perform optimally in spite of negative cognitions and emotions) that contradicts their previously established belief system, clients often resist and/or simply do not understand. As we have suggested in the past (Gardner and Moore, 2007), rather than debating this issue with the client on conceptual grounds, the practitioner can effectively validate the struggle that the client has with the concept of acceptance, possibly even noting his or her own struggle to integrate an acceptance-based rather than change-based perspective despite previous learning. In addition, the practitioner can help the client move toward the understanding and integration of acceptance by asking the client to consider the acceptance alternative. For example, we have asked clients to provide the name of an athlete they know or look up to who never has negative thoughts, negative emotions, or undesirable levels of physiological arousal either independent of or during performance. When examples are not provided, we logically present that no one comes to mind because this is an impossibility. Effective control or elimination of such cognitions and emotions is not possible. In fact, the ironic processes of mental control theory posits that attempting to not think or feel something leads to a scanning process that actually leaves one engaged in the thoughts or feelings it on a regular basis (Wegner, 1994; Wegner, Ansfield, and Pilloff, 1998). We then present to the athlete what, then, *is* possible. This patient Socratic process slowly helps move the client from a change- to an acceptance-based stance, while understanding that the athlete's own paradigm shift will likely require some ongoing struggle.

3. Finally, at the beginning of service provision, it is not uncommon for athletes to note that they have previously had negative experiences with sport psychology and

traditional performance enhancement efforts, especially if traditional PST methods have been ineffective for them. In such cases, the practitioner can validate the client's concerns and briefly describe the history of performance enhancement models and the more recent scientific evolutions (to the acceptance-based behavioral model). At that point, the practitioner can present the substantial differences between the acceptance-based behavioral approach and the traditional change-based approach with which they are likely to be familiar. In our experience, this discussion is often invigorating and exciting for the client, and while brief conceptual resistance based on reflexive patterns is likely, the client is typically ready to try an alternative approach.

CONCLUSION

The field of sport psychology is now over 3 decades old and the traditional performance enhancement paradigm has been maintained despite both insufficient empirical evidence and the fact that the original methodology has long been discarded by the field that originally developed it. However, fueled in the empirical tradition of cognitive behavioral psychology, a new scientific paradigm has emerged which suggests that acceptance rather than change of internal states seems to offer a more effective option for the promotion of enhanced outcomes, including athletic performance. As sport-focused acceptance-based behavioral interventions have garnered empirical standing in a relatively short period of time, mainstream sport psychology has the opportunity to embrace this alternative model. Explained within the context of the typical course of scientific revolutions (Kuhn, 1962), there are challenges that practitioners must naturally overcome to personally adopt this conceptual framework, and subsequently expand their practice opportunities based on this new paradigm. Yet, the athletes with whom we work trust that the techniques in which we engage will be the most effective methods for the promotion and maintenance of their overall psychological wellbeing and athletic functioning. The practitioner's time-limited struggle to embrace the new scientific paradigm pales in comparison to the vast impact the new paradigm can have on the field of sport psychology and most importantly, the athletes with whom we work.

REFERENCES

Bandura, A. (1969). *Principles of behavior modification*. New York: Holt, Rinehart and Winston.

Barlow, D. H. (2010). The dodo bird--again--and again. *The Behavior Therapist, 33*, 13-14.

Barlow, D. H. (1988). *Anxiety and its disorders: The nature and treatment of anxiety and panic*. New York: Guilford.

Beck, A. T. (1976). *Cognitive therapy and the emotional disorders*. New York: International University Press.

Bernier, M., Thienot, E., Cordon, R., and Fournier, J. F. (2009). Mindfulness and acceptance approaches in sport performance. *Journal of Clinical Sport Psychology, 3*, 320-333.

Brefczynski-Lewis, J. A., Lutz, A., Schaefer, H. S., Levinson, D. B., and Davidson, R. J.(2007). Neural correlates of attentional expertise in long-term meditation practitioners. *Proceedings of the National Academy of Science, 104*, 11483-11488.

Crews, D. J., and Landers, D. M. (1993). Electroencephalographic measures of attentional patterns prior to the golf putt. *Medicine and Science in Sports and Exercise, 25*, 116–126.

Csikszentmihalyi, M. (1990). *Flow: The psychology of optimal experience.* New York: Harperand Row.

Davidson, R. J., Kabat-Zinn, J., Schumacher, J., Rosenkranz, M., Muller, D., Santorelli, S., et al. (2003). Alterations in brain and immune function produced by mindfulness meditation. *Psychosomatic Medicine, 65*, 564-570.

De Petrillo, D. A., Kaufman, K. A., Glass, C. R., and Arnkoff, D. B. (2009). Mindfulness for long distance runners: An open trial using Mindful Sport Performance Enhancement (MSPE). *Journal of Clinical Sport Psychology, 3*, 357-376.

Dishman, R. K. (1983). Identity crises in North American sport psychology: Academics in professional issues. *Journal of Sport Psychology, 5*, 123-134.

Ellis, A. (1962). *Reason and emotion in psychotherapy.* New York: Lyle Stuart.

Foreman, E. M., Herbert, J. D., Moitra, E., Yeomans, P. D., and Geller, P. E.(2007). A randomized controlled effectiveness trial of acceptance and commitment therapy and cognitive therapy for anxiety and depression. *Behavior Modification, 31*, 772-799.

Garcia, R. F., Villa, R. S., Cepeda, N. T., Cueto, E. G., and Montes, J. M. G. (2004). Efecto de la hypnosis y la terapia de aceptcion y compromiso (ACT) en la mejora de la fuerzafisica en piraguistas. *International Journal of Clinical and Health Psychology, 4*, 481-493.

Gardner, F. L. (2009). Efficacy, mechanisms of change, and the scientific development of sport psychology. *Journal of Clinical Sport Psychology, 3*, 139-155.

Gardner, F. L., and Moore, Z. E. (2004). A mindfulness-acceptance-commitment approach to performance enhancement: Theoretical considerations. *Behavior Therapy, 35*, 707-723.

Gardner, F. L., and Moore, Z. E. (2006). *Clinical sport psychology.* Champaign, IL: Human Kinetics.

Gardner, F. L., and Moore, Z. E. (2007). *The psychology of enhancing human performance: The Mindfulness-Acceptance-Commitment (MAC) approach.* New York: Springer.

Gooding, A., and Gardner, F. L. (2009). An investigation of the relationship between mindfulness, pre-shot routine, and basketball free throw percentage. *Journal of Clinical Sport Psychology, 3*, 303-319.

Greenspan, M. J., and Feltz, D. L. (1989). Psychological interventions with athletes in competitive situations: A review. *The Sport Psychologist, 3*, 219-236.

Hardy, L., Jones, G., and Gould, D. (1996). *Understanding psychological preparation for sport: Theory and practice of elite performers.* New York: Wiley.

Hayes, S. C., Strosahl, K., and Wilson, K. G. (1999). *Acceptance and commitment therapy: An experiential approach to behavior change.* New York: Guilford.

Hayes, S. C., Wilson, K. G., Gifford, E. V., Follette, V. M., and Strosahl, K. (1996). Experiential avoidance and behavioral disorders: A functional dimensional approach to diagnosis and treatment. *Journal of Consulting and Clinical Psychology, 64*, 1152-1168.

Hill, K. L. (2001). *Frameworks for sport psychologists: Enhancing sport performance.* Champaign, IL: Human Kinetics.

Jacobsen, N. S., Dobson, K., Truax, P. A., Addis, M. E., Koerner, K., Gollan, J. K., et al. (1996). A component analysis of cognitive behavioral treatments for depression. *Journal of Consulting and Clinical Psychology, 64*, 295-304.

Jha, A. P., Krompinger, J., and Baime, M. J. (2007). Mindfulness training modifiessubsystems of attention. *Cognitive, Affective, and Behavioral Neuroscience, 7*, 109-119.

Kabat-Zinn, J. (2005). *Coming to our senses: Healing ourselves and the world through mindfulness.* New York: Hyperion.

Kaufman, K. A., Glass, C. R., and Arnkoff, D. B. (2009). Evaluation of Mindful Sport Performance Enhancement (MSPE): A new approach to promote flow in athletes. *Journal of Clinical Sport Psychology, 3*, 334-356.

Kee, Y. H., and Wang, C. K. J. (2008). Relationships between mindfulness, flow dispositions, and mental skills adoption: A cluster analytic approach. *Psychology of Sport and Exercise, 9*, 393-411.

Kuhn, T. (1962). *The structure of scientific revolutions.* Chicago: University of Chicago.

Longmore, R. J., and Worrell, M. (2007). Do we need to challenge thoughts in cognitive behavior therapy. *Clinical Psychology Review, 27*, 173-187.

Lutkenhouse, J., Gardner, F. L., and Moore, Z. E. (2010). *A randomized controlled trial comparing the performance enhancement effects of Mindfulness-Acceptance-Commitment (MAC) performance enhancement and psychological skills training procedures.* Manuscript in preparation.

Meichenbaum, D. (1977). *Cognitive behavior modification.* New York: Plenum Press.

Meyers, A. W., Whelan, J. P., and Murphy, S. M. (1996). Cognitive behavioral strategies in athletic performance enhancement. In M. Hersen, R. M. Eisler, and P. M. Miller (Eds.), *Progress in behavior modification* (Vol. 30, pp. 137-164). Pacific Grove, CA: Brooks/Cole.

Mindfulness- and Acceptance-based Approaches to Sport Performance and Wellbeing. (2009). *Journal of Clinical Sport Psychology, 3*, 291-395.

Moore, Z. E. (2003). Toward the development of an evidence based practice of sport psychology: A structured qualitative study of performance enhancement interventions (Doctoral dissertation, La Salle University, 2003). *Dissertation Abstracts International-B, 64*, 5227.

Moore, Z. E. (2007). Critical thinking and the evidence-based practice of sport psychology. *Journal of Clinical Sport Psychology, 1*, 9-22.

Moore, Z. E. (2009). Theoretical and empirical developments of the Mindfulness-Acceptance-Commitment (MAC) approach to performance enhancement. *Journal of Clinical Sport Psychology, 3*, 291-302.

Moore, Z., and Gardner, F. (2001, October). *Taking applied sport psychology from research to practice: Integrating empirically supported interventions into a self-regulatory model of athletic performance.* Symposium presented at the annual conference of the Association for the Advancement of Applied Sport Psychology, Orlando, Florida.

Nathan, P. E., and Gorman, J. M. (Eds.) (2002). *A guide to treatments that work.* New York: Oxford University Press.

Roemer, L., and Orsillo, S. M. (2009). *Mindfulness and acceptance based behavioral therapies in practice.* New York: Guilford.

Schwanhausser, L. (2009). Application of the Mindfulness-Acceptance-Commitment (MAC) protocol with an adolescent springboard diver: The case of Steve. *Journal of Clinical Sport Psychology*, *3*, 377-395.

Skinner, B. F. (1953). *Science and human behavior*. New York: MacMillan.

Smith, R. E. (1989). Applied sport psychology in an age of accountability. *Journal of Applied Sport Psychology, 1*, 166-180.

Strean, W. B., and Roberts, G. C. (1992). Future directions in applied sport psychology research. *The Sport Psychologist, 6*, 55-65.

Wegner, D. M. (1994). Ironic processes of mental control. *Psychological Review, 101*, 34-52.

Wegner, D. M., Ansfield, M., and Pilloff, D. (1998). The putt and the pendulum: Ironiceffects of the mental control of action. *Psychological Science, 9*, 196-199.

Whelan, J., Mahoney, M., and Meyers, A. (1991). Performance enhancement in sport: A cognitive-behavioral domain. *Behavior Therapy, 22,* 307-327.

Wolanin, A. T. (2005). Mindfulness-Acceptance-Commitment (MAC) based performance enhancement for Division I collegiate athletes: A preliminary investigation (Doctoral Dissertation, La Salle University, 2003). *Dissertation Abstracts International-B, 65,* 3735-3794.

In: Athletic Insight's Writings of 2012
Editor: Robert Schinke

ISBN: 978-1-62618-120-5
© 2013 Nova Science Publishers, Inc.

Chapter 2

A REVIEW OF THE PEER REVIEW PROCESS AND IMPLICATIONS FOR SPORT AND EXERCISE PSYCHOLOGY

Nicholas L. Holt[1] and John C. Spence[2]*

University of Alberta, Edmonton, Canada
[1]Child and Adolescent Sport and Activity Research Lab,
Faculty of Physical Education and Recreation, University of Alberta, Canada
[2]Sedentary Living Lab, Faculty of Physical Education and Recreation,
University of Alberta, Canada

ABSTRACT

The purpose of this article was to review peer review procedures and related research in order to offer potential implications for sport and exercise psychology. Publication procedures and evaluation criteria from four sport and exercise psychology journals are reviewed. Drawing upon a limited number of studies and editorials in the sport and exercise psychology literature and a much larger body of research in the biomedical and mainstream psychology literatures, a critique of the peer review process is presented. Issues addressed include determinants of publication decisions, evaluations of the effects of peer review, and characteristics of high quality reviews. Suggestions for preparing a review, reviewer training, editors, and publishers are presented.

Keywords: Publication decisions, reviewer training, review quality

As the relatively young field of sport and exercise psychology has grown there has been an expansion in the number of specialist journals in the area. The field has also become more international, evidenced by the emergence of international editorial boards and use of

---

* Corresponding Author: Nicholas L. Holt, PhD, Associate Professor, Faculty of Physical Education and Recreation, University of Alberta, Edmonton, AB T6G 2H9, CANADA. Fax: (780) 492-2364. E-mail: nick.holt@ualberta.ca.

reviewers from around the world (Biddle, 2000). The growing sophistication of sport and exercise psychology research has been demonstrated through studies of publication tendencies, which have provided information that can be used to guide future research (e.g., Conroy, Kaye, and Schantz, 2008; Culver, Gilbert, and Trudel, 2003; Gauvin and Spence, 1995; Spence and Blanchard, 2001). Scholars have also commented on the role of the peer review process in the creation of scientific knowledge (Brustad, 1999). Although the peer review process has received little empirical research attention in sport and exercise psychology, its importance cannot be underestimated.

Given the importance of peer review, the current article is intended to add to the literature by reviewing key issues relating to the peer review process from publications within sport and exercise psychology. It is targeted toward graduate students and neophyte researchers to help them understand some of the vagaries of peer review, but it should also be useful for more experienced researchers and possibly even journal editors and publishers. This paper may therefore be important because, in a sense, one primarily learns about peer review through going through the peer review process, having manuscripts rejected (more often than not) or occasionally accepted.

PROCESS AND PURPOSES OF PEER REVIEW

The publication process in sport and exercise psychology journals is based on the double blind peer review process recommended by the American Psychological Association (APA, 2001a; 2010). Briefly, this involves a journal editor sending a 'blind' manuscript, with the authors' identity removed, to two or more peer reviewers whose identity is masked to the authors. Reviewers' feedback and recommendations have an important influence on which manuscripts editors accept for publication, shaping how knowledge is generated (Brustad, 1999).

Although most readers likely have some idea about what a peer review entails, the purposes of peer review are often vague and misunderstood. For example, having completed a systematic review of peer review research in the biomedical field, Jefferson, Alderson, Wager, and Davidoff (2002) concluded that the aims of peer review have not been properly identified.

Authors have described peer review as a remote and mysterious process with a religious mystique (Goldbeck-Wood, 1999). Smith (2006), the former editor of the *British Medical Journal*, reflected that peer review "… is the method by which grants are allocated, papers published, academics promoted, and Nobel prizes won. Yet it is hard to define. It has until recently been understudied, and its defects are easier to identify than its attributes." (p. 178).

To define the peer review process, Kaplan (2005) argued that peer reviewers are faced with two principle objectives: (a) provide constructive criticism about the study presented in a manuscript and (b) decide on the worthiness of the manuscript for publication.

The point is that the *first* task reviewers face is to provide constructive criticism and their *second* task is to make a recommendation to editors regarding the worthiness of a manuscript for publication. Editors then accept or reject manuscripts based on the accumulated feedback they receive from two or more reviewers, their own opinions about the manuscript, the aims, scope, and publication standards of their journal, and the relative merits of a manuscript in comparison to other manuscripts they receive.

PUBLICATION PROCEDURES IN SPORT AND EXERCISE PSYCHOLOGY JOURNALS

We selected four specialist journals in the sport and exercise psychology literature with the highest impact factors[1], all of which follow the APA guidelines, to provide a context for this paper: namely *Journal of Applied Sport Psychology* (*JASP*), *The Sport Psychologist* (*TSP*), *Journal of Sport and Exercise Psychology* (*JSEP*), and *Psychology of Sport and Exercise* (*PSE*).

Aims and scope of journals reviewed. Aims reflect the objectives a journal is intended to achieve. Scope refers to the breadth of types of research published in a journal. By understanding the aims and scope of a journal, authors can also select the most appropriate outlets for their work. If reviewers also understand the aims and scope of a journal it can help them to focus on most important issues they should target in their review. This is important because there are some subtle, but nonetheless important, variations between the aims and scope of the four journals we selected for review. A summary of key information across four selected journals is presented in Table 1. In the most general terms, *JSEP* and *PSE* focus on basic research whereas *TSP* and *JASP* place more emphasis on applied research.

All four journals have a fairly broad scope in terms of the types of research methods they deem suitable for publication. For example, in his editorial to the first edition of *PSE*, Biddle (2000, p. 1) commented that:

> The journal will also be open to the use of diverse methodological approaches. In other words, we will consider papers on the basis of their contribution to knowledge in psychology and sport/exercise rather than adherence to predetermined methods or approaches.

In summary, all four journals embrace a range of research methods, and are relatively applied; but *TSP* and *JASP* may require reviewers to explicitly evaluate the applied implications of research.

Evaluation criteria. At the time the current paper was written, each journal listed required peer reviewers to provide two types of feedback in addition to their recommendations for the publication of a study; open ended written comments and structured scores on standardized criteria. The standardized evaluation criteria used reflect the aims and scope of the journals (see Table 2). For example, *TSP* and *JASP* both included a criterion of 'applied focus' which reflects the practical aims/scope of these journals. *JSEP* and *PSE* did not include an 'applied focus' criterion. *JSEP* was the only journal that specifically provided peer reviewers a criterion to evaluate the degree to which the article is based on sound theory. These distinctions in evaluation criteria are important because they help authors to identify the most appropriate outlets for their work while also directing reviewers' feedback to the issues most salient for each journal. The criteria provided by *JASP* and *TSP* are more applied, *JSEP* is more theory-based, and *PSE* probably has the broadest scope – all issues reflected by the stated aims of the journals.

---

[1] Impact factor is a measure based on the average number of citations to articles published in journals. Although there are some controversies concerning the value of impact factors for judging a journal, impact factor score is often used as a proxy for the relative importance of a journal in a field. Arguably, journals with higher impact factors are considered more influential than journals with lower impact factors.

Table 1. Main Sport Psychology Journals: Summary of Publication Details

Journal	Organization	Aims and Scope [a]	Publication types [a]	Issues per year	Review [a] Protocol	Impact Factor [b]
JSEP	North American Society for Psychology of Sport and Physical Activity	…to stimulate and communicate research and theory in all areas of sport and exercise psychology… Emphasizes original research reports that advance understanding of human behavior as it relates to sport and exercise. Areas of interest include research in social, clinical, developmental, and experimental psychology, as well as psychobiology and personality.	Review articles and single-study experimental/ methodological reports. Multi-study reports encouraged.	6	APA Double Blind	2005: 1.167 2006: 1.457 2007: 1.719 2008: 2.118 2009: 2.951
PSE	Journal of the European Federation of Sport Psychology	…an international forum for scholarly reports in the psychology of sport and exercise, broadly defined.	High quality research and comprehensive research reviews. Reports of professional practice must demonstrate academic rigour, preferably through analysis of program effectiveness, and go beyond mere description.	6	APA Double Blind	2005: 1.281 2006: 1.394 2007: 1.192 2008: 1.568 2009: 2.152
TSP	N/A	…focuses on applied research and its application in providing psychological services to coaches and athletes… a forum to stimulate thought and disseminate knowledge that focuses on the application and practice of sport psychology… special emphasis on the delivery of psychological services to athletes and coaches.	Applied Research that focuses directly upon application and practice in sport psychology. Review articles, clinical observations, professional practice, case studies, field studies, evaluation research, methodological and measurement issues. Qualitative and other emerging research methods.	4	APA Double Blind	2005: 0.906 2006: 0.887 2007: 0.732 2008: 0.893 2009: 1.345

Journal	Organization	Aims and Scope [a]	Publication types [a]	Issues per year	Review [a] Protocol	Impact Factor [b]
JASP	Association for Applied Sport Psychology	… to advance thought, theory, and research on applied aspects of sport and exercise psychology… to promote the development of psychological theory, research, and intervention strategies in sport psychology.	Position papers, reviews, theoretical developments specific to sport and/or exercise and applied research conducted in these settings or having significant applied implications to sport and exercise.	4	APA Double Blind	2005: 0.906 2006: 1.220 2007: 1.250 2008: 1.093 2009: 1.295

[a] Information obtained from journal websites.
[b] Journal Citation Reports® published by Thomson Scientific.

Table 2. Evaluation Criteria for Four Sport and Exercise Psychology Journals

Journal	Scale	Standardized Evaluation Criteria
JSEP	1-5 Likert scale rating, with 5 indicating greatest degree or best, and 1 indicating least degree or poor.	How relevant is the topic of the article to the field? How clear is the research question? How original is the research question? To what degree is the article based on sound theory? How appropriate in the methodology? How thorough is the data analysis? How informative is the interpretation of results? To what extent does the discussion yield new insights? How clear is the writing?
PSE	1-3 Likert scale rating, with 3 being the highest and 1 being the lowest.	Clarity of objectives Introduction and literature review Method Validity of assumptions Quality of analyses Extent to which the interpretations/conclusions are supported by the data Overall significance of the work
TSP	5 point scale ranging from not applicable, to poor, marginal, adequate, and good.	Applied focus Contribution to knowledge Methodology–design Data analysis Discussion or interpretation Clarity of writing
JASP	6 point scale ranging from not applicable to outstanding, good, adequate, marginal, and poor.	Importance of topic Contribution to knowledge Applied focus Analysis of data Clarity of writing Quality of manuscript

Acceptance rates. Another relevant issue for the peer review process concerns manuscript acceptance rates. As shown in Table 3, the probability of manuscripts making it through to publication is relatively low, with acceptance rates ranging from ~14 to 33% in the past few years.

Table 3. Approximate Manuscript Acceptance Rates 2003-2007

Journal	Manuscript acceptance rates					
	2003-2004	2004-2005	2005-2006	2006-2007	2007-08	2008-2009
JSEP [a]	15%	19.9%	16.8%	16.8%	20.3%	14.7%
PSE [b]	--	30%	32%	16%	33%	At time current paper written: To date: 11%
TSP [c]	--	14%	19.68%	18.26%	24.3[e]	26.1[e]
JASP [d]	--	23%	17%	17.5%	14%	16%

Note: Typical manuscript acceptance year runs from October to following September.
[a] Personal communication from Bob Eklund (Editor, JSEP), February 1 and August 16 2009.
[b]Personal communications from Martin Hagger (Co-Editor, PSE) May 1, 2008 and PSE Editorial staff January 9 and August 15, 2009.
[c] Personal communication from Ian Maynard (Editor, TSP), February 1, 2008.
[d] Personal communication for Stephanie Hanrahan (Editor, JASP), May 2, 2008 and August 16, 2009.
[e] The Sport Psychologist, 2009 Annual Report.

For purposes of comparison, in 2000 approximately 27% of manuscripts submitted to 25 APA journals were accepted for publication (APA, 2001b) and a similar acceptance rate is present in medical journals (Hojat, Gonella, and Caelleigh, 2003). These figures show that most reviewers recommend rejecting manuscripts far more often than they recommend manuscripts be accepted for publication.

Who completes reviews? Peer reviews are completed by editorial board members and guest reviewers. For example, Brustad (1999) reported that of 271 manuscripts submitted to *JSEP* in 1998, 21 editorial board members and 137 guest reviewers completed reviews. From September 1, 2006 to September 1, 2007, *JASP* had 25 board members and used 82 guest reviewers. Clearly guest reviewers serve an important role; without them journals would be unlikely to function efficiently.

Editorial board members are drawn from several countries. For example, in March 2008 the *TSP* board comprised 24 members from the following countries: U.S. (n = 12), Canada (n = 2), U.K. (n = 6), Australia (n = 2), New Zealand (n = 1), and Sweden (n = 1). In 2008 there were 25 members of the *JASP* editorial board with 19 being from the U.S., 3 from Canada, and 3 from the U.K. In September 2008 the *JSEP* board comprised 29 members, with 20 being from the U.S., 4 from the U.K., 3 from Canada, 2 from Australia. In 2008, *PSE* had 22 board members; 5 from the U.K., 3 from the U.S., 2 from Greece, and one from each of the following countries: Australia, Canada, Netherlands, Turkey, Spain, Japan, Finland, Norway, Germany, Sweden, Switzerland, and Belgium.

Whereas Biddle (2000) reflected that editorial boards have become increasingly international, the snapshot of board membership listed above shows that academics from English-speaking institutions, primarily from the U.S., dominate editorial boards. This is not necessarily a criticism as it reflects the North American roots of the journals/professional organizations and the long-standing history of sport and exercise psychology on that continent. Indeed, the *PSE*, as the journal of FEPSAC, reflects the European origins of that professional organization.

Research trends. All four journals selected for this review are open to diverse methodological approaches. However, previous reviews of research trends in sport and exercise psychology have shown that a small number of research designs dominated the literature. For example, Conroy et al. (2008) coded articles published in the first 26 volumes of *JSEP*. They found that over the entire 26-year period an average 84% of articles were original empirical reports (with averages ranging from 67% to 97% across the 26 years). Of those empirical reports approximately 93% were based on quantitative data. In terms of the research designs used in these quantitative studies, 63% were coded as passive observational (i.e., cross-sectional survey) designs, 34% experimental or quasi-experimental, and less than 1% were single case study designs. Biddle (2000) also noted the dominance of cross-sectional survey designs versus experimental and quasi-experimental research, and urged sport and exercise psychology researchers to engage in more randomized controlled trials, large-scale meta-analyses, and in-depth qualitative studies.

Culver et al. (2003) examined qualitative studies published in the leading sport and exercise psychology journals between 1990 and 1999. Having identified 84 articles that used qualitative data, these studies were primarily characterized by the use of one-time interviews and inter-rater reliability tests to ensure the consistency of analysis. Brustad (2008) suggested that the strong reliance on a single type of qualitative research – the individual interview – may limit knowledge generation, and noted that a more diverse range of qualitative methodologies are starting to be published, including grounded theory (e.g., Holt and Dunn, 2004) and ethnography (e.g., Faulkner and Sparkes, 1999). Similarly, over-reliance on cross-sectional designs may limit researchers. Hence, a need remains for researchers to ask a variety of research questions and use a range of research designs (cf. Biddle, 2000). Furthermore, reviewers should be open to novel methodologies and be motivated to learn more about new approaches in order to provide high quality reviews (Brustad, 1999).

RESEARCH EXAMINING THE PEER REVIEW PROCESS

Examined publication determinants. The most important factor in judging the overall merit of a manuscript for publication is the extent to which it makes a unique contribution to the literature in a given area (e.g., the key question for the current paper concerns whether or not it stimulates critical thought, and/or new researchers' knowledge about the peer review process in sport and exercise psychology). However, there is little direct evidence evaluating determinants of publication decisions in sport and exercise psychology. Fortunately, guidance and research have been provided in other disciplines, along with some related studies in the sport and exercise psychology literature.

According to the APA (2001a), editors typically find the following defects in the design and reporting of research: (a) piecemeal publication, which is the separation of a single substantial report into a series of overlapping papers, (b) reporting only a single correlation, because a significant correlation between two variables rarely has any interpretable value, (c) reporting null results without attention to power analyses, (d) lack of congruence between a study's specific operations (including design and analysis) with the authors' discussion of the outcomes (e.g., failure to report the statistical test at the level being claimed), (d) failure to report effect sizes, (e) failure to build in needed controls, and (f) exhaustion of a problem, which is the endless production of papers that report trivial changes to previous research rather than ongoing research which explores the limits of generality of existing findings.

Spence and Blanchard (2001) examined publication bias (i.e., the tendency to publish studies reporting statistically significant findings and rejecting the null hypothesis) in manuscripts published in five sport and exercise psychology journals in 1987, 1992, and 1997. Studies were coded according to whether null hypothesis tests had been conducted and if these tests resulted in a rejection of the null hypothesis. Spence and Blanchard found that 98% of published articles had at least one significant finding and 80% rejected the null hypothesis. They concluded that publication bias existed in sport and exercise psychology and an editor's decision to publish a study was heavily influenced by the direction and strength of study results. Such a focus on statistical significance leads to the file drawer problem (Rosenthal, 1979) whereby studies with non-significant findings are condemned to the authors' file drawers.

Publication bias has implications for theory development and empirical understanding. It may, in fact, influence the evidence base that guides applied sport psychology practice. For example, Weinberg and Comar (1994) reviewed 45 studies that used psychological skills interventions in competitive sport settings. They found that 85% (35 studies) showed positive performance effects. But what if studies with non-significant findings have been condemned to researchers' file drawers? If intervention studies with non-significant findings remain unpublished this could create a false sense of confidence in the use of certain types of psychological skills training techniques. The point is, "More emphasis ought to be placed on the quality of the work (e.g., method and design), the author's reasoning, the magnitude of the effect or relationship measured, and the relevance of the findings" (Spence and Blanchard, 2001, p. 396).

Use of the double blind peer review protocol. Studies examining the effects of double-blind reviews have produced equivocal findings. For example, some studies have revealed that concealing the identity of the reviewer and/or author tended to have a small but positive effect on review quality (e.g., Fisher, Friedman, and Strauss, 1994; McNutt, Evans, Fletcher, and Fletcher, 1990). On the other hand, Jefferson, Alderson et al. (2002) conducted a systematic review of studies in the medical literature and found no conclusive evidence for the effects of double blind review on review quality. In fact, in the absence of compelling evidence supporting the double blind peer review, the journal *Academic Medicine* abandoned its blind review policy (see Shea, Caelleigh, Pangaro, and Steinecke, 2001).

There do not appear to be any studies in the sport and exercise psychology literature testing the effects of blind peer review on review or publication quality. This is likely an issue that requires research attention in the future. Interestingly, some research in other disciplines suggested that blinding manuscripts is problematic because up to 50% of peer reviewers were able to determine the authors' identity by their reputation for conducting research in a particular subject matter (Fisher, et al., 1994). Indeed, authors' reputations in a particular area have also been revealed as a determinant of publication decisions (Coelho and La Forge,

2000). In a relatively small field like sport and exercise psychology reviewers are likely often able to identify authors because of their well-established reputations in particular areas of research. Another problem may be that authors may cite their own work and self-reference (some reviewers may do the same thing). However, the APA (2001a) stated that "authors are responsible for concealing their identities in manuscripts that are to receive a masked review" (p. 361). To help protect the integrity of the blind peer review authors should make every attempt to conceal their identity, and editors may even return manuscripts to authors who failed to fulfill this expectation.

Use of standardized criteria. The leading sport and exercise psychology journals use standardized criteria in addition to open-ended comments. Standardizing criteria is appealing because it provides a means of comparing the perspectives of different reviewers. Furthermore, Arkes (2003) recommended that peer-review ratings sould be converted into z-scores to limit the amount of variance in reviews attributable to manuscript quality (which is a function available to sport and exercise psychology journals that use the Manuscript Central/Scholar One website). However, there is limited empirical evidence for the benefits of using standardized checklists. Gardner and Bond (1990) assessed 45 submissions to *BMJ* and found that using a checklist was associated with improved statistical quality of the published studies. Alternatively, Jefferson, Wager, and Davidoff (2002) found no apparent impact on submission quality due to publishing checklist guidelines for submissions in the medical literature. Jefferson and colleagues speculated that standardized criteria may have some benefits for the 'publication process because they provide editors with consistent and comparable information between reviewers. But there is no clear evidence that standardized criteria improve the quality of peer reviews. One reason for the lack of evidence may be because the extent to which editors use standardized scores to make their decisions is unclear. Editors may rely on reviewers' open-ended comments and criticisms more than the standardized scores provided. An implication for sport and exercise psychology editors could be to ensure the decision-making process is as transparent as possible.

EXAMINING REVIEW QUALITY

Characteristics of good reviews. In his *JSEP* editorial, Brustad (1999) proposed three characteristics of a high quality review. First, the review should be written in a collegial tone. This has been referred to as the 'Matthew Principle' -- do unto others as you would have them do to you (Cummings and Rivara, 2002). Second, reviewers should view themselves as a mentor rather than a judge. Third, good reviews should focus the author's attention on major conceptual, methodological, and interpretative issues that are at the crux of the contribution a manuscript may make to knowledge. Reviewers should not disproportionately comment on minor issues.

Weiss (1994a; 1994b; 1995) provided three editorials on manuscript quality while she was editor of *Research Quarterly for Exercise and Sport* (*RQES*). These editorials provide useful guidelines for authors and may also help guide peer reviewers. In the first editorial (1994a) she provided a series of suggestions for how to structure the introduction section to a manuscript and some key questions authors should reflect upon. In the second editorial (1994b) she addressed ways in which authors should structure their method section in order to provide sufficient information to satisfy peer reviewers. Finally, Weiss (1995) summarized how authors should structure their results section to systematically lead the reader to desired answers. Together, these editorials provide some standards by which the quality of manuscripts may be judged and could provide a foundation for future research in sport and exercise psychology that examines effects of the peer review process.

Interestingly, authors' responses to peer reviews do not appear to be predicated on the quality of the reviews they receive. Weber, Katz, Waeckerle and Callaham (2002) surveyed 576 contributors to the *Annals of Emergency Medicine* between May 1999 and October 2000 to determine authors' perceptions of peer review and the association between quality of review and author satisfaction. Those authors with rejected manuscripts were more likely than those with accepted manuscripts to be dissatisfied with the turnaround time to decision and their communication with the journal editor. Author satisfaction was predicated on manuscript acceptance but not with the quality of the review. Hence, authors appear to be more interested in the outcome (i.e., acceptance) rather than the process (i.e., review quality).

Characteristics of good reviewers. Brustad (1999) suggested that good reviewers possess subject matter expertise and motivation to learn about new methodological techniques that are outside their initial training and knowledge. Researchers in the medical field have empirically examined the personal qualities of a good reviewer. Black, van Rooyan, Godless, Smith and Evans (1998) obtained information (demographics, details of their training, and experience) from 507 reviewers of 420 manuscripts. High quality reviews were identified using authors' and editors' subjective assessment of review quality. Two personal factors were associated with higher quality reviews. First, reviewers trained in epidemiology or statistics provided high quality reviews. Second, younger reviewers received higher quality assessments from editors. In addition to personal characteristics, review quality increased with time spent on the review, but only up to three hours; spending more than three hours on a review was not associated with improved quality.

In a similar study, Evans, McNutt, Fletcher, and Fletcher (1993) examined review quality among 226 reviewers of 131 manuscripts of original research consecutively submitted to *The Journal of General Internal Medicine*. Review quality was judged on a 1 to 5 scale by an editor who was blinded to the identity of the reviewer. Personal characteristics of reviewers were taken from their curricula vitae. Results showed that 43% of reviewers produced good reviews (i.e., their reviews received a score of 4 or 5). Good reviewers tended to be young (< 40 years old), from prestigious academic institutions, and well known to the editor (even though the reviewers' identity was concealed), and blinded to the authors' identity. There was an 87% probability that reviewers with these characteristics would produce a good review. A reviewer who did not possess any of these characteristics had a 7% probability of producing a good review.

Review bias. Review bias is not random error but "any systematic effect on rating unrelated to the true quality of the object being rated" (Blackburn and Hakel, 2006, p. 378). To test review bias Blackburn and Hakel examined ratings of poster quality among reviewers and non-reviewers for 1,983 posters submitted to three psychology conferences. Whereas reviews of conference posters were likely less rigorous than the journal manuscript peer review process, this study did provide some relevant findings concerning reviewer bias. Reviewers who authored posters gave lower average quality ratings than reviewers who did not author posters. Additionally, posters submitted by reviewers were rated of significantly higher quality than posters submitted by non-reviewers. These findings suggest that reviewers may implicitly compare the posters they review to their own work and perceive that their own work is of higher quality. This reflects the tendency for people to believe their own work is 'better-than-average.' Van Lange (1999) applied the better-than-average effect to the manuscript review process and found that reviewers rated their own research significantly higher than that of other authors.

As the better-than-average effect implies, reviewing manuscripts involves subjective factors (Kassirer and Campion, 1994). While reviewers should strive to eliminate any personal bias toward an author's subject matter (APA, 1992), they tend to evaluate manuscripts with reference to their own experience and knowledge of a subject area (Coelho and La Forge, 1996). Reviewers bring a mix of their preferences and moods to the review process (King, McGuire, Longman, and Carroll-Johnson, 1997). Criticisms of reviewer bias have also included accusations of sexism and nepotism (e.g., Della Salla and Grafman, 2002; Jelicic and Merckelbach, 2002; Nylenna, Riis, and Karisson, 1994). Based on the available evidence it is fair to conclude that peer review is not, and never has been, a strictly objective process.

SUGGESTIONS FOR SPORT AND EXERCISE PSYCHOLOGY

Suggestions for Producing a Review

Pre-review. Prior to engaging with the process reviewers should understand the objectives of the peer review; to first provide constructive criticism and, *second*, a recommendation about the worthiness of the manuscript for publication (cf. Kaplan, 2005). Next, given the distinctions between journals in sport and exercise psychology (See Table 1), reviewers should be aware of the aims and scope of a particular journal to help them understand how to evaluate a manuscript and frame their feedback.

Another 'pre-review' issue is the difficult decision of how many peer reviews to accept. A colleague [Dr. Kerry Courneya] uses a type of 'homeostasis principle.' That is, for every first authored paper he submits to a journal he is prepared to complete two peer reviews, because his submission will have inconvenienced at least two other reviewers in his discipline. In this way, equilibrium in distribution of peer reviews across the field is (theoretically) maintained.

Writing a review. Studies have shown that reviewers spend somewhere between 1.5 and 6 hours reviewing manuscripts (Armstrong, 1996; Nylenna et al., 1994), but spending more than three hours on a review was not associated with increased quality (Black et al., 1998). This provides a very rough guide to the amount of time reviewers may wish to set aside to complete their reviews. We suggest that reviewers first read the manuscript, perhaps making rough notes, before they start to write their review. When the writing begins, reviewers should focus on major conceptual issues and avoid disproportionately commenting on minor issues (Brustad, 1999). The editorials provided by Weiss (1994a; 1994b; 1995) provide guidance on specific conceptual issues that require attention. Reviewers should remember the 'Matthew Principle' and ensure they spend adequate time editing and crafting their review for collegial tone.

Finally, reviewers must realize they bring their own personal biases to the review process (e.g., Coelho and La Forge, 1996; King et al., 1997). Drotar (2008) suggested that one safeguard to establish scientific integrity is that reviewers should recognize and appreciate their biases. That is, reviewers need to be aware they are not immune to their own preferences about science and methods. Stating bias would be most relevant if a reviewer's comments are grounded in a particular school of thought where there is some controversy on a matter. For example, sport psychology researchers have debated different views about achievement goal theory in the literature (see Harwood, Hardy, and Swain, 2000; Harwood and Hardy, 2001; Treasure et al., 2001). Reviewers of manuscripts in this area may wish to clarify their own biases toward achievement goals at the beginning of their review, thus providing a context for their feedback and reducing the threat of reviewer bias shaping how knowledge is generated.

Tips for preparing/training peer reviewers. Although short-term training sessions appear to have little influence on review quality (Callaham, Wears, and Waeckerle, 1998), basic methodological expertise acquired during graduate training has been associated with the production of high quality reviews (Black et al., 1998). We agree with Brustad (1999) that peer reviewer training should be a fundamental feature of graduate training programs in sport and exercise psychology.

It seems that the basic infrastructure to provide peer review training is in place among many graduate programs in sport and exercise psychology. For example, Van Raalte et al. (2000) found that of 79 sport psychology programs offered in the U.S., 99% offered a course in research design, statistics, and/or psychological assessment. It is less clear whether peer reviewing forms a part of research methods curricular; but, based on Brustad's (1999) arguments, it seems that most graduates receive little training in peer review.

One suggestion would be to include peer reviewing as an integral part of research methods training courses. Peer reviewing can also be included in sport and exercise topic based courses. For example, a colleague at our university [Dr. John Dunn] includes readings and a class specifically addressing peer review in sport psychology. Students are provided with previous reviews he has received for his own work. They discuss the reviews and subsequently apply peer review to published articles. Our Faculty also holds a monthly meeting for approximately 20 students in behavioral programs (including those working in sport and exercise psychology) and their supervisors. For the past couple of years a minimum of one meeting has been devoted to the peer review process. These training initiatives may represent some ways to integrate peer review training into existing graduate programs without creating prohibitive financial and logistical demands on faculty or students.

Suggestions for Editors

Continually clarify journal expectations for peer reviews. In addition to the editorials provided to date (e.g., Brustad, 1999; Weiss, 1994a; 1994b; 1995), editors could continue to publish advice on the qualities of a good review for their journals. As shown in this article, little empirical evidence exists regarding review quality in sport and exercise psychology. Editors may be able to draw upon their own experience and research in other disciplines to provide suggestions for their reviewers regarding the purposes of a peer review (see Kaplan, 2005) and the specific aims and scope of their journals.

Mentoring. Evidence shows that young reviewers can produce high quality reviews (Black et al., 1998). One possibility for sport and exercise psychology is that younger guest reviewers could be mentored by more experienced reviewers. The mentor reviewer could provide an evaluation of the junior reviewer's comments (and vice versa). This could be a way of providing on-going training and feedback in the peer review process (see Drotar, 2008). Such mentoring could also be provided to graduate students by their supervisors as a cornerstone of graduate training. Some APA journals (e.g., *Emotion*) explicitly ask reviewers to list the names and qualifications of graduate students who assisted with a peer review. At the time of writing, this is not a requirement stipulated by any sport and exercise psychology journals, but we know from personal experience that editors are open to reviewer mentoring.

Provide feedback for reviewers. At present it seems that reviewers are provided with very little feedback, other than perhaps providing the editor's comments to the authors along with the feedback provided by the other reviewer(s). In addition, it would seem important to provide reviewers with specific feedback about the quality of their review. Although editors are already heavily burdened, providing reviewers with feedback could represent an important contribution to the on-going improvement of the process. Editors would require additional support from publishers to support such activities.

Another means of providing reviewers with feedback could be a 'back-review' from authors commenting on the quality of the reviewers' review. This process would be distinct from the revision/rebuttal process. Perhaps, authors could be provided with a standardized checklist and be invited to provide open-ended written comments. Rating items would include good anchors and may reflect issues such as the clarity of comments provided on the introduction, method, results, and discussion sections, collegiality of tone, or appropriate focus on major conceptual issues rather than disproportionate comments on minor issues. Although authors may react negatively to the frustration of a rejection and care less about the quality of a review for accepted manuscripts (Weber et al., 2002), the goal of this back-review process would be a long-term commitment to improving the quality of the peer review rather than creating 'quid pro quo' exchanges. The success of back-review would almost certainly depend on the integrity contributors bring to the process (cf. Drotar, 2008).

Suggestions for Publishers

Although we may be stepping beyond the boundaries of the evidence reviewed above, publishers surely have a responsibility to the peer review and publication process. Securing capable editors for exercise and sport psychology journals may be an ongoing struggle for the professional organizations and publishers because it is time-demanding to serve in editorial roles. Publishers offer small honoraria for editors and associate editors (in our experience somewhere in the range of $750-1500 U.S. per annum). Some universities place a low priority on supporting editorial service, and shouldering editorial responsibilities takes time from responsibilities (e.g., research, teaching) that university administrators prioritize. If publishers provided sufficient resources to buy editors out of teaching duties and hire full-time editorial assistants, editors may be able to commit more time to the continual improvement of the peer review process (such as by evaluating reviews and providing detailed feedback to reviewers).

CONCLUSION

This review revealed little research has been paid to the peer review process in sport and exercise psychology. We were unable to locate any direct empirical studies of the effects of the peer review in the field. For comparison, in the biomedical field Jefferson, Alderson, et al. (2002) were able to complete a systematic review of 135 studies on the effects of peer review. There are clearly gaps in the sport and exercise psychology literature when it comes to evaluating the peer review process.

Given that the goals and process of peer review are ambiguous (Jefferson, Alderson, et al., 2002; Kaplan, 2005), to help remedy these issues editors could be encouraged to provide on-going updates about the specific goals/objectives they wish reviewers to fulfill. Additionally, in sport and exercise psychology journals, there does not appear to be any evidence that items included in standardized checklists are valid and reliable. Given that a great deal of attention has been devoted to creating and validating measures in sport and exercise psychology (see Duda, 1998) there is sufficient expertise in the field to assess manuscript evaluation measures.

Evidence for the positive effects of blind reviews is inconclusive (Jefferson, Alderson, et al., 2002). Indeed, some journals have abandoned the blind review process (e.g., *Academic Medicine*). Given that all the main sport and exercise psychology journals employ a double blind review process it would take a brave editor to abandon this approach. On the other hand, about 50% of reviewers are often able to identify authors (Fisher, et al., 1994), so the peer review process may not conceal authors' identities in the intended manner. Before sport and exercise psychology journal editors abandon the double blind review process, research is required to assess whether or not double blind versus open reviews impact review and/or publication quality.

As this article has revealed, peer review is a relatively unexplored issue in sport and exercise psychology that has received little scholarly attention. A limitation is that some of the suggestions we provide here may add to the workload of already burdened editors, reviewers, and authors. But given the amount of time authors spend conducting their research and the importance of peer review, efforts to evaluate and improve this process should not be overlooked due to logistical constraints. The key would be for authors and reviewers to commit to the long-term advancement of the field, and equally their service must be recognized in their respective annual evaluation reports.

We have provided information that may help reviewers and authors reflect on some issues surrounding the peer review process. This paper may be useful for graduate students and their supervisors as well as researchers, editors, and even publishers. But we also hope to stimulate some discussion, and perhaps even research, about the peer review process more generally. Although we have highlighted some of the problems with peer review, as Smith (2006) suggested, the peer review system might not be perfect, but like democracy, it is probably the 'least worst' option.

ACKNOWLEDGMENTS

We would like to thank the members of the Behavioral Medicine Group in the Faculty of Physical Education and Recreation at the University of Alberta for helping us to explore some of the ideas presented in this paper. During the writing of this manuscript Nick Holt was supported by a Population Health Investigator Award from the Alberta Heritage Foundation for Medical Research.

REFERENCES

American Psychological Association.(1992). Ethical principles of psychologists and code of conduct. *American Psychologist, 47*, 1597-1611.

American Psychological Association. (2001a). *Publication manual of the American Psychological Association* (5th ed.). Washington: American Psychological Association.

American Psychological Association.(2001b). Summary report of journal operations, 2000. *American Psychologist, 56*, 166-167.

American Psychological Association. (2010). *Publication manual of the American Psychological Association* 6th ed.). Washington: American Psychological Association.

Arkes, H. R. (2003). The nonuse of psychological research at two federal agencies. *Psychological Science, 14*, 1-6.

Armstrong, S. J. (1996). We need to rethink the editorial role of peer reviewers. *The Chronicle of Higher Education, 43*(9), B3.

Biddle, S. J. H. (2000). Psychology of sport and exercise: Present and future. *Psychology of Sport and Exercise, 1*, 1-5.

Black, N., van Rooyen, S., Godless, F., Smith, R., and Evans, S. (1998). What makes a good reviewer and a good review for a general medical journal? *Journal of the American Medical Association, 280*, 231-233.

Blackburn, J. L., and Hakel, M. D. (2006). An examination of sources of peer-review bias. *Psychological Science, 17*, 378-382.

Brustad, R. J. (1999). Editorial perspective: The contribution of the manuscript-review process to knowledge development in sport and exercise psychology. *Journal of Sport and Exercise Psychology, 21*, 307-312.

Brustad, R. J. (2008). Qualitative research approaches. In T. S. Horn (Ed), *Advances in sport psychology* (3rd ed., pp. 31-44). Champaign, IL: Human Kinetics.

Callaham, M. L., Waeckerle, J. F., and Wears, R. L. (1998). Effect of attendance at a training session on peer review quality and performance. *Annuls of Emergency Medicine, 32*, 318-322.

Coelho, R. J., and La Forge, J. (1996). Preparing a journal manuscript: A guide for rehabilitation counselor practitioners. *Journal of Applied Rehabilitation Counseling, 27*, 37-41.

Coelho, R. J., and La Forge, J. (2000). Manuscript characteristics affecting reviewers' decisions for rehabilitation counseling related journals. *The Journal of Rehabilitation, 66*, 4-8.

Conroy, D.E., Kaye, M.P., and Schantz, L.H. (2008). Quantitative research methodology. In T. S. Horn (Ed.), *Advances in sport psychology* (3rd ed., pp. 15-30). Champaign, IL: Human Kinetics.

Culver, D. M., Gilbert, W. D., and Trudel, P. (2003). A decade of qualitative research in sport psychology journals: 1990-1999. *The Sport Psychologist, 17*, 1-15.

Cummings, P., and Rivara, F. P. (2002). Reviewing manuscripts for Archives of Pediatrics and Adolescent Medicine. *Archives of Pediatrics and Adolescent Medicine, 156,* 11-13.

DellaSalla, S., and Graffman., J. (2002). Refereeing mortusest, vivat refereeing. *Cortex, 38,* 269-271.

Drotar, D. (2008). Editorial: Thoughts on establishing research significance and preserving scientific integrity. *Journal of Pediatric Psychology, 33,* 1-5.

Duda, J. L. (Ed., 1998). *Advances in sport and exercise psychology measurement.* Morgantown, WV: Fitness Information Technology.

Evans, A. T., McNutt, R. A., Fletcher, S. W., and Fletcher, R. H. (1993). The characteristics of peer reviewers who produce good quality reviews. *Journal of General Internal Medicine, 8,* 422-428.

Faulkner, G., and Sparkes, A.C. (1999). Exercise as a treatment for schizophrenia: An ethnographic study. *Journal of Sport and Exercise Psychology, 21,* 52-69.

Fisher, M., Friedman, S. B., and Strauss, B. (1994). The effects of blinding on acceptance of research papers by peer review. *Journal of the American Medical Association, 272,* 143-146.

Gardner, M. J., and Bond, J. (1990). An exploratory study of statistical assessment of papers published in the British Medical Journal. *Journal of the American Medical Association, 263,* 1355-1357.

Gauvin, L., and Spence, J. C. (1995). Psychological research on exercise and fitness: Current research trends and future challenges. *The Sport Psychologist, 9,* 434-448.

Goldbeck-Wood, S. (1999). Evidence on peer-reviews scientific quality control or smoke screen?*British Medical Journal* 318, 44–45.

Harwood, C. G., and Hardy, L. (2001). Persistence and effort in moving achievement goal research forward: A response to Treasure and colleagues. *Journal of Sport and Exercise Psychology, 23,* 330-345.

Harwood, C. G., Hardy, L., and Swain, A. B. J. (2000). Achievement goals in sport: A critique of conceptual and measurement issues. *Journal of Sport and Exercise Psychology, 22,* 235-255.

Hojat, M., Gonnella, J. S., and Caelleigh, A. S. (2003). Impartial judgment by the 'gatekeepers' of science: Fallibility and accountability in the peer review process. *Advances in Health Sciences Education, 8,* 75-96.

Holt, N. L., and Dunn, J. G. H. (2004). Toward a grounded theory of the psychosocial competencies and environmental conditions associated with soccer success. *Journal of Applied Sport Psychology, 16,* 199-219.

Jefferson, T., Alderson, P., Wager, E., and Davidoff, F. (2002). Effects of editorial peer review: A systematic review. *Journal of the American Medical Association, 287,* 2784-2786.

Jefferson, T., Wager, E., and Davidoff, F. (2002). Measuring the quality of editorial peer review. *Journal of the American Medical Association, 287,* 2786-2790.

Jelicic, M., and Merchelbach, H. (2002). Peer review: Let's imitate the lawyers! *Cortex, 38,* 406-407.

Kaplan, D. (2005). How to fix peer review: Separating its two functions – Improving manuscripts and judging their scientific merit – Would help. *Journal of Child and Family Studies, 14,* 321-323.

Kassirer, J., and Campion, E. (1994). Crude and understudied, but indispensable. *Journal of the American Medical Association, 270*, 96-97.

King, C. R., McGuire, D. B., Longman, A. J., and Carroll-Johnson, R. M. (1997). Peer review, authorship, ethics, and conflict of interest. *Image: Journal of Nursing Scholarship, 29*, 163-167.

McNutt, R. A., Evans, A. T., Fletcher, R. H., and Fletcher, S. W. (1990). The effects of blinding on the quality of peer review. *Journal of the American Medical Association, 263*, 1371-1376.

Nylenna, M., Riis, P., and Karlsson, Y. (1994). The characteristics of peer reviewers who produce good quality reviews. *Journal of the American Medical Association, 272*, 149-151.

Rosenthal, R. (1979). The 'file drawer problem' and tolerance for null results. *Psychological Bulletin, 86*, 638-641.

Shea, J. A., Caelleigh, A. S., Pangaro L., and Steinecke A. (2001). Review process and publication decision. *Academic Medicine, 76*, 911-916.

Smith, R. (2006). Peer review: A flawed process at the heart of science and journals. *Journal of the Royal Society of Medicine, 99*, 178-182.

Spence, J. C., and Blanchard, C. M. (2001). Publication bias in sport and exercise psychology research: The games we play. *International Journal of Sport Psychology, 32*, 386-399.

Treasure, D. C., Duda, J. L., Hall, H. K., Roberts, G. C., Ames, C., and Maehr, M. L. (2001). Clarifying misconceptions and misrepresentations in achievement goal research in sport: A response to Harwood, Hardy, and Swain. *Journal of Sport and Exercise Psychology, 23*, 317-329

Van Lange, P. M. (1999). What authors believe that reviews stress limiting aspects of manuscripts: The SLAM effect in peer review. *Journal of Applied Social Psychology, 29*, 2550-2556.

Van Raalte, J. L., Brown, T. D., Brewer, B. W., Avondoglio, A. V., Hartmann, W. M., and Scherzer, C. B. (2000). An on-line survey of graduate course offerings satisfying AAASP certification criteria. *The Sport Psychologist, 14*, 98-104.

Weber, E. J., Katz, P. P., Waeckerle, J. F., and Callaham, M. L. (2002). Author perception of peer review: Impact of review quality and acceptance on satisfaction. *Journal of the American Medical Association, 287*, 2790-2792.

Weinberg, R. S., and Comar, W. (1994). The effectiveness of psychological interventions in sport. *Sports Medicine, 18*, 406-418.

Weiss, M. R. (1994a). Editor's viewpoint: Why ask 'why?' *Research Quarterly for Exercise and Sport, 65*(1), iii-iv.

Weiss, M. R., (1994b). Editor's viewpoint: Who's on first, what's on second? *Research Quarterly for Exercise and Sport, 65*(2), iii-iv.

Weiss, M. R. (1995). Editor's viewpoint: Do you know the way to San José? *Research Quarterly for Exercise and Sport, 66*(1), iii-v.

In: Athletic Insight's Writings of 2012   ISBN: 978-1-62618-120-5
Editor: Robert Schinke   © 2013 Nova Science Publishers, Inc.

Chapter 3

AM "I" A WORK OF ART(?): UNDERSTANDING EXERCISE AND THE SELF THROUGH CRITICAL SELF-AWARENESS AND AESTHETIC SELF-STYLIZATION

Kerry R. McGannon

School of Human Kinetics, Laurentian University,
Sudbury, Ontario, Canada

ABSTRACT

Scholars in sport psychology have begun to create intellectual spaces for the exploration of the self as dynamic fluid and multiple, using autoethnography whereby researchers tell stories about their own experiences. These reflexive "narratives of self" display multiple layers of consciousness which are intertwined with the socio-cultural realm.

Autoethnography is a useful methodological tool to explore the contradictory and complex interrelationships between society, the body, sport, physical activity and the self. However, these forms of research are on the fringes of sport psychology. This paper extends self-reflexive writing in sport psychology into new theoretical territory by exploring two aspects of Foucault's (1988) technologies of the self: critical self-awareness and aesthetic self-stylization.

Autoethnography and creative non-fiction are combined to produce a self-reflexive story about exercise self-identity and embodied running. Facets of the story are discussed within the context of Foucault's concepts of critical self-awareness and aesthetic self-stylization, illuminating running and embodied experiences as transformational practices of freedom which allow for challenging and changing the limits of exerciser self-identities. The paper concludes with a discussion of the implications of exploring self-reflexive knowledge from a Foucauldian perspective for understanding the self and physical activity participation.

INTRODUCTION

...if we think of our lives as works of art, we regain the ability to think creatively and challenge the limitations of the "natural" identities formed through the games of truth. Aesthetic stylization of the self denotes a self that is open to change and the constant recreation of changing conditions in society

Markula, 2003a, p.102

In her recent paper, *A Sport Odyssey*, sport psychologist Vikki Krane (2009) framed sport as a long wandering journey, using multi-genre writing styles to weave a personal tale of her experiences in sport in relation to her self-identity development. This self-reflexive narrative (i.e., the researcher's self is the site of analysis and subject of critique) explored the physical self as dynamic across personal, social and cultural circumstances, revealing the self to be multiple, socially constructed and negotiated within sport contexts.

In the context of self-reflexive writing, Krane's sport odyssey can be characterized as an autoethnography whereby researchers tell stories about their lived experiences, displaying multiple layers of consciousness connected to culture making individual experience a social experience (Ellis and Bochner, 2000; Sparkes, 2000; 2002a). At the same time, Krane's (2009) self-reflexive narrative is a creative non-fiction (see Sparkes, 2002b), as her real-life short stories were dramatized using fictional techniques such as scenic method (e.g., an emotional tone was created), character development (e.g., real and complicated characters were at the center), and plot (e.g., dramatic tension was built through flashbacks) (Agar, 1995). Krane characterized her story as a "hybrid" whereby she blended diverse—and at times fragmented—yet complementary writing styles (see Sermijn, Devieger and Loots, 2008).

What do self-reflexive tales add to further understanding the self in sport psychology?Because these genres of writing assume personal experience and the self are simultaneously socio-cultural they are useful methodological tools to explore the complex interrelationships between society, the body, physical activity and self-identities (McGannon and Johnson, 2009). In turn, self-reflexive writing allows us to capture the socially constructed self as dynamic and multiple across sport and exercise settings – an endeavor recently advocated within edited volumes in cultural sport psychology (see Ryba, Schinke and Tennenbaum, 2010; Schinke and Hanrahan, 2009). Krane's (2009) tale crystallizes all of these points, as it shows how self reflexive writing contributes toward raising awareness and understanding of the physical self as profoundly gendered, with associated psychological, social, and cultural effects.

Additional examples of self-reflexive writing in sport psychology include confessionals (Carless and Douglas, 2010), creative non-fiction (Gilbourne and Richardson, 2006), poetic representations (Sparkes, Nilges, Swan and Dowling, 2003; Sparkes and Douglas, 2007) and autoethnography (Douglas, 2009; Holt, 2003).

Despite the promise that self-reflexive writing holds for learning more about how individuals integrate aspects of their physical selves into their self-systems and the relationship to life experiences, these forms of research are on the fringes of sport psychology. My own journey in self-reflexive writing is recent whereby I have explored various facets of "self" through writing stories (see Richardson, 2000a, 2000b) to illuminate understandings of power between researchers and research participants (McGannon and

Johnson, 2009), confessional tales (see Van Maanen, 1988) of the research process (McGannon and Metz, 2010) and an autoethnography (see Sparkes, 2000) of my exercise journey and physical self (McGannon, 2004). All of my self-tales have allowed me to theorize and explore the self as post-modern in the sense that the self is conceptualized as historical, multiple, fractured and (re)produced within discourse and power structures (McGannon and Busanich, 2010; McGannon and Spence, 2010).

This paper extends self-reflexive writing within sport psychology into new theoretical territory by exploring two aspects of Foucault's (1988) technologies of the self: critical self-awareness and aesthetic self-stylization. A Foucauldian analysis allows for a more nuanced exploration of the complex interrelationships between power, society, physical activity and the self. To accomplish my purpose, autoethnography and creative non-fiction are used to produce a "hybrid" self-reflexive story about my exercise self-identity and running. Various facets of the story are discussed within the context of Foucault's concepts of critical self-awareness and aesthetic self-stylization. By doing so, I illuminate my running and embodied experiences as transformational practices of freedom (Foucault 1988; Lloyd, 1996; Rail and Harvey, 1995) which allowed me to problematize and change the limits of my self as an exerciser whose prior experiences and fitness practices were primarily constructed within dominant discourses of femininity. I conclude by discussing the implications of exploring self-reflexive knowledge from a Foucauldian perspective for understanding the self and physical activity participation.

THEORETICAL TRAJECTORY: FOUCAULT, POWER AND THE SELF

To accomplish the above, a discussion of the aspects of Foucault's work appropriated in this paper is first necessary. While Foucault's writings are vast and varied sport studies scholars have used Foucault's conception of discourse and power to "deconstruct gendered power relations within sport and physical activity milieus" (Bridel and Rail, 2007, p. 127). For Foucault (1978), discourse refers to an interrelated "system of statements that cohere around common meanings and values…(that) are a product of social factors, of powers and practices rather than an individual's set of ideas" (Hollway, 1983, p. 231). Discourse can also be understood as providing the meanings that constitute everyday practices (e.g., what people think, feel and say about themselves in relation to exercise, the type of exercise one does and/or the types of exercise one avoids). Additionally, discourses not only "systematically form the objects of which they speak" (Foucault, 1978, p. 49) but they have material/concrete implications for bodies and embodiment (Markula et al., 2008). Stated differently, while discourses are resources that people draw upon to explain and/or give meaning to who they are (i.e., self and identity) and what they experience, discourses also shape, enable and/or constrain behavioral practices.

In addition to the discursive articulation of certain kinds of selves and subjectivities, discourses also maintain power relations and patterns of domination and subordination (Potter and Wetherell, 1987). For Foucault, power is contingent upon discourse and tactical usages of discourses by dominant individuals and groups with power working *through* people (i.e., power is diffused throughout the body politic, held by no one, acting on everyone, and articulated or made visible in its various discursive iterations) (Markula and Pringle, 2006). Foucault's view of power is relational and "omnipresent in every relationship and working as a capillary-like network. Within this network, there are multiple points of resistance and struggle" (Markula et al., 2008, p. 11). Foucault's conception of power is neither positive nor negative and power relations are *productive* because they (re)produce subjectivities, economic systems, and social transformation (Markula and Pringle, 2006). Foucault was thus concerned with how power operates through discourse(s) that provides knowledge about how women understand, regulate, and experience their selves and bodies in relation to exercise (Lupton, 1997).

One way that people negotiate discourses and associated practices is through a technology of dominance (Bridel and Rail, 2007; Foucault, 1977; Markula and Pringle, 2006). A technology of dominance is a way in which power and knowledge fuse to produce power relations, setting up what is "normal" or taken for granted with respect to bodies (Foucault, 1977). When discussing the power-knowledge nexus, Markula and Pringle (2006) noted that technologies of dominance are limiting as they "act to constrain and subject people to certain ends, identities and modes of behavior" (p. 8). Relevant to contextualizing my running self-story is research exploring the discursive construction of femininity and ideal body in women's exercise within media texts (e.g., fitness magazines) and individual exercise practices (e.g., aerobics, running). Such research shows that when constructed within discourses of ideal femininity, physical activity emerges as a technology of dominance rarely questioned by women which (re)produces a particular version of the fit female body (e.g., thin, toned) and particular practices (e.g., dieting, avoiding weight training, over exercising) as "normal" and the means to achieve such a body (Chapman, 1997; Chase, 2006; Duncan, 1994; Markula, 1995, 2000, 2001).

Foucault's later work focused on how people may challenge, transform and (re)create themselves within discursive power relations through a technology of self (Foucault, 1988; Markula and Pringle, 2006; Rail and Bridel, 2007; Rail and Harvey, 1995). Known as practices of freedom individuals can use to transform the self and associated practices within power relations, a key to realizing such transformation is that athletes or exercisers first become critically self-aware by problematizing their identities and behavior-governing codes in relation to dominant discourses of femininity and the ideal body (Foucault, 1988; Markula, 2003a, 2004; Thorpe, 2008). By interrogating the limits of one's self, one reconfigures (not dissolves) discursive power relations and "the possibility of transgression emerges and thus, the potential for creating new subjective experiences" (Markula, 2004, p. 308). For example, appearance discourses and associated meanings (e.g., thin is fit, exercise leads to weight loss) and practices (e.g., disordered eating, avoiding particular forms of exercise) used to construct the "fit female body", can be challenged/resisted by *consciously* embracing one's shape as fit and feminine regardless of weight/size, building a muscular body apart from appearance aspirations, or viewing food as nourishment for the self, thus reconfiguring dominant discourses of femininity (Haravon Collins, 2002; Markula, 1995, 2003b, 2004; Markula and Pringle, 2006; Wesley, 2001).

It is important to point out that resistance of dominant discourses through technologies of the self must be *conscious* and make a political statement in order to serve as transformative practices of freedom (Lloyd, 1996; Markula, 2003a, 2004; Thorpe, 2008). An important part of realizing such critical self-awareness is to think of one's relationship to one's self as a process of *aesthetic stylization*, whereby construction, reconstruction and even deconstruction of self, is "like a creative activity, a constant process of invention" (Markula, 2004, p. 102). Thus, instead of viewing the self as fixed and naturally given, we are invited to think of our selves and lives as works of art, open to change, creativity and a process of (re)creation. Given their association with movement and expression, exercise and sport are particularly fruitful contexts within which to accomplish and understand aesthetic self-stylization. Self-asetheticization sport and exercise practices for women may include building a strong body that pushes and challenges the limits of dominant femininity, viewing one's physical activity and performance as artistic and creative expressions, shifting participation motives to less visible exercise benefits such as relaxation and clarity of mind, or feeling free and empowered during movement (Markula and Pringle, 2006). When combined with critical self-awareness, aesthetic self-stylization practices can be used to produce a self that is politically aware and literally *actively* resistant, questioning the limits of "natural" identities and practices in sport and exercise formed through the games of truth that may disempower women (see Markula, 2004 as an example in women's exercise or Thorpe, 2008 in women's sport).

Since Foucault emphasized understanding how people might problematize their self-identities by becoming self-reflexive (Markula, 2003a), employing technologies of the self in conjunction with self-reflexive writing practices opens up additional possibilities for reframing and transforming women's physical selves and sport and exercise practices. In fact, on its own self-reflexive writing can be viewed as a technology of the self, as one becomes critically self-aware through such writing practices and the very act of writing creatively is an aesthetic self-stylization practice. Before I explore these notions in and through my self-story, I next discuss research on distance running to further contextualize my running-story and subsequent analysis/discussion.

DISTANCE RUNNING AND THE SELF

While few studies have applied Foucault's ideas on the body to distance running (an exception is Bridel and Rail, 2007 which will be discussed shortly) certain aspects of distance running can be seen as technologies of dominance. For example, despite running being linked to improved health, personal achievement and acquiring a greater sense of self (Carless, 2008; Major, 2001; Smith, 2000), notions of body modification often emerge as central within running discourse (Bridel and Rail, 2007). When positioned within appearance discourses, the meaning of body modification in running is associated with desiring weight loss, changing one's musculature and/or shape, or to be more "physically attractive" (Chase, 2008; Major, 2001; Smith, 2000; van Ingen, 2004). Such meanings and practices associated with body modification in running may thus serve as disciplinary forms of power through which people construct their running self-identities in limited ways (Bridel and Rail, 2007). These dominant meanings and associated practices are further circulated via the media, reproducing limited representations of healthy running bodies as lean, masculine, and youthful (Abbas, 2004; Greenleaf, 2002). This visual representation of a dominant body type in running texts further contributes to shaping expectations and pursuits in running (Bridel and Rail, 2007; Chase, 2008), which may detract from enjoyment or become linked to unhealthy practices (e.g., dieting, over exercising) (Busanich and McGannon, 2010; Greenleaf, 2002; Thompson, 2007; Weight and Noakes, 1987). This discursively constructed running body further subordinates aging bodies, female bodies, or less lean bodies, despite their growing presence in running communities (Abbas, 2004). Visual representations of certain bodies also reproduce a limited body type often linked with running "success" (Chase, 2008; Johns and Johns, 2000) despite the fact people run for enjoyment or achieve success, or different versions of success, with different body types (Major, 2001; Ogles et al., 1995).

In addition to being a technology of dominance, recent research suggests that running can also be viewed as a technology of self through which people transform and renegotiate their self-identities within, outside of, or in spite of, the aforementioned discourses. In their examination of gay male marathon runners using technologies of dominance and technologies of the self, Bridel and Rail (2007) found that the marathon context was paradoxical. While participants drew upon dominant appearance discourses to construct participation motives (e.g., obtain a lean body), they also used their marathon practices to gain a sense of self-achievement and satisfaction connected to a stronger sense of self and gay identity. However, these same practices also led to psychological distress and/or injury for some runners.

Given the complexity of the discourses, self-related views, and associated outcomes, further research on distance runner's self-constructions and the implications for embodied subjectivity and running practices is needed. Extending this research on women is underscored by Krane (2009) who noted that "sport can provide a space where females defy traditional gender norms and celebrate their bodies; it offers an arena for challenging and transforming social constraints imposed on women" (p. 221).

With this latter point in mind, I now turn to my self-reflexive story. In so doing, I acknowledge as others have in self-reflexive writing, that I may be perceived as narcissistic (e.g., Holt, 2003; Krane, 2009; Sparkes 2000). While that interpretation is ultimately left up to the reader, my intent is not to position my running story as more important or central toward lending understanding of the self than others. Instead, I offer this story in the interest of encouraging qualitative sport and exercise researchers to ask new questions, think differently and allow for the creation of new knowledge (see Sparkes and Smith, 2009).

PREFACE: WHO THE HECK DO I "THINK" I AM?

I am not an elite athlete. I am not a competitive athlete. I am not an athlete period. I do not construct myself in those terms. Yet as a physically active woman, the journey of understanding my physically active self has spanned over 20 years. I see my "self" as a highly committed exerciser. The structure and shape of "me" as a committed exerciser has taken on particular meanings and been dynamic throughout my years of exercise participation. My exerciser-self literally began to take shape through my participation in aerobics in 1987. During this time, my exercise practices were primarily a technology of dominance (Foucault, 1977), as I tried to attain the "fit female body" constructed by dominant discourses of femininity.

By drawing upon such discourses, I engaged in dietary and exercise practices such as counting calories, doing particular exercises (e.g., aerobics, abdominal/sit-up exercises), and avoiding particular exercises (e.g., lifting heavy weights) in order to make my body smaller and a particular shape. I experienced a paradox of feelings in relation to my physical self, such as guilt, anxiety, happiness, elation, a sense of freedom and control, and a loss of control. During this time, I rarely questioned my "body project" and I gained empowerment and enjoyment from exercise when my body conformed to the "normal" ideal body. The reverse happened when my body did not conform. Outside of these discourses my exercise also allowed me to experience myself as skilled and masterful and I thoroughly enjoyed movement through participating in aerobic dance.

From 1994-2002, I was a fitness instructor, imparting my love of aerobics and movement to others. In the year 2000, as a result of my immersion in feminist perspectives during my doctoral work, I became more critically self-aware (Foucault 1988; Markula, 2004) and began questioning the limits of my previously constructed exerciser-self. I began problematizing the rules and taken for granted "truths" of the fitness industry. While I continued to draw upon these discourses to construct myself and exercise, I also challenged taken for granted fitness industry practices at both personal and instructional levels (e.g., I emphasized functional fitness in my own training and classes, avoided body shaping/toning exercises, and educated participants about fitness benefits outside of weight loss).

The result of the foregoing has been a sense of self and subjectivity that is shifting and contradictory; on the one hand I have experienced my physical self as flawed and in need of fixing via various exercise practices. On the other hand I have experienced my physical self as strong because of liberating features of my exercise and/or by liberating others through challenging the "truth games" of women's fitness (Markula, 2004). I would thus characterize my participation in aerobics from 1987-2002 as *both* a technology of dominance and a technology of self – in varying degrees.

As such my exercise practices and self-related views were at times transformational practices of freedom (Foucault, 1988; Markula, 2004; Markula and Pringle, 2006).

When I left teaching group exercise at the end of 2002and began recreational running, I still drew upon weight management and appearance discourses to experience my running as a technology of dominance and familiar experiences followed (e.g., I felt guilty when I didn't run; I felt fat if I ate too much and/or if I didn't run far enough). However, with my feminist consciousness being raised further, I began to train for a marathon fall of 2003 with a particular "mind-set".

As a result, my running practices and exercising-self shifted again. For me this shift was profound as I truly began to construct and experience my physical self and exercise outside of the dominant discourses of femininity, despite their ever-presence in my world (e.g., at the gym, in the media, through conversations other women would have with me about my running in relation to weight and caloric expenditure).

My training experiences and critical self-awareness became a form of resistance and I questioned the limits of my exercising self by framing my physical activity within health and wellness discourses.

In turn, I experienced my running as empowering and my body as fit apart from how it looked, focusing on what my body accomplished and how that felt. Like Bridel and Rail's (2007) runners who engaged in self-transformational running practices, particular psychological experiences (e.g., enjoyment, a sense of accomplishment) and behavioral practices (e.g., not using running as a punishment but as a tool for energy and wellbeing) followed when I drew upon these discourses.

My next autoethnography draws on creative non-fiction as an additional tool to explore my embodied experiences of running "in" the marathon. My experiences were transformational practices of freedom as my self-identity was not only re-negotiated in a broader sense, but also at the local level (Foucault, 1988) with each passing mile-marker in the race. Like other creative non-fictions (see Sparkes, 2002b) my story is the result of having "been there"; the narrative is a conglomeration of my experiences as a seven-time recreational marathoner between the years 2004-2008.

The Big Sur International Marathon (BSIM) in California is also a central character in my story. My experiences with this character are explored using the various milestones to represent facets of the BSIM's "personality" (i.e., marathon course) as "it" fuses and shifts with my physical self.

(UN)BROKEN: FREEDOM THROUGH THE MILESTONES

Miles 1-10: The Start of Something Big

It is almost 7 am and I am standing in the middle nowhere. The air is crisp and I am shivering in my shorts and thin long sleeved top. But "I AM" somewhere – I am in the heart of Big Sur. I see a tiny white sign raised high over an ant-people colony. The sign says, "START" in bold red print, and the colony of people-ants spans back to me and beyond; there are hundreds of people behind me. Eye of the Tiger from Rocky III is booming. This is so cliché! I am singing the words with my friend Todd. Todd and I have a pact to run the BSIM every year, though we only run the first five minutes together, then go our separate ways, reconvening at the finish. It's better this way…

At 6:55 a man in a plaid kilt and running gear plays the U.S. National Anthem on bag pipes. People are silent, people are singing and I am nervous. Six white doves are released into the air and a gun goes off. Yea—here I go! But wait. No one is moving. We are packed like sardines. Finally, we begin to walk in tandem; just me and 3000 friends. I have a sense of walking on air and being carried. At last, there is elbow room as I cross a black mat beneath the start; four minutes have passed since the gun went off.

Paces quicken and I am trotting through the California red woods. Big, thick, tall looming trees line the road on either side. The forest is cool this morning, but it's an enchanted one – laughter, chatter, the pitter patter of little feet…and people urinating in bushes. There are many different bodies – different shapes, wearing different clothing, different ages, all scampering through the enchanted forest. I am also one of those different scampering bodies.

Once Todd veers off .5 miles in claiming he "has to beat P-Diddy's time" I run with two women wearing t-shirts with the Canadian flag on the back. I feel pride and we chat about where I'm from originally in Canada. At mile three, we part ways and I run alone. But I am not alone; there are people for miles in front of me. I don't need to look back to know that hundreds of people are behind me. I can hear them – laughter, chatter, and the pitter patter on the road.

My legs are fresh as I run past stores at mile four –these will be the last buildings I see until mile twenty two. Running is effortless for the next three miles; the scenery keeps me riveted as it changes from forest to rolling green hills and meadows. No ocean yet, but I begin to hear and smell it at mile seven and into mile eight, as my quadriceps contract and tighten and my pace slows– I have hit the first significant hills of the nineteen hill course. After these miles, I glide down a gentle hill. It's on baby, it's on…

Miles 10-13: Hurricane Point: We're Over the Hill!

As I round the bend on the canted road and continue downward, I hear them…the drums, the drums …beating and echoing out toward the ocean and up toward me. As the hill bottoms out at mile ten, there is one last stop; Gatorade…a green, rusty porta- potty (my god what's THAT smell?!)…horrifying but ah, relief…I am running again, turning my stride into a shuffle; it lessens the pain I feel in my tender ankles. I take a deep breath and look upwards. The drums…the drums…I can only see a small part of the two mile hill that will ultimately rise over 500 feet above the ocean below.

I shuffle onward and upward. I hear the voice of my one of mentors from graduate school mocking my whining of grading papers, "you lady you…it's ALWAYS about YOU…" The drums are louder and I can see THEM! Blue shirts, black tops and head bands, they are the Taikodrummers, beating out the rhythms of my hurricane point ascension…I have butterflies in my stomach. I feel elated and energized by the drums. They set my pace.

Suddenly, I am overcome with tears. I breathe deeply, adrenaline is going. I begin my ascension and I look at what is head of me. The tears are gone, replaced with the sight of bodies in colored shirts and shorts; red ones, green ones, blue ones, yellow ones; they are like MandM candies. Head goes down; after this, 13 miles left in the race—run steady but conserve…Steep hill, canted and cracked road. Pace slows, breath quickens. I hear the MandM's breathing—which one am I? I am a blue one in my blue shorts. A cross wind blows from the ocean and my pace slows. I look at my watch and begin a three minute run, one minute walk. Lather, rinse, repeat. I'm almost there – mile twelve is called out by a child wearing a t-shirt that is so big it is a dress on him. I shuffle off to the far side of the road, avoiding the steep cant. This isn't so bad.

Oh f---k! My right leg is sore, pain in my quad. My ankles – they feel like they're creaking. Next walk break. Shake it out. I feel better…and finally a reprieve – I am at the top of the point and the sun is out! Laughter—not me---other runners are laughing. I begin to smile and I hear a grand piano playing Chariots of Fire! It is echoing and I wonder why I didn't notice it before like I had the drums? I look back at what I've just run – a craggy, rocky, winding cliff, rolling green hills with blue, white capped ocean on the right side. I am again overcome. I just ran THAT?! I see the tiny bodies in colored shirts and shorts going up the winding two mile hill; red ones, green ones, blue ones, yellow ones. They are MandM's – time for fuel!

Miles 13-20: Bridges and Troubled Waters

Aide station. Gatorade. Gu. Water. Stomach rumbles. Oh-oh…Miles thirteen and fourteen promise two winding down hills with hair pin turns, and one bridge after each mile. As I run across Bixby Bridge I look over ---and feel sick. Is it the view or my GI? Possibly both. It feels good to go downhill during these miles– but it is pleasure-pain. Quads are sore. Ankles are screaming. Stomach is rumbling. Mile fifteen = porta-potty! There is a line-up. Suddenly, I am twelve years old, on a road trip with my parents in the back seat of a car yelling, "Are we there yet? Are we there yet? I gotta go to the washroom!" But they won't pull over! Awakening me from my day-dream, a rusty-green door flings open with a loud thump and a man standing behind me urges, "are you goin' or what?!" He punctuates his question with a tiny dance – I assume this means he must also use the washroom. I go inside the porta-potty and close out the beauty of Big Sur. I curse my GI-tract, "why, oh why have you forsaken me!"

Relief…I am back on the road running miles fifteen to eighteen. The next four miles are up-down-down-up-down-up-down-up-up-down. Half mile hills go up. Half mile hills go down. Going up, legs and ankles are searing with pain. Going down, legs and ankles are searing with pain. I marvel that my knees are not sore and I am pleased. The McGannon-shuffle brings some relief, or at least lets me continue without stopping. If I stop, I'll become stiff. If I become stiff I won't finish.

I shuffle past a group of walkers and again stake my claim on the side of the road that does not have a steep cant. It seems that others know this "game" I am playing as I find that I am either weaving past someone or being woven past by someone. Aide station. Gu. Gatorade.Water. Stomach again rumbles. Porta-poty. I know this drill…Miles nineteen and twenty bring a flat stretch of road and the ocean scenery is no longer as visible. Many of the MandM's are walking and shuffling along with me, but since candy cannot speak, we are silent. The flat portion allows me to run again, though quads and ankles are still tight and sore.

Miles 21-Finish: Blur and Happiness in the Valley of the Dolls

For the first time, I see and hear people cheering who aren't runners or the volunteers from the aide stations. Big Sur is a solitary rural race with few spectators so it is good to be back in "civilization". My right leg is numb. I stop. I move to the side, shake it out and then stretch my hip flexors. I try it out with a little trot. It works! I can keep going, so I do. Almost there!

The half mile up and downs of miles fourteen to eighteen are now in the past—a blur. These are replaced by a series of short up and down hills until mile twenty two; I am now in the Carmel highlands. I drag my right fatigued leg up hill. I shuffle downhill as gravity propels me forward. I let my right leg float along like a dead slab of meat. The sun is beating down; I feel sun burnt. My stomach is rumbling and churning. Ignore and focus on getting to that next mile marker. The porta-poty and aide stations are mile markers once again – a triumph! At mile twenty three there are fresh strawberries! I eat them and force myself to drink water. Inside of my stomach there is a giant ball of rising dough. The flat portions of miles twenty four and twenty five bring some relief and my right leg is no longer numb.

I keep shuffling. I take a walk break, stretch my right hip flexor. Shuffle again. I am on Mile 26: also known as *D-minor hill at D-major time*. Spectators are out in full force, cheering. My right leg still works! I feel a rush of adrenaline. Good enough to get me to the end.

The finish line is in sight. Heat, tears, pain, and now – push. No more walking, I am running. People line the gates on either side of the road. Unlike the MandM runners, they look like tiny blurry colored pill capsules from the "Valley of the Dolls". The miles behind me are also blurs as I cross the finish line.

Euphoria? No. Happiness and a balance of pleasure and pain. Yes. Todd is there – he proclaims that he finished the marathon a full hour ahead of me. I am salty – literally. We flop down on the grass to stretch and exchange stories about our experiences. They are stories of heroic triumph – "I was down and couldn't go on, but then my super powers kicked in and I overcame adversity!" We make the pact to run the Big Sur again next year. Until then: Bus. Hotel. Ibuprofen. Shower. Food. Hot tub. Beer. (Repeat the last three).

REFLECTIONS ON SELF-TRANSFORMATION

While I am reluctant to tell the reader how to interpret my story – the validity of self-reflexive work lies in the verisimilitude and evocativeness of the story for readers[1] (see Sparkes, 2000)—as set out in my purpose I will offer some theoretical interpretations of my story. Remembering that a first step in viewing physical activity as a technology of the self is to challenge the limits of one's identity via critical self-awareness and make a political statement (Markula, 2003; Markula and Pringle, 2006), choosing the BSIM can be viewed as a technology of the self. First, deciding to do a marathon was a *conscious resistance* practice of my previous physical activity and fitness practices (e.g., aerobics, body shaping and toning exercises). In choosing to run marathons and problematize my exercise identity, I no longer constructed myself and distance running within the dominant discourses of femininity and body modification. I changed the meaning of what it means to "build a fit body" by drawing upon health, wellness and feminist discourses to view and use my running as an aesthetic self-stylized expression. This manifested in other aesthetic stylized practices such as focusing on what my body could do (e.g., run for over two hours without being tired, experience the mental highs and lows of a long run), focusing on enjoyment instead of time (I would just "go" and enjoy the run), getting lost or feeling free in the movement during my runs, and training for mental benefits and mental toughness.

While I pushed my body in training it was never to the point of injury; I was patient and did not berate myself for how I looked or how I did and didn't perform. Instead I marveled in the fact that I ran. With each step during the marathon, no matter how difficult, I was continually in awe and experienced my pain (whether in legs, ankles or GI tract) as a resource that allowed me to use my body as a tool of self-expression and personal self-accomplishment. I also used aesthetic self-stylization to (re)construct my body's relationship with food and exercise whereby food was viewed as a source of fuel and nourishment to stay healthy, rather than as something to be "exercised off". Similarly, exercise was no longer viewed or experienced as a punishment for eating too much or the wrong kinds of food or as a source of guilt when I took a day off to rest.

Additionally, my conscious desire to run the BSIM in order to construct a feminist identity was also a political and critically self-aware practice: I wanted to run a marathon to achieve what only a small percentage of the female population has and breach the so-called norms of the ideal marathon body constructed in running discourse. I was aware of the history

---

[1] Researchers have recently used the termed analytic autoethnography (see Anderson, 2006) to refer to research in which the researcher is (1) an "inside" member in the research group or setting, (2) written into the published text, and (3) committed to developing theoretical understandings of broader social phenomena. At the same time, other researchers are critical of positioning autoethnography within theory and/or interpreting an autoethnography for the reader, as these practices breach the evocative, interpretive and post-modernist intents of the writing genre (see Ellis and Bochner, 2006 or Vryan, 2006). Since my research could be classified as an analytic autoethnography I acknowledge that those who align with the latter "camp" may take issue with some of my methods and interpretations. While I likely cannot appease those individuals, I acknowledge these debates up front and recognize that there are advantages and disadvantages to either approach. Engaging with such debates more fully is beyond the scope of the present paper.

of women's exclusion from the marathon, and when I researched the BSIM, I learned that males always outnumber females. My first year running BSIM in 2004 would record 1044 female vs. 1819 male "finishers". Though not part of my current self-story, scanning the pages after each of my seven marathons always meant looking at the "women's results" – which were segregated by age. I gained a sense of pride and self from being one of those women. At the same time I was aware both outside of, and "in", the marathon that I am a white, educated, middle-class woman who is afforded with this opportunity in light of such privilege.

Another reason I chose BSIM—and indeed why THIS marathon figures as a prominent character in my story--- was because of its resistance potential from other dominant running discourses that often narrowly construct running as conforming to particular "performances" via specific time goals and mileage splits. While I am not suggesting such aspirations are incorrect or bad, I personally found them constraining and limiting with respect to my running self, thus I problematized these discourses. As an international marathon, the numbers of people that BSIM attracts is small because of its treacherous course. The narratives surrounding this marathon—which also figure prominently in my self-construction and experiences during the race-- confirm that if you want a personal record (PR) do not bother signing up, but if you want an *experience*, then that is a different "story". As the race promoters put it, "finishing a marathon is a life-changing experience…finishing Big Sur will enrich your soul. Please join us the last Sunday in April for a run along the ragged edge of the western world". In constructing my running outside of, and within, this BSIM discourse I accomplished a mystical and spiritual experience through my aesthetic self-stylized practices (e.g., using pain as a resource, enjoying how my body felt during various milestones, reveling in what my body could accomplish as I finished each set of milestones).

Additionally, in drawing upon the BSIM narrative, I had numerous paradoxical moments throughout the race. I was in awe of the scenery one minute and cursing the terrain the next. I marveled that the sun was out and was later irritated that it was burning me. I experienced moments of "pleasure-pain" on hills, and had an awareness of my legs and ankles hurting yet I was pleased that my knees were not hurting. These contradictory moments all culminated into a self-identity—of "me" *and* the BSIM--- that was negotiated in similar, different and contradictory ways throughout the milestones. We (i.e., me and BSIM) are tough, we are a conglomeration of experiences, and we transgress the boundaries of what the wider world may expect of us.

Finally, there is a sense in which my body-related experiences and practices during the race (e.g., monitoring food intake, conserving energy, monitoring mile markers, timing myself on hurricane point, monitoring leg and ankle pain) might be viewed as technologies of dominance. Foucault theorized that bodies become sites of domination through technologies of power and practices of discipline and surveillance (Foucault, 1977). The self-regulating and self-monitoring practices that I engaged in throughout BSIM are prime examples of the foregoing. However, one must also keep in mind that according to Foucault (1988) it is not practices in and of themselves that are oppressive, but the discourses that one draws upon to make sense of them and give them meaning. Moreover, surveillance practices *can* be transformed and transgressed when they are reframed and executed within the context of critical self-awareness and self-asetheticization (Lloyd, 1996; Markula, 2003a; Thorpe, 2008).

Given the complexity of the above, I may have been subjecting myself to *both* technologies of dominance and technologies of the self in the case of my self-surveillance practices during the marathon. On the one hand I bought into the notion of eating synthetic food (i.e., Gu) and drink (i.e., Gatorade) as performance enhancement tools, a dominant technology of the body tied to consumerism. At the same time my conscious consumption practices during the marathon were done to enable my body to complete my feminist and mystical quest of running BSIM--a technology of the self and transformational practice of freedom. Additionally, while I viewed my pain and concentration on the broken and unbroken parts of myself as aesthetic forms of self-stylization, I also incorporated the surveillance of my pain and injury into my self-identity. In turn, I was reproducing the taken-for-granted states of pain and injury so often prevalent in distance running discourse (Allen-Collinson, 2003; Bridel and Rail, 2007; Major, 2001).

Regardless, my self-surveillance practices and other critical awareness and self-asetheticization practices engaged in both "in" and out of BSIM, ultimately served as transformational practices of freedom for "me" as I used them to challenge and renegotiate the limits of my exercising-self over time. This latter point underscores the usefulness of exploring the self and exercise relationship through technologies of the self, as *any* practice may potentially serve as a technology of the self, but "to detect athlete's critical awareness, feminists need to ask women to articulate it" (Markula, 2003a, p. 104).

CONCLUSION

In line with emerging research in sport psychology my self-reflexive story shows that the physical self is multiple, dynamic and socially constructed in discourse and power relations (Busanich and McGannon, in press; Krane, 2009; McGannon and Busanich, 2010; McGannon and Spence, 2010; Smith, 2010). As such, there are limitless ways to experience and negotiate ourselves in and through physical activity. People may use technologies of dominance, technologies of the self or a combination of both to navigate the power-discourse nexus, constructing, reconstructing, and deconstructing the physical self. By engaging in technologies of the self through critical self-awareness and aesthetic self-stylization practices we can reconfigure the power-discourse nexus, viewing the self as a work of art (Foucault, 1988, Markula, 2003a). In turn, the physical self is (re)invented in and through one's physical activity practices and experiences. As demonstrated in this paper, when combined with a Foucauldian perspective, self-reflexive writing practices add further understanding to the dynamic physical self, capturing and teasing out the complexity of that process.

Despite the usefulness of combining self-reflexive writing with technologies of the self, the technologies of the self is a complex concept with no clear formula that allows for the detection of which sport and exercise practices serve as transformational practices of freedom (Markula, 2003a). That being said, as I've pointed to in this piece and in-line with other research exploring women's sport and exercise practices as a technology of the self (e.g., Markula, 2004; Thorpe, 2008), a physically active woman must become aware of the limitations of her discursively constructed femininity and exercise-self to reconfigure the dominant discourses that disempower her. Researchers can use self-reflexive writing as a tool to articulate and problematize their own awareness of the often narrowly defined body within women's sport and exercise. Researchers may also invite research participants to write their own self-reflexive stories to contribute toward further understanding and transforming the self and sport and exercise practices.

Additionally, understanding the broader socio-cultural context of women's sport and exercise practices will also be important to realize critical self-awareness and encourage aesthetic self-stylization practices that challenge dominance in women's sport and exercise (Markula, 2003a; Markula and Pringle, 2006). As research has shown, challenging dominant discourses in sport and exercise may prove difficult as female athletes and exercisers may be in power relations reinforced by institutional and material bodies (e.g., governing sport bodies, the fitness industry) that allow women less room for resistance and less desire to construct themselves as feminists (Markula, 2003a, 2003b, 2004; Young, 1997). This last statement points to the value of researchers and practitioners in sport and fitness becoming critically self-aware by using self-reflexive knowledge and experiences as technologies of the self. Doing so has great potential to open up new or additional foundations of resistance and self-transformation in relation to women's physical selves and sport and exercise practices (Markula, 2004).

REFERENCES

Allen-Collinson, J. (2003). Running into injury time: Distance running and temporality. *Sociology of Sport Journal, 20*, 331-350.

Anderson, L. (2006). Analytic autoethnography. *Journal of Contemporary Ethnography, 35*, 373-395.

Abbas, A. (2004). The embodiment of class, gender and age through leisure: A realist analysis of long distance running. *Leisure Studies, 23*, 159-175.

Agar, M. (1995). Literary journalism as ethnography: Exploring the excluded middle. In J. Van Maanen (Ed.), *Representation in ethnography,* (pp. 112-129). London: Sage.

Bridel, William and Rail, Geneviève (2007) Sport, Sexuality, and the Productionof(Resistant) Bodies: De-/Re-Constructing the Meanings of Gay Male Marathon Corporeality. Sociology of Sport Journal, 24, 127-144.

Busanich, R., and McGannon, K. R. (2010). Deconstructing disordered eating: A feminist psychological approach to the body, food and exercise relationship in female athletes. *Quest, 62, 385-405.*

Carless, D. (2008). Serious mental illness: A lifehistory of a runner. *Qualitative Research in Psychology, 5*, 233-248.

Carless, D., and Douglas, K. (2010). Restoring connections in physical activity and mental health research and practice: A confessional tale. *Qualitative Research in Sport and Exercise, 2,* 336-353..

Chapman, G. E. (1997). Making weight: Lightweight rowing, technologies of power and technologies of the self. *Sociology of Sport Journal, 14*, 205-223.

Chase, L. F. (2006). (Un)Disciplined bodies: A Foucauldian analysis of women's rugby. *Sociology of Sport Journal, 23*, 229-247.

Chase, L. F. (2008). Running big: Clydesdale runners and technologies of the bodies. *Sociology of Sport Journal, 25*, 130-147.

Douglas, K. (2009). Storying myself: Negotiating a relational identity in professional sport. *Qualitative Research in Sport and Exercise, 1*, 176-190.

Duncan, M. C. (1994). The politics of women's body images and practices: Foucault, the panopticon, and Shape magazine. *Journal of Sport and Social Issues, 18*, 48-65.

Ellis, C., and Bochner, A. (2000). Autoethnography, personal narrative, reflexivity: Researcher as subject. In N. K. Denzin and Y. S. Lincoln (Eds.), *Handbook of qualitative research* (2nd ed. Pp. 733-768). London: Sage.

Ellis, C. and Bochner, A. (2006). Analyzing analytic autoethnography: An autopsy. *Journal of Contemporary Ethnography, 35*, 429-449.

Foucault, M. (1977). *Discipline and punish: The birth of the prison*. London: Penguin.

Foucault, M. (1978) *The history of sexuality, volume 1: An introduction*. London: Penguin. Foucault, M. (1988). Technologies of the self. In L. H. Martin, H. Gutma and P. H. Hutton (Eds.), *Technologies of the self: A seminar with Michel Foucault* (pp. 16-49). Amherst, MA: University of Massachusetts Press.

Gilbourne, D., and Richardson, D. (2006). Tales from the field: Personal reflections on the provision of psychological support in professional soccer. *Psychology of Sport and Exercise, 7*, 325-337.

Greenleaf, C. (2002). Athletic body image: Exploratory interviews with former competitive female athletes. *Women in Sport and Physical Activity Journal, 11*, 63.

Haravon Collins, L. (2002). Working out the contradictions: Feminism and aerobics. *Journal of Sport and Social Issues, 26*, 85-109.

Holt, N. (2003). Representation, legitimation, and autoethnography: An autoethnographic writing story. *International Journal of Qualitative Methods, 2*, 1-22.

Hollway, W. 1983. Heterosexual sex: Power and desire for the other. In S. Cartledge and J. Ryan(Eds.), *Sex and love: New thoughts on old contradictions* (pp. 124-140). London: Women's Press.

Johns, D. P., and Johns, J. S. (2000). Surveillance, subjectivism and technologies of power: An analysis of the discusrive practice of high performance sport. *International Review for the Sociology of Sport, 35*, 219-234.

Krane, V. (2009). A sport odyssey. *Qualitative Research in Sport and Exercise, 3*, 221-238.

Lloyd, M. (1996). A feminist mapping of Foucauldian politics. In S. Heckman (Ed.), *Feminist interpretations of Michel Foucault*. University park, PA: Pennsylvania State University Press.

Lupton, D. (1997). Foucault and the medicalization critique. In A. Petersen and R. Bunton (Eds.), *Focault, health and medicine* (pp. 94-110). London: Routledge.

Major, W. F. (2001). The benefits and costs of serious running. *World Leisure Journal, 43*, 12-25.

Markula, P. (1995). Firm but shapely, fit but sexy, strong but thin: The post-modern aerobicizing female bodies. *Sociology of Sport Journal, 12*, 424-453.

Markula, P. (2001). Beyond the perfect body: Women's body image distortion in fitness magazine discourse. *Journal of Sport and Social Issues, 25*, 134-155.

Markula, P. (2003a). The technologies of the self: Sport, feminism and Foucault. *Sociology of Sport Journal, 20*, 87-107.

Markula, P. (2003b). Post-modern aerobics: Contradiction and resistance. In A. Bolin and J. Granskog (Eds.), *Athletic intruders: Ethnographic research on women, culture and exercise* (pp. 53-78). Albany: State University of New York Press.

Markula, P. (2004). "Turning into one's self": Foucault's technologies of the self and mindful fitness. *Sociology of Sport Journal, 21*, 302-321.

Markula, P., Burns, M., and Riley, S. (2008). Introducing critical bodies: Representations, identities and practices of weight and body management. In S. Riley, M. Burns, H. Frith,

S. Wiggins, and P. Markula (Eds.), *Critical bodies: Representations, identities and practices of weight and body management* (pp. 1-22). New York: Palgrave Macmillan.

Markula, P., and Pringle, R. (2006). *Foucault, sport and exercise: Power, knowledge and transforming the self.* New York: Routledge.

McGannon, K. R. (2004). Honey, is it just me, or does this research make my AAAS(P) look fat?: An autoethnographical tale of the physical self and exercise participation. Presentation to the annual meeting of the Association for the Advancement of Applied Sport Psychology, Minneapolis, MN.

McGannon, K. R., and Busanich, R. (2010). Rethinking subjectivity in sport and exercise psychology: A feminist post-structuralist perspective on women's embodied physical activity. In T. V. Ryba, R. J. Schinke and G. Tenenbaum (Eds.), *The cultural turn in sport psychology (pp. 203-229).* Morgantown, West Virginia: Fitness Information Technology.

McGannon, K. R. and Johnson, C. R. (2009). Strategies for reflective sport psychology research. In R. J. Schinke and S. J. Hanrahan (Eds.), *Cultural sport psychology* (pp. 57-75). Champaign, IL.: Human Kinetics.

McGannon, K. R., and Metz, J. L. (*2010*). Through the funhouse mirror: Understanding access and (un)expected selves through confessional tales. In R. J. Schinke (Ed.) *Contemporary sport psychology (pp. 153-170).* Hauppauge, NY: Nova Science Publishers.

McGannon, K. R'. and Spence, J. C. (2010). Speaking of the self and physical activity participation: What discursive psychology can tell us about an old problem. *Qualitative Research in Sport and Exercise, 2,* 17-38.

Ogles, B., Masters, K., and Richardson, S. (1995). Obligatory running and gender: An analysisof participative motives and training habits. *International Journal of Sport Psychology,26*, 233-248.

Potter, J., and Wetherell, M. (1987). *Discourse and social psychology: Beyond attitudes and behavior.* London: Sage.

Rail, G. and Harvey, J. (1995). Body at work: Michel Foucault and the sociology of sport. *Sociology of Sport Journal, 18*, 162-180.

Richardson, L. (2000a). New writing practices in qualitative research. *Sociology of Sport Journal, 17*, 5-20.

Richardson, L. (2000b). Writing: A method of inquiry. In N. K. Denzin and Y. S. Lincoln (Eds.), *Handbook of qualitative research* (2nd ed., pp. 923-948). Thousand Oaks, CA: Sage.

Ryba, T. V., Schinke, R. J. and Tenenbaum, G. (2010) *The cultural turn in sport psychology.* Morgantown, West Virginia: Fitness Information Technology. Schinke, R. J. and Hanrahan, S. J. (2009) *Cultural sport psychology.* Champaign, IL.: Human Kinetics.

Sermijn, J., Devieger, P. and Loots, G. (2008). The narrative construction of self: Selfhood as a rhizomatic story. *Qualitative Inquiry, 14*, 632-650.

Smith, B. M. (2010). Narrative inquiry: Ongoing conversations and questions for sport and exercise psychology research. *International Review of Sport and Exercise Psychology, 3*, 87-107.

Smith, S. (2000). British nonelite road running and masculinity: A case of 'running repairs?'*Men and Masculinities, 3*, 187-208.

Sparkes, A. C. (2000). Autoethnography and narratives of self: Reflections on criteria in action. *Sociology of Sport Journal, 17*, 21-43.

Sparkes, A. C. (2002a). *Telling tales in sport and physical activity: A qualitative journey.* Champaign, IL.: Human Kinetics.

Sparkes, A. C. (2002b). Fictional representations: On difference, choice and risk. *Sociology of Sport Journal, 19*, 1-24.

Sparkes, A. C., and Smith, B. (2009). Judging the quality of qualitative inquiry: Criteriology and relativism in action. *Psychology of Sport and Exercise, 10*, 491-497.

Thompson, S. (2007). Characteristics of the female athlete triad in collegiate cross-country runners. *Journal of American College Health, 56*, 129-137.

Thorpe, H. (2008). Foucault, technologies of self and the media: Discourses of femininity in snowboarding culture. *Journal of Sport and Social Issues, 32*, 199-229.

vanIngen, C. (2004). Therapeutic landscapes and the regulated body in the Toronto FrontRunners. *Sociology of Sport Journal, 21*, 253-269.

Van Maanen, J. (1988). *Tales of the field.* Chicago: University of Chicago Press.

Vryan, K. D. (2006). Expanding analytic autoethnography and enhancing its potential. *Journal of Contemporary Ethnography, 35*, 405-409.

Wesely, J. K. (2001). Negotiating gender: Bodybuilding and the natural/unnatural continuum. *Sociology of Sport Journal, 18*, 162-180.

Young, K. (1997). Women, sport and physicality: Preliminary findings from a Canadian study. *International Review for the Sociology of Sport, 32*, 297-305.

Submitted to Athletic Insight: February 20, 2010

In: Athletic Insight's Writings of 2012   ISBN: 978-1-62618-120-5
Editor: Robert Schinke   © 2013 Nova Science Publishers, Inc.

Chapter 4

INTERNET USAGE PATTERNS AND ETHICAL CONCERNS IN SPORT AND EXERCISE PSYCHOLOGY

Jack C. Watson II[*1], *John R. Lubker*[2],
Rebecca A. Zakrajsek[3] *and Alessandro Quartiroli*[4]

[1]West Virginia University, US
[2]University of Notre Dame, US
[3]University of Tennessee, US
[4]West Virginia University, US

ABSTRACT

Changes that occur in technology and the internet have a strong influence upon the provision of teaching, research and practice within the field of sport and exercise psychology (SEP) and other mental health fields. These influences upon SEP are made even more dramatic given the rate of change in these evolving technologies. The purpose of the current research project was to better understand how SEP practitioners (members of the Association for Applied Sport Psychology) utilize the internet in their teaching, research and practice. Participants (N=292) completed an online survey which assessed demographics, time spent using the internet, proficiency, and importance of the internet in one's professional endeavors. Further questions relate to ethical concerns related to the use of the internet in the practice of SEP. Analyses of the data revealed significant differences between students and professionals, certified/licensed and non-certified/non-licensed practitioners, and psychology and physical education professionals with regard to their use of, perceived competence with, and ethical concern for using the internet in teaching research and service.

The increased presence and improved familiarity with computers that has occurred over the past few decades has produced an increase in the attention paid to the use of such

---

[*] Send all correspondence related to this article to: Jack C. Watson II, College of Physical Activity and Sport Sciences, West Virginia University, P.O. Box 6116, Morgantown, WV 26506-6116. (304)293-325 (ext. 5273). Fax: (304)293-4641. jack.watson@mail.wvu.edu.

technology within the daily professional lives of helping professionals who teach courses, conduct research, and consult with clients. Since its initial development in the 1970's, the internet has evolved into a global interconnection of government, education, and business computer networks that the public now depends upon. In fact, the availability of inexpensive and user friendly computer networks is one of the more recent steps in the evolution of computer technology (Sampson, Kolodinsky, and Greeno, 1997). Satisfying the common cultural desire of wanting quick results, the internet allows individuals to obtain answers, solve problems, and communicate with others both quickly and reliably. Further, hardware and software advancements occur so quickly, that it is commonly remarked that computer technology is out of date within three months of purchase.

As technological advancements grow, individuals continue to find new and innovative ways of using technology as an opportunity to go beyond traditional methods of disseminating information and services and furthering professional development (Sampson et al., 1997).

Those working in academia are also attempting to take full advantage of technology with online courses, posting assignments and online readings, and using the internet as a medium to communicate with students. Helping professionals have gone beyond the traditional face-to-face approach to offering services over the internet. Such online services include self-help psycho-educational resources, career counseling, support groups, psychological assessment, counseling, and supervision (Sampson, 2000; Barr, Taylor and Luce, 2003; Schultze, 2006; Miller, Cowger, Young, Tobacyk, Sheets, and Loftus, 2008). Among health care professionals, computers are often considered to be a useful tool with which to provide services (Horgan, Merrick, Reif, and Stewart, 2007; Liss, 2005; Monnier, Laken, and Carter, 2002), as this medium is seen as an innovative and efficient communication channel for providing mental health services and supporting the therapeutic activities of counselors and psychologists (Sampson et al., 1997).

As is true within other professions, sport and exercise psychology (SEP) professionals are finding the internet to be a powerful and cost-effective tool that has the potential to help promote and develop the field as well as change the way SEP professionals conduct research, teach, and provide services (Watson and Etzel, 2000; Watson, Tenenbaum, Lidor, and Alfermann, 2001). Although use of the internet for the application of SEP services has yet to be investigated, other helping professions (e.g. counseling, psychology, assessment and testing) have been using the internet as a resource for over 30 years and may serve as guides for the use of the internet in the field of SEP (Maxmen, 1978; as cited in Fisher and Fried, 2003). Based upon the work being conducted in these other helping professions and basic findings from SEP literature, the authors believe that the internet is an important component of the field that needs to be better understood.

Counseling professionals have identified several benefits related to the use of the internet for mental health practices (Butcher et al., 1985; Marks, Shaw, and Parkin, 1998; Newman et al., 1997). Many of these benefits appear to be transferable into the field of SEP. These potential benefits include: increased awareness of service availability, cost-effectiveness, psychological assessments are updated more easily and scored more quickly, increased access to self-help psycho-educational resources, improved access to services that transcend geographic and physical barriers, improved access for clients who have transportation problems, increased access and promotion of cross-culture communication, improved accessibility to self-help groups, and increased opportunities for supervision, consultation and collaboration among colleagues (Naglieri et al., 2004; Sampson, 1998; Zizzi and Perna, 2001).

In addition to these abovementioned benefits to the use of the internet for SEP service delivery, other advantages to the client may include the relative anonymity of the client and the increased response time (Smiley and Vande Creek, 2005; Zizzi and Perna, 2001). While the first of these additional advantage offers a way to lower the client's perception of stigmatization and embarrassment related to seeking help (Smiley and Vande Creek, 2005; Zizzi and Perna, 2001), the second advantage allows more time for deeper reflections by both therapist and client (Smiley and Vande Creek, 2005).

Sport and exercise psychology information and services on the internet, such as self-help psycho-educational resources (e.g. imagery, goal setting exercises), self-help groups, question/answer services, and professional resources (e.g. books, videos, tapes), provide opportunities for increased awareness amongst consumers (Zizzi and Perna, 2001). Athletes, coaches, and SEP professionals have in the past consulted over the internet and obtained a plethora of information regarding methods for decreasing anxiety, goal setting exercises, imagery, and various other psychological skills (Stoll and Lau, 2003; Zizzi and Perna, 2001).

Further, recent research has shown that after attending a SEP workshop, approximately 40% of coaches accessed a website containing information about sport psychology and sport psychology services during a four-week follow-up period (Zakrajsek and Zizzi, 2008). With roughly 10% - 43% of coaches reporting access to sport psychology services and 2% - 22% reporting working with a sport psychology consultant (Zakrajsek and Zizzi, 2007; 2008), it is apparent that the internet may be a viable option for coaches to learn about, access and use sport psychology services.

The internet can be a cost-effective, time-saving enterprise due to the geographic barriers that are evident in the field of SEP. The number of Association for Applied Sport Psychology (AASP) certified consultants has grown to roughly 300 since its inception in 1986. While this seems like a large number of consultants, many of them are located in cities with universities that have SEP programs. This means that individuals living in many areas around the world have little or no direct access to certified SEP service providers. The internet provides improved access for performance enhancement, counseling, collaboration, and supervision services to individuals living in locations distant to qualified consultants. Furthermore, the internet may provide a means to keep in contact with athletes who travel for training and competitions outside of a consultant's immediate reach.

While many benefits of service delivery via the internet have been identified, several concerns have also been voiced (Skinner and Zack, 2004). Professionals must be held responsible for providing ethical and quality services to consumers (Bloom and Sampson, 1998) with positive results (Barr, Taylor, and Luce, 2003). While the internet has the potential to increase the exposure and viability of SEP through the 21st century, it is important to maintain standards of professional conduct and be aware of potential concerns, problems, and ethical issues (Watson et al., 2001).

Reviews of literature from fields outside of SEP have revealed numerous concerns related to using the internet for service delivery. Bloom and Sampson (1998), Mallen, Vogel, and Rochlen, (2005), and Sampson (1998a) identified issues such as confidentiality, relationship development, competence, limited accessibility, data transmission and storage, credentialing, training, quality and quantity of information, lack of local knowledge, and validating internet resources as important ethical concerns regarding internet use. Additionally, Del Rio Sánchez

(2002) identified concerns related to the difficulty of using and managing technology as it changes so rapidly, as well as the professionalism and the unknown effectiveness of psychological services offered via the internet as major concerns with regard to using the internet for service delivery. Due to the aforementioned concerns, Watson et al. (2001) proposed ethical guidelines for internet use in SEP using information obtained from the American Counseling Association (1999), the National Board of Certified Counselors (1999), and Bloom and Sampson (1998). These proposed ethical standards included, but were not limited to, confidentiality, competence, the online counseling relationship, and legal considerations (Watson et al., 2001).

Professionals in various fields have identified the internet as a powerful tool for service delivery (Sampson et al., 1997). Within the field of SEP, the internet could and is likely being used for marketing and dissemination of information, research, distance learning, individual and group supervision, counseling/performance enhancement, referrals, and as a medium for discussion and collaboration (Watson and Etzel, 2000; Watson et al., 2001).

In addition, new potential ethical concerns are being faced by professionals as technological advancements change the way services are provided. Although the benefits and concerns have been explored by a few SEP professionals (Watson and Etzel, 2000; Watson et al., 2001), how SEP professionals are actually using the internet and what precautionary measures are being taken to ensure quality of care have not been empirically explored.

Therefore, the primary purpose of the current study was to assess the current internet proficiency levels, usage patterns, perceived usefulness, and time spent using the internet by AASP SEP professionals.

A secondary purpose of this study was to assess the perceived ethical problems and concerns of using the internet in the practice of SEP, as well as AASP's need to address these ethical concerns/problems in its ethics code.

METHOD

Participants

Members of the Association of Applied Sport Psychology ($N = 292$) were assessed via an internet survey to determine their use of, perceptions of, and beliefs about the ethicality of using the internet in their work while teaching, researching and applying their skills in SEP. The sample consisted of 147 males and 133 females (ages 21 to 61). Ethnic background was primarily Caucasian ($n = 251$) and a majority resided in the United States ($n = 225$); however, 18 ethnic backgrounds and 23 countries were represented in this sample. The sample consisted of professionals with bachelors ($n = 42$), masters ($n = 96$), and doctoral ($n = 142$) degrees which were primarily focused in physical education/exercise science ($n = 131$) and psychology/counseling ($n = 130$).

Participants primarily worked in university settings ($n = 168$) or private practice ($n = 44$) specializing in performance enhancement ($n = 157$), counseling or clinical psychology ($n = 50$), health or exercise psychology ($n = 41$), or social psychology ($n = 28$). The majority of participants were unlicensed practitioners ($n = 216$) or non-certified consultants ($n = 153$); however, 80 non-certified consultants reported that they planned on becoming certified within the next two years.

A minority of participants were licensed mental health practitioners ($n = 56$) or certified consultants ($n = 58$). Participants reported the following levels of ethical training: none ($n = 25$), undergrad course ($n = 28$), independent readings ($n = 23$), workshops ($n = 25$), and some graduate coursework ($n = 191$).

Instrument

The Internet Use Survey (IUS) was developed by the authors to assess AASP members' impressions of the internet and related technologies with respect to perceptions of personal use and proficiency, usefulness and ethical issues for professional activities, and their specific time and reasons for using the internet in SEP teaching, research and practice. The IUS was separated into nine sections. The first section contained 13 demographic questions about the respondents and their training. The second section consisted of nine, four-point Likert-type items ranging from 1 (*none*) to 4 (*expert*) which assessed respondent perceived proficiency levels for using internet related technology. The third section asked five questions related to the type and frequency of the delivery of applied SEP services to clients and nine, four-point Likert-type items ranging from 1 (*not at all*) to 4 (*very much*) about the use of specific internet related technologies in the practice of applied SEP. The fourth and fifth sections contained 14 items assessing the same issues found in section three, but related directly to the use of the internet for teaching and research respectively. The sixth section included 20 items related to individuals' perceptions of the usefulness of the internet in SEP teaching, research and applied services and the seventh section contained 20 items related to time spent during a normal week using specific internet related technologies, both using the same four-point Likert-type scale from 1 (*not at all*) to 4 (*very much*). The eighth section contained 56 Likert-type items ranging from 1 (*not at all*) to 4 (*very much*) related to perceptions of the potential for ethical problems to evolve from internet related technology, and perceptions of the need for ethical standards to be written to cover these new technologies. The ninth section asked three open ended items about potential uses of the internet in SEP, and ethical concerns related to uses of the internet.

Survey development and security. After developing the internet Use Survey (IUS) and consent form in a paper and pencil format, the documents were translated via the Microsoft FrontPage web-editing program into hypertext markup language (HTML) format. The final survey was then uploaded to a university academic computing server where it could only be accessed by the research team, the academic computing staff, and participating AASP members. The online survey was configured so that once a finished survey was submitted, the data were automatically sent to the university server (i.e., in tab delimited format) and to two members of the research team via e-mail for back-up purposes. Once data collection was completed, the tab-delimited data from the server was converted into a spreadsheet format for input into the SPSS statistical analysis program. This dataset was then double checked to ensure consistency of results and to rule out the possibility of multiple responses from the same person.

Pilot testing. Initial pilot testing of the instrument involved the use of 15 undergraduate students in SEP. These students completed the survey to the best of their ability, providing comments about the wording of instructions and items, and time needed to complete the survey. Minor changes in wording were made as a result of this testing, and an additional pilot test was then conducted using 8 doctoral students who at the time were providing teaching, research and/or practice services within the field of SEP. Feedback again resulted in minor modifications to the format to help make administration easier.

Procedures

Upon approval from the Institutional Review Board for the Protection of Human Subjects and approval from the AASP executive committee, two broadcast e-mails were sent one month apart to all AASP members who had provided the organization with an e-mail address. These messages provided members with an overview of the project and invited them to visit a web page to complete the survey.

Upon opening this web page, participants were presented with informed consent information outlining ethical issues related to internet research. Members who clicked on a box indicating they agreed to participate were automatically transferred to a web page with the survey and completion instructions. Upon completion of the survey, respondents were asked to click on a box to submit the survey, and were transferred to a debriefing and thank you page. The time needed for administration was approximately 15-20 minutes.

RESULTS

Demographic information was used to divide respondents into four groups based upon dichotomous variables: status (student vs. professional), professional specialization (physical education vs. psychology), licensure status (licensed vs. unlicensed), and certified consultant status (certified vs. uncertified). All analyses in this study were conducted using these four groupings as independent variables.

Initial Item Reduction

Initially, the survey consisted of 38 items developed by the researchers pertaining to the ethical precautions, problems, standards, and concerns related to using the internet in SEP. To pare down the number of analyses and reduce the chance for type I error, only items that displayed a standard deviation above 1.0 (where one may assume a high level of variability in the ratings) were included in the analyses (Table 1). This criterion for inclusion was based upon the idea that if an item displayed a high standard deviation, there might be some controversy between certain member groups of AASP concerning this item (Etzel et al., 2004; Petitpas et al., 1994). Due to the skewness of these independent variables, the non-parametric Mann-Whitney test was employed to test the differences in the means of the sample.

Potential Ethical Problems Related to the Internet

There was a significant difference between students (n= 111) and professionals (n = 150) for the ethical problem of advertisement of services (z = -3.03, p < .01). On this item, professionals (M = 2.51) showed more ethical concern than students (M = 2.13). Another significant difference was found between certified consultants (n = 55) and non-certified consultants (n = 205) where certified consultants showed more ethical concern for the advertisement of services than non-certified consultants (z = 2.30, p < .05). Also on this item, licensed psychologists (M = 2.64) showed more ethical concern than unlicensed psychologists (M = 2.28).

Table 1. Items with a Standard Deviation above 1.00 on the IUS Scale

Items	SD
Advertisement of services [a]	1.04
Communications with professionals	1.07
Referrals	1.01
Self-education	1.12
Advice	1.07
Job searching	1.01
Videoconferencing	1.10
Communication with students	1.10
Communication with class	1.05
Scheduling appointments [a]	1.04
Recruiting research participants	1.00
Contacting research participants	1.03
Student grades/feedback	1.16
Reimbursement [a]	1.08
Equality of access to the internet	1.03
Cross-boundary licensure issues	1.09

[a] Significant t-Tests results between athletes and SPCs, p's< .001.

Ethical Standards of AASP

There was a significant difference between licensed psychologists (n = 47) and those who were not licensed psychologists (n = 199) related to opinions about scheduling appointments using the internet (z = 4.10, p < .001).

On this item, licensed psychologists (M = 2.51) indicated more strongly than those who were not licensed (M = 1.81), their belief that AASP should focus an ethical standard on this issue of scheduling clients using the internet.

Ethical Concerns when Using the Internet

There was a significant difference between physical education professionals ($n = 111$) and psychology professionals ($n = 101$) related to reimbursement of services ($z = -2.94$, $p < .01$). Physical education professionals ($M = 2.07$) thought this item less of a concern when using the internet than psychology professionals ($M = 2.50$). There was also a significant difference between physical education professionals ($n = 125$) and psychology professionals ($n = 110$) for the ethical concern of equality of access to the internet for clients ($z = -2.54$, $p < .05$), where physical education professionals ($M = 2.22$) were less concerned about this issue than psychology professionals ($M = 2.55$). Finally, there was a significant difference between physical education professionals ($n = 113$) and psychology professionals ($n = 105$) for the ethical concern of cross-boundary licensure issues ($z = -1.98$, $p < .05$), where physical education professionals ($M = 2.61$) showed less concern about the issue than psychology professionals ($M = 2.90$).

Perceived Proficiency in Internet Features

A perceived proficiency score was calculated for each respondent by summing their self-report scores for the nine proficiency items (four-point Likert-type items) related to the use of the internet in SEP (i.e., chat rooms, data collection, e-mail, list serves, videoconferencing, web browsers, internet security, and instant messaging). By summing these scores, respondents were given a perceived proficiency score which could range from 9-36, with higher scores indicating a higher total perceived proficiency level. Independent sample t-tests were then calculated to determine if differences existed between the independent variables.

Those respondents who were not AASP certified consultants ($M = 23.91$) reported a higher level of perceived proficiency in using the internet than certified consultants ($M = 21.64$) ($t(197) = -2.61$, $p < .01$, $d = -.37$). Professionals without licenses ($M = 23.96$) reported a higher level of perceived proficiency in using the internet than licensed professionals ($M = 21.61$) ($t(196) = -2.71$, $p < .01$, $d = -.39$). Physical education professionals ($M = 24.20$) reported a higher level of perceived proficiency in using the internet than psychology professionals ($M = 22.79$) ($t(197) = 1.70$, $p < .05$, $d = .24$). Although students ($M = 24.09$) reported a higher level of perceived proficiency in using the internet than non-students ($M = 22.94$), there was no significant difference between the means ($d = .24$).

Precaution Taken Using the Internet: Teaching, Research, and Practice

Participants were asked to assess the "level of precaution" taken in each area of internet use: teaching, research, and service in three separate, singular questions. Independent samples t-tests were used to assess the differences in these levels of precaution. No significant differences were reported between any of the four dichotomous groupings on the level of precaution taken using the internet in SEP teaching, research, or practice ($p > .05$). However, when the means of these items where investigated, ethical precaution taken in SEP practice were non-significantly more elevated than those for research and teaching; this was evident in all four dichotomous groupings (Table 2).

Internet Use in the Practice of Sport and Exercise Psychology

In this study, 52% of the sample reported using the internet for zero hours a week in their practice of SEP, followed by 41% reporting 1-5 hours of weekly use and 5% reporting 6-10 hours of weekly use. Ninety-six percent of the sample reported "in person" to be the preferred method of contact, and only 1.7% reported preferring to use the internet as the primary method of contact in the practice of SEP. Amongst respondents, 36% reported that the internet was only "slightly important" in the practice of SEP. Twenty-two percent of the sample reported the internet to be of moderate importance to the practice of SEP, while 14% reported that the internet was "not at all important" and 13% indicated that it was "very much important."

Table 2. Precaution Taken Using the Internet: Teaching, Research, and Practice Means and Standard Deviations

		Teaching	Research	Practice
Status				
	Student	2.67 (.92)	2.82 (.94)	3.18 (.97)
	Professional	2.62 (.93)	2.88 (1.03)	3.07 (1.04)
Professional Specialization				
	Physical Education	2.62 (.95)	2.85 (1.02)	3.03 (1.08)
	Psychology	2.72 (.87)	2.88 (.94)	3.26 (.89)
Licensure Status				
	Licensed	2.75 (.88)	2.96 (.92)	3.33 (.82)
	Non-licensed	2.62 (.93)	2.84 (1.00)	3.06 (1.06)
Certified Consultant Status				
	Certified	2.80 (.87)	3.03 (1.03)	3.31 (.85)
	Non-certified	2.59 (.94)	2.81 (.98)	3.05 (1.06)

Respondents who were not AASP Certified Consultants reported a significantly higher score for the usefulness of the internet in the practice of SEP than certified consultants ($t(197) = -2.08$, $p < .05$, $d = -.30$). No significant differences in the reported usefulness of the Internet in practice were reported between non-licensed and licensed consultants, physical education and psychology professionals, or students and non-students.

Those professionals who were not AASP Certified Consultants reported a significantly higher level of frequency in using the internet in practice than certified consultants ($t(213) = -2.27$, $p < .05$, $d = -.31$). There were no significant differences reported between non-licensed and licensed practitioners, physical education and psychology professionals, or students and non-students. Although no significant differences were found, the reported means for the frequency of use of the internet features in the practice of SEP were quite low (between 13.94 and 15.57; 9-36 point scale for self-reported proficiency score).

Internet Use in Teaching Sport and Exercise Psychology

In the current study, 52% of the respondents reported using the internet for zero hours a week in their teaching of SEP. Thirty-seven percent reported using the internet for 1-5 hours a week and 7% reporting 6-10 hours of use each week. Eighty percent of the sample reported "in person" to be the preferred method of contact, 18% reported preferring to use the internet as the primary method of contact in the teaching of SEP. The importance of the Internet in the teaching of SEP was reported as "moderately" important by 22%, "slightly" important by 21%, "very" important by 14%, and "not at all" important by 7% of the respondents. There were no significant differences reported between non-certified and certified consultants, non-licensed and licensed consultants, physical education and psychology professionals, or students and non-students in the frequency of their use of the internet in teaching. Although no significant differences were found, the reported means for the frequency of use of the internet features in the teaching of SEP were quite low (between 14.17 and 15.40; 9-36 point scale for self-reported proficiency score). No significant differences were found between non-certified and certified consultants, non-licensed and licensed consultants, physical education and psychology professionals, or students and non-students in the perceived usefulness of the Internet in the teaching of SEP.

Internet Use in Sport and Exercise Psychology Research

In this study 46% of the sample reported using the internet between 1-5 hours a week in their SEP research, followed by 32% reporting zero hours and 14% reporting 6-10 hours of weekly use. Eighty-four percent of the sample reported their preferred method of research contact to be "in person". Of the remaining participants, 14% reported preferring to use the Internet as their primary method of contact in SEP research. For the deemed importance of the Internet in SEP research, 28% reported it was "very" important, followed by "moderately" (21%), "slightly" (18%), and "not at all" (7%) important. There were no significant differences reported between non-certified and certified consultants, non-licensed and licensed consultants, physical education and psychology professionals, or students and non-students in their frequency for using the Internet for SEP research. Although no significant differences were found, the reported means for the frequency of use of the internet in SEP research were quite low (between 14.23 and 15.52; 9-36 point scale for self-reported proficiency score). Sport psychology students reported a significantly higher score for the usefulness of the internet in SEP research than non-students ($t(241) = 2.82$, $p < .01$, $d = .36$). No significant differences were found between non-certified and certified consultants, non-licensed and licensed consultants, and physical education and psychology professionals.

Ethical Issues Related to the Internet

Licensed professionals reported a significantly higher level of belief that the ethical standards of AASP should address the use of the internet than non-licensed professionals for the practice ($t(198) = 2.95$, $p < .01$, $d = .42$), teaching ($t(228) = 2.49$, $p < .05$, $d = .33$), and research ($t(232) = 2.12$, $p < .05$, $d = .28$) of SEP. Non-students reported a significantly higher level perception of potential ethical problems related to using the internet than students for the teaching ($t(233) = -2.02$, $p < .05$, $d = -.26$) of SEP. There were no significant differences between certified and non-certified consultants on these items.

DISCUSSION

This was the first study that investigated internet usage patterns of professionals in the field of SEP. This study also provides a "baseline" assessment of how professionals in SEP are using the internet in their teaching, research, and practice.

Perceived Proficiency in Internet Features

Participants in this study reported moderate to moderately high perceived proficiency levels related to uses of the internet within professional practice. However, the proficiency levels of certified consultants and licensed professionals for using the internet were lower than uncertified and unlicensed professionals. Physical education professionals also reported a higher level of perceived proficiency with internet technology when compared to psychology professionals. This is cause for concern because the internet is becoming a more useful and common avenue for consultation and those who are certified and/or licensed to engage in consultation perceive themselves as less proficient than professionals who may have less training or fewer credentials to practice SEP. While practicing SEP without licensure or certification may not always be unethical, it could lead to boundary confusion or competency issues. These causes for concern may be even more valid if unlicensed and non-certified practitioners use the internet for service delivery more often due to their higher levels of perceived competency. Because of the vastness of the internet, it is difficult to keep track of all SEP services being provided on it. Further, if unlicensed or non-certified consultants have more perceived proficiency with service delivery over the internet, they may appear to potential clients to offer better services. It would behoove governing bodies such as AASP to require coursework related to the internet and/or a fraction of the 400 hours needed for certification to be completed through the use of the internet. Further, professional organizations may also be wise to offer a mentorship or continuing education program for certified professionals who are not proficient in the use of the internet to assist in ensuring effective and efficient use of the internet in practice. Because of the speed of change related to the internet and other technologies, the provision of teaching, research and practice in the field of SEP is likely to continue changing at a rapid pace.

Sport and Exercise Psychology Practice, Teaching, and Research

Of the total sample, 48% reported using the internet in the practice of SEP. This statistic highlights the usefulness of the internet in SEP consulting. Because of the paucity of certified and licensed SEP consultants in the United States and world-wide, there are geographical barriers that pose a problem in reaching clients who could benefit from SEP services. Although the internet is being used for consultative purposes, 96% of the participants in this study reported "in person" as the preferred method of contact and only 1.7% preferred using the internet as their primary method of contact. More research is needed to parcel out why the vast majority of practitioners prefer to consult in-person, and what factors would need to change to help them feel more comfortable with internet related consultations. While the internet can be a useful resource, only 13% reported that the internet was "very important" in the practice of SEP and 71% reported that the internet was either slightly, moderately, or very important in the practice of SEP. Given that non-certified consultants reported the internet as being more useful and reported a higher frequency use of the internet in the practice of SEP compared to certified consultants, it makes sense that they would also view themselves as having higher proficiency in internet usage.

In this sample, 48% of the participants reported using the internet in their teaching of SEP. Once again, "in-person" was the preferred method of contact (80%). The internet is becoming a larger part of teaching at the university level and 57% reported that the internet was either slightly, moderately, or very important in the teaching of SEP. Lastly, 68% of the sample reported using the internet in their SEP research. Eighty-four percent of the sample reported "in person" as their preferred method of research contact. However, using the internet in research is seen as a valuable tool where 67% reported that the internet was either slightly, moderately, or very important in SEP research. Within this study, respondents identified research as the professional endeavor where they most use the internet.

Ethical Issues in Using the Internet in Sport and Exercise Psychology

Overall, the total sample of participants reported a higher level of ethical precaution when using the internet for SEP practice as compared to research and teaching. It is important that governing bodies such as AASP continue to promote ethical practice in SEP. Because the internet is currently being used to consult with athletes and exercisers, and will only become a more widely used avenue for contact, ethical standards for using the internet in the practice of SEP need to be developed and promoted.

If SEP professionals and programs deem ethical behavior to be important, and want the internet to be a place where ethical behavior is warranted, coursework might be a necessary step for AASP certification. Within this sample, licensed psychologists reported a stronger belief that AASP should focus on ethical standards.

These individuals may be more sensitive to ethical concerns which, as stated previously, may be related to their lower frequency of using the internet and perceived proficiency. Educating professionals in the practice of using the internet in SEP may increase the perceived proficiency of certified and licensed professionals. In this study, it was found that the more training a person had, the higher level of ethical concern they had for using the internet for service delivery.

While ethical behavior has some origin in one's personality, training in psychology and specifically ethics can aid professionals in becoming more conscious of potential ethical pitfalls, especially in a new medium like the internet. In addition to educating certified and licensed professionals, it would be equally important to promote ethical guidelines of internet usage to non-certified and certified professionals especially since they seem to be using the internet in practice.

Ethical Issues Related to AASP Governance

At the professional level, licensed professionals reported a higher belief that AASP ethical standards should address the use of the internet compared to non-licensed professionals for the practice, teaching, and research of SEP. However, based upon the differences found between students and professionals, the next wave of future professionals seem to be more proficient and less concerned about using the internet. This may be a concern of over confidence or lack of knowledge of the potential ethical pitfalls of using the internet in the teaching, research, and practice of SEP. Either way, with the rapid growth of SEP, the "peeling away" of the stigma of using a sport psychologist, and the increasing belief in the benefits of SEP – the internet can either positively or negatively affect the future growth of the field.

LIMITATIONS AND FUTURE DIRECTIONS

There were a few limitations to this current study. First, this study assessed participants' level of perceived internet proficiency using an internet-based survey. Therefore, participants who might have little to no proficiency using the internet or completing surveys on the internet might not have completed this survey, in turn skewing the data. Also, this sample was limited to AASP members and; therefore, is not necessarily generalizable to the greater or worldwide population of SEP professionals.

Three major themes/future directions that have come to light via this study. First, there needs to be some establishment of ethical guidelines and/or standards for using the internet in the practice of SEP. While teaching and research are important areas in which ethical standards need to be adhered to, participants in this study believed that there was more of an ethical concern in the practice of SEP. Second, new professionals (who are much more inexperienced) seem to be moving in the direction of using the internet in their practice; therefore, it would be beneficial for AASP to establish certification standards related to the internet to ensure that all interested parties are being protected. Finally, more consistent research needs to be conducted in this area to help ethical codes and knowledge keep up with practice trends.

REFERENCES

American Psychologist Association.(2002). Ethical principles of psychologists and code of conduct. Retrieved from http://www.apa.org/ethics/code2002.html.

Barr Taylor, C., and Luce, K. H. (2003).Computer- and Internet-based psychotherapy interventions.*Current Direction in Psychological Science*, 12(1), 18-22.

Butcher, J. N., Keller, L. S., and Bacon, S. F. (1985). Current developments and future directions in computerized personality assessment.*Journal of Consulting and Clinical Psychology, 53,* 803-815.

Del Rio Sánchez, C. (2002).Psicoterapia online: Consideraciones Éticas y deontologicas. *Revista de PsicologiaUniversitasTarraconensis, 24*, 111-131.

Etzel, E. F., Watson II, J. C., and Zizzi, S. J., (2004). A web-based survey of AAASP members' ethical beliefs and behaviors in the new millennium.Journal of Applied Sport Psychology, 16, 236-250.

Fenichel, M., Suler, J., Barak, A., Zelvin, E., Jones, G., Munro, K., et al. (2002).Myths and realities of online clinical work.*Cyberpsychology and Behavior, 5*, 481-497.

Griffiths, M. (2001). Online therapy: A cause for concern? *Psychologist, 14*, 244-248.

Mallen, M. J., Vogel, D. L., and Rochlen, A. B. (2005). The practical aspects of online counseling: Ethics, training, technology, and competency. *The Counseling Psychologist*, 33, 776-818.

Marks, I., Shaw, S., and Parkin, R. (1998).Computer-aided treatments of mental health problems.*Clinical Psychology: Science and Practice, 5*, 151-170.

Newman, M. G., Consoli, A., and Taylor, C. B. (1997). Computers in assessment and cognitive behavioral treatment of clinical disorders: anxiety as case in point. *Behavior Therapy, 28*, 211-235.

Petitpas, A. J., Brewer, B. W., Rivera, P. M., and Van Raalte, J. L. (1994). Ethical beliefs and behaviors in applied sport psychology: The AAASP ethics survey. *Journal of Applied Sport Psychology, 6*, 135-151.

Sampson Jr., J. P., Kolodinsky, R. W., and Greeno, B. P. (1997). Counseling on the information highway: Future possibilities and potential problems. *Journal of Counseling and Development*, 75, 203-212.

Shaw, H. E., and Shaw, S. F. (2006). Critical ethical issues in online counseling: Assessing current practices with an ethical intent checklist. *Journal of Counseling and Development, 84*, 41-53.

Skinner, A., and Zack, J. (2004). Counseling and Internet. *The American Behavioral Scientist, 48*, 434-446.

Smiley, P. A., and VandeCreek, L. (2005). Problems and solutions with online therapy. In L. VandeCreek, and J. B. Allen (Eds.), *Innovations in clinical practice: Focus on health and wellness* (pp. 187-197). Sarasota, FL: Professional Resource Press/Professional Resource Exchange.

Stoll, O., and Lau, A. (2003). Online-counsulting in the field of Sport Psychology – Experience, Opportunities and Limitations. *Psychologie und Sport, 10*(4), 144-149 [Abstract].

Watson II, J. C., Tenenbaum, G., Lidor, R., and Alfermann, D. (2001). Ethical uses of the Internet in sport psychology: A position stand. *International Journal of Sport Psychology, 32*, 207-222.

Zakrajsek, R. A., and Zizzi, S. J. (2007). Factors influencing track and swimming coaches intentions to use sport psychology services. *Athletic Insight: The Online Journal of Sport Psychology, Vol 9(2)*. Retrieved from http://www.athleticinsight.com/Vol9Iss2/CoachesIntentions.htm.

Zakrajsek, R. A., and Zizzi, S. (2008). How do coaches' attitudes change when exposed to a sport psychology workshop? *Journal of Coaching Education, Vol 1(1)*. Retrieved from http://www.aahperd.org/naspe/jce/pdf_files/Zakrajsek_Zizzi_JCE_2008.pdf.

Zizzi, S. J., and Perna, F. M. (2002). Integrating web pages and e-mail into sport psychology consultations, *The Sport Psychologist*, 16, 416-431.

Zizzi, S. J., Quartiroli, A., and Vosloo, J. (2007, October). A worldwide survey of the training of sport psychology professionals. Paper presented at the annual meeting of the Association for Applied Sport Psychology, Louisville, KY.

Submitted for publication to Athletic Insight: February 26, 2010

In: Athletic Insight's Writings of 2012
Editor: Robert Schinke

ISBN: 978-1-62618-120-5
© 2013 Nova Science Publishers, Inc.

Chapter 5

STRIKING GOLD:
MENTAL TECHNIQUES AND PREPARATION
STRATEGIES USED BY OLYMPIC GOLD MEDALISTS

*Vanessa R. Shannon[1], Noah B. Gentner[*2],*
Ashwin Patel[3] and Douglas Muccio[4]
[1]West Virginia University, US
[2]Georgia Southern University, US
[3]Western State College of Colorado, US
[4]Kent State University, US

ABSTRACT

Athletes have suggested they use a variety of mental training and preparation techniques in their quest for Olympic glory, including: goal-setting (Weinberg, Burton, Yukelson, and Weigand, 2000), pre-performance routines (Gould, Eklund, and Jackson, 1992a), attentional focus and performance imagery (Orlickand Partington, 1988). However, few studies to date have retrospectively asked Olympic champions what they did to prepare for Olympic gold. The purpose of this study was to gain a better understanding of Olympic gold medalists' use of psychological skills during preparation for their Olympic gold medal performance. Both team and individual Olympic gold medal winners participated in semi-structured interview sessions. Analyses revealed that all athletes in the current study utilized strategies and techniques previously identified in the literature. Specifically, analyses revealed four major themes: process focus, imagery, self-talk, and goal-setting.

For many athletes, an Olympic gold medal represents the ultimate conquest, to the extent that some athletes are willing to admit that they would do anything within or outside of the legal limits of the game to be successful. Every two years from 1982 to 1998, Chicago

---

* Correspondence to: Noah Gentner, Ph.D. Georgia Southern University, Department of Health and Kinesiology, P.O. Box 8076. Statesboro, GA 30460. (912) 478-7900; ngentner@georgiasouthern.edu.

physician Bob Goldman conducted an informal survey among U.S. Olympians or aspiring Olympians (Blair, 1998). In 1995, Goldman surveyed 198 athletes (e.g, swimmers, power lifters, and other assorted athletes) and asked the athletes if they would take a banned, performance-enhancing substance, with two guarantees: 1) they would not be caught and 2) they would win. Of the 198 athletes surveyed, 195 of the athletes answered "yes". When asked if they would take a banned performance-enhancing substance that would kill them in five years but enable them to be successful and win every competition until that point, more than half of the athletes still said "yes" (Blair, 1998). These results suggest that athletes are willing to do anything to be successful.

Researchers in the field of sport and exercise psychology have been studying the factors that influence Olympic performance and success for over two decades. During that time, researchers have examined psychological factors related to performance in Olympic athletes from a number of angles. Morgan and colleagues (1978; 1980) were among the first researchers in the area and examined the personality characteristics of national and Olympic athletes. Results of the study, using the Profile of Mood States with runners, rowers, and wrestlers, supported the iceberg profile -- where athletes who were more successful had more positive mental health compared to less successful athletes.

Other researchers have utilized qualitative methods to investigate the psychological variables that influence the performance of Olympians (Gould, Dieffenbach, and Moffett, 2002; Gould, Eklund, and Jackson, 1992a; Gould, Eklund, and Jackson, 1992b; Greenleaf, Gould, and Dieffenbach, 2001; Orlickand Partington, 1988). Orlick and Partington (1988) reported a number of common psychological variables among successful Olympians. Specifically, Orlick and Partington found that the best athletes: (a) were committed to the pursuit of excellence, (b) employed quality training (e.g., imagery, competition simulation, and goal-setting), and (c) engaged in quality mental preparation (e.g., focus plan, distraction plan). Furthermore, Orlick and Partington found that of the variables common to Olympic athletes, the control and quality of performance imagery and effective attentional focus were significantly related to performance at the Olympic Games.

In a study involving all 20 members of the 1988 U.S. Olympic Wrestling Team members, Gould and colleagues (1992a; 1992b) utilized extensive qualitative interviews to examine affect, precompetition cognition, and mental preparation strategies. Results revealed that all 20 members of the team perceived the use of mental preparation techniques to have a positive influence on their performance. The athletes were asked to discuss their worst Olympic match, their most crucial Olympic match, and their all-time best match. Analysis of the interviews revealed commonalities across responses regarding each type of match. Specifically, before their best matches, athletes reporting following preperformance routines and feeling optimally aroused, confident, and focused.

More recently, Greenleaf and colleagues (2001) examined factors influencing the performance of eight Atlanta and seven Nagano Olympians. Athletes were asked a series of open-ended questions regarding the overall Olympic experience and factors that influenced Olympic performance both positively and negatively. Results revealed that athletes perceived mental skills and preparation to have positively influenced their performance. Specifically, athletes reported that (a) using psychological skills training, (b) maintaining high levels of confidence, (c) working with a sport psychology professional, (d) eliminating distractions, (e) being committed to excellence, (f) utilizing relaxation techniques, (g) staying process focused, (h) discussing strategies and mental skills with team members, and (i) using a previous unsuccessful performance as motivation all positively influenced their performance.

To further understand the way in which psychological variables might influence elite performance, Gould and colleagues (2002) identified psychological characteristics of Olympic champions and examined the development of such characteristics. Gould and colleagues interviewed athletes, coaches, and significant others (e.g., parent, guardian, etc) regarding the development of psychological characteristics. Results suggest that a number of psychological characteristics were common to Olympic champions including: anxiety regulation, confidence, mental toughness, sport intelligence, focus and concentration, competitiveness, work ethic, goal-setting, coachability, hopefulness, optimism, and adaptive perfectionism. In addition, the results revealed that the development of these characteristics was influenced by a number of entities including the individual, family, community, sport and non-sport personnel, and the sport process itself. Similarly, Durand-Bush and Salmela (2002) interviewed 10 World and Olympic champions to examine factors that influence the development and maintenance of expert athletic performance. Results revealed that the development of expert athletic performance was influenced by a number of factors including family, friends, school/education, teammates, other athletes, coaches, and support staff members. Additionally, participants suggested that competitiveness, confidence, and motivation had a significant impact on the maintenance of expert athletic.

Although a number of researchers have examined the way in which psychological variables influence performance in Olympic athletes, only a limited number of studies have focused on understanding the specific mental skills and preparation strategies used by Olympic champions in their pursuit of Olympic gold. In fact, few studies to date have retrospectively asked United States Olympic champions what they did to prepare for Olympic gold medal performances. As a result, the purpose of this study was to gain an in-depth understanding of U.S. Olympic gold medalists' use of mental training and preparation techniques throughout their quest for gold.

METHODS

Participants

Participants were 6 gold medalists from the Summer Olympic Games (2000, n = 2, 2004, n = 4). Three of the participants were men and three participants were women. Participants represented six sports, which will not be disclosed to protect the anonymity of the participants. Of the six sports represented in the study, five were team sports while only one was an individual sport.

Access and Entry Procedures

Coaches and/or administrators for national level teams of each sport winning a gold medal across both Olympiads were contacted by telephone and email and asked to disseminate information regarding the study to those individuals who met the inclusion criteria. If an athlete agreed to participate in the study, their contact information was forwarded from the team contact to the researchers. Each athlete was provided an informative letter via email and asked to schedule a time for the interview.

Data Collection

Rationale for using a qualitative methodology. A semi-structured interview format was used in this study. According to Creswell (1998) qualitative research places a greater emphasis on understanding an individual's experience by examining an individual's words, actions, and records. Whereas, the traditional, or quantitative, approach to research quantifies the individual's experience into a set of numbers. Rainer Martens (1987), a pioneer in the field of sport psychology called for the acceptance of new and diverse methods of research in sport psychology over 20 years ago. Other researchers in the field began to follow suit and sport psychology researchers began to criticize the positivistic way in which knowledge in the field was being produced (Dewar and Horn, 1992). Although positivism and quantitative research are appropriate methods for some research questions in sport psychology, researchers asserted they may not be the best approach to study all experiences. As such, Dewar and Horn issued a challenge to researchers to find different ways to examine the experiences of athletes and suggested that researchers in the field "abandon the belief that there is only one legitimate way of knowing in sport psychology" (p. 17). Furthermore, Dewar and Horn suggested that researchers in sport psychology should embrace "the importance of studying the whole, subjective experience of individuals by examining the way people perceive, create, and interpret this world" (Dewar and Horn, 1992, p. 17). As a result of the challenges proposed by Martens and Dewar and Horn, researchers in the field of sport psychology have attempted to change the face of research design in the field. Over the past decade, the field of sport psychology has produced increasing discussion of qualitative methods, a greater reception of qualitative methods, and a boost in the number of qualitative studies investigating the athlete's experience of sport (Dale, 1996; Krane, 2001; Krane, Andersen, and Strean, 1997).

Interview procedures. The interviews were all conducted by phone and by one member of the research team to provide consistency. The interviews ranged in length from 40 to 60 minutes, with the average interview taking 50 minutes. Before the interview began, the researcher reminded the athletes of the purpose of the study and informed them that the interview would be audiotaped. The researcher also assured the athlete that his/her confidentiality would be preserved by deleting all identifiers, such as the athlete's name (athletes chose pseudonyms), the name of any teammates or coaches mentioned, and the name of the sport, from the resulting transcripts. After the athlete agreed to participate, and prior to the start of the interview, the researcher asked the athlete to read and sign a consent form. After the interviews, the researchers sent each participant a summary of his/her interview transcript via email. Participants were asked to read the summary and, if the participants felt any part of the summary was a misrepresentation of what they shared during the interview, the participants were asked to make changes accordingly. Three of the athletes indicated that the summary was accurate; however, the researchers did not receive replies from the other three participants, implying that they did not see any need for changes.

Interview guide. A semi-structured interview format was used. Interviews began with questions regarding specific background information. Then the participants were asked to answer a series of open-ended questions regarding their used of mental skills and preparation techniques prior to and during: a)training for the Olympics, b) participation in the Olympic Trials, c) performances leading up to their gold medal performance, and d) their gold medal performance. Questions were asked one after the other in a semi-structured fashion allowing the participant time to exhaust the question with his/her answer. In order to foster fluency of the interview and augment the richness of the information garnered, the order of in which questions were asked varied from the guide for some participants (Patton, 2002). If the participants' responses directed the researcher to further explore relevant issues, those issues were explored at that time. A priori probes, such as clarification and elaboration, were used to cultivate more consistency in the depth and complexity of participants' responses (Patton, 2002). Clarification probes included, "You said ' ------------------', would you mind telling what you mean by that?"Elaboration probes included, "Anything else?" and "Would you mind telling me more about that?" (Patton, 2002, p. 373-374).

Data Analysis

Memos were recorded during and immediately after each interview to note details of the interview setting, nonverbal behaviors of the participant, and potential emerging themes. These notes regarding the quality of the information provided by the participant were helpful during the interpretation process (Patton, 2002).

Two forms of analysis were used to examine the data. First, to examine the data from questions based on previously identified mental strategies and preparation techniques used by elite athlete, a typological analysis was conducted (Hatch, 2002). Specifically, typologies were identified using the interview questions, interviews were read and relevant data were highlighted, patterns and relationships within typologies across participants were identified, and data were combed for quotes to support the findings. It should be noted that if the participant suggested one of the proposed mental strategies and preparation techniques used by elite athletes before he/she was asked about that question in the interview guide, then that data were also included in the second analysis.

Second, a modified interpretive analysis was used to extract meaning from the data (Hatch, 2002). Interpretive analysis allows for themes to emerge from the text rather than being identified by the use of predetermined categories. This type of analysis also permits the researcher to interpret the text to better explain the experiences of the participants. In order to give accurate voice to the experiences of the participants, the research team immersed themselves in the data and constantly referred back to the text for affirmation of interpretations. Based on the procedures outlined by Hatch (2002, p. 181) the research team member who conducted the interviews: 1) personally transcribed the interviews word for word to become more familiar with the data; 2) read the transcript to achieve "a sense of the whole"; 3) created a case study analysis for each participant; 4) re-read the transcript and identified common words and impressions; 5) bracketed interpretations of the coding within the text and highlighted words and quotes that supported interpretations; 6) noted possible themes and subthemes in the margins of the transcript; 7) compiled a draft summary for each participant based on the initial findings, possible themes, and support for those themes; and 8) reviewed each individual draft summary and conducted a cross case analysis to compare possible themes and muster support for interpretations across participants. In order to further establish the integrity of the data, the other three research team members, all of whom are familiar with qualitative data analysis, independently examined the transcripts (Patton, 2002). These research team members were asked to read the transcripts and identify emergent themes or ideas that were expressed by the participants. When possible, the research team members used the participants' words or ideas for the title of themes. Afterward, the research team member who conducted the interviews and initial data analysis reviewed the interpretations of the other researchers and reanalyzed the data to portray the most truthful representation of the participants' experiences. As a final step in the data analysis process, the three research team members who did not participate in the initial data analysis, were asked to confirm the analysis by matching supportive quotes with appropriate themes.

RESULTS

Typological analysis of the interview data revealed that significant use of mental training techniques and preparation strategies by all of the participants. In fact, all participants reported using a number of different mental training techniques prior to and during gold medal performances including: focus cues, self-talk, goal-setting, imagery, and relaxation.

The findings that were derived from the interpretive data analysis of the participants' responses are classified into 4 themes: (a) process focus, (b) imagery, (c) self-talk, and (d) goal-setting. A discussion of all the major themes, including a rationale for each theme and quotes from the athletes to support the findings are presented below.

Process Focus

The ability to manage attentional focus prior to and during competition is a difficult skill to learn. Ideally, athletes should focus on the process knowing and stay present-centered knowing that the outcome will come. All of the athletes in the study identified as process focused. They each talked about focusing on the process and the details rather than the outcome and the medal. One athlete described this process focus by saying, "I tried to visualize myself playing well. I tried to keep my emotions in check and tried to really focus on the little things it takes to be successful. Instead of focusing on the fact that it was the gold medal race" (Brittany).

Another athlete described his process focus as staying in the moment when he said, "My goal was to enjoy the moment. I had spent a long time waiting for an opportunity like this. I just wanted to enjoy the moment and play with confidence" (Chris).

Imagery

It is difficult to assess the actual use of imagery in athletes. As a result, sport psychology professionals rely on anecdotal evidence to prove that athletes do in fact use imagery to enhance performance. The athletes in the current study all suggested that they used imagery to improve confidence and prepare for performance. One athlete described her use of imagery by stating,

I think that just thinking about how you want the [performance] to go, goes a long way in how it actually goes. I think a couple days leading up to the [performance] are the heaviest point of visualization for me and that just entails relaxing and thinking about how the [performance] is gonna go and trying to put yourself in an imaginative position and living the [performance] in your mind and just kind of remembering all of the little things that you want to do in the [performance] and then trying to execute them in the [performance]. (Janelle)

Similarly, another athlete described exactly what he imaged in preparation for a competition, he said,

And then in terms of the [performance], I picture myself [prior to the performance] and having a perfect start and having everything go right off the start and feeling great as soon as I [begin the performance]. And during [beginning of the performance] feeling fast but not hard and having a perfect [transition] and hopefully separate myself from the competition a little bit right there. And then, the second [part of the performance] would kind of feel the same as the first [part of the performance] and I just add a little bit more power and as soon as I hit that [transition] I want to explode out of that [transition] and really start to try and separate from the [competition]. And then, that third [part of the performance] put everything I have into it and hit that last [transition] perfectly and come off the [transition] and whatever I have left I bring home the last [part of the performance] with a perfect finish.(John)

Yet, another athlete described her use of imagery as a tool to enhance self-confidence, she said, "I had a huge confidence issue during the Olympics as far as with my [performance]…so I would find myself mentally trying to see myself [performing] and [being successful]" (Lacey).

Self-Talk

Athletes can be their own worst critics, at times without even realizing it. Many athletes will acknowledge the impact of the voices around them but forget about the impact of the voice in their head. Often times, athletes are unaware that they even utilize self-talk until they are asked to become aware of the things they are saying to themselves. Each of the athletes in the current study used self-talk, however, several of the athletes were not aware of what they were saying to themselves until they were asked to think about it. One athlete below describes the way in which he used self-talk to improve his confidence, he said,

With the whole confidence issue I had to do a lot of self-talking just to keep reminding myself that I am a great [athlete] and that if I wasn't a good [athlete] I wouldn't be here and I wouldn't be on the Olympic team and I wouldn't be a starter for the Olympic team and just trying to constantly remind myself that I could do it and that I was good enough to be there. When the coach would say something, I had plenty of practices where I was on the verge of tears and I just had to keep talking to myself like 'hey, you're good'. (Steve)

Goal-Setting

> Every game I set a goal and I would look at how [successful my competition was] and I would try to base my goal on what I could do and how [do I want to limit their success], I based it on how [I could keep them from performing well against me]. (Lacey)

DISCUSSION

The purpose of the current study was to examine the mental techniques and preparation strategies used by Olympic champions. Results of the typological analysis revealed that all of the athletes in the current study reported using specific psychological skills in training for, prior to, and during their gold medal performance; specific skills included: focus cues, self-talk, goal-setting, imagery, and relaxation. Results of the interpretive analysis revealed that athletes perceived that the most often and effectively used mental techniques and performance strategies throughout their Olympic journey were a process focus, imagery, self-talk, and goal-setting. The athletes in the current study maintained a process focus throughout their quest for Olympic gold. First, each of the athletes felt that it was important to stay focused on the process in order to achieve the outcome. The athletes in the current study reported using imagery to enhance both performance and confidence. Second, each of the athletes described using imagery as either a means of mental practice and simulation of a performance and/or a way to image successful performances in order to augment self-confidence. The athletes in the current study used self-talk to maintain motivation, enhance confidence, and/or stay committed to goals. Third, each of the athletes reported using self-talk, although several of the athletes were not aware of the amount of self-talk they employed or the impact that the self-talk had on their performance until they were asked to reflect on the self-talk they employed. Finally, each athlete in the current study reported setting goals. All of the athletes in the current study suggested that they used goal-setting as a means to measure progress, evaluate performances in route to their gold medal performances and make adjustments when necessary, and stay motivated along the exhaustive journey to Olympic success.

All of the techniques and strategies identified by athletes in the current study are consistent with reports from previous research examining psychological variables associated with performance of Olympic athletes. Specifically, results of previous research suggests that athletes use a variety of mental training and preparation techniques in their quest for Olympic glory, including: goal-setting (Weinberg et al., 2000), preparation routines, focus strategies, motivational strategies (Gould et al., 1992a), attentional focus, and quality and controlled performance imagery (Orlickand Partington, 1988).

In addition, the results of the current study are in agreement with results of studies examining the development and maintenance of psychological characteristics in Olympic champions. Athletes in the current study utilized a process focus and goal setting to remain motivated and stay committed to excellence. Additionally, athletes in the current study employed imagery and self-talk to enhance confidence. Previous research suggests that Olympic champions may be characterized by a number of attributes including confidence, motivation, perseverance, focus, and commitment (Durand-Bush and Salmela, 2002; Gould et al., 2002).

Limitations

The current study had several limitations. First, the study was conducted retrospectively. Therefore, there is a chance that some of the athletes may have had trouble recalling their experiences. In addition, athletes may have had a more positive recollection of their experiences leading up to the Olympics since the end result was a gold medal. If an athlete had not succeeded in accomplishing their goal of winning a gold medal, then they may have been more likely to retrospectively identify challenges along the way and the strategies and techniques they used to overcome those challenges. Since the current sample of athletes did win gold medals they may have been more likely to focus on the positive aspects of their experience thus providing less information about the challenges and difficulties they faced. Secondly, the sample was limited as a result of the difficulty associated with accessing former gold medalists. In order to respect the athletes' right to privacy, they were not contacted directly. Athletes were only contacted once they had granted the researchers permission to contact them through a third party (e.g., coach, team liason, etc). Consequently, the sample was considerably smaller than the researchers had hoped. However, despite this small sample size saturation was reached during data collection and it has been suggested that for a qualitative study 6 participants can be sufficient (Patton, 2002).

RECOMMENDATIONS FOR FUTURE RESEARCH

Per the limitations identified above, it would be useful in future studies examining the mental techniques and preparation strategies used by Olympic gold medalists for athletes to be interviewed as close to the completion of the event as possible. This will increase the likelihood that their recollection of their journey is as accurate as possible. Furthermore, based on the fact that the athletes in the current study may have had a more positive recollection of events due to their success it would be useful to interview athletes who were less successful to identify any differences in their preparation. It would also be beneficial to gather an in-depth understanding of Olympic athletes' preparation and use of mental techniques throughout their training. Therefore, future research might include interviews with Olympic athletes on several occasions leading up to the Games as well as after.

The current study identified several mental techniques utilized by successful athletes. While these results can be beneficial for athletes, coaches, and consultants it would be valuable to gather more in-depth information about each skill. Therefore, future research could further investigate each individual mental skill.

Finally, future research should look outside the Olympic arena and examine the mental techniques and preparation strategies used by other elite athletes (e.g., professional, international level, etc). It would be interesting to explore the differences in the preparation and strategies used by athletes at different levels and across different sports.

PRACTICAL APPLICATIONS

The findings of the current study should be useful for athletes, coaches, and sport psychology professionals who are interested in improving athletic performance. The gold medal winning athletes in the current study utilized several mental techniques throughout their training and competitions. While the results of this qualitative study cannot be generalized to all athletes, it can be assumed that the skills identified by these successful athletes may be beneficial for other athletes as well. More specifically, while other athletes may not be able to use these skills in the exact manner employed by the Olympians in this study they can find ways to personalize them. In other words the skills used by the athletes in the study can be used as a guide for other athletes looking to improve their mental game. As such, the techniques identified in this study would be useful for coaches and sport psychology professionals to help athletes implement throughout their preparation for a competition. However, it is important to remember the need to personalize the skills for each individual athlete.

CONCLUSION

The purpose of this study was to gain an in-depth understanding of U.S. Olympic gold medalists' use of mental training and preparation techniques throughout their quest for gold. The athletes in this study identified the use of process focus, imagery, self-talk, and goal-setting as critical to their success.

These skills are consistent with those identified in previous research (Durand-Bush and Salmela, 2002; Gould et al., 2002; Gould et al., 1992a; OrlickandPartington, 1988; Weinberg et al., 2000). This suggests that athletes who utilize these skills might be more successful than those who neglect to use them. Furthermore, the current study lends further support for the notion that mental training is a critical component to athletic success.

In conclusion, in elite athletic competitions where the difference between success and failure can be miniscule, athletes are continually searching for ways to gain an edge. The results of this study, coupled with previous research, suggest that mental training and preparation may be one way for athletes to increase their chances of success.

REFERENCES

Blair, T. (1998, July 27). Just say go: The latest performance-boosting drugs are impossible to detect – and, for many athletes, impossible to resist. *Time Magazine: International Addition, 152,* (4). Retrieved from http://www.time.com/time/magazine/1998/int/ 980727/sport.just_say_go.the_la5.html.

Creswell, J. (1998). *Qualitative Inquiry and Research Design: Choosing Among Five Traditions.* Thousand Oaks: Sage.

Dale, G. A. (1996). Existential phenomenology: Emphasizing the experience of the athlete in sport psychology research. *The Sport Psychologist, 10,* 307-321.

Dewar, A., and Horn, T. (1992).A critical analysis of knowledge construction in sport psychology. In T. Horn (Ed.), *Advances in sport psychology* (pp. 13-22). Champaign, IL: Human Kinetics.

Durand-Bush, N., and Salmela, J. H. (2002). The development and maintenance of expert athletic performance: Perceptions of World and Olympic Champions. *Journal of Applied Sport Psychology, 14,* 154-171.

Gould, D., Dieffenbach, K., and Moffett (2002). Psychological characteristics and their development in Olympic champions. *Journal of Applied Sport Psychology, 14*, 172-204.

Gould, D., Eklund, R. C., and Jackson, S. A. (1992a). 1988 U.S. Olympic wrestling excellence: I. Mental preparation, precompetitive cognition, and affect. *The Sport Psychologist, 6*, 359-382.

Gould, D., Eklund, R. C., and Jackson, S. A. (1992b). 1988 U.S. Olympic wrestling excellence: II. Thoughts and affect occurring during competition. *The Sport Psychologist,6*, 383–402.

Greenleaf, C., Gould, D., and Dieffenbach, K. (2001). Factors influencing Olympic performance: Interviews with Atlanta and Nagano US Olympians. *Journal of Applied Sport Psychology, 13*, 154-184.

Hatch, J. A. (2002). *Doing qualitative research in education settings*. New York: State University of New York Press.

Krane, V. (2001). One lesbian feminist epistemology: Integrating feminist standpoint, queer theory, and feminist cultural studies. *The Sport Psychologist, 15*, 401-411.

Krane, V., Andersen, M., and Strean, W. B. (1997). Issues of qualitative research method and presentation. *Journal of Sport and Exercise Psychology, 19*, 213-218.

Martens, R. (1987). Science, knowledge, and sport psychology. *The Sport Psychologist, 1*, 39-55.

Morgan, W. P. (1980). The trait psychology controversy. *Research Quarterly for Exercise and Sport, 51*, 50-76.

Morgan, W., and Johnson, R. (1978). Personality characteristics of successful and unsuccessfuloarsmen. *International Journal of Sport Psychology, 9*, 119-133.

Orlick, T., and Partington, J. (1988). Mental links to excellence. *The Sport Psychologist, 2*, 105-130.

Patton, M. (2002). Qualitative interviewing. In M. Patton (Ed.), *Qualitative evaluation and research methods (pp. 277- 368) (2^{nd}ed).* New York: Sage Publications.

Weinberg, R., Burton, D., Yukelson, D., and Weigand, D. (2000). Perceived goal setting practices of Olympic athletes: An exploratory investigation. *The Sport Psychologist, 14*, 279-295.

Submitted to Athletic Insight: December 6, 2010.

In: Athletic Insight's Writings of 2012   ISBN: 978-1-62618-120-5
Editor: Robert Schinke   © 2013 Nova Science Publishers, Inc.

Chapter 6

THE PSYCHOLOGICAL COMPONENTS
OF ELITE CYCLING[*]

Timothy Baghurst[†*]
Health and Human Performance
Oklahoma State University, Stillwater, OK, US

ABSTRACT

Current expertise theory suggests that while variables such as genetics and environmental factors are likely to play a role in the development of an expert, other mediators such as deliberate practice and an adaptation to task constraints lead to expertise. However, empirical research describing the underlying mechanisms responsible for expertise in sport is limited. Therefore, the purpose of this study was to gain an understanding of the psychological components of elite cycling. Five cyclists (4 male, 1 female) from the British national and junior cycling squads were interviewed to determine expertise from a psychological perspective. Interviews revealed that both deliberate physiological training and overcoming psychological obstacles were of particular importance. Specifically, the interpretation of anxiety and pain as being debilitative or facilitative as well as social support concerns were found to effect performance. Implications for expertise development and future psychological intervention protocols in cycling are discussed.

INTRODUCTION

The usefulness of investigating the nature and function of expertise has been well documented (Proctor, 1995). Its worth is derived from being able to determine what separates elite from novice, what segregates great from good, and what distinguishes outstanding from normal. Investigation into expertise typically proceeds in three steps (Ericsson and Smith, 1991). The first step is to identify characteristics of elite athletes or their performances which

---

[*] Note: This research was conducted at the Bangor University, Wales.
[†] Direct correspondence to: Timothy Baghurst, Health and Human Performance, Colvin 189, Oklahoma State University, Stillwater, OK, 74078. E-mail: tbaghurst@live.com. Phone: (405) 744 4346.

distinguish them from others within that sporting domain. This is often accomplished by testing both elite and novice athletes in a controlled condition. The second step involves conducting a thorough analysis of the expert's performance in an attempt to determine the nature of the cognitive processes involved. This is generally undertaken by comparing elite and novice performers' cognition in relation to a task or set of tasks that determine superior performance. The third and final step requires developing an account of the expert's processes and knowledge structures. This account should provide an insight into the performer's understandings, thoughts, and practices that enable him or her to function as an expert.

According to Abernethy (1993), the knowledge generated from expertise research has an immediate relevance to coaches, sport and exercise scientists, and the practitioners concerned with testing, training, and identifying of potential elite performers. Thus, the aim of this study was to investigate the third step of the strategy suggested by Ericsson and Smith (1991) in order to develop an understanding of psychological functioning of elite cyclists. Expert in this study was defined as 10 years of deliberate practice (Ericsson, Krampe, and Tesch-Römer, 1993), and an assumption was made that having an elite status in a sport was associated with expertise. Thus, the aim was to compile and mapelite performers' thought processes in order to provide a potential method for the acceleration of skill acquisition in the non-elite performer.

QUALITATIVE OR QUANTITATIVE METHODOLOGIES

Qualitative research holds an advantage over quantitative research when investigating individuals through its use of a more "human" approach (Reason and Rowan, 1981). While quantitative results may provide substantial evidence for a particular aspect, humans are complex and multiple interpretations might be derived from the information provided by an individual (Pidgeon, 1996). In addition, a qualitative approach allows for the discovery of new theories and ideas. This is seen as equally important because, if previous theory has been developed through a positivist approach, then there is the likelihood that knowledge has been distorted in some way leading to "false" theories and conclusions (Kuhn, 1962).

Although quantitative research plays a significant role within scientific research, methods must be chosen according to the purpose of the investigation (Bryman, 1988). Therefore, in consideration of the aim of this investigation, open-ended interviews, a qualitative measure, was employed in the present study.

Interviews were based on the premises of grounded theory, but did not strictly adhere to grounded theory structure. Glaser and Strauss (1967) developed grounded theory for the purpose of generating theories that are derived from a sound setting and grounded in or generated by qualitative research. Although grounded theory may be applicable in the acquisition of new information, Reissman (1993) suggests that in order for the researcher to dissect the information given, some form of theoretical backing must be in place in order to interpret the results. Glaser and Strauss (1967) recommend that, "the researcher does not approach reality as "tabula rasa" or blank sheet" (p. 3). However, these recommendations question whether grounded theory can be used to develop new theory when it relies on previous theory in the first place. Pidgeon and Henwood (1997) answer this question succinctly:

The resolution of this conundrum is to recognise that it makes no sense to claim that research can proceed either from testing theory alone, or from a pure, inductive analysis of data ....the value of grounded theory approach is that it suggests a set of procedures which facilitate the operation of subjectivity (and in particular the researcher's interpretation and creativity) in the process of qualitative data analysis. (p. 255)

Thus, grounded theory should be used as a means of constantly comparing what previous research suggests and what emerges from the data to develop new theory in a 'flip-flop' design (Eccles, Walsh, and Ingledew, 2002).

Within the framework of this study and based on Reissman's (1993) recommendations, prior to data collection some understanding of expertise research and its fundamental basis was investigated. Expertise has been studied in many forms; however, a summation of previous research may be found in the conclusions of Ericsson and Lehmann's (1996) study which suggests that experts are more likely to adapt to the constraints of the task. Although previous research has revealed many factors that are relevant to elite performance acquisition in many sports, little research has investigated the underlying mechanisms responsible for expertise in sport (Shea and Paull, 1996).

With specific reference to cycling, the psychological nature and demands of the sport are not well known. Thus, the purpose of this study was to investigate the psychological cognitions and actions of elite cyclists through semi-structured interviews. Essentially, the aim was to determine what elite cyclists think immediately prior to and during a competitive race. The mapping of this information can be utilized in the development of less experienced cyclists by accelerating skill acquisition within the sport.

METHOD

Participants

Participants were five cyclists from the British national and junior cycling squads (see Table 1); this participant size was not chosen prior to data collection, but was limited by participant access; however, data saturation was achieved. Each had completed a minimum of ten years deliberate practice as recommended by Ericsson and colleagues (1993).

As this was the first investigation of its type to explore the psychological components of cycling, the rationale for choosing elite athletes was to obtain data that could be extrapolated across elite cycling and further be applied to more novice cyclists. Also, expert, experienced cyclists would be able to more accurately describe and recount detail. The aim was to employ purpose sampling for more information rich cases of study (Lincoln and Guba, 1985).

Table 1. Participants' Demographics

Cyclist Name	Age	Gender	Specialty	Years Experience
Jason	24	M	Road Racing	12
Heather	20	F	Time Trials	10
Brian	22	M	Time Trials	11
Liam	20	M	Road Racing	10
Asa	23	M	Road Racing	12

Procedures

Following university IRB approval, cyclists were contacted to request an interview. As cyclists 1 and 5 were known to the researcher, they were initially contacted via phone. Both agreed to be interviewed and times were arranged. For the remaining three cyclists, their coach was contacted via phone and with his assistance interviews were arranged while they attended a training camp.

Each participant was asked to sign a consent form before being interviewed. All interviews lasted between 40 and 50 minutes and were conducted within a two month period either face-to-face ($n = 4$) or via phone ($n = 1$). The phone interview was necessary due to the location of the athlete at the time of interview which is a limitation, as the interviewer did not have the opportunity to pilot a phone interview. A micro cassette recorder was used to record all interviews in their entirety. All interviews were transcribed verbatim using a *Sanyo memo-scriber*. Transcripts were sent to the respective athletes for confirmation and for the allowance of possible follow-up questions and elaboration of statements/context by the athletes. No adjustments were made by the athletes.

Interview Guide

The interview. guide (Patton, 1990) was designed to allow for open-ended questions with elaboration probes. This guide was designed from a pilot study undertaken with one male 23 year old semi-professional cyclist (Category 1-2; 1 is elite, 5 is beginner). During the pilot interview, the cyclist was asked to re-tell a recent race in as much detail as possible from which further elaboration probes were made.

From this interview a general interview guide was developed which included elaboration probes that could be employed in a generic sense such as: "You mentioned … Can you tell me in a little more detail what happened?" Further questions were organically derived whereby analysis of an interview allowed for the development of new questions and the next step of the data collection process. However, the overall structure of all interviews was based on the athlete describing a recent race in chronological order from several hours before it began to several hours after it finished.

The open-ended questions were designed to acquire as much information as possible. For example, the typical request that the researcher asked the cyclist at the beginning of the interview followed in this format:

> I would like you to go back to a recent race and tell me in as much detail as you can everything that happened in the race. Maybe start a couple of hours before on the way to the race and just tell me as much as you can about what happened, what you thought about etcetera, etcetera. Okay?

Thus, the aim was to employ open-ended questions to generate an overall picture which would allow for further probing. For example, one cyclist mentioned his father several times in his description of the race. Noting this allowed for further questioning. "Okay, something that you mentioned several times was your dad. How much does he influence what you do?"

Data Reliability and Analysis

Critics of qualitative data collection question its credibility and trustworthiness (Jackson, 1996). Trustworthiness, according to Lincoln and Guba (1985), is when the researcher must demonstrate to him or herself as well as the audience that the findings of the study are worth consideration. They suggest that the terms credibility, transferability, dependability and conformability are the equivalent of the terms, internal validity, external validity, reliability, and objectivity. Credibility comes from those who took part in the study agreeing to what has been found. Transferability is only proven or disproved based on the results of future studies. However, it is the responsibility of the researcher to provide sufficient information about the conditions and context in which the study took place to allow the reader to make an informed choice as to whether the information provided is relevant to his or her situation. While it is not possible to replicate any one study exactly, dependability assesses whether the enquiry was conducted appropriately and in a methodologically sound manner. Finally, conformability examines the extent to which the data and its subsequent interpretations have been influenced by the researcher. Essentially, the goal is to demonstrate that the conclusions from the data are derived from the data (Jackson).

In order to increase the quality and trustworthiness of the research (Lincoln and Guba, 1985; Patton, 1990) three strategies were used in the present study comprising of, (1) the use of stringent techniques for gathering and analysing data while observing the issues of reliability, triangulation and validity, (2) the credibility of the researcher, and (3) an appreciation of qualitative methods and holistic thinking. Each of the three strategies is discussed and includes the procedures employed in this investigation to enhance trustworthiness in the present study.

For the first strategy (1), several techniques were employed including a reflexive journal, negative case analysis, triangulation, and an audit check to ensure credibility, transferability, dependability, and confirmability of the data. A reflexive journal is aimed at maintaining stringent techniques, credibility, and qualitative methods by ensuring that the investigator keeps a diary in which he or she records information concerning self and method (Lincoln and Guba, 1985). In this way, decisions regarding method and analysis and the reasons behind each decision can be recorded. As recommended by Lincoln and Guba, the primary researcher kept a journal that consisted of three parts. Part one contained a daily schedule detailing logistics, part two contained personal reflection and insight, and part three contained a methodological log where methodological decisions and their rationale were recorded.

Negative case analysis can be used as a means of testing for alternative paradigms (Jackson, 1996). This form of analysis involves searching for anything that does not conform to the conclusions and patterns already discovered. Kidder (1981) suggests that negative case analysis is to qualitative research as statistical analysis is to quantitative research. While true negative analysis involves the revision of a hypothesis until all known cases are considered and outliers eliminated (Lincoln and Guba, 1985), there is a fear of eliminating what could be important and potentially interesting data. Thus, this study employed the use of negative case analysis, but did not eliminate outliers.

Triangulation is often employed as a credibility check (Jackson, 1996) and can occur through employing a variety of data sources, employing multiple methods to study a single problem, using multiple perspectives to interpret each piece of data, and employing more than one researcher (Patton, 1990). Triangulation occurred in the present study through the use of multiple methods of analysis and the employment of more than one researcher.

The purpose of an audit check is to obtain an outside perspective of the dependability and credibility of the study (Lincoln and Guba, 1895). In this particular case, 30 participant quotations (25% of the total number) were given to an independent expert in qualitative research methods, experienced in research, and who also possessed a background in endurance sports. These quotations had already been assigned to one of five concepts identified by the primary researcher. The independent expert was asked to match each quotation to one of the five possible category concepts to determine inter rater reliability. Analysis using Cohen's kappa between the primary researcher and the expert resulted in a score of .91.

The credibility of the researcher is the second strategy (2) used to enhance that the quality and trustworthiness of the research. As the researcher is essentially the instrument of the qualitative research, a qualitative study should include information concerning the researcher (Patton, 1990). All personnel who have been involved in the data collection and evaluation of the research should be recorded within the study. The primary method of ensuring that this took place was the inclusion of a reflexive journal.

In addressing the third strategy (3), the researcher must consider the individual/topic under study as a complex system that is more than the sum of its parts (Patton, 1990). Caution must also be taken to ensure that the researcher is aware of the questions what and why to the extent that they are able to explain to other researchers the study's value both from a holistic perspective as well as a more detailed view. In the present study, the researcher attempted to maintain a holistic approach to the data, but was aware that specific topics may need a more reductionistic approach. The purpose of including Patton's interpretive research paradigm was to provide support for the methods of investigation that were used in this study.

The primary researcher transcribed all interviews, which allowed for a general familiarisation of the transcribed interviews and verbal inflections of the participants' responses. An awareness of verbal inflections assisted in determining whether a comment was intended as sarcasm, for example. Following confirmation from each athlete, interviews were fully coded and managed using QSR NUD*IST computer software. This reduces thechance of information loss and produces an audit trail thereby increasing validity (Pigeon, 1996). Initially, the primary researcher printed out each statement and aligned similar participant statements together. From this alignment, five core concepts emerged. The direction and influence of each concept with each other was ascertained from statements made by the participants that linked the concepts to each other. This provided an overall map of the psychological components of participants' competitive experiences with supporting statements.

RESULTS

The premise of this study was to develop an understanding of the psychological components of elite cycling. This task was undertaken through the use of semi-structured interviews to develop an overall analysis of expert thinking. The analysis revealed a number of concepts pertaining to the psychological perspectives of cyclists. The properties of each concept and their links to other concepts are explained in terms of their influence on one another and the direction of that influence (Figure 1).

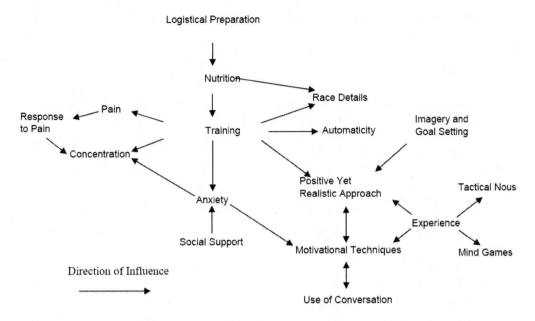

Figure 1. The psychological perspectives of cyclists immediately prior to and during a race.

Prominence was determined by a combination of the number of participants who referenced the concept in addition to how frequently that concept was referenced. Pathways refer to the direction of influence shown, but not the importance of the link. Each concept is explained and then supported by athlete quotes. Unless otherwise stated, all cyclists provided evidence for the concept.

Training

Training, within the area of cycling is seen to be paramount. Its central placement within the map indicates its prominence within the cyclists' thinking. For example, Heather mentioned how she would, "... be doing my absolute best and I've done everything possible to get the best out of me so if I hadn't have prepared then it would be a shadow of what I can actually do…" (Heather). "The more you train, the more confident you are going into a race. Therefore, I take training as being very, very important," said Brian.

Nutrition

Both training and race performance can be affected by nutrition, as nutrition is important prior to and during a race (pathway 1). It requires both timing and planning. Nutrition can also play a key role post performance, as often races are strung over a period of days resulting in the necessity to be at the same physiological level on each day.

I might reflect on my course, what it's like, how it will suit me, where to attack, what to do, where to speed, where to eat, where to drink so that you're not going to put yourself at a disadvantage because if you want to feed, you can't just feed anywhere on the course. If you're hungry and you like eat and then like, ten seconds later you're going up a big climb or something like that then you're not going to be able to breathe properly and you're still going to be chewing food and it's just kind of schoolboy errors that you're trying to avoid by having a good preparation. (Asa)

> … if you do a race and you don't eat the right food afterwards and you just eat tons and tons of lettuce and tomatoes and that, that won't give you enough energy for the next day and you will be knackered (extremely tired). After say half an hour you'll be off the back. You just need to get the carbohydrates straight in there… (Liam)

Logistical Preparation

Logistical preparation can influence event success (pathway 2). This includes ensuring that the cyclist arrives at the event in plenty of time, the bike is set up, drinks are made, race numbers collected, and the body is properly warmed up and ready to go. Brian described his pre service checks. "I went and checked my bike get it clean, pump the tires up then got my kit together and then I got everything all ready…" Heather explained how not arriving on time effected her warm up. "We turned up late so I didn't get a proper warm up. I had to do that on the turbo…I did that to warm up which I never do."

Race Details

Both training and nutrition can influence race details (pathways 3 and 4). If either training or nutrition is not optimal, a race is unlikely to be successful, and may not be completed or even attempted. In addition, other details such as environmental conditions need to be considered.

> You have to know where to go, where the wind is coming from. That's very important as well because it's best to attack into a headwind because no one else wants to chase you into a headwind so if you feel strong, go there and by the time you've got to a tail wind, you've got a gap and then they've lost heart or whatever so weather conditions definitely. (Jason)

Automaticity

Also linked to training comes an automaticity that enables all parts of the body to function in a rhythmic fashion (pathway 5). The whole body working together is how Liam described it. "You're just thinking... you're just thinking and doing stuff all at the same time so your brain's working as well as your body so really the whole of you is working at the same time."

Positive yet Realistic Approach

The training that a cyclist has done is likely to affect his or her outlook and it enables the athlete to approach the race with a realistic outlook (pathway 6).A positive approach is also necessary; without the training, a positive approach is unlikely to be realistic.

> I thought I'd just drill it because I didn't have the legs for a sprint. You need to be really sharp to have a sprint and I'm talking about flat out sprinting.I didn't have that so I thought, 'I'll just use my strength and whatever I've got left', so I just drilled it to the front and only a couple of lads came round so I was really pleased with that. (Jason)

In this race I had done a fair bit of work. Like every time there was a sprint off I'd be catching up, bringing the group back together again apart from the leading group like, the bunch gave up in the end on the front. They just sort of went, 'Ah they're going to win it so we just might as well leave them. 'They shouldn't have thought that. They should have thought, 'Ah close them down, get the places'. (Liam)

Imagery and Goal Setting

While employed by only four of the five cyclists, imagery and goal setting were strategies employed as a means of improving performance while remaining realistic (pathway 7). Both imagery and goal setting were used before and during an event. Although these are often considered separate psychological skills, there was some overlap in the participants' responses. Thus, they were included in the same category. Heather gave an example of goal setting. "But usually or fortunately I suppose, I'm usually able to catch my minute man. That's always in my head that I have to catch at least two people" (Heather).

If there is a time trial and I want to do a certain time before it and I kind of go over the course in my head and I come up with a schedule so at a certain point I have got to do it in a certain time in order to achieve it. I go through the course and sort of think what gears I might need for certain climbs, which way the wind will be coming from, corners, and if there's village in it then if there is (sic) any cars parked on the side of the road. And if it's a road race the same again; the terrain. (Brian)

Motivational Techniques

Motivational techniques employ some form of method to induce greater task effort. Psyching up is a method much employed by the cyclists in this study, and sometimes other cyclists within the race or a significant other can help induce this motivation. Heather used a dislike for competition to serve as a motivator. "But then I remembered one girl that was riding and I have a passionate dislike for her and I think, 'She isn't beating me!' So I just pushed myself just to beat that girl."

Although a significant other or any other individual may help to motivate a cyclist, the motivation stemmed predominantly from within (pathway 8). While getting an extra push from an external source may aid performance, internal motivation was seen as more stable and significant, as it generates a hunger for success.

… the psychological disappointment of not achieving what I want will last longer than the pain that I'm in the moment. Because once I cross the line the pain stops, you throw up a few times and go have a shower and then half an hour later I'm okay. But if I didn't do it then I'd be going for weeks, 'Should have gone harder. 'It's only an hour and when it comes to it there's twenty four hours in a day. (Brian)

Use of Conversation

The influence of conversation and motivators was found to be bi-directional (pathway 9). Whether verbal or nonverbal, it appears to affect a cyclist's motivation. Likewise, the motivation of the cyclist may affect their use of conversation. If a cyclist is demotivated then conversation is unlikely to be motivational. Specifically, nonmotivational conversation was considered to be classed as chat or banter in contrast to motivational chat or tactical conversation. Consider the comments of Jason concerning the difference between the two.

They chat because they're not doing that much and that really annoys me because it's like, personally I don't think that you should ... If there's two or three people on a break, you know, it's like shouting, 'Come on', you know, 'Really go for it, dig in there, we've got a gap', or whatever. Everyone who's there to seriously race, they chat like that, you know. They sort of say, 'We've got a gap, we've got ten seconds so let's work hard and get away from them', or whatever, you know. It's more sort of motivational shouting and there's not much chat going on to be honest. But it's good to get other people saying it because you know they mean business as well. You know, they could be there just for the fun of it.

Experience

Experience also plays a large part in successful performance. Experience of both course and competitor can be both a motivator and tactical advantage (pathways 11 and 13). However, it also allows for a greater self-confidence in a cyclist's ability and thereby influences his or her approach (pathway 10). Said Heather, "Because I'd won another university championships a few weeks prior, I knew what to expect from the other competitors."

…they come up to talk to you and saying what training they've done and they're to make out that they're better than everybody else. But I don't think I'm being bigheaded or anything but I know I'm better than them. (Asa)

Mind Games

This experience also plays a key role in the mind games that go on prior to and during a cycling race (pathway 12). These mind games can be self-imposed – only one cyclist mentioned this – or are employed as means of psyching out another competitor. However, psyching out another competitor is a two-way thing, as he or she is just as keen to be the one to gain a psychological advantage. For example, Jason was aware of the mind games occurring before an event. "I don't know, especially confident people who walk around and you're going, 'Oh, how you doing?' and you know and I know they're thinking 'Ah' and I know they're just checking you out to see what you've done…"

Because if they're breathing out their arse and they are in so much pain they can hardly ride the bike anymore and you're just like, out of the saddle dancing on the pedals looking like it's totally easy, but really underneath you are going through so much pain you wouldn't believe then it's such a blow to them that, and it uplifts you so much because you can block out the pain and you can win the race hopefully. (Asa)

Tactical Nous

Experience can also influence tactical nous (pathway 13). While seemingly very similar to the Mind Games category, subtle differences exist that involve planning tactics before and during the race, controlling the race, monitoring energy reserves, and being able to analyze positions. The frequency of comments about this issue suggest its importance to the cyclist, as races can be both won and lost through the monitoring of self and others."If you're feeling good then you'd be attacking and watching people come after you and then sitting up if everyone came after you and like going back into the group again," said Asa. Jason explained how he could avoid taxing himself on a breakaway as much as others to conserve energy. "But I wasn't going through all my turns. You sort of slide in and miss the odd turn to save yourself a bit."

Anxiety

Anxiety is something that all the cyclists reported as being important both prior to and within a race. The causes of anxiety have a resultant effect that can be either negative or positive. It is how the cyclist interprets the anxiety that appears to be vital.

Anxiety prior to a race is often apparent. All the cyclists mentioned how nervous they get prior to a race. However, once the race begins nerves appear to dissipate. For example, Brian described how nervous he could get before a race. "Sometimes I feel nervous before the start of the race on the way there. I've done national time trial championships a few times and before then I'm almost throwing up with nerves."

Unfortunately, anxiety prior to the race can be costly, but strategies are devised to control this anxiety by either avoiding it altogether or by using it in a motivational sense (pathway 20). Nervousness is particularly evident toward the end of a race, particularly if the cyclist is in contention for a good finish. Again these nerves can be interpreted as either a positive or negative thing.

Like, say if you're nervous it's gives you an adrenaline rush and like the blood's flowing properly, flowing faster through your legs and your legs feel like weak but then like stronger and it like, sort of energizes you and sort of like, '(vocal breathing) Surprised I'm here! I'm up near the front. 'It does make you go harder when you do feel a bit nervous. Like you think about, 'Ah what if I come first? What if I do this, that and the other?' And it's like, you're thinking about that and it makes you nervous. It's just one of those things that sort of gets you hyper kind of thing. (Liam)

Social Support

Social support refers to the influences of parents, family and coaches. Unfortunately, it is seen by the cyclists as something that can influence anxiety in both a positive and negative manner (pathway 15). While a parent or coach may provide psychologically what the cyclist needs at that time, they are also capable of hindering the cyclist's performance.

I do go quiet a lot before a race, particularly a big race, and my parents start butting in and my mum's saying, oh like, if we're going round a course an hour before the race when I've got there and before I get changed and my mom's like, 'You know you've got to watch out for the pot hole here and the pot hole there and there's a bit of gravel on that bend.' And I tell her to shut up because I don't need to be told how to ride a bike, because I know how to race. And that's probably when I'm like handling my bike and everything so I don't need that, and that annoys me sometimes. (Asa)

Concentration

Concentration is influenced by anxiety, training, and pain (pathways 16 and 17). It is seen to play a major part in successful performance. Rather than success being drawn from maintaining concentration throughout a race, it appears that success is drawn from being able to avoid losing concentration less often than other competitors or at critical times in the race. For example, Jason mentioned how easy it is to miss something. "Someone might go shoot up a hill, 'I missed that just because I switched off for a minute.' But that's luck because everyone switches off. I'm sure they do."

The middle of the race is reported to be the most frequent time that lapses in concentration occur. These lapses vary from thinking about family or work, to noticing things completely unrelated to the race itself.

But you do often tend to find yourself wondering, you know, just losing concentration maybe because you're fatigued just because it's two hours on the bike so your mind might wander a bit so you've got to keep stuck in there and sort of, it's just a matter of focusing. Just keep focusing when nothing much is happening or you're just going through the motions for a while. (Jason)

Pain

Pain, according to the cyclists, is something that all must face if they are to succeed, but can come in more than one form. Good pain refers to the pain that occurs when a cyclist is in contention for a good finish. However, bad pain occurs more often when a high finish is unlikely, or if physically the cyclist is unable to continue working at that same rate. This appears to link quite heavily with fatigue and thereby can be influenced by training (pathway 18).

...there's sort of good pain as well. When you going fast and you know you've only got a couple of miles to go and you're really going well but you legs are burning but you know you're going to do well sometimes that drives you on.(Brian)

If I'm unfit then I'll be grovelling so I'm more likely to think, 'I'm in absolute agony. Oh no, I hope I... shall I quit? Shall I pull out on the next section?' And I go, 'No, no, no, no.'

And then I start thinking really bad things like, 'Oh remember when I got beaten by such and such a person.', or, 'If they were here now they would be giving me a kicking.' But when you're quite fit you kind of just click out of it and you just remember all the good rides you've done and it doesn't hurt. (Asa)

Response to Pain

Responses to pain tend to surround methods of blocking it (pathway 19). For example, Heather explained how she tried to ignore it. "Well, I learnt to just not think about it, just think about what you're doing or instead of the pain which I did."

While predominantly the case, sometimes pain can be thrived off, as Brian mentioned in reference to good pain. The danger in responding to pain inappropriately, however, is that it causes a loss of focus (pathway 21).

Well, that's something you have to deal with in cycling all the time. Even in training you might go through very bad phases where you feel very bad and you just have to bite the bullet and get on with it. Keep your head down and ride through it. (Jason)

DISCUSSION

The purpose of this study was to obtain an understanding of elite cycling taken from a psychological perspective. This was accomplished by analyzing interview data of elite cyclists to generate a description of expert psychological thinking in cycling. This research conducted an analysis of the expert's performance in an attempt to develop an account of the expert's processes and knowledge structures, step three of Ericsson and Smith's (1991) strategy for expertise research.

The findings of this research confirm and support much of the findings from previous research into expertise in endurance sports. Although physiological training is understood to be of clear importance in attained expertise in a sport, this study would suggest that psychological variables such as tactical experience, perception of anxiety, and control of and response to pain may also be tantamount in achieving expert or elite status.

Prior to performance, training is seen to be crucial to a successful race. This comes as no surprise considering the physiological demands placed on cyclists, and deliberate practice is necessary to develop the physiological body and cardiovascular body necessary for endurance event success (O'Toole and Douglas, 1995).

There is evidence to suggest that training not only affects physiological relationships such as pain tolerance and automaticity, but can also affect many psychological issues that arise during a race. For example, Heather reported that a lack of training had an effect on her outlook and her response to pain.

While deliberate practice may have only targeted physiological aspects of cycling, it is apparent that psychological training is accrued as a by-product. Ericsson and colleagues (1993) define expert performance as, "acquired characteristics resulting from extended deliberate practice..." (p. 363). However, not only does this research support the claim for deliberate practice, it also provides support for the notion that domain specific deliberate practice can be influenced by other factors such as psychological skills training. In the present research, all cyclists gave evidence for the necessity of deliberate physiological practice. However, only Jason gave mention of any deliberate psychological practice. Thus, this discussion aims to highlight some of the areas of the specific use of psychological strategies that have occurred without the use of specific, psychological deliberate practice.

Anxiety is a factor that, if perceived as negative, can have catastrophic consequences. However, when perceived as something positive, it is found to motivate and reassure the cyclist of the race's importance. This is in agreement with current psychological understanding that anxiety, when perceived to be a positive attribute of an event, can enhance motivation to the task (Hardy, Jones, and Gould, 1996). Research into facilitative and debilitative anxiety has found that elite athletes have a predisposition to interpret anxiety as being facilitative (Jones and Swain, 1995). Hardy and colleagues state that, "the control of stress and anxiety is a very salient factor in elite performers' abilities to produce peak performance at really important competitions" (p. 159).

Social support is another factor that must be controlled effectively if the performer is to perform at his or her best. Rees, Hardy, and Freeman (2007) found that social support increased performance in high level golfers. Furthermore, Buman, Omli, Giacobbi, and Brewer (2008) reported that some marathon runners used another competitor as a means of social support when they "hit the wall". However, the present research reports social support as being a double-edged sword. Parents, coaches, and significant others can be seen as a calming influence in many situations, but sometimes they may be a negative distraction. Although the participants in this study were younger than most participants in other endurance based studies, this perception, regardless of the social support involved, can have an adverse affect (Whitsett, Almvig, and Shoda, 2010). Within endurance based sports, coping with competitive stress and the expectations of others can be significant. For example, Baltzell (1999) found that elite rowers who retold their least effective coping experiences expressed high levels of worry regarding the expectations of others. Therefore, sport psychologists, coaches, and parents should ensure that social support is perceived to be a positive factor. Positive social support derived from a coach is particularly important for adolescent athletes (Kristiansen and Roberts, 2010). This can be accomplished through greater communication with the athlete and understanding that what the supporter may view as helpful may be perceived by the athlete as detrimental.

The response to pain reported in this study also warrants further mention. Kress and Statler (2007) reported that former Olympic cyclists had multiple strategies for coping with pain and associated rather than dissociated the pain. Association is a cognitive strategy that monitors the body's sensations and pays attention to all its cues and signals (Morgan, 1980). This cognition allows the individual to alter their movement pattern according to how they feel. Examples of body sensations include body awareness, racing strategy, and muscular tension (Tammen, 1996). Dissociation, on the other hand, is a cognitive strategy that focuses on external cues thus restricting the sensory input from the body (Morgan). As an example of dissociation, one marathon runner in Morgan's study stated that in order to dissociate, he focused on the shadow of either himself or the runner in front so that he could leave his body and join the shadow that experienced no pain.

Determining the most effective cognitive strategy for coping with pain has been mixed (Masters and Ogles, 1998). In Morgan's (1980) study, for example, marathon runners reported employing a dissociative form of coping in order to overcome 'Heartbreak Hill', a particularly difficult section of the Boston marathon. Conversely, Stevinson and Biddle (1999) found that those marathon runners who hit 'the wall' were more likely to have employed an internal dissociation.

Contrary to the research of Kress and Statler (2007), the present research highlights claims for the use of both association and dissociation as a means of coping and responding to pain. Cyclists reported using pain as a positive factor but also as something which just had to be dealt with. Thus, it is possible that an individual's preferred attentional style may be an indicator of which cognitive strategy is most effective (Baghurst, Thierry, and Holder, 2004). Future research may wish to highlight this area further by examining when and how pain is dealt with, as the onset of pain and its subsequent psychological response could be mediated by the pace of the exercise (Tammen, 1996).

Several methodological limitations of this study must be noted. First, the use of retrospective data is somewhat controversial (Jackson, 1996; Davids, 2000). Results are based on the understanding of the researcher and concepts may not have been developed due to the nature of the study. However, as many safeguards as possible were employed to ensure that the data retrieved and recorded were as accurate and unbiased as possible. Second, participant numbers were small and the cyclists had not yet reached their competitive peaks; therefore, generalisations must be considered with caution, but these findings should provide a well-grounded platform for future research. Third, this study did not employ the traditional expert-novice paradigm (Ericsson and Smith, 1991) that has been the basis of most expertise research. However, every attempt was made to ensure that while these limitations do exist, results were obtained using strict guidelines set out by Lincoln and Guba (1985) and Patton (1990). Such strategies included the inclusion of a reflexive journal, the triangulation of data, and an audit check. In addition, every effort was made to ensure that the data was valid, was obtained reliably, and retained its credibility in order to ensure that the conclusions drawn from the data were derived from the data (Jackson).

To conclude, this research has investigated the psychological components of elite cycling. The research highlights the importance of physiological training within cycling, but also shows the apparent neglect of specific psychological training. This training is necessitated by the number of psychological factors reported as being salient within the race domain. Future research may wish to study the effects of a psychological training intervention programin younger or novice athletes in order to determine whether performance can be enhanced through consistent and systematic psychological skills training. With respect to cycling, this training should be focused on anxiety, coping with pain, and social support.

REFERENCES

Abernethy, B. (1993). *The nature of expertise in sport*. Paper presented at the 7th International Society of Sport Psychology Conference, Lisbon, Portugal.

Baghurst, T., Thierry, G., and Holder, T. (2004). Evidence for a relationship between attentional styles and effective cognitive strategies during performance. *Athletic Insight-The Online Journal of Sport Psychology*, 6. Retrieved from http://www.athleticinsight.com/Vol6Iss1/AttentionalStylesandEffectiveCognitiveStrategies.htm.

Baltzell, A. (1999). *Psychological factors and resources related to rowers' coping in elite competition.* Unpublished doctoral dissertation, Boston University School of Education, Boston, MA.

Bryman, A. (1988). *Quantity and quality in social research.* London: Unwin Hyman. Buman, M. P., Omli, J. W., Gicobbi, P. R., and Brewer, B. W. (2008). Experiences and coping responses of "hitting the wall" for recreational marathon runners. *Journal of Applied Sport Psychology, 20,* 282-301.

Chi, M. T. H., Glaser, R., and Rees, E. (1982).Expertise in problem solving. In R. J. Sternberg (Ed.), *Advances in the psychology of expertise* (Vol. 1, pp. 7-76). Hillsdale, NJ: Erlbaum.

Davids, K. (2000). Skill acquisition and the theory of deliberate practice: It ain't what you do it's the way that you do it! *International Journal of Sport Psychology, 31,* 461-466.

Eccles, D. W., Walsh, S. E., and Ingledew, D. K. (2002). A grounded theory of expert cognition in orienteering. *Journal of Sport and Exercise Psychology, 24,* 68-88.

Ericsson, K. A., and Lehmann, A. C. (1996). Expert and exceptional performance: Evidence of maximal adaptation to task constraints. *Annual Review of Psychology, 47,* 273-305.

Ericsson, K. A., Krampe, R. Th., and Tesch-Römer, C. (1993). The role of deliberate practice in the acquisition of expert performance. *Psychological Review, 100,* 363-406.

Ericsson, K. A., and Smith, J. (1991). Prospects and limits of the empirical study of expertise: An introduction. In K. A. Ericsson, and J. Smith (Eds.). *Toward a general theory of expertise: Prospects and limits.* (pp. 1-38). New York: Cambridge University Press.

Glaser, B., and Strauss, A. (1967). *The discovery of grounded theory: Strategies for qualitative research.* New York: Aldine.

Hardy, L., Jones, G., and Gould, D. (1996). *Understanding psychological preparation for sport: Theory and practice of elite performers.* Chichester: John Wiley and Sons.

Jackson, S. A. (1992). Elite athletes in flow: The psychology of optimal sport experience. (Doctoral dissertation). *Dissertation Abstracts International,54,* 124-A. Jones, G., and Swain, A. (1995). Predispositions to experience debilitative and facilitative anxiety in elite and nonelite performers. *The Sport Psychologist, 9,* 201-211.

Kidder, L. (1981). *Research methods in social relations.* New York: Holt, Rinehart and Winston.

Kress, J. L., and Statler, T. (2007). A naturalistic investigation of former Olympic cyclists' cognitive strategies for coping with exertion pain during performance. *Journal of Sport Behavior, 30,* 428-452.

Kristiansen, E., and Roberts, G. C. (2010). Young elite athletes and social support: Coping with competitive and organizational stress in "Olympic" competition. *Scandinavian Journal of Medicine and Science in Sports, 20,* 686-696.

Kuhn, T. S. (1962). *The structure of scientific revolutions.* Chicago: University of Chicago Press.

Lincoln, Y. S., and Guba, E. G. (1985). *Naturalistic inquiry.* Beverly Hills: Sage Publications.

Masters, K. S., and Ogles, B. M. (1998). Associative and dissociative cognitive strategies in exercise and running: 20 years later, what do we know? *The Sport Psychologist, 12,* 253-270.

Morgan, W. P. (1980). The mind of the marathoner. In R. M. Swinn (Ed.), *Psychology in Sports*, (pp. 297-303). Minneapolis, MN: Burgess Publishing Company.

O'Toole, M. L., and Douglas, P. S. (1995). Applied physiology of triathlon. *Sports Medicine, 19*, 251-267.

Patton, M. Q. (1990). *Qualitative evaluation and research methods*. Newbury Park, CA: Sage Publications Inc.

Pidgeon, N. (1996). Grounded theory: Theoretical background. In T. E. Richardson (Ed.), *Handbook of qualitative research methods*, (pp. 75-101). Leicester, UK: British Psychological Society.

Pidgeon, N., and Henwood, K. (1997). Using grounded theory in psychological research. In N. Hayes (Ed.) *Doing qualitative analysis in psychology*(pp. 245-273). Hove, UK: Psychology Press.

Proctor, R. W. (1995). *Skill acquisition and human performance*. London: Sage Publications.

Reason, P., and Rowan J. (1981). *Human inquiry: A sourcebook of new paradigm research*. Chichester, UK: Wiley.

Rees, T., Hardy, L., and Freeman, P. (2007). Stressors, social support, and effects upon performance in golf. *Journal of Sports Sciences, 25*, 33-43.

Reissman, C. (1993). *Narrative analysis*. Newbury Park, California: Sage Publications. Shea, J. B., and Paull, G. (1996). Capturing expertise in sports. In K. A. Ericsson (Ed.). *The road to excellence: The acquisition of expert performance in the arts and sciences, sports and games.* (pp. 321-336). Mahwah: Lawrence Erlbaum Associates.

Singer, R. N., and Janelle, C. M. (1999). Determining sport expertise: From genes to supremes. *International Journal of Sport Psychology, 30,* 117-150.

Stevinson, C. D., and Biddle, S. (1999). Cognitive strategies in running: A response to Masters and Ogles (1998). *The Sport Psychologist, 13,*235-236.

Tammen, V. (1996). Elite middle and long distance runners associative/dissociative coping. *Journal of Applied Sport Psychology, 8,*1-8.

Whitsett, D. D., Almvig, T., and Shoda, Y. (2010). Identifying the distress cues that influence support provision: A paired comparison approach. *Journal of Social Psychology, 150,* 503-520.

Williams, M., and Davids, K. (1995). Declarative knowledge in sport: A by-product of experience or a characteristic of expertise? *Journal of Sport and Exercise Psychology, 17,* 259-275.

In: Athletic Insight's Writings of 2012
Editor: Robert Schinke

ISBN: 978-1-62618-120-5
© 2013 Nova Science Publishers, Inc.

Chapter 7

TIME, MONEY AND SUPPORT: STUDENT-ATHLETES' TRANSITION TO HIGH ACHIEVEMENT SPORTS

Sverker Bengtsson[*1] *and Urban Johnson*[1,2]
[1]Malmö University, Malmö, Sweden
[2]Halmstad University, Halmstad, Sweden

ABSTRACT

The aim of this study was to examine the perceptions of within-career transition, as experienced by student-athletes striving to reach the international level. Interviews were used to examine the perceptions of 26 Swedish student-athletes with a mean age of 22.5 years practicing individual sportsa the national elite level, involved in a career assistance program. Categories identified through them at iccontent analysis were changes experienced in the transition, the career assistance program, resources to adjust to the new level in sport, satisfaction with their current situation, and strategies to adjust to the new level in sport. The athletes highlighted the value of interpersonal support and commitment, and recognized the need to develop further coping strategies, such as stress and time management. Practical implications for promoting successful within-career transitions are discussed.

Keywords: Within-career transition, achievement sport, thematic content analysis, student-athlete, career-assistance

The transition from national to international level in competitive sport is a stressful but challenging experience for many athletes. Previous research has suggested that athletes experience a number of sport-specific (Haninand Stambulova, 2004; Salmela, 1994) and social-related issues (Pummell, Harwood, and Lavallee, 2008; Wylleman and Lavallee, 2004)

---
[*] Corresponding author: SverkerBengtsson. Department of Sport Sciences, Nordenskiöldsgatan 10, 205 06 Malmö, Sweden. Phone: (46) 406658301; Fax: (46) 406658310; e-mail: sverker.bengtsson@mah.se.

during their transition, such as higherperformance expectations and changes in interpersonal relationships. Consequently, there is a need to further understand the specific demands of particular transitions, in order to assist athletes in making their transitions as successful as possible (MacNamara and Collins, 2010; Stambulova, Alfermann, Statler, and Côté, 2009). The literature concerning athletic career transitions has traditionally focused on the transition out of sport; not as much attention has been paid to specific within-career transitions. To assist athletes in making their transitions successful, it is crucial to understand the specific demands of within-career transitions.

Athletic career is a term for a multi-year sport activity voluntarily chosen by the person and aimed at achieving his or her individual peak in athletic performance in one or several sport events (Alfermannand Stambulova, 2007). According to Schlossberg (1981) a transition is defined as an event that causes "a change in assumptions about oneself and the world and requires a corresponding change in one's behavior and relationships" (p.5). Within-career athletic career transitions include the transitions that occur during the athletic career (Wyllemanand Lavallee, 2004), such as the transition to a higher competitive level. Moreover, Stambulova (1994) has identified three normative phases of within-career transition: the transition from junior to senior sports, the transition from amateur to professional sport, and the transition from the peak to the final stage of the athletic career. In her research, Stambulova (2000) showed that athletic transition has the potential to be a crisis, a success, or a combination of the two, depending on the individual's perception. Normative athletic within-career transitions have also been covered within the developmental model (Wyllemanand Lavallee, 2004), which takes a holistic, whole-person approach, considering how transitions and development in different spheres of an athlete's life overlap and interact. Organized across four levels, it includes stages and transitions in athletic, psychological, psychosocial, and academic/vocational development. Evidence for such a holistic, whole-person approach to career transition comes primarily from career transition research, which has particularly studied the interaction between developments in different spheres. For example, in an investigation of parental involvement and within-career transition in youth sport, Wuerth, Lee, and Alfermann (2004) demonstrated a link between psychosocial development and athletic development. Furthermore, Salmela, Young, and Kallio (1998) have demonstrated, in research on youth sport, that a positive social support system created by the parents and the coaches is important for commitment to progress to later stages of athletic development. Finn and McKenna (2010) recognized through their research that the career transition from academy-to-first-team in elite English male team sports was perceived as potentially very demanding, with athletic and social sources of strain.

Pummell, et al. (2008) used the human adaption to transition model as proposed by Schlossberg (1981) to examine the perceptions of 10 young event riders who had made a transition from local to regional level. Their research revealed that the transition was facilitated by substantial social support. Furthermore, it showed that the athletes made considerable sacrifices during their transition, such as in academic and social areas of life. More specifically, Schlossberg's model demonstrates how the characteristics of a particular transition and the individual's transition environment interact to produce a unique experience for the individual, making the subjective perception of a transition all-important.

In later research, Schlossberg, Waters, and Goodman(1995)recognized four major factors that influence an individual's ability to cope with a transition, offering an explanation of inter- and intra-individual differences in transition experiences: the situation (e.g., feelings of personal control over the transition); the self (e.g., psychological characteristics, such as self-efficacy); support (i.e., social support available); and strategies (i.e., the individual's coping strategies and resources). Each variable acts as a resource or a deficiency during a within-career transition, with the ratio of resources to deficiencies determining ease of adaptation.

The developmental model arises from sport, and can recognize possible coexisting developmental tasks for an athlete in transition, but it does not make any predictions concerning the transition experience between the stages. Athletes will also experience other normative and non-normative transitions within a stage, which are not detailed in the model. The human adaption to transition model does not originate in sport, and focuses more on the individual, subjective perception of a transition, which in this context means that it can be used to overlap the athlete's experience between the stages of transition in the developmental model. Although both models have their deficiencies, combining them may offer a possibility to explain the holistic perspective of a within-career transition, as experienced by athletes.

Research has also examined the non-athletic life transitions of athletes. For instance, Giacobbi, Lynn, Wetherington, Jenkins, Bodendorf, and Langley (2004) studied the sources of stress and coping strategies of student-swimmers during their transition to university, exposingseveral sources of stress associated with this transition, including performance expectations, training intensity, interpersonal relationships, relocation, and academic demands. For instance, in a study by CecićErpić, Wylleman, and Zupančić (2004), it was found that both athletic and non-athletic factors have an impact upon the athletic transition. CecićErpić et al. conclude that athletic and non-athletic aspects of life interact to affect an athlete's experience of career transition.

There is some research regarding the transition of athletes to university. MacNamara and Collins (2010) studied the role of psychological characteristics in managing the transition to university in high-level athletes, and concluded that the transition to university is perceived as a process that needs considerable pre-emptive work in the lead-up to the move, focusing on systemic and interpersonal resources. This has also been acknowledged by Petitpas, Brewer, and Van Raalte (1997), who conclude that student-athletes are faced with establishing new relationships, making important career and life decisions, and balancing academic and social priorities while trying to improve their athletic career. This has also been acknowledged in later research by Miller and Kerr (2002), whose research on Canadian student-athletes revealed that the athletes' lives revolved around athletic, academic, and social demands, and that the athletes were forced to make a number of compromises to cope with the demands.

The importance of social support during a career transition has been studied in a number of reports, including normative (see e.g., Parker, 1994; Thomas, Gilbourne, and Eubank, 2004; Wuerth et al., 2004) and non-normative career transitions (see e.g., Alfermann and Stambulova, 2007; Woods, Buckley, and Kirrane, 2004; Wylleman, Alfermann, and Lavallee, 2004). Social support and social support networks are important for developing informed practices (Côté, Ericsson, and Law, 2005), and facilitating athletic career transitions at various stages (Martinelli, 2000; Wylleman et al., 2004).

Despite the vast amount of research recognized in the area, few studies specifically examine athletic career assistance programs. According to North and Lavallee (2004), there appears to be some reluctance among younger athletes, and those who perceive themselves to have a significant amount of time before they retire, to develop concrete plans about their future career prior to their retirement. Regarding transition out of sport, in evaluating a career assistance program for elite athletes, Mateos, Torregrosa, and Cruz (2008) concluded that satisfaction levels were high, and the level of career decision-making difficulties tended to diminish in relation to the amount of time spent in the program.

Researchers have also examined athletic identity and its relationship to career transition. Brewer, Van Raalte, and Petitpas (2000) found that athletic career transition affects patterns and levels of an individual's identity. According to Lally (2007), decreasing the prominence of athletic identities can preclude a major identity crisis or confusion upon and following athletic retirement. In a study including intercollegiate students, those who failed to explore alternative roles and did identify strongly and exclusively with the athlete role (Murphy, Petitpas, and Brewer, 1996) were associated with delayed career development.

The study of adolescent development has been of great interest to researchers, theorists, and practitioners. Numerous publications have brought to the forefront various defining features of adolescence. One such defining element is the array of developmental changes that occur and mark this period as unique (see, e.g., Erikson, 1963; Erikson, 1968; Safyer, Leahy, and Colan, 1995). Safyer et al. (1995) have described adolescence as a transition period that bridges childhood and adulthood, a period during which major physical, cognitive, and psychological changes occur.

SUMMARY AND OBJECTIVE OF THE STUDY

It is evident from the literature that a within-career transition affects athletes from an inside- as well as an outside-sport perspective. Athletes at the national elite level have already passed a number of career transitions and are at a point where their athletic careers probably are close to their peak. For many national elite level athletes; this point coincides with other, non-athletic, career transitions that demand attention, such as transition to higher education or a vocational transition. Consequently, it is important to understand this adaptation process— how student-athletes cope with transitions demands—because of its influence on successful and unsuccessful within-career transitions. However, such studies are sparsely documented. The aim of this study was to examine the experience of national elite level student-athletes striving to reach the international elite level, during a normative within-career transition.

METHOD

A qualitative design was chosen as appropriate for study of phenomena of "student-athletes' transition to high achievement sport," due to the underlying naturalistic paradigm's ontological notion that numerous and subjective realities do exist and that, epistemologically, it is possible to acquire knowledge by examining people's life worlds. The qualitative method consisted of narrative interviews, which are based on the assumption that people give meaning to events by telling stories (Clandini, 2007), and thematic content analysis (Baxter, 1991). Qualitative approaches to content analysis have their roots in literary theory, the social sciences, and critical scholarship (Krippendorff, 2004), and are commonly used in health and sport psychology research (Chamberlain and Murray, 2008; Smith and Gilbourne, 2009).

Participants

Twenty-six Swedish student-athletes, 14 men and 12 women, were contacted, to gain understanding of the process by which the athletes approached a normative within-career transition. That is, a purposive sample was chosen, to be able to explain some of the issues of the transition (Gratton and Jones, 2004). All the athletes were, at the time of data gathering, enrolled in a career assistance program in Sweden, which presupposed that the athletes were at a national elite level in their sport. The athletes all participated in individual sports: canoeing (4), badminton (4), squash (1), athletics (9), swimming (2), taekwondo (2), rowing (1), boxing (2), and triathlon (1), and were between 19 and 28 years of age (mean age 22.5 years, SD 2.6). The athletes had been competing in their sport for an average of 10.3 years (SD 3.8). They spent about 20 hours per week on training (SD 4.2), and had been competing at the senior level for an average of 4 years (SD 2.8), although some of the athletes were still competing in junior sports as well.

Interview Guide

A semi-structured interview guide was developed, focusing on the conception and process of operationalizing knowledge in content analysis (Krippendorff, 2004; Kvale, 2007). The interview guide was developed to allow the interviewer to explore the experience of the transition as experienced by the participant, and in this regard, drew on the conceptualization of human transition as defined by Schlossberg and colleagues (Schlossberg, 1981; Schlossberg et al., 1995). Open-ended questions pertaining to psychosocial and academic influences were also included, reflected by the developmental model (Wyllemanand Lavallee, 2004). The interview guide was pilot-tested using two athletes of the same level as the participants, resulting in only minor changes. The final interview guide, which altogether consisted of 30 questions, was used in the interviews.

The interview questions were all related to a) changes experienced in the transition (perceptions of the transition, degree of stress, concurrent pressures, and transition changes); b) the career assistance program (perceived support and expectations); c) resources to adjust to the new level in sport (sport/life balance, perception of the impact of the transition on their psychological skills, and readiness for competition); d) satisfaction with their current situation (inside and outside of sport); e) strategies to adjust to the new level in sport (perception of social support and development of athletic skills).

Procedure

Potential participants were contacted by the researchers in an information meeting initiated through the career assistance program. The purpose and rationale behind the study, assurances of confidentiality, and an explanation of the upcoming interview process was explained to the participants. The participants were also presented with an information letter and a consent form, and were given the opportunity to ask questions about the study. Participants who returned the completed consent form signified agreement to participate in the study. The participants also provided the approximate date at which they felt their transition to international elite level commenced, the indication being their first major international competition. The regional ethical review boards serving universities in the southern part of Sweden approved the ethical standards in the study. All interviews were conducted by one of the authors. Each interview lasted between 35 and 70 minutes and was digitally recorded to provide an accurate record.

Data Analysis

All interviews were transcribed verbatim. Data analysis was done through thematic content analysis and progressed from an inductive to a deductive process. Content analysis is used to make replicable and valid inferences from texts (or other meaningful matter) to the contexts of their use (Krippendorff, 2004), and therefore, is well-adapted for this study. In the inductive phase, new themes were drawn from the interview transcripts, while in the deductive phase; pre-existing categories (based on existing research) were used to organize the quotes (Kvale, 2007). The first stage consisted of microanalysis, which involves examining the data phrase by phrase and sometimes word by word, as defined by Graneheimand Lundman (2004). Corresponding parts of the interviews were copied into a separate file called "raw data file." Individual meaning units were then identified and coded from the interview transcripts to identify preliminary themes within the data. To ensure that the results were grounded in the data, raw data themes were derived from, rather than forced upon, the data (Graneheimand Lundman, 2004). Once this first stage of coding was completed, the most frequently cited raw-data themes were identified and grouped into categories that represented their meaning (high-order themes and low-order themes). The analysis, in this way, became increasingly deductive, with links being made to existing literature. Data analysis was initiated by the authors and subsequently verified by two senior researchers who were, at the time, unfamiliar with the data and, therefore, able to give an unbiased opinion regarding the validity of the analysis. In instances where there was a disagreement regarding an analytic decision, interpretations were discussed until agreement was reached regarding the representation of the results. In addition, to further increase dependability, two participating athletes confirmed that they recognized the findings, as suggested by Krippendorff (2004). Each category was structured as a profile, in which themes were ordered according to the number of raw data units related to them, from those with the biggest number of raw data units to those with the smallest. Complete versions of category profiles, tables, and raw data are available on request from the corresponding author. Deductive analysis was then used again to verify the validity of the analysis, by rereading the transcripts to ensure that all identified categories were present in the data, providing a true representation of participant perceptions. The findings are summarized in Table 1.

RESULTS

From the raw data themes, 48 low-order themes, 12 higher-order themes, and five general categories emerged. Each of these general categories: a) changes experienced in the transition, b) resources to adjust to the new level in sport, c) the career program, d) satisfaction with the current situation, and e) strategies to adjust to the new level in sport are presented in a temporal manner from common factors evident prior to transition and factors related to the transition phase.

Table 1. Overview of the low order themes, high order themes and categories "Student-athletes' transition to high achievement sport"

Low order themes	High order themes	Categories
- Changes in practice - Changes in competition - Changes in relationship to coach - Changes in lifestyle - Difficulties in adjusting - Environmental factors	Changes experienced at the higher level	Changes experienced in the transition
- Season goals - Long-term goals - Intrinsic motivation - Motivation-related behavior - Non-motivational factors	Goals and motivation	
- Financial support - Social support	Support to adjust	Resources to adjust to the new level in sport
- Technical skills - Tactical skills - Mental skills - Communication skills - Physical conditions - Personal characteristics - Health conditions	Perceived athletic skills	
- Support areas - No clear expectations	Expectations of the career assistance program	The career assistance program
- Financial support - Have a support site/location - Sponsor aid - Support in combining sport with studies	Areas to develop in the career assistance program	
- Current positive experience in practice - Inconvenience during practice - Optimistic view on results - Not reaching goals	Practice and competition	Satisfaction with current situation
- Encouraging practice environment - External nuisances - Significant others' support - Struggle to maintain relationships	Relationships inside and outside sport	
- Organizational support - Pressure of combining sport participation and vocational career - Social advantages of transition - Negative influence on social life	Work/studies and leisure activities	
- Intrinsic motivation/enthusiasm - Non-motivational factors	Life in general	
- Raise level in practice - Raise level in competition - Improve communication - Combine sport with other activities	Strategies to develop/ improve	Strategies to adjust to the new level in sport
- Mental skills - Physical condition - Experience - Structure/planning	Strategies to meet requirements at new level	

Changes Experienced in the Transition

The transition to higher competitive sport (international elite level) had triggered several changes in the life of the athletes, both inside and outside sport.

Changes experienced at the higher level. In sport, the most apparent changes at the higher level were the greater intensity, duration, and quality of the athletes' training. One athlete stated that "the training volume picked up tremendously, from 4 sessions a week to sometime 10 sessions a week"; this answer exemplified a common theme among the athletes. Another change in the sporting environment related to the higher level was that many of the athletes could observe that few of their former teammates remained in the sport, due to tougher opposition and competitions at the new level. Several athletes mentioned that "the training group has diminished," and that "many of my former teammates have dropped out," The fact that the opposition in competition now was becoming more challenging was also evident among the athletes.

Possible obstacles to adjusting to the higher level consisted of both internal factors (e.g., risk of injuries) and external factors (e.g., academic demands), and the athletes were quite aware of the difficulties in adjusting. As one athlete stated, "it's a constant struggle to keep your balance"

Goals and motivation. All athletes had as a long-term goal to reach and perform on an international elite level in their sport. Thirteen of the athletes mentioned the Olympics as a prime goal, and it was also evident that goal setting was an important issue for the athletes.

Motivation and dedication to the sport were high among the athletes, two of the athletes stated that "it is my primary drive" and another stated that "it's the most important thing for me," although some of the athletes also mentioned other areas of interest outside of sport, such as school, and some mentioned difficulties connected to the changes experienced, such as injuries.

Resources for Adjusting to the New Level in Sport

When the athletes were reviewing their resources for adjusting to the new level in sport, it became apparent that they felt that their support system, as well as their athletic skills, was of great significance, and they recognized the importance of developing both(see Table 1).

Support to adjust. Most of the participating athletes perceived themselves to have sufficient social support. Eighteen athletes acknowledged their family as an important source of social support; some athletes said, "They have always supported me," and "My family supports me all the way." Coaches and friends were also mentioned as important social supports. Eight athletes stated, "My coach gives me all the support I want." If the athletes were content with their social support, the opposite was true about their financial support. Only two athletes stated that they felt they had enough financial support. "I could really use more financial support" was a common comment, as well as "I struggle to make ends meet." Support from the club, and in some cases, the national federation was acknowledged as important and appreciated, but it was not considered to be enough financial assistance to adjust to the new level in sport.

Perceived athletic skills. In relation to perceived athletic skills, all athletes felt they could develop further, especially in skills directly related to their sporting performance, with focus on technical, tactical, and mental skills, and physical conditioning. Much of the perceived shortcoming was attributed to a lack of experience of the new level in sport. However, most of the athletes stated that they "were working on improving their skills." Determination, dedication, and focus were personal characteristics that were mentioned by most of the athletes. Several athletes stated, "I am very headstrong," and this was considered an important personal characteristic that would serve as a resource in adjusting to the new level in sport. Injuries were also considered a problem by some. Five athletes reported that they were not able to train due to injuries, although the vast majority of the athletes reported that they were in good health.

The Career Assistance Program

The career assistance program was something new to the athletes, and they were not completely sure what it would mean for their endeavor to reach the higher level (see Table 1).

Expectations of the career assistance program. The expectations of the career program were to receive assistance in order to further strengthen their athletic skills, although the athletes were not completely certain of how much support they could really receive from the career program. On the other hand, the athletes had plenty of ideas with respect to areas that could be developed in the career assistance program to help them.

Areas to develop in the career assistance program. Concurrent with the athletes' perception of financial support as a means to obtain resources for adjusting to the new level in sport, financial support and sponsor aid were considered important areas to develop in the career assistance program. Several athletes mentioned "money for travelling to competitions" and "help to get sponsors." A place or location to meet other athletes in the same situation was also considered an area to develop, further to the issue of social support, or as one athlete stated; "somewhere to meet, train, and hang with the other athletes would be great." Some of the student-athletes also brought up the notion of getting more support in combining sport with their studies.

Satisfaction with Current Situation

The athletes seemed to be quite content with their current situation in sport and in life, but they felt that, to cope, they had a lot of things to manage. This generated several higher order themes (see Table 1).

In practice and competition. In relation to practice, there appear to be both positive experiences and some inconveniences, such as problems with time management and injuries. The athletes' views on their competition performances were divided, some athletes were optimistic, but some were disappointed in their results at the higher level; however, a lot of the athletes were in off-season at the time of the interview and had not taken part in many competitions in the season yet.

Relationships inside and outside of sport. Relationships in sport were also considered important for the athletes, and a majority of the athletes' comments in this regard were positive: "It's a good atmosphere at the club" and "My coach always backs me up," as two athletes stated. Regarding relationships outside sport, it became clear that most of the athletes perceived themselves to have good support from their significant others, but outside the circle of closest friends and family it was perceived as much harder to keep up contacts, due to all the time the athletes devoted to their sport.

Work/studies and leisure activities. Several athletes stated that they were having a hard time combining sport participation and vocational career, including difficulties in combining sport and studies. "I have to work to be able to continue in my effort to reach higher in my sport" and similar statements were common among the athletes who were working. The most common reason that athletes were experiencing problems was due to a perceived lack of time, and this was also the case when the athletes talked about their leisure activities.

Life in general. The athletes exhibited strong intrinsic motivation and satisfaction with life in general. A lot of the athletes stated "I love my sport," "sport is my life," and "I really like what I do." These comments also imply that the athletes have a strong identity in their sport, although some also feel that sometimes it's tough, especially when injured.

Strategies to Adjust to the New Level in Sport

The athletes had developed a number of strategies to adjust to the new level in sport, and the athletes had similar views on what they needed to work on to make the transition (see Table 1).

Strategies to develop/improve. The strategies the athletes felt they needed to improve were mainly focused on training and competition, combined with planning and structuring their life situation. In training and competition comments such as "work harder," "stay focused," and "get more experience" were common. Communication and maintaining a good dialogue with their coach and teammates was also considered important.

Strategies to meet requirements at new level. The athletes were also convinced that the ability to plan their life and structure their time around their training, competitions, and all other activities were a crucial part of making the transition, and which they also had to develop further. Other strategies the athletes stated as important to meet requirements at the new level were physical conditioning and experience, or as several athletes believed, "It takes a long time and a lot more training to reach the highest level."

DISCUSSION

The transition-related experiences described by athletes are consistent with the path of athletic development hypothesized by Wylleman and Lavallee (2004), with increase in dedication and training, evidence of a strong athletic identity, recognition of achievements, and striving for a more expert status. Consistent with Schlossberg (1981) and Stambulova (2000), the athletes' perceptions of transition indicate a process rather than an event. A high level of commitment was demonstrated by the athletes who, collectively, showed significant personal investment, drive, and effort in the pursuit of transition success. A range of social-environmental and intrapersonal factors played key roles in the quality of each athlete's transitional experience, providing the athletes with a basis of resources for the transition. Additionally, Schlossberg has attributed to most transitional experiences elements of both positive and negative effect, and the participants' perceptions of this transition were congruent with this observation.

Changes Experienced in the Transition

At the social level, the time pressures and competitive demands inherent in the sport seemed to restrict the athletes' social activities. Such social restriction is likely to have negative consequences at career termination, when social support is important for readjustment (Grove, Lavallee, and Gordon, 1997), and is also likely to affect social development at a time when mature peer relationships and social skills should be developing. Given that training for the international elite level in an individual sport often is solitary in nature, these athletes may have less contact with their peers than other athletes who may train and compete regularly together or participate in team sports. Social development is also important for athletic performance (Rees and Hardy, 2000; Wylleman, 1995), as well as for adaptation in other areas of life. Thus, individuals with a strong commitment and defined goals, which were displayed by a clear drive towards achievement of athletic goals and motivation-related behavior, may be more at risk for sport-related stress when faced with difficult situations such as a sport injury (e.g., Johnson, 2000). The athletes' subjective perceptions of the transition were important, as outlined by Schlossberg (1981). For example, perceptions of personal control over the transition process were associated with the degree of stress experienced.

Resources to Adjust to the New Level in Sport

The support the athletes received was multi-dimensional in nature and included emotional, tangible, and informational types of support. The importance of social support as a causal factor in successful transition has also been emphasized in the existing literature (Lavallee, 2005; Schlossberg, 1981), as have the quality of athletes' interpersonal relationships in predicting whether they will reach the national elite level (Vanden Auweele, De Cuyper, Van Mele, and Rzewnicki, 1993). In this study it was also shown that athletes emphasize emotional support as an important factor in their interpersonal relationships. Moreover, athletes seemed to know what athletic skills were needed, and, although they felt they had to develop further, athletic abilities were also perceived as important resources for adjusting to the new level in sport. Adaption to a new level based on control of athletic skills or self-enhancement is consistent with previous research (Martinelli, 2000; Wylleman and Lavallee, 2004).

The Career Assistance Program

The athletes had modest expectations of the career assistance program; however, this was mainly attributed to the fact that they were only just starting the program and they did not know what to expect. The athletes collectively perceived that they did not have enough financial support at the time of the interview. A transition to the international elite level presents a significant time and financial burden on the athlete, and therefore, an athlete is unlikely to be able to progress in the sport without such support. Student-athletes also hoped to receive support in combining sport with their studies, which is a common problem for many student-athletes (Giacobbi et al., 2004; Lanning, 1982). The importance of support from institutional service units, and formal and intentional programming at times that are convenient for student-athletes, has also been acknowledged in previous research (MacNamara and Collins, 2010; Martinelli, 2000). Further research needs to address the type of financial (and organizational) support that facilitates this type of transition, especially in relation to career assistance programs.

Satisfaction with Current Situation

Several athletes perceived that they did not have enough leisure time, and time to be with friends outside sport, although a majority of the athletes were content with their experiences, in practice. Social isolation can be detrimental to sporting performance (Rees and Hardy, 2000), as the support received from coaches, other athletes, family, and friends outside sport is important during transition, as well as the support from within the sport. Consistent with previous research, significant others played an important role in the athletes' transition (e.g. Pummell et al. 2008). Families, and social affiliation with peers, were key elements in the development of the athletes' motivation for transition, as well as their continued participation in sport, and social support from significant others acted as a key coping resource used to facilitate the athletes' transition. The pattern of significant-other involvement was also consistent with the developmental model (Wyllemanand Lavallee, 2004), which implies that significant others play important roles throughout within-career transitions. Sources of stress for participants included organizational issues, as well as competitive outcome expectations, which can influence athletic performance and development (Fletcher and Hanton, 2003), and have the potential to affect the process of adaptation to transition negatively. This relationship is consistent with the model of human adaptation to transition, since the degree of stress associated with a transition has an important effect on the outcome of adaptation to the transition (Schlossberg, 1981). Athletes driven to make the transition to a higher competitive level may also be at greater risk for transition-related stress, since individuals highly identified with their sport have been shown to experience greater sport -related stress, for example, in reaction to injury (Brewer, 1993). Results from this study confirm the athletic injury situation, since some of the athletes had vast problems due to injuries, and a majority experienced transition-related stress.

Strategies to Adjust to the New Level in Sport

Again, increased dedication and training, including attempting to improve communication and taking control by means of planning and structuring their everyday life, were the main focuses of the athletes' strategies to adjust to the higher level in sport, which is consistent with previous research on athletic development (Stambulova, 1994; Wylleman and Lavallee, 2004). The importance of structure has also been highlighted by, for instance, Galotti (2001), who concluded that students who report themselves to be good planners are significantly more certain they have made the right decision, more comfortable with the process, more satisfied with the information they have gathered, more likely to consider future consequences of their decision, and more likely to make their decision based on their overall values or principles.

A developing athletic identity was evidenced in this sample through the importance the athletes placed on their sport and the priority given to athletic development. Concurrent pressure to excel in academic, vocational, and athletic arenas can sometimes have negative consequences for athletes (Lanning, 1982), including academic problems and delays in social and psychological development (Wylleman and De Knop, 1997). The current study provides support for this, since the athletes reported a reciprocal (negative) influence regarding the combining of sport and academics, primarily because of time pressures.

The combined usefulness of the career transition frameworks used in this study offers possibilities to merge processes inside and outside sport, analyzing within-career transition experience among athletes involved in career assistance programs. In particular, it emphasizes developmental, as well as individual, differences in transition experiences, such as the value of coping resources, time management and interpersonal support.

Many questions remain to be addressed, in order to provide appropriate support to athletes in transition situations, such as outlined in this study. Academic institutions, career assistance programs, clubs, and national sport federations should cooperate to promote all-around development and a well-rounded identity.

Methodological Considerations

This study represents an examination of a small sample of student-athletes in the midst of a normative transition to top-elite level sport. The interviewees' differences in gender, age, sport, and length of sporting career contributed to a rich variation in the experience of within-career transition. It is possible that, if part of the study had been conducted in another country or in a different cultural context, the variation could have been even richer. The trust-worthiness also relates to the transferability of the findings (Graneheimand Lundman, 2004). However, it is argued that the reader can make a realistic assessment of whether or not the findings are transferable to other, similar contexts. Some athletes' memory recall may have been deficient, but the relatively high congruence of the findings with previous research speaks to the credibility of the results. The findings of the study represent one possible interpretation of many variables affecting within-career transition, influenced by the authors' roles as sport psychologists and background as former athletes, having passed some of the career transitions the athletes in the study face. However, this influence could also be counted as a benefit to the study, since researchers performing content analysis are served by some level of familiarity with what they are looking for and sharing of similar backgrounds to those of the participants in the study (Krippendorff, 2004).

Practical Implications

Consistent with existing literature (especially Schlossberg et al., 1995; Stambulova, 2003; Wyllemanand Lavallee, 2004), this study demonstrates the importance for student-athletes during within-career transition to be equipped with the necessary coping resources to successfully manage their transition, especially a career assistance program. The athletes highlighted the value of resources such as interpersonal support, commitment, and motivation. Through their transition experience, they recognized the need to develop coping strategies, such as time management, as well as the ability to cope with stress and setbacks, which is congruent with Finn and McKenna (2010), suggesting that meaning-focused coping is an important technique for successful transitions. This is also consistent with the findings of MacNamara and Collins (2010), who suggest that development of capabilities, abilities, and behaviors that are requisites for learning and development is important in the transition to university. Various transition-related pressures have also emerged in the text, which need to be planned for, to promote successful transition. The insights offered by the athletes suggest a number of psychological support activities that may assist members of the athlete's family and organization with the necessary resources for successful transition. Firstly, by educating the organization, the athletes, their coaches, and significant others, a practitioner can prepare athletes for the challenges associated with a particular transition at the athletic, academic, social, and psychological levels (Wylleman and Lavallee, 2004). For example, in this study, the role of the organization and career assistance program in helping to decrease feelings of uncertainty may be enhanced by ensuring greater informational support to the athletes. Older athletes, noted as a useful source of informational support, could contribute to a mentoring or role model system set up by the sporting organizations and the career program to ensure this provision. Such pre-transition planning may reduce feelings of uncertainty and increase feelings of personal control over the transition process. The findings support the importance of considering pre-emptive work with athletes and coaches, which is acknowledged by Petitpas, Champagne, Chartrand, Danish, and Murphy (1997). For example, attention to stress management strategies or goal setting may enable athletes to cope more effectively with increased competitive pressure and expectations. In addition, it is important to work to maintain a healthy level of athletic identity and prevent identity foreclosure through the exploration of other life roles, and it is recommended that athletes be encouraged to acknowledge their achievements in non-athletic areas. This process provides essential buffering, in case of failure or premature career termination (Wylleman and Lavallee, 2004). Student-athletes will also benefit from time management training to minimize the athletic-academic conflict (Lavallee and Andersen, 2000). Self-help guides for career and life planning could also be presented at an early stage, such as suggested by Petitpas et al. (1997). At the coaching level, following education regarding the demands of the transition and their role in terms of support, coaches may be given specific tasks to help them manage the changing nature of the coach-athlete (and peer) relationships. During times of change, coaches can be an important source of pressure, as well as support, although many coaches remain unaware of the pressure that they sometimes place on their athletes (Hawkins and Blann, 1996).

FUTURE RESEARCH AND CONCLUSION

It would be valuable to examine the processes of adaptation when comparing perceived successful and non-successful within-career transitions in the latter stages of athlete development. The student-athletes in this study suggested a high level of coping resources, having the potential to promote successful adaptation to transition. Less successful individuals may show a greater degree of deficits compared to resources. In addition, longitudinal studies involving measurements of student-athletes at several occasions during their career would provide a deeper understanding of the transition process as it unfolds over time. A follow-up study on the athletes in this study is scheduled. In such research, intervention programs could be developed and implemented to prepare athletes for within-career transition.

Overall, the present study suggests that a within-career transition affects not only the sporting context, but also psychosocial development and academic and vocational transitions, both inside and outside of sport. Evidence suggests that the extent of an individual's identification with their sport has a profound effect on the development of self-identity transition (Brewer et al., 2000), and at the extreme, these athletes may be at risk for identity foreclosure. Within-career transitions create particular challenges, expectations, and pressures, along with the need to balance demands from other life domains. This study represents an effort to expose the characteristics that promote successful within-career transition and successful all-around development for student-athletes. A career assistance program should take these aspects into consideration, in order to become a real source of support in the transition to high achievement sport, because "it is a lot tougher at the higher level."

REFERENCES

Alfermann, D., and Stambulova, N. (2007). Career transitions and career termination. In G. Tenenbaum and R. C. Eklund (Eds.), *Handbook of sport psychology* (3rd ed., pp.712–736). New York:Wiley.

Baxter, L. A. (1991). Content analysis. In B. M. Montgomery and S. Duck (Eds.), *Studying interpersonal interactions* (pp. 239–254). London: Guilford Press.

Brewer, B. W. (1993). Self-identity and specific vulnerability to depressed mood. *Journal of Personality, 61*, 343–363.

Brewer, B. W., Van Raalte, J. L., and Petitpas, A. J. (2000). Self-identity issues in sport career transitions. In D. Lavallee and P. Wylleman (Eds.), *Career transitions in sport: International perspectives* (pp. 29–43). Morgantown, WV: Fitness Information Technology.

CecićErpić, S., Wylleman, P., and Zupančić, M. (2004). The effect of athletic and non-athletic factors on the sports career termination process. *Psychology of Sport and Exercise, 5* (1), 45–59.

Côté, J., Ericsson, K. A., and Law, M. P. (2005). Tracing the development of athletes using retrospective interview methods: A proposed interview and validation procedure for reported information. *Journal of Applied Sport Psychology, 17*, 1–19.

Chamberlain, K., and Murray, M. (2008). Health psychology. In C. WilligandW. Stainton-Rogers (Eds.), *The Sage handbook of qualitative research in psychology* (pp. 390–406). London: Sage.

Clandini, D. J. (2007). *Handbook of narrative inquiry: Mapping methodology.* Thousand Oaks, CA: Sage.

Erikson, E. (1963). *Childhood and society* (2nd Ed). New York: Norton.

Erikson, E. (1968). *Identity: Youth and crisis.* New York: Norton.

Finn, J. and McKenna, J. (2010). Coping with academy-to-first-team transitions in elite English male team sports: The coaches' perspective. *International Journal of Sport Science and Coaching, 5,* 257-279.

Fletcher, D., and Hanton, S. (2003). Sources of organizational stress in elite sports performers. *The Sport Psychologist, 17,* 175–195.

Galotti, K. M. (2001). Helps and hindrances for adolescents making important real-life decisions. *Journal of Applied Developmental Psychology, 22,* 275–287.

Giacobbi, P. R., Lynn, T. K., Wetherington, J. M., Jenkins, J., Bodendorf, M., and Langley, B. (2004). Stress and coping during the transition to University for first-year female athletes. *The Sport Psychologist, 18,* 1–30.

Graneheim, U. H., and Lundman, B. (2004). Qualitative content analysis in nursing research: concepts, procedures and measures to achieve trustworthiness. *Nurse Education Today, 24,* 105–112.

Gratton, C., and Jones, I. (2004). *Research methods for sport studies.* New York: Routledge.

Grove, J. R., Lavallee, D., and Gordon, S. (1997). Coping with retirement from sport: The influence of athletic identity. *Journal of Applied Sport Psychology, 9,* 191–203.

Hanin, Y., and Stambulova, N. (2004). Sport psychology, Overview. In C. Spielberger (Ed.), *Encyclopedia of applied psychology* (pp. 463–477). New York: Elsevier.

Hawkins, K., and Blann, F.W. (1996). *Applied Sports Research Program; National Sports Research Centre.* Belconnen: Australian Sports Commission.

Johnson, U. (2000). Short-term psychological intervention: A study of long-term injured competitive athletes. *Journal of Sport Rehabilitation, 9,* 207–218.

Krippendorff, K. (2004). *Content analysis: An introduction to its methodology*(2nd Ed.). Thousand Oaks, CA:Sage.

Kvale, S. (2007). *Den kvalitativaforskningsintervjun.(The qualitative research interview).* Lund: Studentlitterattur.

Lanning, W. (1982). The privileged few: special counseling needs of athletes. *Journal of Sport Psychology, 4,* 19–23.

Lally, P. (2007). Identity and athletic retirement: A prospective study. *Psychology of Sport and Exercise, 8,* 85–99.

Lavallee, D. (2005). The effect of a life development intervention on sports career transition adjustment. *The Sport Psychologist, 19,* 193–202.

Lavallee, D., and Andersen, M. (2000). Leaving sport: Easing career transitions. In M. B. Andersen (Ed.), *Doing sport psychology* (pp. 249–261). Champaign, IL: Human Kinetics.

Mateos, M., Torregrosa, M., and Cruz, J. (2008). Evaluation of career assistance programs me for elite athletes: satisfaction levels and exploration of making career decisions and athletic identity. *KinesiologiaSlovenica, 14,* (1), 14–27.

MacNamara, A., and Collins, D. (2010). The role of psychological characteristics in managing the transition to university. *Psychology of Sport and Exercise, 11,* 353–362.

Martinelli, E. A. (2000). Career decision making and student-athletes. In D. A. Luzzo (Ed.), *Career counseling of college students—an empirical guide to strategies that work* (pp. 201–215). Washington DC: American Psychological Association.

Miller, P. S., and Kerr, G. (2002). The athletic, academic and social experiences of intercollegiate student athletes. *Journal of Sport Behavior, 25,* 346–367.

Murphy, M. G., Petitpas, A. J., and Brewer, B.W. (1996). Identity foreclosure, athletic identity and career maturity in intercollegiate athletes. *The Sport Psychologist, 10,* 239–246.

North, J., and Lavallee, D. (2004). An investigation of potential users of career transition services in the United Kingdom. *Psychology of Sport and Exercise, 5,* 77–84.

Parker, K. B. (1994). "Has-beens" and "wanna-bes": Transition experiences of former major college football players. *The Sport Psychologist, 8,* 287–304.

Petitpas, A. J., Brewer, B. W., and Van Raalte, J. L. (1997). Transitions of the student-athlete: Theoretical, empirical, and practical perspectives. In E. F. Etztel, A. P. Ferrante, and J. W. Pinkney (Eds.), *Counseling college student athletes: Issues and interventions* (pp. 137–156). Morgantown, WV: Fitness Information Technology.

Petitpas, A. J., Champagne, D., Chartrand, J., Danish, S., and Murphy, S. (1997). *Athlete's guide to career planning.* Champaign, IL: Human Kinetics.

Pummell, B., Harwood, C., and Lavallee, D. (2008). Jumping to the next level: A qualitative examination of within-career transition in adolescent event riders. *Psychology of Sport and Exercise, 9,* 427–447.

Rees, T., and Hardy, L. (2000). An investigation of the social support experiences of high-level sports performers. *The Sport Psychologist, 14,* 327–347.

Salmela, J. H. (1994). *Phases and transitions among sport careers.* In D. Hackfort (Ed.), Psycho-social issues and interventions in elite sport (pp. 11–28). Frankfurt: Lang.

Salmela, J. H., Young, B. W., and Kallio, J. (1998). Within career transitions of the athlete-coach-parent triad. In D. LavalleeandP. Wylleman (Eds.), *Career transitions in sport, International perspectives* (pp. 181–193). Morgantown, WV: Fitness Information Technology.

Safyer, A. W., Leahy, B. H., and Colan, N. B. (1995). The impact of work on adolescent development. *The Journal of Contemporary Human Services, 76,* 38–45.

Schlossberg, N. (1981). A model for analyzing human adaptation. *The Counseling Psychologist, 9* (2), 2–18.

Schlossberg, N., Waters, E. B., and Goodman, J. (1995). *Counseling adults in transition: Linking practice with theory.* New York: Springer.

Smith, B., and Gilbourne, D. (2009). *Qualitative Research in Sport and Exercise, 1,* 1–2.

Stambulova, N. (1994). Developmental sports career investigations in Russia: A post-perestroika analysis. *The Sport Psychologist, 8,* 221–237.

Stambulova, N. B. (2000). Athlete's crises: A developmental perspective. *International Journal of Sport Psychology, 31,* 584–601.

Stambulova, N. (2003). Symptoms of a crisis-transition: A grounded theory study. In N. Hassmén (Ed.), *SIPF yearbook 2003* (pp. 97–109). Örebro: Örebro University Press.

Stambulova, N., Alfermann, D., Statler, T., and Côté, J. (2009). ISSP position stand: Career development and transitions of athletes. *International Journal of Sport and Exercise Psychology, 7,* 395–412.

Thomas, M.J., Gilbourne, D., and Eubank, M.R. (2004). Young athletes in pursuit of excellence: The bi-directional nature of stress, coping and social support in close family relationships. Communication to the Annual Conference of the British Association of Sport and Exercise Sciences (BASES). *Journal of Sports Sciences, 22,* 313–314.

VandenAuweele, Y., De Cuyper, B., Van Mele, V., and Rzewnicki, R. (1993). Elite performance and personality: From description and prediction to diagnosis and intervention. In R. E. Singer, M. Murphy, and L. K. Tennant (Eds.), *Handbook of research on sport psychology* (pp. 257–289). New York: MacMillan.

Woods, C.B., Buckley, F., and Kirrane, M. (2004). The role of social support in the career transitions of young footballers. Communication to the Annual Conference of the British Association of Sport and Exercise Sciences (BASES). *Journal of Sports Sciences, 22,* 313–314.

Wuerth, S., Lee, M. J., and Alfermann, D. (2004). Parental involvement and athletes' career in youth sport. *Psychology of Sport and Exercise, 5,* 21–34.

Wylleman, P. (1995). *Talented young athletes and the interpersonal relationships in the athletic triangle.* Doctoral dissertation, Vrije UniversitiesBrusselBrussels, Belgium.

Wylleman, P., Alfermann, D., and Lavallee, D. (2004). Career transition in sport: European perspectives. *Psychology of Sport and Exercise, 5,* 7–20.

Wylleman, P., and De Knop, P. (1997). *The role and influence of the psycho-social environment on the career transitions of student-athletes.* In Bangsbo, J., Saltin, B., Bonde, H., Hellsten, Y., Ibsen, B., Kjaer, M., and Sjøgaard, G. *Book of abstracts: 2nd Annual Congress of the European College of Sports Science* (pp. 90–91). Copenhagen: University of Copenhagen.

Wylleman, P., and Lavallee, D. (2004).A developmental perspective on transitions faced by athletes. In M. Weiss (Ed.), *Developmental sport psychology.* Morgantown, WV: Fitness Information Technology.

In: Athletic Insight's Writings of 2012
Editor: Robert Schinke

ISBN: 978-1-62618-120-5
© 2013 Nova Science Publishers, Inc.

Chapter 8

THE ROLE OF SUPERSTITION AMONG PROFESSIONAL FOOTBALLERS IN GHANA

Patrick Kwaku Ofori[1], Stuart Biddle[2] and David Lavallee[1]*
[1]Aberwystwyth University, UK
[2]Loughborough University, UK

ABSTRACT

Superstitious behavior and beliefs are evident in all sports. The present study examines the self-report of superstitious behavior among 120 male professional footballers in Ghana. The Superstitious Ritual Questionnaire and Sport Attribution Style Scale were the instruments used to measured superstitious behavior and attribution styles of elite Ghanaian footballers. Significant negative correlations ($p < .05$) were found between number of rituals and scores for positive-internality (-0.27) and negative-internality (-0.17). A significant positive correlation was found between superstitious behavior and positive-controllability (0.20). Simple correlations and multiple regression showed that scores for attribution styles significantly but weakly predicted scores on the Superstition Ritual Questionnaire, accounting for 11% of the variance with the latter measured. This is important in understanding professional footballers' usage of superstitious rituals. Follow up work needs to address cross-cultural differences among Africans and Western professional athletes.

Keywords: Superstitious behavior, attribution style, rituals, professional footballers, sport, pre-performance routines and Ghana

Superstition and pre-game rituals remain in sport despite advancement in sports science and technology. The presence of superstition permeates all major sports worldwide (Vyse, 1997). Superstitious behaviors are clearly prevalent and have been extensively discussed in

---

*Corresponding author: Patrick KwakuOfori, Department of Sport and Exercise Science. Carwyn James Building, Aberystwyth University.Penglais Campus, Aberystwyth, Ceredigion, SY23 3FD, UK. Email: bainkoop @hotmail.co.uk /pko09@aber.ac.uk. Phone: +44(0) 1970 621947. Fax: +44(0) 1970 628557.

the popular media. From professional organizations to the local league team, the use of superstitious behavior is evident from the media reporting of sporting events.

Superstition in sports can be defined as "actions which are repetitive, formal, sequential, and distinct from technical performance and which the athlete believes to be powerful in controlling luck or other external factors" (Bleak and Frederick, 1998, p.2). The repetitive nature of such events allows for the term 'ritual' to be used to describe these superstitious behaviors. A ritual in sport is usually defined as conscious activity involving heightened arousal with focused attention that provides a way of coping with a high stress situation (Wormack, 1992).

Superstitious practices in sports have been linked to the theoretical perspectives of attribution (Heider, 1958), achievement motivation (Weiner, 1990), reinforcement (Skinner, 1948), and locus of control (Rotter, 1966). Attribution theory is based on individual perceptions about success and failure and relates to the need for achievement. Weiner (1990) believed that when achievement is aroused, we tend to attribute our performance to a variety of possible causes or attribution elements, such as ability, effort, or luck.

Because of the diversity of attributions possible in sporting situations, some writers have suggested that research in sports should focus on causal dimensions rather than the four basic elements (Hanrahan, 1995). Such dimensions include locus of causality (internal, external), stability (stable, unstable), and controllability (controllable, uncontrollable). However, the nature of attribution dimensions in sport has not been studied much in relation to athletes' ritualistic or superstitious behaviors. Research has found that participants who indicated on a measure of locus of control (LOC) that they believe their actions can control chance events were more likely to develop superstitious behavior (Van Raalte, Brewer, Nemeroff, and Linder, 1991). In contrast, Bleak and Frederick (1998) found little support for the significant role of LOC in conjunction with several other constructs (level of competition, duration of play, type of sport, Type A personality, athletic identity, personal control, optimism and pessimism) in predicting overall use of superstitions among athletes.

Skinner (1948) discussed the acquisition of superstition as a conditioning process. However, the mere fact that reinforcement coincides temporally with a response does not always mean that it is contingent upon the response. For instance, if a favorable consequence happens to coincide with a particular set of behaviors (i.e., rituals); it could serve as an accidental reinforcement that leads to the belief in a causal relation between the two. This connection might explain why athletes continue with their pre-game rituals especially after successful outcomes. Consequently, ritualistic behaviors are reinforced and maintained as a superstition, even though it may just be a coincidence as far as performance is concerned. Matute (1994) stated that superstitions are utilized to give the illusion of control over reinforcement in an uncontrollable situation.

Superstition may provide a means for athletes to cope with stress associated with competition and the uncertainty of sporting events. Superstitious behaviors, therefore, are associated with management of anxiety and building confidence. The element of chance in sport contributes to player's feelings of uncertainty and lack of control. Such feelings may detract from confidence and contribute to elevated levels of anxiety (Van Raalte et al., 1991). It has been acknowledged that to feel some sense of certainty and to provide a means of feeling in control during competitive situations, many athletes practice some form of superstition (Wormack, 1992). Despite the apparent prevalence of superstitious behavior in sports, literature on this subject is scant. Recent studies have examined superstitious behavior as related to types of behavior, athletic identity (AI) and locus of control among college athletes (Todd and Brown 2003; Bleak and Frederick, 1998). Todd and Brown (2003) found track and field athletes with an external locus of control were more likely to utilize superstitious behaviors. Perhaps the greatest problem is that much of the literature has been based on the above mentioned psychological constructs which does not allow the participants to state how they perceive their attribution styles in relation to their ritualistic behavior in professional football. According to sports lore, some playing positions have more rituals associated with them than others. In baseball, pitching and hitting are more likely to be associated with ritual than fielding (Gmelch, 1971). Gmelch's findings support the contention that risk is the primary factor in ritual, because pitching and hitting are "riskier" than fielding. In hockey, the goaltenders are considered to be more superstitious than other hockey players. Not much of the literature has been based on the ritualistic behavior in professional football. Football is the most popular sport in Ghana and arguable the world as whole, this informed our interest in this study. The purpose of the present study is to investigate the role of superstition and how it is perceived to be effective among professional Ghanaian Footballers, and assess whether the degree of superstitious behavior practiced by footballers varies according to the position of the players. A secondary purpose of this study is to investigate how attribution styles of athletes can predict superstitious behavior. It was hypothesized that sports attribution style relate to the use of superstitious behavior and rituals in professional football. It was also hypothesized that attackers are more likely to practice superstitious behaviors than goalkeepers.

METHOD

Participants

The participants were 120 male professional footballers who play their sport in the elite league in Ghana. The participants comprised 34 defenders, 19 midfielders, 13 goalkeepers and 54 attackers. The participants represent all the sixteen premier clubs in Ghana, with ages ranging between18-32 (mean age=21 years, SD=3.2).

Measures

Superstitious behavior. The Superstitious Ritual Questionnaire (SRQ; Bleak and Frederick, 1998) was slightly modified to measure superstitious beliefs, behavior, and rituals. The minor modifications were made because some of the items were not relevant to football (soccer). The wording was also changed to make it culturally relevant to the Ghanaian footballer, examples being 'shake net after failing to score' and 'wear lucky charm on game days'. The original measure comprises 45 items, three of which were excluded because they do not apply to football. The questionnaire consisted of 42 questions separated into seven categories of superstitious behavior including Clothing and Appearance (n= 14, e.g., wear a particular jersey number); Lucky Signs (n=7, e.g., discarding lucky charms); Pre-Game (n= 5, e.g., listening to music during warm-up); Game (n= 5, e.g., perform a sign of the cross); Team

Rituals (n= 4, e.g., team cheer); Prayer (n= 4, e.g., team has a team prayer); and Superstition of the Coach (n= 3, e.g., coach takes a lucky charm to the game) by Bleak and Frederick, (1998). Each ritual was measured using a five-point Likert scale ranging from not at all effective (1) to very effective (5). The sum of the number of rituals used by the participant was defined as the total "number of rituals". The averages of the sub-scales were determined by dividing the total of the categories by the number of ticked questions (rituals engaged in). This was done to find out which of the rituals were relevant to each participant. Buhrmann, Brown, and Zaugg (1982) reported a test-retest reliability coefficient of .95 on the original scale. The SRQ (Bleak and Frederick, 1998) was developed based upon the work of Buhrmann, and Zaugg (1981) however, the psychometric properties have not been established (Burke, et al., 2006).

Sport attribution styles. The Short Form of the Sport Attribution Style Scale (Hanrahan and Grove, 1990) was modified for this study. The modification was necessary to allow the scale to be administered in the field when time was short and to reword some items to make them more understandable to the participants. The wording was changed from sports to football specific. The original scale has inter-item reliability coefficient averages of .74 and .72 for both positive and negative events, respectively. Test-retest reliability over an eleven week period averages .58 across the causal dimensions. It consists of six positive and six negative events in football. All items permitted participants to use their own definitions of success and failure. For example, instead of stating "You win a match" one item said "You perform very well in a match". Participants were asked to write down the single most likely cause of a positive and negative event in football that was presented to them. Then they were asked to rate their open-ended causal attributions along the dimensions of internality, stability and controllability. Ratings reflected the extent to which the participant believed the cause exhibited these dimensional properties on 7-point scales. The 12 items were presented in random order with restriction that positive and negative versions of the same situation were never placed next to each other.

Procedure

The data collection took place in Ghana in compliance with the host University Ethics Committee and the Ghana Football Association. Directors of the sixteen premiership clubs in Ghana were formally contacted through letters and followed up with telephone calls. Permission was granted to solicit professional footballers to voluntarily participate in the study during a regular scheduled team meeting. The participants were given a brief explanation of the purpose of this study before being provided with the questionnaires. After explanations in both English and Asante Twig (participants' local dialect), all players were asked to read and sign an informed consent form. The questionnaires were administered by the first author because he can communicate in both languages and have in-depth understanding of the psychological constructs under investigation. This was to reduce the chance of any translation difficulties. No coaches were present during the administration of the questionnaires. The inventories were administered in the following order: one- page background questionnaire (age, playing position etc), SASS, and SRQ. Although data were collected from 120 professional footballers, nine were excluded from the results due to incomplete information.

RESULTS

Descriptive statistics are presented in Table 1. Positional differences were present only in the total number of superstitious behaviors players engaged in. An examination of the categories of superstitious behaviors endorsed by professional footballers revealed that the top three categories were Clothing and Appearance, Prayer and Team rituals (see Table 1).

Pearson correlations were obtained among measures of attribution styles and superstitious behavior (see Table 2). Significant negative correlations (p<. 01) were found between superstitious behavior and total scores for positive –internality (-0.27). A significant positive correlation was found between superstitious behavior and positive-controllability (0.20). Players who are high on both positive and negative internality are less likely to engage in superstitious rituals. Overall, there was a significant relationship between attribution style and superstitious behavior.

Table1. Descriptive statistics for Superstitious Ritual Questionnaire (SRQ) Subscales

	N	Mean	Standard Deviation
Clothing and Appearance	115	18.94	9.93
Lucky signs	88	8.65	6.86
Pre-game rituals	111	12.04	5.86
Game rituals	110	12.67	5.11
Team rituals	114	14.53	4.39
Prayer	113	16.89	3.43
Coach	114	7.75	2.83

Note: N represents the number of players who subscribed to that particular ritual.
For example, of the total 120 players sampled, 115 players used the Clothing and Appearance ritual.

Table 2. Correlation of attribution styles and superstitious ritual practice (N = 120)

	Total (Superstition Scale)	Positives-Internality	Positive-Stability	Positive-Controllability	Negative-Intern ability	Negative-Stability	Negative-Controllability
Total (Superstition Scale)		-0.27**	-0.09	0.20	-0.17	-0.03	0.18
Positives-Internality			0.33**	-0.20	0.351**	0.36**	-0.27**
Positive-Stability				-0.37**	0.50**	0.38**	-0.24*
Positive-Controllability					-0.45**	-0.29**	0.62**
Negative-Intern ability						0.24**	-0.54**
Negative-Stability							-0.28**
Negative-Controllability							

** Correlation is significant at .01 levels (2 tailed).
* Correlation is significant at .05 levels (2 tailed).

Attribution Style as Predictors of Superstitious Behaviors

A Multiple Regression analysis was performed to determine the extent to which the scores for Attribution style predicted scores on the SRQ. For total superstition scale and attribution style, the findings revealed a significant multiple correlation of 0.33, which was statistically significant (R=.33, F (df 6,106) = 2.21, $p<$. 05). Positive-internality, negative-internality and negative controllability were significant predictors of the practice of superstitious behavior. These constructs accounted for 11.1% of the total variance in the practice of superstitious behavior in this sample of professional footballers.

In order to determine whether the strength of this significant relationship varied as a function of a particular sub-scale or categories, separate multiple regression analyses were conducted for each of the top three categories (Clothing and appearance, Team ritual and Coach) as the dependent variable and Attribution styles constructs as Independent variables. The findings revealed that Attribution styles measures were significant predictors of Clothing and Appearance (R=0.41, F=3.60, $p<$. 05). These constructs accounted for 16.9% of the variance in the practice of Clothing and Appearance as a ritual.

An independent t-test was employed to examine if there were any differences among Goalkeeper's (n=12) and Attacker's (n=52) beliefs and usages of superstitious behaviors (See Table 3). Overall, no significant differences existed between Goalkeepers and Attackers in how they subscribed to superstitious behavior practice. In hockey, the goaltenders are considered to be more superstitious than other hockey players, this study sought to find out whether such claims existed in professional football.

DISCUSSION

One purpose of this study was to examine the relationship between attribution style measures and the usage of superstitious behavior among professional footballers. Differences in superstitious behaviors were also examined by position. It was hypothesized that attackers are more likely to practice superstitious behaviors than goalkeepers. Overall, no significant differences existed between Goalkeepers and Attackers in how they subscribed to superstitious practices. This finding is contrary to claims by Gmelch (1971) that in baseball and hockey, individuals assigned to certain positions are likely to engage in superstitious behaviors than others. The reason why positions like hitting and pitching in baseball and goalkeeping in hockey are associated with ritualistic behaviors is that these positions are riskier. Perhaps the risk component in football does not vary by position. A second possibility relates to the nature and size of sample tested. The sample comprised of only male footballers in Ghana and a sample size of 12 goalkeepers and 52 attackers.

The findings of the second research question investigating the extent to which attribution styles predicted superstitious practice in elite footballers are discussed herein. The negative relationship that emerged between Internality (positive and negative) and superstitious behavior implies that players, who scored highly on both positive and negative Internality, are less likely to engage in superstitious rituals. In other words, players who tended to believe that events occur due to their own internal capabilities were less likely to practice superstition in football.

Table 3. Differences among goalkeepers and attackers and superstitious behavior statistics
Independent Samples Test

		Levene's Test for Equality of Variances		t-test for Equality of Means						95% Confidence Interval of the Difference	
		F	Sig.	t	df	Sig. (2-tailed)	Mean Difference	Std. Error Difference		Lower	upper
Total (Superstition Scale)	Equal variances assumed	0.453	0.503	-1.021	62	0.311	-9.5385	9.34646		-28.22177	9.14485
	Equal variances not assumed			-.932	15.049	0.366	-9.5385	10.23116		-31.33947	12.26255

This finding is in contrast to research by Van Raalte et al. (1991) who found that participants who endorsed internal responses on a measure of LOC were more likely to develop superstitious behavior. These conflicting findings may be explained by the nature of the competitive situation as reported by Van Raalte et al (1991) study, which was conducted with a laboratory-controlled golf putting task. It is possible that the artificial settings coupled with participants with less athletic experience may have potentially created different results than a realistic, uncontrolled setting.

The present study also revealed that a positive correlation exists between Controllability (Positive and Negative) and superstitious behavior. This indicates that the more a player scores high on both positive and negative controllability, the more likely it is for them to engage in superstitious practice. Perhaps, they use it to gain control. The current finding confirms Womack's (1992) assertion that superstition provides athletes with the means of feeling control in competitive situations. The inherent competitiveness of elite footballers and the societal pressure to succeed at the professional level can influence a player to resort to external means, (Bleak and Frederick, 1998) such as superstitious behavior, to control the outcome of a football match. Again, the ambiguity inherent in professional soccer may cause players to seek control and certainty through the use of superstition. Thus, a player with a high need to succeed seeks to develop control over his performance, injury, and luck through uses of ritual to gain control over chance elements or events under other's control. Perhaps, they use it to gain control.

A significant finding from the SRQ was that elite footballers had a higher incidence of engaging in superstitious rituals associated with their clothing and appearance. This finding is contrary to the view point of Ciborowski (1997) who found that collegiate baseball players had a higher incidence of possessing a lucky object or charm. The discrepancy found between these two studies may be attributed to the difference in competitive level of participants. Thus, the level of competitiveness can be an emerging factor that can differentiate particular groups of athletes from ascribing to a different sport ritual. Although clothing and appearance seemed to be the widely used ritual, it was prayer rituals that garnered the highest effectiveness ratings across the board. The conclusion can be drawn that it is not necessarily effectiveness of a superstitious sports behavior which determines its popularity among professional soccer players.

It is a widely held view that superstitious behaviors have been used to reduce anxiety, build confidence, and cope with uncertainty (Neil, 1980), and the findings of this study are no different. However, research has begun to show that some athletes engage in superstitious behavior not for any of the above benefits but as means to conform to peer-pressure and to demonstrate commitment towards the team cause (Vyse, 1997). Further research is needed in the area of cognitive dissonance, how an individual athlete's superstitious beliefs conflict with that of the team's superstitious beliefs.

Another finding from this study was the importance of team prayers. All the participants reported feelings of alertness, strong team bond, cohesion, and confidence just after team prayers before kickoff. A possible explanation for this finding may be that players pray together before matches with a common foe (opponents). With victory in mind, team players often forgo any difference and focus on winning, which in team settings will demand the maximum contribution from other team members.

At the very least, players of different religious faith wanted to adopt different means of Prayer that were in line with their faith. This supports previous research which indicated that it is difficult to distinguish clearly between religious and superstitious beliefs and practices (Buhrmann and Zaugg, 1983; Jahoda, 1969). It can be concluded that superstitious beliefs and practices are partly a function of religion.

Additionally, it was inferred from the survey that players attributed at least 30% of their success and failure to an element of luck. This corroborates the findings of Ciborowski (1997) that during almost every game, one or more of the players made comments about luck as a deciding factor. Although players gave credence to skills and techniques in the game as important factors, it will interest readers to know that especially in the course of defeats, players resorted to luck eluding them as a defense mechanism. Confronted with the pain of defeat, stress, and uncertainty about making the squad for the next game, players may suppress their normal judgment and logic as a means of gaining control over the desire outcome (Gmelch, 1971, Womack, 1981).

As individuals from various cultures have different socialization experience (i.e., behavior influenced by the support or pressures of the social context) it is suggested that superstition could be, in part, a function of culture. More research involving individuals from various cultural perspectives is warranted to provide a comprehensive understanding of superstitious behavior in the sporting context. Further research is necessary in the area, and should consider comparing individual sports and team sports, professionals and amateurs, objective sports and subjective sports on the usage of superstition. There is also the need for future studies investigating superstition among athletes to include playing experience, starters and reserves, and the educational background of the players.

Some of the findings of the present study contradicted previous research results and conclusion and may be explained by this difference in the type of sport context and culture. For instance, participants of this study comprised of professional footballers from Ghana, whereas previous research include college athletes from North America and Western Europe. An understanding of the differences that naturally occur between athletes of different cultural and sport contexts may be used to cultivate certain behaviors that would enhance training and performance.

LIMITATIONS

There are a number of limitations that need to be kept in mind when assessing the results of the present study. The study employed a quantitative approach and understanding of superstitious and ritualistic behaviors would be strengthened by qualitative research. The second limitation relates to language and translation difficulties, as some of the constructs used in the questionnaire had no exact word or meaning in the participants local dialect or language. Another limitation with this study is the self-report protocol of measuring superstition. It should be noted that a test for the order effects could not be conducted because the questionnaires were not counterbalanced.

Overall, this study expands upon the existing literature concerning use of superstition in a number of ways. First, the study sampled professional footballers in Ghana. Second, this study examined, how attribution style constructs predicted superstitious behavior. Again the study investigated how positional differences can influence superstition usage in football. Lastly, the study made an attempt to test some of the underlying assumptions about why footballers use rituals. Results of the study indicated that attribution style were significant predictor of superstitious behavior. In addition, no significant differences were found for positional differences in the usage of superstition. More so, support was shown for fear of injury, culture and religiosity playing important roles in determining the overall use of superstition in sport. However, these factors were also important in distinguishing use of specific rituals. Based on these findings it is suggested that not only the desire to win will motivate athletes to subscribe to superstitious behavior but also fear of injury, culture, religiosity and pressure from team officials.

REFERENCES

Bleak, J. L., and Frederick, C. M. (1998). Superstitious behavior in sport: levels of effectiveness and determinants of use in three collegiate sports. *Journal of Sport Behavior, 21,* 1-15.

Buhrmann, H.G., Brown B., and Zaugg, M.K. (1982). Superstitious beliefs and behavior: A comparison of male and female basketball players. *Journal of Sport Behavior, 5,* 75-185.

Buhrmann, H. G., and Zaugg, M. K. (1983). Religion and superstition in the sport of basketball. *Journal of Sport Behavior, 6,* 146-157.

Buhrmann, H. G., and Zaugg, M. K. (1981). Superstitions among basketball players: An investigation of various forms of superstitious beliefs and behavior among competitive basket balers at the junior high school to university level. *Journal of Sport Behavior, 4,* 163-174.

Burke, K. L., Joyner, A. B., Czech, D. R., Knight, J. L., Scott, L. A., Benton, S.G., and Roughton, H.K. (2006). An exploratory investigation of superstition, personal control, optimism and pessimism in NCAA division I intercollegiate student-athletes. *AthleticInsight, 8(2).* Retrieved from http://www.athleticinsight.com/Vol8Iss2/Superstition.htm

Ciborowski, T. (1997).Superstition in the collegiate baseball player.*The Sport Psychologist, 11,* 305-317.

Cohn, P. J. (1990). Preperformance routines in sport: Theoretical support and practical applications. *The Sport Psychologist, 4,* 301-312.

Gmelch, G. J. (1971). Baseball magic.In J. Spradely and D. McCurdy (Eds.), *Conformity and conflict* (pp 346-352). Boston: Little, Brown, and Co.

Hanrahan, S. J. (1995). Attribution theory.In T. Morris and J. Summers (Eds.), *Sport psychology* (pp.122-142). Brisbane, Australia: Wiley.

Hanrahan, S. J., and Grove, J. R. (1990b).A short form of the Sport Attribution Style Scale. *Australian Journal of Science and Medicine* in Sport, *22,* 97-101.

Heider, F. (1958). *The psychology of interpersonal relations.* New York: Wiley.

Jahoda, G. (1969). *The psychology of superstition.* London, Allen Lane: The Penguin Press.

Lusthberg, R. (2003). http://www.psychologyofsports.com/guest/superstitions2.htm

Matute, H. (1994). Learned helplessness and superstitious behavior as opposite effects of uncontrollable reinforcement in humans.*Learning and Motivation, 25,* 216-232.

Reid, K. S. (1978). *Rodeo rituals: A look at the superstitions of the rodeo.*Mid-South Sociological Association (MiSSA), 1978.

Rotter, J. B. (1966).Generalized expectancies for internal versus external control for Reinforcement.*Psychological Monographs, 80*(1, Whole No. 609).

Skinner, B.F. (1948). "Superstition" in the pigeon. *Journal of Experimental Psychology, 38*, 168-172.

Todd, M., and Brown, C. (2003). Characteristics associated with superstitious behavior in track and field athletes: Are there NCAA divisional level differences? *Journal of Sport Behavior, 26*, 168-187.

Van Raalte, J L, Brewer, B. W., Nemeroff, C. J., and Linder, D. E. (1991). Chance orientation and superstitious behavior on the putting green. *Journal of Sport Behavior, 14*, 41-50.

Vyse, S. A., (1997). *Believing in magic.* New York, NY: Oxford University Press.

Weiner, B. (1990). History of motivational research in education. *Journal of Educational Psychology, 82*, 616-622.

Womack, M. (1992). Why athletes need a ritual: A study of magic among professional athletes. In S. Hoffman (Ed.), *Sport and religion* (pp. 191-202). Champaign, IL: Human Kinetics.

In: Athletic Insight's Writings of 2012   ISBN: 978-1-62618-120-5
Editor: Robert Schinke   © 2013 Nova Science Publishers, Inc.

Chapter 9

PERFORMANCE ENHANCEMENT AND STRESS REDUCTION USING BIOFEEDBACK WITH WOMEN COLLEGIATE VOLLEYBALL PLAYERS

Cindy J. Tanis[*]

Azusa Pacific University,
Department of Innovative Educational Technology
and Physical Education, Azusa CA, US

ABSTRACT

Biofeedback training prepares athletes for activities requiring concentration and motor coordination. It assists in controlling competition anxiety, which is necessary for quality performance (Rozman and Rosch, 2004). The purpose of this research was to investigate the effects of heart rhythm variability (HRV) biofeedback training with emotional regulation on the athletic performance of women collegiate volleyball players. Individual biofeedback training using Heart Math's emWave® PC (1.0) was provided to 13 student-athletes during six weekly sessions. The emWave® PSR, a portable biofeedback device, was given to each player for independent self-regulation rehearsal. The quantitative results suggested the athletes recruited for this study were of high athletic caliber, but it did not support the intervention improved performance. However, the qualitative analysis revealed numerous benefits of the intervention including a reduction of physical and mental stress, and an enhancement of physical and mental states improving academic and athletic performance.

Keywords: Biofeedback, self-regulation, volleyball, performance enhancement, stress reduction

---

[*] E-mail: ctanis@apu.edu.

BIOFEEDBACK AND SPORT

Biofeedback is used to assist one in developing awareness of internal physiological processes that are not consciously controlled (Zaichkowsky and Fuchs, 1988). Through a variety of feedback modalities, clients observe the relationship of their current psychological state and physiological response. In biofeedback training, the clinician assists the client in identifying incoherent, or unhealthy biological responses, and implements adaptive practices such as paced breathing, positive self-talk, and emotional regulation (De Witt, 1980; McCraty, Atkinson, and Tomasino, 2001). The goal of biofeedback training is for the client to learn to gain voluntary control, or self-regulation of biological responses, and to transfer this ability to everyday situations without any instrumentation (Blumenstein, Bar Eli, and Tenenbaum, 1997).

Biofeedback training with athletes has resulted in the enhancement of self-control (Miller, 1994), the prevention of overtraining, the enrichment of injury treatment, the reduction of competition anxiety (Sime, 2003), and the increase in perceived control (Kavussanu, Crews, and Gill, 1998).

Improved performance was the result of the following biofeedback studies. Galloway and Lane (2005) integrated muscle contraction (EMG), electroencephalography (EEG), and galvanic skin response (GSR) biofeedback with five elite, junior tennis players. The result was the same or improved success in serves. Davis and Sime (2005) applied diaphragmatic breathing, cognitive exercises, imagery, and EEG biofeedback with an injured baseball athlete. The result was increased confidence and improved hitting and fielding percentages. De Witt (1980) incorporated EMG biofeedback with six collegiate football and twelve collegiate basketball players. The results were decreased muscle tension and improved game performances. Daniels and Landers (1981) implemented heart rate biofeedback with Olympic and collegiate rifle shooters. The results were a 51% improvement in shooting accuracy for the treatment group, compared to a 2% increase in the control group. Landers, Han, Salazar, Petruzzello, Kubitz and Gannon (1992) conducted another study with archers using heart rate variability training (HRV). After 12 weeks of training, there was a 62% improvement in shooting accuracy.

The Heart Math Institute developed a HRV biofeedback system known as the emWave® PC. HRV dynamics are sensitive to changes in one's physiological and emotional state as positive and negative emotions are distinguished by smooth or erratic heart rhythm patterns, respectively (McCraty and Tomasino, 2004). Constant heart beat variations with rhythmical patterns are desirable because they demonstrate a healthy heart, psycho physiological coherence, and a balanced autonomic nervous system (ANS; Gevirtz and Lehrer, 2003). This balance promotes healthy perceptions and beliefs, and physical well-being (Salovey, Rothman, Detweiler and Steward, 2000).

The goal of bio feedback training with the emWave PC® is to instruct the client to recognize faulty and healthy heart rhythm patterns on the screen. Through self-regulation, the individual learns to initiate a smooth heart rhythm with variability, ultimately creating psycho physiological coherence and a balanced ANS (Culbert, Martin, and McCraty, 2004). In sport, high coherence relates to the experience of flow or playing in the zone as automatic movement initiates efficient performance (Cooper, 1998). This study was designed to (a) investigate volleyball players' ability to self-regulate using HRV biofeedback; (b) analyze the effect of biofeedback training on volleyball performance; and (c) explore the participants' perception of the biofeedback intervention.

THEORIES AND MODELS

According to Zaichkowsky and Baltzell (2001), Hanin's Zone of Optimal Functioning (ZOF) represents the interaction of emotional states and optimal performance. This theory considers differences in arousal levels and emotions and their influence on ideal performance states. Some athletes thrive on higher levels of arousal for optimal performance, whereas others find this state to be counterproductive to performance. During biofeedback training, the clinician assists the athlete in identifying the zone of optimal performance. The athlete visualizes the psycho physiological response to emotions on the heart rhythm screen, and learns self-regulation strategies to control the effects of dysfunctional emotions (Sime, 2003).

Blumenstein et al. (1997) developed a model for psychological training with biofeedback. The psycho physiological equipment and protocol is introduced to the athlete. Initial sessions include guided instruction in self-regulation as the athlete learns how to consciously control psycho physiological responses. Independent self-regulation exercises are also included between biofeedback sessions. During sessions, visual and auditory feedback is provided. The athlete practices the self-regulation technique in both natural and competitive situations. Portable biofeedback devices assist the athlete to regulate arousal states in competitive environments. Realization is the transfer of guided learning and independent rehearsal into competition. Blumenstein et al. stated: "the ultimate goal of mental preparation in sport is to teach the athlete to independently monitor his or her arousal state as required" (p. 449). The authors emphasized the modification of these steps as needed, depending upon the sport and population.

METHOD

Participants

An HRV intervention was implemented with 14 collegiate volleyball athletes who were also full-time students. This population was chosen because biofeedback in sport is limited. The proposal was submitted and approved by the Institutional Review Board (IRB). The athletic director and the head coach of the women's volleyball team consented to the intervention. The athletes were requested, but not coerced to participate during the second half of their competitive season. After the second week of the biofeedback intervention, one participant voluntarily removed herself from the volleyball team, which subsequently excluded her from the intervention. Although a few players needed to reschedule their biofeedback session, no appointments were missed. There was an average of 5.58 days between each biofeedback session ($SD = 1.56$), with an average of 27.12 minutes required to complete each session ($SD = 4.73$).

Apparatus

The emWave PC® heart rhythm variability (HRV) biofeedback system was used in this study. An earpiece device was attached to the participant to detect her heartbeat, and the biofeedback software was launched using a PC and Microsoft Windows XP system. A portable biofeedback device known as the emWave PSR® was given to each participant to use for independent self-regulation. Journals were provided to each participant to record independent self-regulation rehearsal between biofeedback sessions.

Procedure

The study was proposed to the players at the midpoint of the season after the team had played ten conference matches. The participants attended an individual biofeedback session once a week for six consecutive weeks. Each participant received her first HRV biofeedback session before the beginning of the second half of the season. A customized, scripted biofeedback protocol was developed and used for each session. The protocol conforms to the biofeedback guidelines established by Culbert et al. (2004) and Blumenstein et al. (1997). The self-regulation process used in the study is known as the Quick Coherence Technique® (QCT), and consists of focusing on the heart, while breathing slowly and deeply, and recreating a positive emotion (Heart Math Institute, 2008).

Heart rhythm variability (HRV) biofeedback was used to analyze the participant's heartbeat waveform while she rehearsed the self-regulation steps. The goal of the biofeedback training was for the participant to learn how to create a smooth, orderly heart rhythm, which reflects autonomic nervous system balance. The researcher administered the sessions and taught each student-athlete the process of self-regulation with the use of feedback. The participants were also taught how to independently self-regulate with and without a portable biofeedback device. They journal their independent practice sessions each week, and reported their affect before and after self-regulating.

To promote group regulation, the "link up" signal, consisting of interlocking the thumb and index fingers into two conjoined rings, was integrated to assist the team in self-regulating simultaneously while on the court, and without the use of the feedback device. The participants were taught the signal during their biofeedback session and were encouraged to "link up" during practices and games to encourage team cohesion and performance.

Measures

In volleyball, the closed skill is serving, whereas the open skills included in this measure were passing off the serve, digging, and hitting. Serving occurs when the player stands behind the end line and drives the ball over the net in an attempt to make the ball land inside the opponent's court. Hitting, also referred to as spiking, occurs when the player attacks the ball so that it lands on the opponent's court. Passing is considered a serve-receive skill as the player attempts to pass the ball to the setter from the opponent's serve. Digging is the attempt to pass the ball to the setter after the opponent spikes (Lenberg, 2006).

In many studies measuring volleyball performance, the serve is the only evaluated skill (Gabbett, Boris, Anderson, Cotton, Savoic, and Nicholson, 2006; Kitanas, Masaon, and Zimmerman, 2002; Lidor and Mayan, 2005). However, this is only one of six major skills conducted on the court. For the performance measure used in this study, a rubric was designed by the coaches and researchers to evaluate four volleyball skills using a 5-point Likert-scale. The evaluation ranged from 1 to 5, which characterized an error to a perfectly performed skill, respectively. The two assistant coaches administered the rubric during 12 preseason matches. One coach evaluated passing and hitting, and the other digging and serving. Setting and blocking were not evaluated, as these skills are performed by only a few specialty players. Psychometric evaluation was conducted on the rubric during the preseason matches using Cronbach's alpha reliability statistic. The results demonstrated a moderate alpha (.6). Further analysis revealed that the four skills are not correlated with each other and are considered independent of each other. This is demonstrated by the low inter-item correlation scores between passing and hitting (.07), digging and hitting (.23) and serving and hitting (.20). The coefficient correlation revealed the following: passing and hitting accounted for approximately 4.5% of the variance, digging and hitting accounted for 53.8 %, and serving and hitting accounted for 41.2%. This suggests that the rubric for each skill measures only the specific properties of that skill.

Perception was considered the participant's personal understanding of the biofeedback treatment as it related to her experiences with the intervention including the guided and independent self-regulation rehearsal. Perception was investigated using an open-ended interview, and the participant's self-regulation journals.

Data Collection and Design

A quasi-experimental research design was incorporated using a mixed-methodology approach. The two assistant volleyball coaches evaluated the volleyball players' performance during each game using the skill rubric. Each coach evaluated the same two skills throughout the season. Upon the completion of each game, the results were given to the researcher who copied the data, but substituted each player's name with her randomly assigned participant code. Raw and mean scores were utilized for each of the four skills the players conducted during each game using the 5-point Likert-scale. Team and individual analyses were conducted by comparing the scores from eight conference games before the intervention to the same eight conference games during the intervention.

At the end of the sixth and final biofeedback session, an audiotape interview was administered to each participant, individually. The interview transpired in the same private office where the biofeedback sessions occurred and was the final component of the sixth biofeedback session. The interview lasted 20-30 minutes. The three questions were provided for the participant to read so she could anticipate the content of the interview. The researcher proceeded to ask each question using follow-up probing questions only if the response was unclear.

1. What was your experience attending the six biofeedback sessions and independently practicing the self-regulation techniques?
2. Did you experience any benefits from the biofeedback intervention?
3. Did you experience any negative aspects from the biofeedback intervention?

Following this interview, the researcher transcribed the audiotape into hardcopy text for data analysis. Initially, all 13 transcripts were read separately to acquire a sense of the whole of each transcript. To begin the process of theme recognition, the transcripts were subsequently read line by line according to the responses from each question. Codes from the initial participant data were grouped into themes as relationships were noted. This is referred to as pattern coding (Breakwell, Hammond, and Fife-Shaw, 2000). Groups of initial themes were derived from the three interview questions for each individual (Glaser, 1978). Following this, the themes from the separate transcripts were merged and compiled for all 13 participant interviews with direct quotes drawn from each transcript to support the themes (Agar, 1996). Finally, the syntheses of all themes were merged into a collective description of the biofeedback experience (Patton, 1990).

A practice diary and tracking system was provided for each participant during the six-week biofeedback intervention. The participant was requested to write in the journal each day to record her feelings before and after she independently rehearsed the self-regulation technique. She returned the completed journal at each subsequent session, and her responses were reviewed with the researcher/clinician. Each entry was assigned to the category of activities of daily living (ADL) and volleyball practices/games (VPG). Themes from the responses were recognized and percentages of responses were calculated. The ATLAS software program was also used to verify and assist with the accuracy of determining the number and percentage of participants who responded within each of the major themes. The ATLAS data analysis was consistent with the researcher's coding procedures.

RESULTS

To investigate the participant's ability to self-regulate, the data provided by the emWave® PC (1.0) from each of the six biofeedback sessions was used. The highest score, reflecting ability in self-regulation is 100. The lowest score, reflecting difficulty in self-regulation is 0. Results suggested the participants were able to self-regulate immediately in the first session with coherence scores ranging from 67-100% (Table 1).

To investigate the ability level of the team during the first and second part of conference play, separate one sample t-tests were calculated to compare the raw scores with the criterion score of three. The criterion score of three is the midpoint of the five-point performance scale (1-5). The raw scores originated from the coach's evaluation rubric. They reflect the overall performance of some of the players more accurately than the mean scores because they represent the amount of times the player actually contacted the ball in each game. Results were statistically significant for both the preintervention scores t (3495) = 19.57, p < .01 and intervention scores t (3106) = 16.27, p < .01. The total mean scores for the preintervention (M = 3.43, SD = 1.3) and the intervention (M = 3.39, SD = 1.34) were greater than the criterion score of three. Estimate of Cohen's magnitude of the difference was d = .33 and .29 respectively. These scores suggest the advanced ability level of the team before and after the biofeedback intervention.

To investigate the ability level of the individual players during the first and second part of the season, separate one sample t-tests were calculated to compare the raw scores with the criterion score of three. Raw scores were used rather than mean scores, as a couple of players did not have ample playing time to warrant the use of mean scores for the test. The results of the one sample t-test for the individual players are listed in Table 2. The results indicated that five of the thirteen players (38%) had performance mean scores greater than three during the preintervention and intervention (Participants 1, 2, 6, 7, 9). Four (31%) had scores greater than three in preintervention (Participants 3, 4, 5, 14), and one (8%) had a performance score greater than three during the intervention (Participant 8). These scores were considered significant at the $p < .01$ or $p < .05$ levels with small to medium effect sizes. The results of the one sample t-test suggest the high caliber of play associated with this volleyball team and its individual members.

To assess the effect of the biofeedback intervention on the team's athletic performance, two separate paired sample t-tests were calculated using both raw and mean scores. Using the raw scores, the results indicated a .04 reduction comparing preintervention scores ($M = 3.43$, $SD = .1.30$) to the intervention scores ($M = 3.39$, $SD = 1.34$) which was not significant t $(3105) = 1.6$, $p > .05$. Using the mean scores, the results indicated a .18 reduction comparing preintervention scores ($M = 3.44$, $SD = .78$) to the intervention scores ($M = 3.26$, $SD = .73$) which was significant t $(222) = 2.50$, $p < .05$. Estimate of Cohen's magnitude of the difference was $d = .29$, which is considered small (Howell, 2004). Using the raw scores, these results imply no change in performance. Using the mean scores, these results suggest a possible reduction in team performance in the second part of conference play with minimal practical significance.

To assess the effect of the biofeedback intervention on the individual player's athletic performance, a paired sample t-test was calculated using the raw scores. The results of the paired sample t-test for the individual players are listed in Table 3. Of the 13 participants, only Participant 10 demonstrated a significant score reduction (preintervention $M = 3.33$, $SD = 1.35$; intervention $M = 2.78$, $SD = 1.20$ t $(3.02) = 2$ $p < .01$ $d = .33$). Overall, the results of the individual t-tests do not reflect an improvement in performance in the second part of conference play during the biofeedback intervention. The results do reflect a reduction in performance for one participant, with minimal practical significance.

To assess the participants' perception of the biofeedback intervention, an interview was conducted. The interview questions examined the participants' experiences of the biofeedback intervention. Three major themes emerged from the participants' responses to the interview questions: Overall Experiences, Intervention Benefits, and Intervention Detriments. The length of the participants' responses to the audiotape interview questions ranged from five to seventeen minutes. The following sections outline the specific themes and give direct quotes from the participants' responses.

Overall Experiences

The first theme, *Overall Experiences,* involved the participants' thoughts about attending the six biofeedback sessions and practicing the self-regulation technique independently using the em-Wave PSR®. This theme described the participant's perception of the intervention and included the following concepts: a) the dynamic of the experience; b) the process of learning; and c) the product of control. Consider the following four examples:

I enjoyed going to the sessions. (P8)

It was fun. I have never done anything like this before. It is cool you can give us a technique and we can do it on our own and on the volleyball court. (P12)

The participants identified the learning process as an important component of the experience. They emphasized the benefit of gaining knowledge about self-regulation and understanding the influence of feelings and emotions. Participants also recognized the importance of understanding the context of biofeedback and how it influenced the mind and body.

[The biofeedback] taught me to control my emotions…and just control myself a little bit better…and learn about my feelings and how to relax more. (P1) I seem to have a better understanding of how to calm myself just through the three-step process. (P11)

Some participants emphasized that heightened awareness and insight were important aspects of the biofeedback intervention.
It made me more aware of coherence because I never even knew about any of that. (P5)

It kind of gave me new insight on how I can better become coherent…be balanced in all aspects of life. (P8)

The participants experienced increased self-control as it related to the process of identifying unhealthy psychophysiology and balancing the mind-body at will through the process of self-regulation. Consider the following examples:

It's been a good experience to learn about how to control your own emotions…you have a choice in everything you do. (P1)

It really helped me to take a step back and see that I CAN calm myself down through the whole heart-felt, heart breathing thing [emphasis from participant's interview]. (P4)

Intervention Benefits

The next theme, *Intervention Benefits,* depicted the positive results of the biofeedback intervention for the participants in their roles as college students, individual athletes, and team members. This theme described the benefits of the intervention and included: a) physical and mental stress reduction; b) improved academics; c) healthy relationships and sleep; d) enhanced physical and mental performance; and e) increased energy, team camaraderie and composure. The following participants' comments illustrate the benefits:

It was a stress reliever. I have so many things on my mind. If you have something that worries you, take time for yourself to focus on your heart and your feelings. (P1)

Just being able to calm myself down…during stressful situations and just focusing on the moment rather than sometimes I get wrapped up in all the stuff…I just sit and relax and think about my coherent state and I feel a little bit more calm. (P11)

When I would drive…in traffic, I would put it (emWaveearpiece) on my ear and that helped a lot, … it just calmed me down. (P12)

The benefits of the biofeedback intervention also contributed to the participants' effort with coursework, presentations, and tests as explained by the following:

When I was stressed with homework…I would put it all away and sit there and do it [The Quick Coherence Technique] even without the hand-held. It would definitely help me not to stress so much about it.

I can step back and think about it… OK, this isn't that big of a deal…It's a paper…it will be done tomorrow. (P12)

Before tests and presentations, I noticed it becoming more automatic like the breathing aspect because I'll get nervous before it. The result is relaxed, calm, at ease. [sic] (P14)

The participants also identified three benefits of the intervention with relationships outside the team: a) family; b) friends and c) boyfriends.

With the whole boyfriend thing and friends, there's no need to freak out about things…It's like, whenever that happens, I'm like, 'OK, deep breathing, calm down'. (P4)

Being aware of the effects of breathing and positive emotion in just everyday life.

With an experience happening in your life with family or friends or just something you're thinking about or that's either bothering you or making you anxious. (P14)

Enhanced sleep was also reported by the participants, as depicted in the following:

Sometimes when I go to bed, if I have a lot on my mind, or restless, or whatever, I would do my deep breathing and positive thinking and I would seem to fall asleep quicker. (P11)

As individual athletes, the participants reported an improvement in the physical and mental aspects of performance that potentially enhanced their play.

For the second half of the season, I think my game improved a little bit more…I became a little bit stronger as a player. (P1)

In serve-receive, I felt like it's all you and the server, and it's just the two of you…if you can just calm yourself down and focus to make that one pass…it's so much better. I felt like my passing got better. I was able to stay a lot more relaxed, and I tend to get tense during serve-receive, and I was able to stay more relaxed. (P2)

The mental enhancement described the participants consisted of improved concentration, confidence, and control. Consider the following statements.

I didn't really trust myself, but then the breathing and biofeedback helps you to trust yourself and be coherent. I think that it helped overall as an individual player. (P1)

I could control myself better, and know what I'm focusing on. (P3)

It helped me keep myself together, knowing that I can't play [due to injury]….able to control myself and my negative emotions. (P3)

When I'm passing, and if you shank a couple balls or you're not doing very well, you're like, 'Oh gosh, I need to relax and focus' and you breathe a couple times and think about it. I thought that was helpful, because it just refocuses you. (P10)

Mindfulness is a heightened state of attention and perspective associated in athletic participation. It is a transcendent experience that goes beyond the conscious or the typical play (Cooper, 1998). The participants recognized mindfulness as a benefit of the intervention, as the following comments illustrate:

…tuning out the noise. I always thought was a huge deal and never thought I could do it. And that's something I've noticed that I can do now. I felt like I better understood the game. I was looking for more things because I wasn't so scattered and nervous. (P4)

If I would miss a serve, or double a ball, or whatever the goof-up, I'd just deep breathe and get myself together with the steps you have taught us. The result was a clear state of mind. (P11)

Go into the zone, and focus on what you need to do. Don't think about what's really going on…think about yourself and breathe deep…just focus on what you need to do to get the next play. (P8)

The responses regarding the benefits of the biofeedback intervention also related to the team as a whole. Many participants reported increased positive energy, team camaraderie, and composure as the following comments suggest.

We had fun with the linking. I think it was helpful to be able to [link] as a team. We all know what we're working toward and so it was able to help us in that aspect. (P2)

…Well that worked, why don't we always do this? When we link up, we just so surpass everything that we ever think we could. (P4)

…everyone 'link up' and we were playing really well at the times that we were doing that. (P6)

"Link up" made us feel happy…calming effect…more together…on the same page. (P6)

Intervention Detriments

The theme, *Intervention Detriments,* included the participants' negative experiences of the intervention. Although 54% of the participants didn't identify any detrimental effects, some participants felt unwanted relaxation, a disruption in skill performance, and competition with or reliance on the emWave PSR®. Consider the following comments:

When I was excited and energetic I would avoid doing it…right before a game because I wanted to keep my energy up…It made me too relaxed or groggy. (P9)

Sometimes when I would do it, it would make me tired, but I think that's just because I have a lot going on. When I would breathe regularly, it would make me yawn. (P10)

When I focused on being coherent, I would forget about the techniques [serving] and what I was supposed to be doing...and really not thinking for instance about my service. Because my jump-serve isn't second nature yet, if I'd do that, sometimes I would forget on focusing on keeping my arm high...I like to do the QCT before, and think about my technique. (P1)

At the beginning, it was a little bit frustrating because I was, 'I can't do this.' Sometimes I can't get the thing to turn green [emWave PSR], and it stays blue. (P2)

Trying hard to think about my breathing...and the emWave would still be red and it would worry me... I was competing against the emWave... I needed it to change to green before the game. (P6)

The participants completed a weekly journal recording their feelings before and after they rehearsed the self-regulation techniques. There were a total of 65 journals collected over the 6-week intervention. Each entry was transcribed from its original content and assigned to its related category: a) activities of daily living (ADL); and b) volleyball practices/games (VPG). There were 394 and 292 entries related to ADL and VPG, respectively.

Themes from the responses were recognized and the percentages of responses correlating to each theme were calculated. Within the category ADL, the three common feelings the participants noted before self-regulation training were as follows: a) stressed (35%); b) tired (24%); and c) anxious/nervous (15%). The five feelings after self-regulation training were as follows: a) relaxed (30%); b) calm (20%); c) less stressed (8%); d) able to fall asleep (16%); and e) more focused/centered (9%). For the responses relating to VPG, the four common feelings the participants noted before self-regulation training were as follows: a) stressed/overwhelmed (26%); b) physically and emotionally tired (13%); c) anxious/nervous (16%); and d) frustrated (10%). Their feelings after self-regulation training were as follows: a) relaxed (29%); b) calm (23%); and c) re-focused (12%).

DISCUSSION

The recruited team was ranked fifth in the nation representing the National Association of Intercollegiate Athletics. They won and lost to the same teams before and during the treatment intervention. These losses occurred to teams ranked second, third and fourth in the nation. The results of the one sample t-test using the midpoint of the performance rubric revealed the advanced ability level of the team with 77% of the athletes having performance scores greater than three. This demonstrates the high caliber of athletes recruited for this intervention.

The data from the biofeedback device suggests the participants were able to self-regulate at will. Without this ability, the participants would not be able to transfer the skill into athletic performance, nor could their performance be positively affected. As Crews, Lochbaum, and Karoly (2001) stated, motivation contributes to successful self-regulation. The primary researcher believes the participants were motivated to attend the biofeedback sessions, and practice the self-regulation independently as supported by the 100% attendance and the submission of journals. Their interviews also revealed enthusiasm and a positive response to the intervention.

The quantitative results from the performance rubric did not support the hypothesis that athletic performance would improve with the biofeedback intervention. However, many participants during the interview reported an improvement in physical and mental performance. A statistical and performance ceiling effect may be one contributor to the quantitative results as most players exhibited above average scores before and after the intervention. According to Breakwell, et al. (2000), ceiling effects occur when individuals score too close to the top of the rating scale. As a result, the dependent variable cannot accurately measure the full range of the independent variable. Therefore, small increases in improvement with advanced athletes are considered meaningful because the ceiling effect leaves only a small margin of improvement (Behncke, 2004).

Other potential confounders reflected in the performance results include the following. First, the intervention was initiated at the middle of conference play. This allowed eight of the ten games to be used in preintervention and during the intervention. Before conference play, the team competed in 12 preseason games. The intervention transpired after the team had already played 22 games, which suggests the team might have reached a peak in performance before the intervention began. Second, team dynamics and circumstances during the treatment intervention may have contributed to the performance results. One of the starting athletes did not play in most of the second half of the season due to injury. Another participant was suspended for two games, and a third player voluntarily removed herself from the team. These situations required other players to compete in unfamiliar positions and receive more playing time than expected. Such team dynamics may have contributed to their overall performance. This observation is supported by Munroe, Estabrooks, Dennis, and Carron (1999) who state a team's performance may fall short of its potential due to the complexity and climate of the group.

Although a direct relationship between the biofeedback intervention and improved performance was not confirmed by the quantitative analysis, the athlete's perception of the intervention was positive. Overall, the participants described the biofeedback experience using affirmative terminology. The process of learning about biofeedback and self-regulation while visualizing their heart rhythm variability was an important component to its success. Realizing that they have control over their emotions, and ultimately psycho physiological balance was emphasized. The participants identified the benefits of the intervention for them as students, individual athletes, and team members. As students, the participants experienced a reduction in both mental and physical stress, as seen by increased relaxation, and for some, improved sleep. The biofeedback intervention promoted a focused and calm state helpful for academic rigors, and test taking. In relationships outside the team, the process of self-regulation was noted to enhance interactions with significant others. As individual athletes, some participants noted an improvement in physical performance, others commented of mental enhancement, while a few made note of zone play and mindfulness. As a team, the participants reported "linking up" as a means to improve performance, or a process to promote calm and team unity. A few detrimental experiences of the intervention were also noted. Some felt it made them too relaxed. A few participants shared concern regarding their reliance on or competitiveness with the emWave PSR®. The inability to focus on volleyball skills while self-regulating was also noted by one participant.

The participants gained greater awareness into their student-athlete lives, especially in areas of academic and athletic stress. They became aware of the benefits of positive emotions, and the detriments of negative ones. They learned how to control their emotions and transfer the negative feelings of stress into positive energy for academic and athletic involvement. This may have resulted in improved academic and athletic performance. This finding aligns with the ZOF theory which considers the differences in arousal levels and emotions and their influence on ideal performance states (Zaichkowsky and Baltzell, 2001). Although this finding was consistent with these participants, it cannot be generalized with other athletic populations. This heart rhythm variability biofeedback intervention warrants investigation in other athletic venues, in both individual and team sports. It would be intriguing to evaluate performance outcomes with a less skilled team to negate the performance ceiling effect. Furthermore, as individual biofeedback sessions were used in this study, it would be helpful to investigate the effects of the same intervention using group sessions.

In summary, this study evaluated the effects of heart rhythm variability biofeedback on the athletic performance of women collegiate volleyball players. The benefits of the intervention included the following: (a) Learning about biofeedback and self-regulation while visualizing the heart rhythm on the computer screen; (b) Improving self-awareness and increasing self-control; (c) Reducing the effects of physical and mental stress relating to academic and athletic rigors; (d) Experiencing enhanced physical and mental states; (e) Improving academic and athletic performance; and (f) Enriching team composure and camaraderie. Sport psychology personnel, coaches, and athletic trainers are qualified practitioners for implementing HRV biofeedback in sport, and this intervention has the potential to enhance academic and athletic performance for collegiate athletes.

REFERENCES

Agar, M. (1996). *Speaking of ethnography* (2nd Ed.). Thousand Oaks, CA: SAGE.

Behncke, L. (2004). Mental skills training for sports: A brief review. *Athletic Insight, 61*(1).

Blumenstein, B., Bar-Eli, M., and Tenenbaum, G. (1997).A five-step approach to mental training incorporating biofeedback. *The Sport Psychologist, 11*, 440-453.

Breakwell, G. M., Hammond, S., and Fife-Schaw, C. (2000). *Research methods in psychology* (2ndEd.). Thousand Oaks, CA: SAGE.

Cooper, A. (1998). *Playing in the Zone: Exploring the spiritual dimensions of sports.* Boston, MA: Shambhala.

Crews, D. J., Lochbaum, M. R., and Karoly, P. (2001). Self-Regulation: Concepts, methods, and strategies in sport and exercise. In R. N. Singer, H. A. Hausenblas, and C. M. Janelle (Eds.), Handbook of sport psychology (2nd ed., pp. 566-584). New York, NY: John Wiley and Sons.

Culbert, T., Martin, H., and McCraty, R. (2004).A practitioner's guide: Applications of the *freeze-framer interactive learning system.* Boulder Creek, CA: Heart Math Institute.

Daniels, F. S., and Landers, D. M. (1981). Biofeedback and shooting performance: A test of deregulation and systems theory. *Journal of Sport Psychology, 4,* 271-282.

Davis, P. A., and Sime, W. E. (2005). Toward a psychophysiology of performance: Sport psychology principles dealing with anxiety. *International Journal of Stress Management, 12*, 363-378. doi: 10.1037/1072-5245.12.4.363.

De Witt, D. J. (1980). Cognitive and biofeedback training for stress reduction with university athletes. *Journal of Sport Psychology, 2*, 288-294.

Gabbett, T., Borris, G., Anderson, S., Cotton, B., Savovic, D., and Nicholson, L. (2006). Changes in skill and physical fitness following training in talent-identified volleyball players. *Journal of Strength and Conditioning Research, 20*, 29-35.

Galloway, S., and Lane, A. (2005). The effects of biofeedback training on elite junior tennis players. *Journal of Sport Sciences, 23*(11-12), 1247.

Gevirtz, R. N., and Lehrer, P. (2003). Resonant frequency heart rate biofeedback. In M. Schwartz and F. Andrasik (Eds.), *Biofeedback: A practitioner's guide* (3rd ed., pp. 245-250). New York, NY: Guildford Press.

Glaser, B. G. (1978). *Theoretical sensitivity*. Mill Valley, CA: Sociology Press.

Heart Math Institute (2008). http://www.heartmath.org/.

Howell, D. C. (2004). *Fundamental Statistics for the Behavioral Sciences (5th Ed.)*. Belmont, CA: Brooks/Cole.

Kavussanu, M., Crews, D. J., and Gill, D. L. (1998). The effects of single versus multiple measures of biofeedback on basketball free throw shooting performance. *International Journal of Sport Psychology, 29*, 132-144.

Kitanas, A., Masaon, G., and Zimmerman, B. J. (2002). Comparing self-regulatory processes among novice, non-expert, and expert volleyball players: A micronalytic study. *Journal of Applied Sport Psychology, 14*, 91-105.

Landers, D., Han, M., Salazar, W., Petruzzello, S., Kubitz, K., and Gannon, T. (1992). Effects of learning on electroencephalographic and electrocardiographic patterns in novice archers. *International Journal of Sport Psychology, 25,* 56-70.

Lenberg, K. S. (2006). *Volleyball skills and drills/ American volleyball coaches association*. Champaign, IL: Human Kinetics.

Lidor, R., and Mayan, Z. (2005). Can beginning learners benefit from pre-performance routines when serving in volleyball? *The Sport Psychologist, 19*, 343-355.

McCraty, R., Atkinson, M., and Tomasino, D. (2001). *Science of the heart*. Boulder Creek, CA: Institute of Heart Math.

McCraty, R., and Tomasino, D. (November, 2004). Heart rhythm coherence feedback: A new tool for stress reduction, rehabilitation and performance enhancement. *Proceedings of the First Baltic Forum on Neuronal Regulation and Biofeedback*, 1-6.

Miller, L. (1994). Biofeedback and behavioral medicine: Treating the symptom, the syndrome, or the person? *Psychotherapy: Theory, Practice, Training, 31*(1), 161-169.

Munroe, K., Estabrooks, P., Dennis, P., and Carron, A. (1999).A phenomenological analysis of group norms in sport teams. *The Sport Psychologist, 13*, 171-183.

Patton, M. Q. (1990). *Qualitative evaluation and research methods* (2nd Ed). Newbury Park, CA: SAGE.

Rozman, D., and Rosch, P. (2004). *Managing emotions*. http://www.pga.com/improve/features/mentalgame/improve_heartmath102604.cfm.

Salovey, P., Rothman, A. J., Detweiler, J. B., and Steward, W. T. (2000).Emotional states and physical health.*American Psychologist, 55*, 110-121.

Sime, W. (2003).Sports psychology applications of biofeedback and neurofeedback. In M.S. Schwartz and F. Andrasik (Eds.), *Biofeedback: A practitioner's guide* (3rd ed., pp. 560-588). New York, NY: Guildford Press.

Zaichkowsky, L. D., and Baltzell, A. (2001).Arousal and performance. In R. N. Singer, H. A. Hausenblas, and C. M. Janelle (Eds.), *Handbook of sport psychology* (pp. 319-339). New York, NY: John Wiley and Sons.

Zaichkowsky, L. D., and Fuchs, C. Z. (1988).Biofeedback applications in exercise and athletic performance.*Exercise and Sport Science Review*, *16*, 381-421.

January 9, 2011

In: Athletic Insight's Writings of 2012
Editor: Robert Schinke

ISBN: 978-1-62618-120-5
© 2013 Nova Science Publishers, Inc.

Chapter 10

MEASURING MOTIVATION FOR PHYSICAL ACTIVITY: AN EXPLORATORY STUDY OF PALMS – THE PHYSICAL ACTIVITY AND LEISURE MOTIVATION SCALE

Sima Zach[*1], *Michael Bar-Eli*[2, 1], *Tony Morris*[3] *and Melissa Moore*[3]

[1]Zinman College of Physical Education and Sport Sciences at the
Wingate Institute, Netanya, Isreal
[2]Guilford Glazer School of Business and Management,
Ben-Gurion University of the Negev, Beer-Sheva, Israel
[3]Institute for Sport, Exercise and Active Living and School of Sport and
Exercise Science, Victoria University, Melbourne, Australia

ABSTRACT

This study was designed to validate a new instrument created to measure motives for physical activity (PA) – the PALMS (Physical Activity and Leisure Motivation Scale), which was found to yield sound psychometric properties. Regular exercisers, ages 9 – 89 (M = 28.65; SD = 16.48), from over 30 different fitness and recreational facilities in Israel were invited to participate in this study. A total of 678 completed the PALMS questionnaire consisting of 40 items rated on a 5-point Likert scale from 1 (*strongly disagree*) to 5 (*strongly agree*). Exploratory factor analysis yielded nine factors that explained 73.29% of the variance: mastery, physical condition, affiliation, psychological condition, appearance, family and friends' expectations, health professionals' and employers' expectations, enjoyment, and competition/ego. We propose the PALMS as a comprehensive and reliable measure of participation motivation in PA.

[*] Corresponding author: Dr. Sima Zach, Head, School of Education.Zinman College of Physical Education and Sport Sciences. Wingate Institute. Netanya, 42902. Israel. Tel. 972-9-8639247.Fax 972-9-8639320. e-mail: simaz@wincol.ac.il.

Keywords: Physical Activity and Leisure Motivation Scale (PALMS), exercise, participation motivation, validation, questionnaire

The importance of physical activity (PA) and its benefits to a variety of important physical, psychological, and social aspects of life have been well-documented in an extenstive line of research (e.g., ACSM, 2009; Lloyd-Jones et al., 2010; McKenzie, 2001; Pangrazi, 2000; Sibley and Etnier, 2003). The recommended dose of PA for health benefits is also quite well-documented. For example, adults aged 25-64 should perform 150 minutes of moderate-intensity aerobic activity (e.g., brisk walking) or 75 minutes of vigorous-intensity aerobic activity (e.g., jogging or running), or an equivalent mix of moderate- and vigorous-intensity aerobic activity, per week (ACSM, 2009; DHHS, 2008). Nevertheless, a large proportion of the population in countries such as Australia (Australian Bureau of Statistics, 2000; Australian Sports Commission, 2005), the U.S. (Butcher, Sallis, Mayer, and Woodruff, 2008), 24 countries in Europe (Armstrong and Welsman, 2006), and Israel (Zach and Netz, 2007) are still insufficiently active or maintain a sedentary lifestyle.

To evaluate why some people are physically active while others are not, researchers have examined their motives for sport and exercise involvement (see Bartholomew, Ntoumanis, and Thøgersen-Ntoumani, 2009; Biddle, Wang, Kavussanu, and Spray, 2003; Frederick-Recascino and Morris, 2004). In general, current measures of participation motivationpresent two main approaches. The first involves developing possible motives for PA on the basis of a particular theory. This method has been adopted in the development of the Sport Motivation Scale (SMS; Fortier, Vallerand, Briere, and Provencher, 1995), the Exercise Motivation Inventory (EMI; Markl and and Hardy, 1993; EMI-2; Markland and Ingledew, 1997), the Exercise Motivation Scale (EMS; Li, 1999), the Motivation for PA Measure (MPAM; Frederick and Ryan, 1993; MPAM-Revised; Ryan, Frederick, Lepes, Rubio, and Sheldon, 1997), and the Perception of Success Questionnaire for Exercise (POSQ-E; Zizzi, Keeler, and Watson, 2006).

Each of these measures takes a somewhat different theoretical approach to the concept of motivation for PA, resulting in a variety of motives spread across the different measures. For example, the POSQ-E is based on task/ego motivation theory, and the SMS and the EMS are questionnaires that are based on self-determination theory (SDT), in particular, the intrinsic/extrinsic component of this theory (Deci and Ryan, 1985; 1991). Because these measures are based on SDT, they cover motives for exercise related solely to this theory, and do not include motives that participants could provide in an open interview. An open interview enables people to elaborate, give examples, and introduce personal aspects. Further, some of these questionnaires were found to have weak psychometric properties. For example, Markland and Hardy (1997) suggested that the Intrinsic Motivation Inventory (IMI) should not be used for assessing levels of intrinsic motivation due to conceptual and operational problems (for example, six of its items were considered to be redundant, and the incremental R for each item over 4 for any given dimension was small). Others, such as the EMI, did not acknowledge motives related to competitive aspects. The EMI also did not assess some obvious fitness-related reasons for exercising (e.g., strength, endurance). In addition, the health-related subscales focused on the avoidance of ill-health, neglecting potential positively-oriented health-related motives (Markland and Ingledew, 1997). The MPAM-R (Ryan et al., 1997) presented a limited number of motives. The POSQ was designed specifically to measure only two goal orientations: competition and mastery. Variations of the POSQ only accounted for approximately 50% of the variance in the data, suggesting that other variables need to be considered. Furthermore, the POSQ was designed specifically for use in the competitive sport context. As a result, the first approach, based on theories, in particular SDT or goal orientation theory, has generated questionnaires with a quite narrow focus, thus lacking comprehensiveness. Research suggests that movement towards health could be a more positive, intrinsically-oriented motivational force (e.g., Lavigne et al., 2009; Puente and Anshel, 2010).

The second approach to the study of motives for participation in PA has been relatively atheoretical, and starts with the empirical exploration of participation motives. The principal example of this approach is probably the work of Gill, Gross, and Huddleston (1983), who asked adolescents to state their reasons for participation, using open-ended questions. Drawing on this information, they devised a 30-item questionnaire called the Participation Motivation Questionnaire (PMQ), which presented those reasons preceded by the phrase "I want to" or "I like to" (for example, "I like to have fun", "I want to develop my skills"). The PMQ was administered to 1,138 youth participants at a multi-sport summer camp. Using exploratory factor analysis, Gill et al. identified eight factors for use in the PMQ, namely achievement, team (affiliation/social), fitness, energy release, being with others, skill, friends, and fun. Researchers used different versions of the PMQ to examine motives for participation in a range of contexts, such as youth multi-sport, youth specific sport, a specific sport or exercise activity across the life span, and multi-sport across the lifespan (e.g., Buinamano, Cei, and Mussino, 1995; Kolt et al., 1999; Weinberg et al., 1999). Taken together, and considering that the numerous versions of the PMQ do indeed cover a breadth of motives for participation in PA, the main motives and questionnaire factors still vary across the different versions. Thus, a stable version of the questionnaire has not yet been established with a set number of items that can be used in various PA contexts. In addition, it remains a disadvantage that the PMQ is not related to a theory of motivation.

To address the disadvantages of both the theory-based and the atheoretical approaches, Rogers, Morris, and Moore (2008) attempted to create a new instrument merging both approaches. As the first step they conducted a qualitative study that involved in-depth, semi-structured interviews with exercise participants, to examine the reasons why people participate in non-competitive PA. Their study involved 11 participants (seven female, four male), aged from 21-50 years. As is common in qualitative research (Miles and Huberman, 1994; Patton, 2002), they selected participants purposively, rather than at random. They selected regular exercisers who engaged in exercise most weekdays for at least 30-60 minutes, and who had done this consistently over the preceding year.

Following the interviews, Rogers et al. (2008) asked two experts to examine each statement made by the participants and interpret them in terms of achievement goal themes. The results were then compiled into a set of raw data themes that comprised 40 goal statements. In the next stage, Rogers et al. (2008) grouped goal statements into seven meaningful concepts: competition/ego, extrinsic rewards, social health, physical health, psychological health, mastery, and enjoyment, as well as two general dimensions: intrinsic and extrinsic goals. They argued that SDT would provide an appropriate theoretical framework for the results obtained in the qualitative study. Based on the findings from the Rogers et al. (2008) qualitative research, we developed the Physical Activity and Leisure Motivation Scale(PALMS), to be investigated here.

There are three advantages of the PALMS over earlier PA motivation measures: 1) The motives that emerged from the qualitative research fit a theoretical framework, namely intrinsic-extrinsic motivation, as characterized in SDT; 2) The empirical process of generation of motives supported a broad framework; 3) Although the motives were generated in a recreational exercise context, they reflected considerable similarities with the items in the PMQ, which was developed in a sport context. To examine whether the 40-item PALMS that we have developed capitalizes on these advantages, it is important to examine its reliability and validity.

The aim of this study was to examine the psychometric properties of the PALMS as a measure of leisure-time PA in a diverse sample of exercisers. Leisure-time physical activity for children was defined as time spent participating in physical activities outside of the regular school day; it did not include activities that took place during physical education classes (Kerner, Kurrant, and Kalinski, 2004). As for adults, leisure-time physical activity is typically characterized as an activity chosen with relative freedom, undertaken during free time, with the potential to provide a feeling of enjoyment, control, or mastery (Mannell and Kleiber, 1997). Data gleaned from this measure will enable the development of appropriate and effective interventions to promote PA involvement. In this study we aimed to administer the PALMS to a diverse sample in terms of age, gender, and type of PA, then to examine the internal consistency, test-re-test reliability and factor structure of the 40-item PALMS. We hypothesized that the factor structure that would emerge from the analysis would be similar to results obtained in the qualitative research (Rogers et al., 2008).

METHOD

Participants

Exercisers who exercised regularly during the last year on most weekdays, ages 9 – 89 (M = 28.65; SD = 16.48; males = 350; females = 316; 12 gender not specified), from over 30 different fitness and recreational parks and facilities in Israel, were asked to participate in this study. A total of 678 people voluntarily completed the questionnaire.

Measures

The PALMS (see Appendix) examines motives for participating in leisure-time PA. It consists of 40 items comprising the following eight sub-scales: mastery, physical condition, affiliation, psychological condition, appearance, others' expectations, enjoyment, and competition/ego, generated from in-depth interviews, each rated on a 5-point Likert scale from 1 (*stronglydisagree*) to 5 (*stronglyagree*). Participants were asked to think of the motives they had for the activity they were doing, and to indicate how much they agreed with the motives expressed in each item. Each participant received a summed score for each sub-scale, as well as a total score for all 40 items. The possible range of scores for each sub-scale is 5-25.

Procedure

Prior to the beginning of the study, the Ethical Review Board approved the study proposal. We obtained permission for collection of data from each of the venues, and standard consent procedures were as follows: Each participant read a statement in which he/she had to decide whether they were willing to complete the questionnaire or not. It was emphasized that participation was on a voluntary basis. The procedure was similar for all participants. The PALMS was handed out to the participants as they entered or left group exercise classes, as they left the sports centers, or, occasionally, while they were exercising. Participants were asked to fill in the questionnaire and return it to the researchers. Seven hundred men and women were approached, and 22 refused to participate. Participants completed the questionnaire within 10-15 minutes.

Data Analysis

Reliability was assessed by means of test-retest, intra-class correlation coefficients, and by means alpha coefficients. Test-retest reliability was examined by means of administration of the PALMS twice, two weeks apart, with a sample of 67 recreational-exercise participants age 19-32, who exercised regularly at two fitness clubs. They were chosen due to their availability. The range of Intra-class Correlation Coefficient (ICC) that was conducted for the questionnaire sub-scales was between .68 and .92, and for the 40 questionnaire items between .27 and .92 (only four items were under .50).

In addition, an exploratory factor analysis was administered. A principal-components analysis followed by a Varimax rotation with Kaiser Normalization was conducted on the 40 items of the PALMS to determine each item's strength of association, minimize the possibility of error variance, optimize the number of zero loadings, and simplify the interpretation of each factor, using SPSS software edition No. 18.

RESULTS

Descriptive statistics of the PALMS factors and the correlations between them are presented in Table 1. As presented, the highest mean was found for the physical condition sub-scale, indicating that physical condition was reported to be the most strongly endorsed motive for PA, with a relatively low standard deviation indicating low variability for this factor. The lowest mean was observed for the get paid sub-scale, indicating that getting paid to exercise was the least strongly-endorsed motive for PA.

Reliability

We assessed reliability in the form of internal consistency, using Cronbach's alpha coefficient (see Table 1). The Alpha values for each of the sub-scales were between .63 and .96, with seven of the nine values reaching .84 or above. In addition, Table 1 presents correlations among the sub-scales. As expected, in most cases correlations among the sub-scales were significant but not high (r = -.05 − .45).

Table 1. Descriptive Statistics, Cronbach's Alpha, and Correlations for the Functions of the PALMS Questionnaire Subscales (N = 678)

Fs	Descriptive statistics		Reliability	Correlations								
	M	SD	Alpha	1	2	3	4	5	6	7	8	9
1	2.65	1.29	.96	1								
2	2.96	1.01	.91	.43**	1							
3	3.57	.94	.90	.20**	.22**	1						
4	3.88	.87	.90	.15**	.04	.30**	1					
5	4.29	.74	.89	.35**	.31**	.44**	.11**	1				
6	4.45	.59	.84	-.002	.02	.27**	.38**	.25**	1			
7	3.96	.80	.84	.45**	.37**	.20**	.10**	.42**	.33**	1		
8	1.90	1.16	.83	.31**	.20**	.28**	.10**	.24**	.03**	.22**	1	
9	2.26	.84	.63	.19**	.19**	.19**	.25**	-.05***	.18**	.09***	.31**	1

F1 = competition/ego; F2 = affiliation; F3 = psychological condition; F4 = appearance; F5 = enjoyment.

F6 = physical condition; F7 = mastery; F8 = family's and friends' expectations.

F9 = health professionals' and employers' expectations; ** = p < .01.

Table 2. Exploratory Factor Analysis for the Factors of the PALMS (N = 672)

PALMS Items	Factors									Communalities
	1	2	3	4	5	6	7	8	9	
PALMS-38	.886									.88
PALMS-39	.873									.88
PALMS-37	.869									.87
PALMS-40	.862									.84
PALMS-36	.842									.85
PALMS-12		.849								.84
PALMS-11		.849								.80
PALMS-15		.834								.77
PALMS-14		.826								.77
PALMS-13		.777								.67
PALMS-19			.837							.79
PALMS-20			.812							.71

PALMS Items	\multicolumn{9}{c}{Factors}									Communalities
	1	2	3	4	5	6	7	8	9	
PALMS-18			.810							.74
PALMS-17			.808							.74
PALMS-16			.733							.66
PALMS-22				.886						.82
PALMS-23				.848						.78
PALMS-24				.807						.72
PALMS-21				.801						.75
PALMS-25				.749						.67
PALMS-32					.878					.86
PALMS-33					.847					.83
PALMS-31					.829					.74
PALMS-35					.685					.66
PALMS-34					.651					.65
PALMS-8						.853				.79
PALMS-7						.802				.74
PALMS-6						.772				.71
PALMS-9						.719				.61
PALMS-10						.545				.60
PALMS-1							.804			.71
PALMS-5							.757			.71
PALMS-2							.721			.70
PALMS-3							.711			.64
PALMS-4							.535			.42
PALMS-29								.888		.83
PALMS-28								.795		.76
PALMS-26									.792	.73
PALMS-27									.633	.62
PALMS-30									.432	.44
Variance (%)	11.18	9.77	9.43	9.31	9.05	8.27	7.88	4.57	3.84	
Eigenvalue	9.80	5.10	3.18	2.92	2.47	2.04	1.46	1.33	1.02	
Alpha	.958	.914	.902	.899	.893	.843	.843	.831	.633	

F1 = competition/ego; F2 = affiliation; F3 = psychological condition; F4 = appearance; F5 = enjoyment; F6 = physical condition; F7 = mastery; F8 = family's and friends' expectations; F9 = health professionals' and employers' expectations.

Correlations among the sub-scales were expected because all the sub-scales measure the same theoretical construct, motivation for physical activity, but because each sub-scale measured a different characteristic, the correlations were not predicted to be too high. It should be noted that correlations approaching zero were observed for the physical condition sub-scale and competition/ego and affiliation sub-scales, and the appearance and affiliation sub-scale. The sub-scale structure was created by orthogonal rotation (Varimax), which aims to maximize zero correlations.

Factor Analysis

We applied an exploratory factor analysis to the 40 items of the PALMS for 678 participants. A principal-components analysis was conducted followed by a Varimax rotation with Kaiser Normalization. Regarding this procedure we followed Costello and Osborne's(2005) observation that researchers using large samples and making informed choices from the options available for data analysis are most likely to come to conclusions that will generalize beyond a particular sample, to either another sample or to the population of interest. After examining the items constituting each factor, the loading values of each item, the cross-loadings, and the internal consistencies for each factor, we retained all 40 items, representing nine factors with eigen-values over 1. These nine factors explained 73.29% of the total variance. Each factor was labeled according to the theme of motives for PA that the items in the factor represented. The results of the exploratory factor analysis for the PALMS are presented in Table 2.

The final nine factors were competition/ego, appearance, family and friends' expectations, health professionals' and employers' expectations, affiliation, physical condition, psychological condition, mastery, and enjoyment. The factor structure that emerged from the analysis was very similar to the structure we had hypothesized prior to the study on the basis of the qualitative research. The factor labeled others' expectations was originally hypothesized to relate to meeting the expectations of friends, family, work, and health professionals, but emerged from the analysis as two distinct factors: (1) family and friends' expectations, and (2) health professionals' and employers' expectations.

DISCUSSION

In this study, we conducted an exploratory investigation of the psychometric properties of the PALMS – a new measure we developed for measuring the motives for PA. It can be concluded that the generally good performance of the items provides quite strong support for their construction within the PALMS, as well as the factors into which they were grouped. Furthermore, the structure produced here supports the proposition that existing questionnaires do not cover all the motives people have for participating in recreational exercise and sport. In this study, we argue that the PALMS is a more comprehensive measure of participation motivation in recreational exercise and sport than other measures. For example, the nine factors that emerged from the factor analyses encompass and expand upon the five factors of the MPAM-R (Ryan et al., 1997). In the MPAM-R, two scales measure intrinsic motivation: the competence scale and the interest/enjoyment scale, and three measure extrinsic motives:

the fitness motives, the appearance-based motives, and the social scales (Ryan et al., 1997). The PALMS includes these factors as well as additional factors not covered by the MPAM-R, including competition/ego, psychological condition, and others' expectations.

In the present study, the others' expectations factor derived previously split into two factors, one related to the expectations of family and friends and the other related to employers' and health professionals' expectations. Although the factor health professional and employers' expectations may be surprising, it could be that exposure to mass media emphasizes health professionals' opinion and recommendations for PA. In addition, in many work sites PA is encouraged by establishing fitness corners or by subsidizing fitness center memberships, which might increase people motives for these expectations.

The close correspondence between the 40-item PALMS factors and the 50-item PMQ factors lends support to the status of the factors, given that the origins of the two questionnaires and the specific items in them are quite distinct: The PMQ was developed on the basis of an exploratory qualitative study of youth sport participants (Gill et al., 1983), whereas the PALMS emerged from the examination of the achievement goals of mainly adult exercisers (Rogers et al., 2008). Specific items within factors differ to some extent between the PALMS and the PMQ, due to variations in their origins, but there appears to be a substantial degree of correspondence.

The factor analyses we performed confirmed the new factors of the PALMS as concepts not covered by the MPAM-R. The diversity of the factors indicates the value of using a questionnaire, such as the PALMS, that measures a wide range of motives. Thus, the results of this research encourage the use of this questionnaire as a more comprehensive, yet reliable measure of motives for participating in recreational exercise and sport than the MPAM-R.

Past research has shown that motivation for participation varies across different cultures (see Duda, 1985, 1986; Li, Harmer, Chi, and Vongjaturapat, 1996). For example, competition is less important and cooperation is more highly valued in some cultures than others. Similarly, the emphasis on a healthy lifestyle is not as prevalent in some global cultures as it is in those in the Western world. Cultural perspectives also vary on what is considered to represent an attractive appearance, and the extent to which it is considered appropriate or important to commit time and effort to improving appearance. Therefore, the PALMS questionnaire should be further investigated, taking cultural differences into account. For example, comparisons between PALMS sub-scale scores for samples from carefully-selected cultures, identifying well-established cultural differences in advance, would provide a valuable test of the construct validity of the PALMS. From the applied aspect, understanding cultural differences in motives for participation in PA may result in more appropriate advice being given about assignment of people to types of PA experiences.

We acknowledge that our study has some limitations. Factor nine (health professionals' and employers' expectations) had an alpha value (.63) that was somewhat below the recommended level for sound internal consistency of .7 (DeVellis, 1991), so this Factor might be considered questionable. We retained Factor 9 for two reasons. First, it is not a long way below the threshold, lying within an area that can be considered borderline. Second, the aim of the present research is to explore the psychometric characteristics of the PALMS and Factor 9 is considered worthy of further consideration. In addition, Factor 8 consists of two items whereas it is recommended to employ a minimum of three items per sub-scale. However, since its alpha was high, and it had low correlations with other factors, which means that it can stand as an independent factor, we decided not to drop it. Lastly, we included a large range of ages in our sample. Often the wording of items in self-report questionnaires needs to be adjusted for children, but we did not adjust the wording of items in the PALMS. We had no reports from administration of the PALMS in the present study that younger participants had problems understanding the items or the instructions. Nor was there any evidence of questionnaires that were completed incorrectly, that is, no participants were excluded for this reason. On the other hand, however, a large age range is considered to be an advantage that enables one to generalize, due to the sample representativeness.

In the future, the PALMS should be further investigated in other contexts (e.g., different countries and/or activities), or with other properties (e.g., with empty lines at the end to be filled in where participants think of other motives not included, or in a version with four items per sub-scale to see if the PALMS can be further reduced in length with little reduction in sensitivity. However, for the time being it can be concluded that our exploratory study of the PALMS demonstrated quite a sound factor structure, as well as reliability, by providing a more comprehensive analysis of participant motives than previous questionnaires, which are based on either achievement goals or SDT. The factor structure within the PALMS provides valuable information for health authorities and fitness professionals concerning the range of motives people have for participation in PA. This information should assist them in matching people to appropriate sport and exercise activities and programs, which hopefully will lead to greater long-term adherence to PA. Moreover, it might be useful to match participants' individual motives to certain physical activities. As Morgan (2001) suggested, the questions "how much physical activity", "what kind of physical activity", "when", "where", "how", and others, should be addressed related to individual preferences. Other researchers have also supported the notion that people are likely to prefer and participate in exercise programs that are designed giving consideration to their preferences (e.g., Courneya, and Hellsten, 1998; Slade, Molloy, and Keating, 2009). Hence, identifying individuals' motives for exercise can help in tailoring a suitable PA program, which should give a greater chance of people adhering to it. As suggested by Slade et al. (2009), such information should be collected systematically. Using the PALMS is one way of accomplishing such data collection.

APPENDIX: ITEMS AND SUB-SCALES IN THE PALMS

Sub-Scale	Item Wording
Mastery	Improve existing skills
	Do my personal best
	Obtain new skills/activities
	Maintain current skill level
	Get better at an activity
Physical condition	It keeps me healthy
	It helps maintain a healthy body
	It helps maintain physical health
	It improves cardiovascular fitness
	I will be physically fit
Affiliation	Be with friends
	Do activities with others
	Enjoy spending time with others while doing exercise

Sub-Scale	Item Wording
	Talk with friends while exercising
	Do something in common with friends
Psychological condition	Because it acts as a stress release
	It's a better way of coping with stress
	It takes my mind off other things
	It helps me relax
	It helps me to get away from pressures
Appearance	Improve appearance
	Improve body shape
	Define muscles, look better
	Maintain trim, toned body
	Lose weight, look better
Health professionals' and employers' expectations	It was prescribed by doctor, physiotherapist
	To manage a medical condition
Family and friends' expectations	I can earn a living
Health professionals' and employers' expectations	I get paid to do it
	People tell me I need to
Enjoyment	I have a good time
	It is fun
	I enjoy exercising
	It is interesting
	It makes me happy
Competition / Ego	Perform better than others
	Be more fit than others
	Work harder than others
	Be best in the group
	Compete with others around me

REFERENCES

American College of Sports Medicine (ACSM) (2009). Exercise and physical activity for older adults. *Medicine and Science in Sports and Exercise,41*, 1510-1530.

Armstrong, N., and Welsman, J. R. (2006). The physical activity patterns of European youth with reference to methods of assessment. *Sports Medicine, 36,* 1067-1086.

Australian Bureau of Statistics.(2000). *National centre for culture and recreation statistics survey.*www.abs.gov.au.

Australian Sports Commission.(2005). *Participation in exercise recreation and sport.*Annual Report, 2004. Canberra: Department of Communications, Information Technology and the Arts.

Bartholomew, K., Ntoumanis, N., and Thøgersen-Ntoumani, C. (2009). A review of controlling motivational strategies from a self-determination theory perspective:

implications for sports coaches. *International Review of Sport and Exercise Psychology*, *2*, 215-233.

Biddle, S., Wang, C., Kavussanu, M., and Spray, C. (2003). Correlates of achievement goal orientations in physical activity: A systematic review of research. *European Journal of Sport Science*, *3*(5), 1-20.

Buinamano, R., Cei, A., and Mussino, A. (1995). Participation motivation in Italian youth sport. *The Sport Psychologist, 9*, 265-281.

Butcher, K., Sallis, J. F., Mayer, J. A., and Woodruff, S. (2008). Correlates of physical activity guideline compliance for adolescents in 100 U.S cities. *Journal of Adolescent Health, 42*, 360-368.

Costello, A. B., and Osborne, J. W.(2005). Best practices in exploratory factor analysis: Four recommendations for getting the most from your analysis. *Practical Assessment, Research and Evaluation, 10*(7), 1-9.

Courneya, S. K., and Hellsten, M. L. (1998). Personality correlates of exercise behavior, motives, barriers and preferences: An application of the five-factor model. *Personality and Individual Differences, 24*, 625-633.

Deci, E., and Ryan, R. (1985). *Intrinsic motivation and self-determination in human behaviour*. New York: Plenum.

Deci, E., and Ryan, R. (1991). A motivational approach to self: integration in personality. In R. Dienstbier,(Ed.), *Nebraska symposium on motivation (1990)* (pp. 237-288). Lincoln, NE: University of Nebraska Press.

Department of Health and Human Services (DHHS) (2008). *Physical activity guidelines for Americans*. Rockville, MD: U.S. Department of Health and Human Services.

DeVellis, R. F. (1991). *Scale development* (pp. 85). Newbury Park, NJ: Sage Publications.

Duda, J. (1985). Goals and achievement of Anglo and Mexican-American adolescents in sport and the classroom. *International Journal of Intercultural Relations, 9*, 131-150.

Duda, J. (1986). Perceptions of sport success and failure among white, black and Hispanic adolescents. In T. Riley, J. Watkins, and L. Burwitz (Eds.), *Sports science* (pp. 214-222). London: E and S. F. Spon.

Fortier, M., Vallerand, R., Briere, N., and Provencher, P. (1995). Competitive and recreational sport structures and gender: A test of their relationship with sport motivation. *International Journal of Sport Psychology, 54*, 5-12.

Frederick-Recascino, C., and Morris, T. (2004). Intrinsic and extrinsic motivation in sport and exercise. *Chapter 5*. In T. Morris and J. Summers (Eds.), *Sport psychology, theory, applications and issues* (2nd ed., pp. 121-151). Melbourne, Australia: Wiley.

Frederick, C., and Ryan, R. (1993). Differences in motivation for sport and exercise and their relations with participation and mental health. *Journal of Sport Behaiour, 16*, 124-146.

Gill, D., Gross, J., and Huddleston, S. (1983). Participation motivation in youth sports. *International Journal of Sport Psychology, 14*, 1-14.

Kerner, S. M., Kurrant, A. B., and Kalinski, M. I. (2004). Leisure-time physical activity, sedentary behavior, and fitness of high school girls. *European Journal of Sport Science, 4*, 1-16.

Kolt, G., Kirby, R., Bar-Eli, M., Blumenstein, B., Chadha, N., Liu, J., and Kerr, G. (1999). A cross-cultural investigation of reasons for participation in gymnastics. *International Journal of Sport Psychology, 30*, 381-398.

Lavigne, G., Hauw, N., Vallerand, R., Brunel, P., Blanchard, C., Cadorette, I., and Angot, C. (2009). On the dynamic relationships between contextual (or general) and situational (or state) motivation toward exercise and physical activity: A longitudinal test of the top-down and bottom-up hypotheses. *International Journal of Sport and Exercise Psychology, 7*, 147-168.

Li, F. (1999). The Exercise Motivation Scale: Its multifaceted structure and construct validity. *Journal of Applied Sport Psychology, 11*, 97-115.

Li, F., Harmer, P., Chi, L., and Vongjaturapat, N. (1996). Cross-cultural validation of the task and ego orientation in sport questionnaire. *Journal of Sport and Exercise Psychology, 18*, 392-238.

Lloyd-Jones D. M., Yuling, H., Labarthe, D., Mozaffarian, L. J., Appel, L., and Van Horn, K. (2010). Defining and setting national goals for cardiovascular health promotion and disease reduction. The American Heart Association's strategic impact goal, through 2020 and beyond. *Circulation, 121*, 586-613.

McKenzie, T. L. (2001). Promoting physical activity in youth: Focus on middle school environments. *Quest, 53(3)*, 326-334.

Mannell, R. C., and Kleiber, D. A. (1997).*A social psychology of leisure.* State College, PA: Venture.

Markland, D., and Hardy, L. (1993). The exercise motivations inventory: Preliminary development and validity of a measure of individuals' reasons for participation in regular physical exercise. *Personality and Individual Differences, 15*, 289-296.

Markland, D., and Hardy, L. (1997). On the factorial and construct validity of the intrinsic motivation inventory: conceptual and operational concerns. *Research Quarterly for Exercise and Sport, 68*, 20-32.

Markland, D., and Ingledew, D. (1997). The measurement of exercise motives: Factorial validity and invariance across gender of a revised Exercise Motivation Inventory. *British Journal of Health Psychology, 2*, 361-376.

Miles, M., and Huberman, A. (1994). *Qualitative data analysis* (2nd ed.). Thousand Oaks, CA: Sage.

Morgan, W. P. (2001). Prescription of physical activity: A paradigm shift. *Quest, 53*, 366-398.

Pangrazi, R. (2000). Promoting physical activity for youth. *ACHPER Healthy Lifestyles Journal, 47(2)*, 18-21.

Patton, M. (2002). *Qualitative research and evaluation methods* (3rd ed.). Thousand Oaks, CA: Sage.

Puente, R., and Anshel, M. (2010). Exercisers' perceptions of their fitness instructor's interacting style, perceived competence, and autonomy as a function of self-determined regulation to exercise, enjoyment, affect, and exercise frequency. *Scandinavian Journal of Psychology, 51(1)*, 38-45.

Rogers, H., Morris, T., and Moore, M. (2008).A qualitative study of the achievement goals of recreational exercise participants. *The Qualitative Report*, 13, 706-734.

Ryan, R., Frederick, C., Lepes, D., Rubio, N., and Sheldon, K. (1997). Intrinsic motivation and exercise adeherence. *International Journal of Sport Psychology, 28*, 335-254.

Sibley, B. A., and Etnier, J. L. (2003). The relationship between physical activity and cognition in children: A metaanalysis. *PediatricExercercise Science, 15*, 243-256.

Slade, S. C., Molloy, E., and Keating, J. L. (2009). People with non-specific chronic low back pain who have participated in exercise programs have preferences about exercise: a qualitative study. *Australian Journal of Physiotherapy, 55,* 115-121.

Weinberg, R., Tenenbaum, G., McKenzie, A., Jackson, S., Anshel, M., Grove, R., and Fogarty, G. (1999). Motivation for youth participation in sport and physical activity: relationships to culture, self-reported activity levels, and gender. *International Journal of Sport Psychology, 31,* 279-333.

Zach, S., and Netz, Y. (2007). Like mother like child: Three generations' patterns of exercise behavior. *Families, Systems, and Health, 25,* 419-434.

Zizzi, S. J., Keeler, L. A., and Watson II, J. C. (2006). The interaction of goal orientation and stage of change on exercise behavior in college students. *Journal of Sport Behavior, 29,* 96-110.

In: Athletic Insight's Writings of 2012
Editor: Robert Schinke

Chapter 11

SHREDS OF MEMORY: A FIRST-PERSON NARRATIVE OF SEXUAL ACQUAINTANCE-EXPLOITATION IN A YOUTH SPORT EXPERIENCE

Lars Dzikus[*]

Department of Kinesiology, Recreation, and Sport Studies,
The University of Tennessee, US

ABSTRACT

Studies on childhood sexual abuse often represent perpetrators and survivors as faceless "them" with brief excerpts from interviews, removed from the person who lived the experience. This study provides an in-depth, first-person narrative from a survivor of sexual exploitation in sport. Inspired by autoethnography, the narrative draws on personal memories to illustrate the profile of the groomer/seducer and his target. The text discusses the processes of gaining access, grooming, seducing, resisting, doubting, and distancing, as well as long-term effects. The paper is aimed to help raise awareness about the significance of sexual exploitation in youth sport for sport psychology professionals. Whereas previous research has mostly provided "snippet" accounts across cases, this narrative allows the reader to follow the development of an abusive coach-athlete relationship from beginning to end. The author calls practitioners to action and for further research to examine how the culture of sport contributes to sexual exploitation.

In this paper, I share experiences of being sexually exploited in youth sports by one of my coaches. This is a topic matter that might be upsetting for some, especially those who have had similar experiences. If you continue to read, be aware of the reactions this narrative may stir in you. It may help to know someone you trust with whom you can talk about your

---

[*] Correspondence concerning this article should be addressed to Lars Dzikus, Department of Kinesiology, Recreation, and Sport Studies, The University of Tennessee, 1914 Andy Holt Avenue, Knoxville, TN 37996. Phone: (865) 974-0451. Fax: (865) 974-8981. Email: ldzikus@utk.edu.

thoughts and emotions. In most areas, there are several resources available to help you process your experience. Universities often offer a variety of services to its students, faculty, and staff. For example, the Counseling Center at the University of Tennessee is accredited by the International Association of Counseling Services and provides individual and group counseling and psychotherapy (Counseling Center, n.d.).

My memories of abuse are somewhat splintered. I sometimes compare them to the old buildings around my childhood home. Every time I go home, they are there. The building and the mold don't change, but pieces of it, shreds really, have fallen to the ground and have been lost amidst the hustle and bustle of life. The memories I do have are like those shreds. As I think back I am aware of certain things, certain fragments of time that seem to gingerly grasp at my mind. I wonder if these pieces will ever become fully lost like those shreds of the old buildings…

One such memory is from a very early experience with Frank when I was about eight or nine years old. He was my coach and 17 years older than I was. I recall my excitement in our exchanges at the time:

> "Hey Lars, great job today at practice!" The praise by my swimming coach makes me glow.

> *I am so excited that he noticed me! Sweet!* "Thank you!"

> "Claudia," Frank looks over at my mother, "I know that Lars is coming to practice by bus and subway. If you want to I can pick him up and give him a ride. It's on my way anyway."

> My mother, knowing her son would find this exciting, smiles at Frank, "That would be great! Lars." She glances my way. "Do you want to go with Frank?"

> I can barely hold back my enthusiasm, "Yes!" Wow, I'll get to ride in his cool car with our club's sponsor on it; it'll be just like the pros!

This memory should be one that is remembered with a particular kind of softness—a softness reserved for memories about a person you look up to—similar to an essay I wrote in fourth grade. I am sure we all remember that hero essay that we were asked to write. We want to write about someone who is helping us become who we want to be; the person who is changing our lives, even though we may not be fully aware of it yet. For me, Frank was not only a hero, but an older man I admired—somewhere between a father figure and an older brother.

"My Role Model"

> Frank is my role model. He is twenty-five years old and my coach at our swimming club. He can swim faster than anyone I know. Last year he won the state title in the 100m freestyle. He looks very athletic with broad shoulders. He is teaching me to swim like him and he is the nicest person I know. He really cares about children and he is my best friend. Frank is studying to be a social worker. I want to become a social worker too. I think Frank is a great role model.

Isn't this something. I wish I could look back and say I still have the same respect for this man as I did as a fourth grader. I wish I could say that he was and is a great man who helped children, but I know better now. I know that Frank, and many that seem like it, are not great men but are just examples of people who take advantage of our naiveté and "the commonly accepted view of sport as an unproblematic site of youth empowerment and positive development" (Leahy, 2010b, p. 303).

PURPOSEFUL METHODOLOGY/METHODICAL PURPOSE

In recent years, childhood sexual abuse in the realm of sports has received increased attention from a variety of sources. A number of athletes have spoken out about their abuse (Fleury and McLellan Day, 2009; Kennedy and Grainger, 2006; Kiehl and Hernandez, 2010; Lee, 2010); research has emerged about the prevalence of sexual abuse in sport, its consequences for survivors, and implications for sport professionals (Brackenridge, 1997, 2001; Leahy, 2010a, 2010b; Leahy, Pretty, and Tenenbaum, 2002, 2003, 2004, 2008); and even the International Olympic Committee has adopted a statement on "sexual harassment and abuse in sport" including recommended prevention strategies (International Olympic Committee, 2007). Previous research, however, tends to focus on sexual victimization of women (Boen et al., 2008; Brackenridge, 1997; Fasting and Brackenridge, 2005; Fasting, Brackenridge, and Borgen-Sundgot, 2003; Fasting, Brackenridge, and Walseth, 2007; Lenskyj, 1992a, 1992b) and few studies examine male targets of sexual abuse in sport (Brackenridge, 2001; Kirby, Demers, and Parent, 2008).

Several studies about sexual harassment and abuse in sport provide brief thematized excerpts from interviews (e.g., Brackenridge, 1997; Leahy et al., 2004). Fasting and Brackenridge (2005) were the first to use a biographical approach to provide more nuanced and contextual accounts of two female athlete-survivors, but the researchers still mediated those narratives in their roles of interviewers, interpreters, and ultimate authors of how the athletes were represented. In most studies, quotations of athlete-survivors stand alone, removed from the person who said the words and lived the experience. We read about perpetrators and survivors as faceless "them." Thus, I want to add my own case study— literally my own. It is not a detached, clinical discussion about abstract victims and perpetrators, but rather, a highly personalized one (Douglas and Carless, 2009; Sparks, 2002).

Is this an autoethnography? A narrative of self? Personal narrative? Is it an "ethnographic autobiography, autobiographical sociology, critical autobiography, analytic autoethnography, reflexive autoethnography"? (Collinson and Hockey, 2007, p. 385). My account borrows from and is empowered by this range of methods. For the time being, I call it a first-person narrative. It is in some ways like autoethnography an "appropriate research approach for uncovering and analysing subjective, lived-body experiences" that focuses on "specific experiences within [my] life [and aims] to uncover and illuminate wider cultural or subcultural processes" (Collinson and Hockey, 2007, p. 384).

To protect the confidentiality of the abuser, I chose "Frank" as a pseudonym, changed other identifying features, and fictionalized certain aspects of my story (Douglas and Carless, 2009). By "(a) altering specific characteristics, (b) limiting the description of specific characteristics, [and] (c) obfuscating case detail by adding extraneous material," I am following the guidelines of the American Psychological Association (2010) to "disguise some aspects of the case material so that neither the subject nor third parties...are identifiable" (p. 17).

At times this text appears to be fragmented for several reasons. Child molesters often gain control over their targets in a progressive grooming process that works in stages (Brackenridge, 2001; Fasting and Brackenridge, 2005; Lanning, 2010). Thus my experience itself was fragmented, because it was not a single, stand-alone episode. Most of all, however, this narrative is fragmented, because my memories are broken and scattered into pieces. I want this narrative to be evocative because I need to remember. I want to feel. I want you to feel. And I want us to do something about it—about men sexually molesting and abusing children in sports.

Reading Lanning's (2010) behavioral analysis of child molesters has provided me with information and language that is helping me to process my experience. I was, I am the survivor (Brackenridge, 2001) of sexual abuse, or more precisely "sexual acquaintance-exploitation" (Lanning, 2010, p. 66). According to Lanning (2010), many investigators prosecutors, and social workers still tend to associate child sexual abuse with cases that involve intra-familial, situational offenders who coerce a small number of girls. In contrast, in child sexual exploitation more boys tend to be the targets, the perpetrators more often tend to come from outside the family, and they tend to use seduction more so than coercion (Lanning, 2010).

The decision to confront and share my story with a wider audience was inspired by the accounts of athletes and survivors like Sheldon Kennedy (2006), Courtney Kiehl, and Alexa Hernandez (2010), as well as the work by such trailblazers as Lenskyj (1992a, 1992b), Brackenridge (1997, 2001), and Leahy (Leahy, 2010a, 2010b). These authors have helped me to capture lost memories and put my experience into words. Reading them, I continue to find myself and the man who abused me. They allow me to look back and remember...

SHREDS OF CHILDHOOD

Traditional studies typically can't provide us with images of childhood abuse survivors. I want to use these pages to give you "a face," a person, someone to care about beyond the usual research report.

When I share my experience with students in our sport sociology class, it is in the context of our discussion of sports, violence, and gender. We first cover these topics in general earlier in the course. I tell the students ahead of time what day I will share my experience, which is typically toward the end of the semester, when we have established better relationships. I tell them that they don't have to be in class that day, that there are several good reasons not to attend, and that they won't have to tell me why they won't be in class. I do not want to place other survivors in a situation where they may have to relive their own experience without feeling safe and some students may not feel comfortable to hear their instructor talk about such personal matters. I also make a similar statement as you find at the beginning of this paper and I take the opportunity to share local resources, such as the counseling services available on our campus (Counseling Center, n.d.). Following my sharing in class, it is important to have time not only for questions and discussion, but also for sharing what it was like for the students to listen to my account and what I feel like when I talk to them about the abuse.

I begin with passing around two photographs from my childhood. In one picture, I am six years old. It was taken on my first day of school; during the same year I joined the swimming club where I met the man who changed my life. Next to me in the picture stands my mom from whom I inherited my enthusiasm for sports in general and swimming in particular. The parents of the man who became my coach that year had been her swimming coaches when she was young. Thus the man who abused me was not a stranger, but rather a trusted friend of the family, as is often the case (Lanning, 2010).

In the second photograph, I am about 12 years old. It shows a close-up of my face and as I look at it today, I think I looked tired and sad. The best I can remember, I was still being abused when that photograph was taken; sexually abused by the man who took that picture, my swimming coach. He held the camera, looked through the lens, and saw me, the boy.

When I invite the students to pass the photographs around, I tell them to handle the pictures with care. Rather than projecting the images on a screen, I want the audience to have a sense of shared responsibility in taking care of them, because we have a shared responsibility in taking care of children in sports. The pictures are precious to me, because they allow me to be in touch with my past, to hold on to those shreds of memories.

Access

In my youth, I participated in a variety of sports, including tennis and track and field, in different clubs. Apart from one coach, I had great experiences with everyone else. My athletic career began shortly after I entered first grade. This I do remember like it was yesterday:

> *Finally home!* I quickly toss the book back in the corner. The words burst out of my mouth, "Mom, the gym teacher said I should join a sports club. I'm the fastest kid in the class! Can I play soccer? Pleeeease?"

> My mother hesitates, but gives me a cautious smile, "You are only six. That's a little young for soccer. It's a pretty violent sport, you know? How about swimming? I used to swim. It's fun!"

> I struggle to hide my disappointment. *Swimming? Really?*

When I joined the swimming club shortly after that, Frank soon became one of my primary coaches. I would see him two to three times a week for practices and for competitions, during trips with the team around the country and abroad for competitions and just for fun. As a child molester, Frank was a classic groomer (van Dam, 2006) and seducer (Lanning, 2010). Our swimming club gave him perfect access to me and possibly other victims:

> The most dramatic behavioral characteristic of the Groomers…is the frequency and intensity of offending. They do not coach only one soccer team; they coach five teams, and tutor dozens of children when they are not leading the youth group at church. There is no room in their life for anything but making a living, grooming parents and communities and accessing children. (van Dam, 2006, p. 121)

The institutionalized relationship between coach and athletes provide child molesters like Frank the necessary long-term access to their targets for the grooming and seducing process (Brackenridge, 2001; Fasting and Brackenridge, 2005; Lanning, 2010). From the perspective of the perpetrator, sport clubs provide target rich environments.

Who would be suspicious of Frank? He was immensely popular in our club and the wider swimming community. Groomers are excellent at image management and are frequent recipients of such awards as "Volunteer of the Year," or "Coach of the Year" (van Dam, 2006, p. 64).

Grooming

I don't remember exactly when and how the sexual activity started. There is a lot that I have blocked out from those years. Leahy (2010b) noted about the work with adult athlete survivors of sexual abuse, "Dissociation, avoidance, and motivated forgetting are likely to be extensively used as defense and coping mechanisms to keep painful material…at a distance" (p. 307). I do know that I quickly became an athletic standout in our club. I even won a state title in the 8-10 year-old division. Frank was a well-known coach in our region and his extra attention made me feel special.

Frank started to groom me early. At first he gave me free equipment, swim wear, running shoes and so forth, then there were personal gifts for birthdays and holidays. And before long I constantly received little tokens of appreciation. Frank acted much like a man who is romancing a woman during the courting phase of their relationship. It made me feel loved and special. As described above, he volunteered to give me rides to and from practices; he started to take me to watch other sporting events together. Increasingly we spent more time together, alone outside of practices and competitions. Over time, he groomed me "with attention, affection, and gifts" (Lanning, 2010, p. 57).

I don't think the touching and the kisses started until I was about 10 or 12 years old. I believe it happened after my parents had gotten divorced, my older siblings had moved out, and I was living alone with my mom. Perhaps that gave Frank the green light.

Seduction

Reading the behavioral profile of the seducer (Lanning, 2010), I realize that Frank understood my emotional needs. According to Lanning (2010), "Almost any child can be seduced, but the most vulnerable children tend to be those who come from dysfunctional homes or are victims of emotional neglect.... A favorite target victim is a child living with a single mother" (p. 72). In my parents' strained relationship, I had never felt close to my father. After the divorce I saw my dad only on occasional weekends and for summer vacations. I ended up spending more time with Frank than with either of my parents. *Take note:* "Parents/guardians should beware of anyone who wants to be with their children more than they do" (Lanning, 2010, p. 55). I think Frank knew I was longing for a father figure and that I would fall for him. Almost every weekend, Frank took me out to do fun things that a father and son might do together—or a romantic couple on a date. According to Lanning

(2010), offenders like Frank "seduce children much the same way adults seduce one another" (p. 27).

Frank seduced me; he didn't force me physically. There was no violence or aggression. There were no bruises that someone could have seen on my body. But, could someone have noticed the bruises on my psyche and spirit? Like other survivors who have experienced the bystander effect (Leahy, 2010a; Leahy et al., 2003), I wonder if those around me could have and should have noticed something. But at the time, I didn't tell anyone. Frank didn't even have to threaten me about that. His control over me was subtle and complete. Some abusers secure secrecy by using threats like: "If you tell anyone I'll hurt you/tell others what you've done/hurt someone you care about/drop you from the team" (Brackenridge, 2001, p. 35).

Most of all I relished the attention. I thought Frank cared for me like nobody else. He listened to me. And according to Lanning (2010), the ability to listen makes pedophiles "exceptionally good teachers, coaches, and youth volunteers" (p. 57). He knew my emotional needs. Like other victims, I developed positive feelings for the offender (Lanning, 2010). To outsiders I may have appeared "loving, needy, wiling to please, and protective of the perpetrator" (Leahy, 2010b, p. 306). In letters, I even called him my "großer Wunschbruder," the big brother I was wishing for.

He almost made me feel like an adult, which is ironic. Child molesters take advantage of the fact that their targets are nowhere near being adults and unable to give consent—real, informed consent—to what they do with the adults (Lanning, 2010). In my case, there were massages after practice and playful wrestling in the beginning. Then there were sleepovers at his apartment with cuddling; later he started to kiss me; we kissed. There was touching, petting, and no: never penetration. I didn't resist. And what may be hard to understand: I enjoyed the sexual activity. I had my first orgasm with him and it felt good at the time. As Lanning (2010) pointed out, "Once a victim is seduced, each successive sexual incident becomes easier and quicker. Eventually the child victim may even take the initiative in the seduction" (pp. 72-73).

As I continue to recall these events I have a foggy recollection of pivotal scenes. Was it when I was about 12 years old? Frank and I are spending increasingly more time together outside of practice and competitions. On weekends when school is out, I am spending hours alone with Frank. One day we play miniature golf and eat ice cream.

It is another of those moments that I should be able to remember fondly. It hurts to know that I have these moments that could have been great but were, and are, the exact opposite. This particular evening we decide to watch a movie.

Frank puts the video in, "Come on, let's watch from the futon." He lies down and makes room for me.

I reply naively, "Sure, that way I can stretch out my legs. I am still sore from practice yesterday"

"Really?" Frank scoots over, "I can give you a massage. That will help you relax. Take off your pants and lay over there. I'll get the oil."
What did I feel here? What did I think? Did I have any questions about his motivation? If I had shared this with my family, my friends, would they have questioned this? My memories may, at some points, be clouded by time and uneasiness, but I do question the "could have's" and the "what if's."

Today I wonder what I was thinking. *Why didn't somebody wake me up? Why didn't anyone protect me? How did my mom not know what was going on? Did she? Did the other coaches notice something?* There is the bystander effect again (Leahy, 2010a; Leahy et al., 2003).

Bystander beware:

Passive attitudes/non-intervention, denial and/or silence by people in positions of power in sport (particularly bystanders) increases the psychological harm of sexual harassment and abuse. Lack of bystander action also creates the impression for victims that sexually harassing and abusive behaviours are legally and socially acceptable and/or that those in sport are powerless to speak out against it. (International Olympic Committee, 2007, p. 4)

Resistance

As with the beginning, I don't know exactly when the sexual exploitation ended. I think it was around the age of 15, after my mother had died from cancer and at a time when I was actually drawing even closer to Frank for support. But somehow I started to resent the physical contact. Today, I am aware of feelings that I would not have been able to consciously express then, but, looking back, I can see that those feelings were gut reactions to things that were wrong.

It is just another Saturday; similar to so many other Saturdays in those days that I am surprised it sticks out in my mind. Frank organized tickets for a hockey game and has invited me to join him. I nervously approach his house. I am not sure what I am going to do, but I feel that I must do something different. With hindsight, I know I was not aware that what I did this day was going to change my life for the better; that this was the moment in which I made sure I would be a better man than my "idol." Shortly after I ring the doorbell Frank opens the door.

He smiles at me, "Hello! Ready for the game?"
His smile freezes on his face after he leans in for the usual kiss and I back up. My mind, somewhat blank until this moment, grips this show of courage, *Not today, Frank! Never again!*

I think somehow I made it stop right then. I don't remember us ever talking about it. Without verbalizing my resistance, I think I drew a line and he stopped trying. Just like that. I wonder if he knew that too much was at stake for him and that pushing me more could have caused me to talk to someone. But I don't know.

The physical exploitation had ended, but the psychological continued, because for a number of years our "friendship" continued as if nothing had happened. Frank continued to be my coach and even the gifts kept coming. But I started to feel that I'd been keeping a secret, a dirty secret. I became increasingly aware of what had happened and I became angry. I started to resent him. At practices I started to scream at him, blaming my lack of progress on his poor coaching. Eventually, at age 16 constant injuries had piled up and my shoulders were so run down that my doctor advised me to quit. I think that was my way out. I quit sports all together. I left not only my swimming club, but also tennis and track and field. Today, I wonder if some of that pain was psychosomatic. Somatic effects related to anxiety are common among sexually abused children (Finkelhor and Browne, 1985). I never had shoulder pain after I quit swimming, even when I started to play American football a year later. Perhaps the break just allowed me to heal in more ways than one.

Doubts

I wish I could say I was a happy young man after I stopped the physical exploitation; that what Frank did to me was in my past and was something I learned from but was able to leave behind. I know now that abuse, no matter what kind, is something that does change us, leaves us different and, at times, uncertain about ourselves, or at least, our actions and reactions (Romano and De Luca, 2001).

Around age 16, I fell in love. A girl, Natalie, had transferred into our school that year. Through the fall we had met and hung out in groups, going to movies and dancing. Finally, we had our first date. Sparks had been flying (*remember those wonderful times of teenage love*) and our friends had been asking if "something was going on" between the two of us.

Wow, tonight is the first time we are alone, just the two of us! Talk about nerves! We have been hanging out, holding hands and kissing all day. *I am sure Natalie is open for more.* She has not been shy about it. But I feel weird. I keep feeling that this is strange; I am super uncomfortable. *Why am I so nervous? I have dreamt about this! I want to touch her. Boy, do I want to touch her.*

"Natalie, I can't do this. I am sorry. I'm gay."

My mind blanks; I am just as shocked as she is. *Where did that come from? What did I just say?? Gay? I am not gay. Why did I say that? I will tell her later that it was just a joke. What was I thinking???*

Today, I understand that avoidance of physical intimacy—but also hypersexual behavior—can be effects of sexual abuse. Similarly, it is not uncommon for male survivors to doubt their sexual orientation (Dhaliwal, Gauzas, Antonowicz, and Ross, 1996; Romano and De Luca, 2001). But at the time, I was just confused and eventually I just wanted to get away from it all.

Distance

The imagination of a child is sometimes filled with visions of what could be and sometimes scarred from the reality of what can be. I lived through a childhood that holds fragmented memories, but those memories are still scarred. These have followed me across countries and other dividing lines.

I was already living miles away that summer, when I was in my mid-20s. I had moved on in many ways, but all it took was just one glance for me to become that scared and confused boy. The only difference was that I was also a more confident and composed man now. A decade later, yet my past and present were at war when I saw Frank. During a summer break, my usual visits home, I stopped by to see some of my old friends at the PE department at the university where I studied as an undergraduate.

The university swimming pool is busy with students taking summer classes. I see Dr. Mueller, one of my former professors.

> "Lars, it's great to see you!" Dr. Mueller shakes my hand (a moment of clear adulthood when I find myself interacting with my old professors as a peer). "How are things going for you in the States? Are you missing us yet?"
>
> "Things are going great, but I do miss home." I hear Dr. Mueller asking about my classes but his voice fades as I stumble back into my childhood. My eyes are fixed across the pool; I can't seem to pull myself back. The man I am now is defensive and protective of the boy I once was. *Shit, Frank, of all people, what is he doing here???*
>
> "Lars? Lars, are you okay?" Dr. Mueller's concerned voice finally breaks through my tension.
>
> My mind, still somewhat scattered, pulls in enough to share a shaky, if not hurried, goodbye. "Sorry Doc, I forgot I had to be somewhere. I gotta go. I will stop by some other time. Promise!" *Damn, I have to get out of here. This is why I had to leave in the first place. This is why I had to get as far away as possible. I can't take this; I can't face him. I can't live here always having to wonder if I'll run into him somewhere.* I want to yell at him, *"You jerk! You took my home from me, my family. Screw you!"* But I don't. *Not yet. Not today.*

I think back to this time, this moment when I could have said something and didn't. Could I have made a difference? I won't know how this could have changed me; I don't know what difference in my life it could have made. I do know that it is now one of those splintered pieces of paint that could be so easily lost.

Effects

How has all of this affected me since then? I'm just starting to realize that; more discovery lies ahead. It is a long journey. Common long-term effects of childhood sexual abuse can include problems with sexual functioning; confusion about sexual identity; feeling stigmatized and isolated; a general sense of betrayal, disillusionment, and powerlessness; anger; substance abuse.... The list is long (Brackenridge, 1997; Dhaliwal et al., 1996; Finkelhor and Browne, 1985). A group of researchers led by Leahy studied the effects on adult athlete survivors of sexual abuse and the implications for those working with them (Leahy, 2010a, 2010b; Leahy et al., 2003, 2004, 2008). For example, "clinically distressed" athlete-survivors reported "difficulties with trust and intimacy in the relational domain," which can have consequences for the way in which these athletes relate to authority figures (e.g, coaches, administrators, sport psychologists, team mates) and significant others in their lives (Leahy et al., 2003, p. 661).

I seem to exhibit some of these effects; I may have escaped others. In addition to a pessimistic outlook and negative self-talk, not always being able to fully enjoy sexual activity and general trust issues are the most negative effects I experience. I tend to trust men less than women. I am especially uncomfortable with older, male authority figures, which has made building personal and professional relationships challenging.

"Lars, I would really like to help you. But it is up to you. Let me know if and when you are ready. You have my number. Call me, if you want to start therapy," says Father Tim at the end of our conversation.

The offer is sincere and promising. I'm sitting in an office in our church, alone with one of my favorite priests. Earlier, I asked him if I could talk to him about something. When he came to our parish a little over a year ago, I learned that he was also working at our university clinic as a licensed psychologist. Turns out he is a leading authority on working with adult survivors of childhood abuse. *What are the odds? Perhaps God does have a plan for me?*

"Thank you, Father. Thank you for listening to me. It felt good to talk about it," I say and I mean it. But I also feel very uncomfortable in this space alone with this man, although—and perhaps because—I actually like him. *I wish I could follow up on your offer. I want to trust you, but I don't.*

And then there a sense of guilt and anxiety; in my case not so much blaming myself for "going along," as other survivors experienced (Dhaliwal et al., 1996), but for not having done more to stop sexual abuse since then. Brackenridge (2001) shared that "researching sexual abuse in sport has exacted a toll on me as an individual" (p. 152). She spoke of anxiety, insomnia, and "the general emotional contagion of listening to and reading about dozens of cases of sexual exploitation and feelings of guilt or blame that I should or could have done more to prevent these" (p. 153). From the experience I have so far with researching this topic, I can relate to her feelings.

Boy, can I relate! From a recent email to a colleague: "I'm sorry this is taking me so long to write. I'm almost done. I'll get the draft to you asap. The tears have dried [for the time being]. I know I can do this!" Picking up these shreds of memories and writing this paper is exhausting. It is taking me to the edge of what I feel I can bear.

CONCLUSION BUT NOT CLOSURE

What does my story mean for you? What are the implications for researchers and professionals in sport like you? If you are familiar with the literature on childhood sexual abuse and work with survivors, my story probably tells you little or nothing new. It is unique, because every person's experience is unique, but it is also somewhat stereotypical.

In many ways, my personal story, characteristics, and circumstances echo the findings of previous research. My coach, Frank, groomed and seduced me. Through the grooming process the perpetrator isolates, prepares, and entraps the target. It may even create the appearance that the target is consenting to the abuse (Brackenridge, 2010). Coming from a broken family, low self-esteem, and longing for attention and confirmation made me a target for any predator (Brackenridge, 2001; Lanning, 2010). My motivation to achieve in sport with its single-minded commitment and hierarchical power structure made me an especially easy target for a predator-coach (Brackenridge, 2001). Sexual abuse and acquaintance-exploitation happen in many contexts, but the socio-cultural context of sport provides especially fertile ground for abuse. The Sexual Harassment Task Force of Women Sport International (WSI, n.d.), summarized:

Risk of sexual harassment or sexual abuse arises from a complex interplay of factors including: weak organisational controls within sport clubs, dominating and controlling behaviour by coaches and vulnerability, low self esteem and high ambition amongst athletes. Particular dangers arise where such athletes become emotionally reliant on or obsessed with their coaches and where their coaches are not subject to independent monitoring. (para., 5)

If you have not thought much about sexual victimization in youth sports before, now is the time to be reminded that "eliminating child abuse requires additional prevention and intervention strategies that can only happen when everyone becomes familiar with the true dynamics of child abuse" (van Dam, 2006, p. xiii). According to Leahy (2010), "the sport psychologist has a key safeguarding role" (p. 315), but the professional training for this role is often lacking. This is alarming, since "research and clinical evidence indicates that athlete survivors of sexual abuse…form a significant percentage of the athlete population with which sport psychologists will come into contact" (p. 328).

Brackenridge (1997) urged, "*all* stakeholders to recognize that they have responsibilities within the system and to overcome their tendency to deny the reality of the issue" (p. 115). What will you do to make a change? What is your/our responsibility? How do we prevent abuse? The literature mentioned in this text provides much needed answers to these questions. I especially recommend Leahy's (2010a, 2010b) and Brackenridge's (2001) insights for practitioners. In the center of their discussions is the concept of power.

Brackenridge's (1997) work on sexual abuse includes a broader examination of the role power and authority within the culture of sport. I believe the sociologists of sport and sport psychologists of the cultural turn among us (Ryba, Schinke, and Tennenbaum, 2010) should continue this line of research to critically examine how the culture of youth sport contributes to sexual exploitation. In this context, Brackenridge (2001) asked, "What is it about sport that promotes and condones sexually exploitive behavior by men?"

As Coakley (2009) argues, today's youth sport system is based on an adult-centered power and performance model that stresses rule conformity. Without adult supervision, children typically organize their games as high-scoring, action-packed affairs that keep the players involved. These games often allow the children to reaffirm friendships and practice conflict resolution. Without an adult coach or referee to make decisions for them, the players learn to regulate their own interactions. On the other hand, when adults organize youth sports, they tend to emphasize skill development, adherence to rules, and listening to the coaches (Coakley, 2009). According to Coakley, normative behavior in the power and performance model requires the athlete to make sacrifices, accept risks, play through pain, and push the (physical) limits. Learning how to legitimately question the authority of a coach is typically not one of these norms. In many ways the system of organized youth sports is set up to function as a catalyst for sexual acquaintance-exploitation. As Brackenridge (2001) remarked, "Wherever there is a power imbalance…there is potential for abuses to occur. In a sports culture that thrives on authoritarian leadership the climate is ripe for individual exploitation" (p. 121). The empowerment of children in and through organized sports requires meaningful adult involvement, but also a less controlling environment for the children (Coakley, 2009). Perhaps those in need for more control and supervision are the coaches.

To help prevent sexual harassment and abuse, WSI (n.d.) provides the following advice for sport organizations:

1. Prepare and implement codes of ethics and conduct for coaches, whether they work with adults or children.
2. Foster a climate of open discussion about the issues of sexual harassment and abuse so that athletes with problems feel confident enough to speak out.
3. Develop athlete autonomy wherever possible including adopting coaching styles which give optimum autonomy and responsibility to athletes.
4. Become involved in coach education programmes which inform and advise about the ethical and interpersonal issues of sexual harassment and abuse and about the technical aspects of physical touch in coaching the sport
5. Adopt athlete and parent education programmes which inform and advise athletes on their rights and how to maintain their integrity and autonomy
6. Introduce and use reporting and mediation systems for both athletes and coaches, ideally with the assistance of trained social work or counselling professionals
7. Ensure that parents are fully informed of the whereabouts of their children at all times and are involved as fully as possible in supporting the work of coaches
8. Adopt rigorous screening procedures for the appointment of all personnel, whether coaching staff or voluntary workers
9. Be constantly vigilant and avoid complacency and expect and demand the highest standards of accountability at all levels of the sport
10. Celebrate the good work of athletes and coaches on a regular basis. (para., 6)

Practical measures like criminal background checks and screening procedures for coaches may add a layer of protection, but they do not fundamentally change the socio-cultural context that facilitates sexual abuse in youth sport. In addition to codes of ethics and training that emphasizes building and maintaining ethical relationships, Leahy (2010) stressed that we have to address "the way power is constructed within the sociocultural milieu of competitive sport. The development of an ethical, psychologically safe, power-sharing coaching system may offer [a] considerable challenge to existing systems and practices" (p. 330).

Here, Brackenridge's (2001) point deserves to be repeated: "by changing the power relations between athletes and authority figures, and between men, women, and children in sport, we can prevent sexual exploitation" (p. 230). This means making sport systems more democratic as well as empowering athletes from a young age to become informed decision-makers and critical thinkers. My first-person narrative responds, in part, to Brackenridge's call for more biographical work on coach-predators and athlete-targets/survivors. Still needed are case studies of coaches who (sexually) abuse and ethnographies of sport settings in which abuse occurs (Brackenridge, 2001). These narrative accounts can help us to put together the pieces of "the big picture" of sexual-acquaintance exploitation in youth sport.

ACKNOWLEDGMENTS

The author would like to thank Nichole M. Dzikus, Kate F. Hays, and Leslee A. Fisher for their help in preparing this manuscript.

REFERENCES

American Psychological Association. (2010). *Publication manual of the American Psychological Association* (6th ed.). Washington, DC: American Psychological Association.

Boen, F., de Martelaer, K., van Nierkerk, L., Opdenacker, J., vanden Auweele, Y., Vertommen, T., & de Cuyper, B. (2008). Unwanted sexual experiences in sport: Perceptions and reported prevalence among Flemish female student-athletes. *International Journal of Sport and Exercise Psychology, 16*, 354-365.

Brackenridge, C. (1997). 'He owned me basically...': Women's experience of sexual abuse in sport. *International Review for the Sociology of Sport, 32*, 115-130. doi: 10.1177/101269097032002001.

Brackenridge, C. (2001). *Spoilsports: Understanding and preventing sexual exploitation in sport*. London: Routledge.

Coakley, J. (2009). *Sports in society: Issues and controversies* (10th ed.). Boston: McGraw-Hill.

Collinson, J. A., & Hockey, J. (2007). 'Working Out' identity: Distance runners and the management of disrupted identity. *Leisure Studies, 26*, 381-398. doi: 10.1080/02614360601053384.

Counseling Center. (n.d.). Welcome. Retrieved May 31, 2011, from http:// counseling center.utk.edu/

Dhaliwal, G. K., Gauzas, L., Antonowicz, D. H., & Ross, R. R. (1996). Adult male survivors of childhood sexual abuse: Prevalence, sexual abuse characteristics, and long-term effects. *Clinical Psychology Review, 16*, 619-639.

Douglas, K., & Carless, D. (2009). Exploring taboo issues in professional sport through a fictional approach. *Reflective Practice, 10*, 311-323. doi: 10.1080/14623940903034630.

Fasting, K., & Brackenridge, C. (2005). The grooming process in sport: Case studies of sexual harassment and abuse. *Auto/Biography, 13*(1), 33-52.

Fasting, K., Brackenridge, C., & Borgen-Sundgot, J. (2003). Experiences of sexual harassment and abuse among Norwegian elite female athletes and nonathletes. *Reserach Quarterly for Exercise and Sport, 74*, 84-97.

Fasting, K., Brackenridge, C., & Walseth, K. (2007). Women athletes' personal responses to sexual harassment in sport. *Journal of Applied Sport Psychology, 19*, 419-433.

Finkelhor, D., and Browne, A. (1985). The traumatic impact of child sexual abuse: A conceptualization. *American Journal of Orthopsychiatry, 55*, 530-541.

Fleury, T., & McLellan Day, K. (2009).*Playing with fire*. Chicago, ill.: Triumph Books.

International Olympic Committee. (2007, February 8). IOC adpots consensus statement on 'sexual harassment and abuse in sport'. Retrieved January 16, 2011, from http://multimedia.olympic.org/pdf/en_report_1125.pdf

Kennedy, S., & Grainger, J. (2006).*Why I didn't say anything: The Sheldon Kennedy story*. Toronto: Insomniac Press.

Kiehl, C., & Hernandez, A. (2010). A.C.H.E. Retrieved December 29, 2010, from http://achefoundation.com/

Kirby, S. L., Demers, G., & Parent, S. (2008). Vulnerability/Prevention: Considering the Needs of Disabled and Gay Athletes in the Context of Sexual Harassment and Abuse. *International Journal of Sport and Exercise Psychology, 6*, 407-426.

Lanning, K. V. (2010). Child molesters: A behavioral analysis. Alexandria, VA: National Center for Missing and Exploited Children.

Leahy, T. (2010a). Sexual abuse in sport: Implications for the sport psychology profession. In T. V. Ryba, R. J. Schinke and G. Tennenbaum (Eds.), *The cultural turn in sport psychology* (pp. 315-334). Morgantown, WV: Fitness Information Technology.

Leahy, T. (2010b). Working with adult athlete survivors of sexual abuse. In S. J. Hanrahan and M. B. Andersen (Eds.), *Routledge handbook of applied sport psychology: A comprehensive guide for students and practitioners* (pp. 303-312). New York: Routledge.

Leahy, T., Pretty, G., & Tenenbaum, G. (2002). Prevalence of sexual abuse in Australia. *Journal of Sexual Aggression, 8*, 16-35.

Leahy, T., Pretty, G., & Tenenbaum, G. (2003). Childhood sexual abuse narratives in clinically and nonclinically distressed adult survivors. *Professional Psychology: Research and Practice, 34*, 657-665. doi: 10.1037/0735-7028.34.6.657

Leahy, T., Pretty, G., & Tenenbaum, G. (2004). Perpetrator methodology as a predictor of traumatic symptomatology in adult survivors of childhood sexual abuse. *Journal of Interpersonal Violence, 19*, 521-540. doi: 10.1177/0886260504262963

Leahy, T., Pretty, G., & Tenenbaum, G. (2008). A contextualized investigation of traumatic correlates of childhood sexual abuse in Australian athletes. *International Journal of Sport and Exercise Psychology, 6*, 366-384.

Lee, V. (2010). Lawsuit alleges sexual abuse in youth swimming. Retrieved January 10, 2011, from http://abclocal.go.com/kgo/story?section=news/sportsandid=7340263

Lenskyj, H. (1992a). Sexual harassment: Female athletes' experiences and coaches' responsibilities. *Science Periodical on Research and Technology in Sport 12*, 1-5.

Lenskyj, H. (1992b). Unsafe at home base: Women's experiences of sexual harassment in university sport and physical education. *Women in Sport and Physical Activity Journal, 1*, 19-34.

Romano, E., & De Luca, R. V. (2001). Male sexual abuse: A review of effects, abuse characteristics, and links with later psychological functioning. *Aggresssion and Violent Behavior, 6*, 55-78.

Ryba, T. V., Schinke, R. J., & Tennenbaum, G. (Eds.). (2010). *The cultural turn in sport psychology*. Morgantown, WV: Fitness Information Technology.

Sparkes, A. C. (2002). *Telling tales in sport and physical activity: A qualitative journey.* Champaign, IL: Human Kinetics.

van Dam, C. (2006). *The socially skilled child molester: Differentiating the guilty from the falsely accssed.* Binghampton, NY: Haworth Press.

WomenSport International. (n.d.). WSI Task Forces Retrieved June 1, 2011, from http://www.sportsbiz.bz/womensportinternational/taskforces/harassment_brochure.htm.

March 7, 2011

In: Athletic Insight's Writings of 2012
Editor: Robert Schinke

Chapter 12

EXPLORING FLOW OCCURRENCE IN ELITE GOLF

Christian Swann[*], Richard Keegan, David Piggott,
Lee Crust and Mark F. Smith
School of Sport and Exercise Science, University of Lincoln,
Brayford Pool, Lincoln, Lincolnshire, UK

ABSTRACT

Research on flow (Csikszentmihalyi, 1975) has traditionally focused on reactive, externally-paced sports (e.g., tennis) without exploring those that are self-paced and stop-start in nature. This study investigated the occurrence of flow in a sample of thirteen elite golfers by conducting semi-structured interviews discussing: (i) their experiences of flow, (ii) factors that influenced flow occurrence, and (iii) the controllability of these experiences. Results shared similarity with existing research in terms of the majority of influencing factors reported, including motivation, preparation, focus, psychological state, environmental and situational conditions, and arousal, and that flow was reported to be at least potentially controllable. Golf-specific influences were also noted, including pre-shot routines, use of psychological interventions, standard of performance, and maintenance of physical state, suggesting that flow may have occurred differently for this sample. Findings are discussed and applied recommendations are made that may help golfers put relevant factors in place to increase the likelihood of experiencing flow.

Keywords: Sport psychology, optimal experience, qualitative research, elite athletes, self-paced sport

The term flow is used to describe a harmonious and intrinsically rewarding state of effortless excellence, in which one is completely absorbed in an activity, attention is totally invested, and the person functions at his/her fullest capacity (Csikszentmihalyi, 1975; 1990). Flow has been reported in domains ranging from surgery to art and music, as well as everyday activities such as reading (Csikszentmihalyi, 1990). However, because both

---

[*] Correspondence concerning this article should be addressed to Christian Swann, Tel. (+ 44) 1522 886030 or e-mail cswann@lincoln.ac.uk.

performance and experience are believed to be enhanced in flow (Jackson and Roberts, 1992), this area of research is particularly relevant in sport.

Csikszentmihalyi outlined nine different dimensions of flow, and it is the experiencing of several of these characteristics together that makes the flow experience so special (Jackson, 1996). Flow usually occurs in situations of *challenge-skills balance,* where one subjectively perceives that the situation he or she is in requires them to extend beyond their normal capabilities, but is still achievable. Hence they require specific, *clear goals* to strive to achieve, while also receiving *unambiguous feedback* that either informs them that they are progressing towards these goals or tells them how to adjust in order to do so. Therefore, the individual requires complete *concentration on the task at hand*, with no extraneous or distracting thoughts, which can also lead to *action-awareness merging*, whereby the person becomes totally absorbed or immersed in the activity. A *loss of self-consciousness* can also occur in the form of an absence of negative thoughts or doubt, as can a *sense of control* over the performance or outcome of the activity, and a *transformation of time*. The combination of these first eight dimensions makes the flow experience enjoyable and intrinsically rewarding, making up the ninth dimension which Csikszentmihalyi (1975) termed *autotelic experience.*

However, because flow is such a subjective experience, it is acknowledged as being difficult to accurately and reliably measure and no approach is trouble-free (Kimiecik and Jackson, 2002; Kimiecik and Stein, 1992). Approaches such as the Experience Sampling Method (Csikszentmihalyi and Larson, 1987) and the Flow Scale questionnaires (Jackson and Ecklund, 2004) have been noted as problematic to the exploration of flow states (see Kimiecik and Jackson, 2002; Kimiecik and Stein, 1992); however, the exploration of subjective experience lends itself to qualitative methods. A qualitative approach can provide important information regarding the subjective nature of flow experience and can overcome quantitative restraints, providing information, interpretation, and understanding of flow phenomena from an athlete's point of view (Stavrou, Jackson, Zervas, and Karteroliotis, 2007). Hence "valuable and often reliable information comes from athletes' subjective description and interpretations" (Chavez, 2008, p.72), and qualitative, open-ended interviews are the most widely used and appropriate method of exploring these elusive experiences (e.g., Chavez, 2008; Jackson, 1992, 1995, 1996; Sugiyama and Inomata, 2005).

This existing qualitative research on flow occurrence in sport has tended to explore the factors perceived to influence (i.e., facilitate, prevent, and disrupt) these states, as well as investigate their controllability (e.g., Chavez, 2008; Jackson, 1995, 1996). Elite athletes, defined by Jackson and Kimiecik (2008) as "those who participate in U.S. Division 1 collegiate sport or higher" (p. 508), have primarily been used because: (i) they have been involved in competitive situations for substantial amounts of time (Jackson, 1996); and (ii) are theoretically more likely to perform in states of automaticity without the need for conscious thought (Hatfield and Hillman, 2001), which may make it easier to become absorbed in the activity and experience flow. This means that elite athletes are likely to be more familiar with these experiences than recreational participants.

Furthermore, certain sports may be more conducive to flow than others: "a structured type of event, and one that is continuous in nature may facilitate flow, in comparison to more unstructured, stop-start events where there are potentially more uncontrollable factors for the athlete to deal with" (Jackson, Thomas, Marsh, and Smethurst, 2001, p.149). Hence, it could be the case that such stop-start sports are less conducive to flow than other sports, and that flow occurs differently in these sports than more structured events. However, existing research (e.g., Jackson, 1992, 1995; Chavez, 2008) has used athletes from sports that are faster and externally paced, and have not yet focused specifically on slower, self-paced sports (Singer, 2002). Previous literature has also tended to combine athletes from various team and individual sports in one sample (e.g., Chavez, 2008; Jackson, 1995, 1996; Russell, 2001), or combine athletes from different forms of one sport (e.g., singles and pairs athletes in Jackson, 1992; Young, 2000). Instead, a sample isolating one single context of athletes is likely to provide a more specific understanding of flow occurrence in that context, in turn providing athletes and coaches within that domain with more specific and relevant information.

One such self-paced sport from which it is possible to isolate a single context of athletes is golf. Elite golfers compete individually, and commonly in tournaments involving up to 150 players. This provides a suitable setting to gain potential access to a sample of players competing in the same sport and at the same level. It has also been suggested that the game of golf is heavily reliant on the mental and emotional control at the highest level, illustrated by the anecdotal quote: "Golf is "90% mental. The other 10% is mental" (Flick and Waggoner, 1997, p.43). This could be because of the self-paced nature of golf, which affords the player time for potential over-thinking, distraction, perceptions of inadequacy, overly elated emotions such as anxiety or fear of failure, and possibly even ironic processes (e.g., thinking about not hitting the ball in a bunker near the green while standing over the ball, and then doing just that; Singer, 2002). Therefore, golf is an interesting domain in which to study the occurrence of optimal psychological states such as flow.

Two empirical studies have been conducted in this area (Cohn, 1991; Catley and Duda, 1997). Cohn (1991) interviewed 19 competitive golfers ranging from NCAA Division 1 collegiate players to PGA Tour professionals about their peak performances, which he defined as a time when they were playing to the best of their ability and shot their best score. While some of the results resonated with dimensions of flow experiences (e.g., narrow focus, automatic and effortless performance, immersion, sense of control), differences between flow and peak performance have been suggested (see Jackson and Kimiecik, 2008; Jackson and Roberts, 1992). Therefore these results may be relevant to elite golfers, but do not focus explicitly on experiences of flow. Catley and Duda (1997) administered questionnaires to 163 recreational golfers in order to assess pre-round readiness variables and frequency and intensity of flow post-round. Results suggested that pre-round readiness was significantly related to the experience of flow, as was skill level. This suggests that elite participants are the most appropriate sample from whom to gain rich descriptions of flow experiences. It also appears that elite golf has not been explored previously in flow research, highlighting the need for an exploratory investigation to help establish an understanding of flow experiences in this domain.

Therefore, using qualitative, semi-structured interviews in order to gain rich accounts and insights, this study aimed to investigate the occurrence of flow specifically in elite golf, and explore whether flow could occur differently in golf than in the faster paced and more generic sports studied previously. Although it is acknowledged that flow research in sport needs to go beyond description of the elements of a flow experience and begin explaining the occurrence of these states (Kimiecik and Stein, 1992), this study also aimed to be exploratory in nature, intending only to establish a description rather than attempting to explain flow. In doing so, it followed the example of previous studies of flow in other elite sports (e.g., Jackson, 1992; Young, 2000). It is hoped that once this introductory understanding is established, future studies can build upon this and begin to investigate "the potential psychosocial mechanisms and variables that may be causally related, or, at the very least, positively or negatively associated with the flow experience" (Kimiecik and Stein, 1992, p.149).

METHOD

Participants

This sample included 13 male professional golfers from the Republic of Ireland, Northern Ireland, and England. These individuals had competed internationally in either European Tour ($n = 8$), Challenge Tour ($n = 4$), or Europro ($n = 1$) tournaments. The European Tour is the flagship professional golf tour in Europe, and one of the major tours worldwide, involving world-class playing standards and the highest level of competition; just below this standard is the Challenge Tour, a European-based developmental Tour used as a training ground for promotion to the European Tour (PGA European Tour, 2010); and the Europro Tour is another European-based developmental Tour that is used as a training ground for promotion to the Challenge Tour. These participants had a mean age of 33.5 years ($SD = 9.28$) ranging from 20 to 51 years, and mean of 11.8 years experience as a professional ($SD = 10.28$) with a range or 1 to 32 years.

Procedure

Ethical approval for the study was granted by the departmental ethics committee at a British university. Nine of the participants were approached at two Professional Golfer's Association (PGA) Irish Region pro-am tournaments, and were asked to take part in a study exploring the occurrence of flow in elite golf. This setting was chosen because it provided access to a large number of competitive professional golfers at the same time and in one location. Initially, one professional known to have competed on the European Tour was approached and agreed to take part. This process snowballed, and more participants were interviewed until a point was reached where no new information or themes were observed in the data (Lincoln and Guba, 1985). Hence, a mixture of purposive (Patton, 2002) and snowball sampling were used to obtain participants.

Due to this tournament setting, time spent with these players was limited and the interviews were kept purposeful and concise. In order to obtain more data, the other four participants in the sample (independent of these original interviews) later took part in member-checking discussions away from a tournament setting (see p. 9).

Interview Guide and Protocol

An interview guide was developed based on previous qualitative research on flow in sport (e.g., Chavez, 2008; Jackson, 1992, 1995; Russell, 2001), and pilot-tested on two amateur golfers with handicaps of one and three before the present sample was interviewed. The pilot study led to changes in the wording of questions, providing a clear explanation and definition of flow at the beginning, and expanding the scope of the interview from one isolated experience to the golfer's general experience of flow in golf in order to gather more data. This concise guide adopted a semi-structured, open-ended approach to ensure that sufficient relevant data could be collected through the use of further probing questions where necessary, while also permitting the participant to elaborate and develop areas of perceived importance (Patton, 2002). All participants gave written consent after the researcher explained the purpose of the study and asked for permission to audiotape the interview. The interviewee's age and number of years' experience as a professional was ascertained, before discussing the highest standard at which he had competed. Following explanation of the concept of flow as an experience that "felt like everything clicked into place on the golf course, or that you were playing on auto-pilot", the participants were asked to describe a performance in which they had one of these experiences. They were then asked three questions relating specifically to the occurrence of flow, in terms of what factors: (i) facilitate flow experiences, (ii) disrupt these states, and (iii) prevent flow from occurring more often. Finally, the interviewees were asked to discuss whether or not they perceived flow to be a controllable state. The interviews were conducted face to face; were digitally recorded, while brief notes were also taken; ranged between 8 and 25 minutes ($M = 14.22$, $SD = 5.33$); and were later transcribed verbatim. Following this, member checking (Lincoln and Guba, 1985) was conducted in order to increase trustworthiness. This process involves taking data and interpretations back to the participants so that they can confirm the credibility of the information by asking if the themes or categories make sense, whether they are developed with sufficient evidence, and whether the overall account is realistic and accurate (Creswell and Miller, 2000). Member checking took place in two stages: first, the transcripts and a copy of the results were returned to the original nine interviewees for verification. None of these golfers reported any problems, and deemed the transcripts to be an accurate reflection of the interviews that took place. Second, follow-up member checking discussions were conducted with the other four participants, and there was no disagreement between these discussions and the data originally obtained.

Analysis

The investigator was sensitised to the game of golf through a number of years' experience at a relatively high amateur standard, and was hence familiar with the terminology used by these participants. This author was most familiar with the data and conducted an exploratory analysis, reading the transcripts and recording the in-vivo codes, before using open then axial coding (Strauss and Corbin, 1998) to establish salient *concepts*, and integrating these around core *categories*. In order to increase trustworthiness, a process of establishing inter-rater reliability was undertaken. This involves giving the same data to a number of analysts and asking them to analyse the data according to an agreed set of categories (Silverman, 2001). In the present study, the second and fourth authors separately and independently analysed the transcripts and generated codes, concepts, and categories in order to establish inter-rater reliability. There was a high level of agreement between all analyses, and where differences emerged, these were discussed and clarified in accordance with Silverman (2001). After this initial analysis was compiled, it was given to the third author (independent to the data until this point) for subsequent analysis, who provided feedback relating to the coding and labelling of concepts and categories.

RESULTS

Data are presented in terms of the categories that (i) facilitate, (ii) prevent, and (iii) disrupt flow occurrence, as well as (iv) the controllability of these experiences, as perceived by elite golfers. In line with recommendations for qualitative research, quotes are used in order to let the participants' voices emerge and describe these experiences through the eyes of the elite golfer (Silverman, 2001). Each participant will be referred to by a pseudonym randomly chosen and assigned by the investigator.

Golfers' Descriptions of Flow

Participants provided rich insights into their experiences of flow in elite golf. Rory described flow as "basically a state of mind where nothing can go wrong. You're just comfortable in everything you're doing, and you think you can't wait to go and play the next shot, and just everything comes very easily." This alluded to a sense of automaticity that other researchers have associated with flow (e.g., Canham and Wiley, 2003), which Luke also referred to: "You don't think about anything at all, you just kind of play golf. You get your yardage, you aim and that's it. You're sensing what to do with the putts, not thinking it." This sensory element was further illustrated by Paul;

> I could just see the ball, you know I had great visualisation on it. I could hear the ball hit the bottom of the hole, I could hear it coming off the putter, I could nearly hear it scraping across the grass…it was really, really like, magnified to me.

These responses resonate strongly with Csikszentmihalyi's flow theory, suggesting that this sample of elite golfers were aware of, and had experienced, flow states.

Factors Influencing Flow Occurrence

Emerging from the analysis were eleven facilitators, six preventers, and four disruptors of flow for this sample of elite golfers; these are presented in Tables 1, 2, and 3, as well as the number of interviewees reporting each category.

This section is structured around these tables: the categories are discussed below in relation to the concepts from which they are comprised.

Factors Facilitating Flow Occurrence

Motivation to perform related to the players' desire to perform well or achieve their goals in the event they were about to compete in. Events that challenged them more than normal were particularly facilitative, as discussed by Luke: "the bigger the competition for me, the more immersed you get."

Effective preparation was an important facilitator of flow, as illustrated by Oliver, who noted that "performance is always reflected in the practice…the zone is really just a reflection how your preparation has been." Such preparation was physical and mental in nature, while efficient organisation in terms of planning and scheduling helped prevent fatigue and burn-out.

Table 1. Factors found to facilitate flow

Concepts	Categories	Number of participants
Bigger competition Personal challenges/negative motivation Motivating self talk	Motivation to perform	4
Pre-round preparation Golf-specific practice/preparation Mental preparation Efficient organisation Practice for tension/pressure Form/recent success	Effective preparation	7
Heightened focus and concentration Focus on present and immediate future Lack of extraneous thought	Appropriate focus	9
Enjoyment Mentally positive Rhythm/tempo Comfort zone	Positive state	6
Surrender/letting go Confidence Trust/belief in self Acceptance Sense of freedom	Letting it happen	6
Positive self talk Breathing exercises Visualisation	Psychological interventions	5
Comfortable in personal life Comfortable in surroundings Positive perception of the course or conditions	Optimal environmental and situational conditions	3
Adrenaline Feeding off nerves Calm/relaxed	Optimal arousal	3
Hydration Snacking	Maintenance of physical state	2
Pre-shot routine Physical cues Target oriented focus Commitment to the shot/confidence in shot selection Pre-shot visualisation Pre-shot self-talk	Pre-shot routine	7
Playing well Hitting good shots Swinging well Momentum	Playing well	7

Table 2. Factors found to prevent flow

Concepts	Category	Number of participants
Non-optimal playing conditions Problems in personal life Organisational stressors Playing partners Opposition Negative perception of the place/course	Non-optimal environmental and situational conditions	6
Lack of practice/preparation Rushing preparation Physical problems	Non-optimal preparation and readiness	6
Lack of confidence/self-belief Anxiety Negative attitude Fear/worry	Negative state	5
Mind drifting Lack of focus Inappropriate thinking	Lack of, or inappropriate, focus	5
Excessive motivation Lack of motivation	Non-optimal motivation	3
Getting off to a bad start Not performing as well as you could	Not playing well	3

Table 3. Factors found to disrupt flow

Concepts	Category	Number of participants
Inconsistent weather Stoppage in play Change in pace of play Distracting interactions with others "Normal" distractions Don't like the shot shape or hole Bad Luck	Non-optimal environmental and situational conditions	5
Loss of focus Awareness of the situation Negative focus	Loss of, or inappropriate, focus	4
Fear/worry Anxiety Loss of self-belief	Negative state	3
Feeling uncomfortable about hitting it Not committing to the shot Rushing the shot Getting out of routine	Hitting bad shots	3

Appropriate focus represented a state of heightened but specific focus, in which the player is concentrating in the moment and on the task at hand. James discussed the influence of this factor, and perceived a close relationship between focus and being in flow: "When I'm really focused that makes it easy to get in the zone. To me there's not much difference between being really focused and in the zone." The concept of process or task focus also appears to revolve around the next shot these golfers face, as described by Nick: "I never ever think about the previous shot I've hit, whether it be good or bad...the next shot is the most important shot."

Positive state referred to the positive, enjoyable, and harmonious characteristics associated with flow, as Matt illustrated: "That's definitely when I play my best...when I'm perfectly happy on the course...I'm just enjoying being there". Other golfers referred to being "comfortable" or in a "comfort zone."

Letting it happen relates to the paradoxical nature of flow, and was illustrated by Oliver: "Because you're not looking for (flow) you're more likely to make it happen", and Jack: "When you're in the zone just let it happen, don't try to fight it or rush it, just go with the flow." With this comes a sense of freedom in terms of playing and swinging freely, and an element of acceptance in that bad shots don't matter as much and are much easier to recover from when in flow.

Psychological interventions referred to techniques or exercises that these players used to maintain an optimal state during the period between shots, when distractions or disrupting influences were likely to occur. Hence this category appears to be a golf-specific difference due to the nature of golf. These interventions were generally used to reduce tension and maintain concentration, and included positive self-talk and visualisation, while breathing exercises were used most widely used. These involved slow, deep, diaphragmatic breathing, the importance of which, were discussed by Jack: "It's impossible to be nervous when you're breathing correctly...when you're breathing correctly you're in a relaxed state of mind."

Optimal environmental and situational conditions referred to elements outside of the actual performance that were favourable for the athlete, and in turn facilitated flow. These could be outside of golf, such as their personal life: "If everything else is comfortable, like your family, whatever, money wise, then I think it's a lot easier to get in the zone" (Rory). Being comfortable in your surroundings was also facilitative, such as returning to a place or course that you like or have played well on before. Or if the player has been used to tougher conditions, a perception that the present course or conditions are easier can lead to a sense of positivity, and similarly facilitate flow.

Optimal arousal varied depending on the golfers' individual differences, and was hence very personal. For some, a more energised state involving adrenaline, and feeding off nerves facilitated flow, relating to optimal motivation/challenge in that "you have to be nervous to get in the zone" (James). For others, a more calm/relaxed state facilitated flow, e.g. Luke, who said that "when I find I'm relaxed I find it much easier."

Maintenance of physical state was comprised of the concepts snacking and hydration, which enabled these participants to function properly throughout their rounds, which can last up to five or even six hours at the elite level. For example, Luke stated that "just being hydrated enough helps...if I'm not, I tend to find (that) physically I get tired or just lose focus a little bit." Again, this was a golf-specific difference due to the nature of golf.

Pre-shot routine described the process through which these golfers execute each shot, which appeared to help the player get into an optimal frame of mind immediately prior to and during the execution of the shot. The link between these pre-shot routines and flow was described by Paul: "The pre-shot routine for me is what triggers (flow)…the one thing that allows you to get into that frame of mind."

These routines were also very individual: for some, triggers or physical cues were used to start their routines: "anything to say 'show time'" (Oliver); while a narrow, specific focus on the target was also important, illustrated by Luke: "When I feel like I'm in the zone…all I think about when I'm hitting the shot is "target"…I can kind of picture the shot before I hit it, and then all you have to do is aim." Most of these golfers also referred to pre-shot visualisation, in being able to picture the shot before they hit it, while pre-shot positive self talk was also an important factor for some players. A final concept was that of committing to the shot and being absolutely certain about the shot they want to hit before beginning their routine.

Playing well described the players' awareness that their overall performance was going to plan and they were on track to achieve their goals. The concepts of swinging well and hitting good shots helped the players feel like they were performing well, and in turn facilitated flow. Some players also discussed a link between psychological momentum and flow. For example, Matt described that if you "start to hit good shots that drags you into the zone", and Oliver discussed that "you do get absorbed in the moment, you get competitive and momentum builds."

Factors Preventing Flow Occurrence

Non-optimal environmental and situational conditions referred to interfering elements outside of the golfer's control. Non-optimal playing conditions could prevent flow, either through tough weather or course-set up, as could a negative perception of the place or course, particularly if the player hasn't played well there previously. For some golfers, competing against better opposition could prevent flow by distracting them from their own performance and focusing more on the presence of these competitors. Similarly, playing partners were also reported as being able to prevent flow experiences, especially those in pro-am tournaments such as amateurs and high-handicappers. Non golf-related factors could also prevent flow, including problems in your personal life (e.g., breaking up from a long-term relationship), or organisational stressors (e.g., doing a lot of travelling or having another job, such as coaching) that take time and focus away from golf.

Non-optimal preparation and readiness captured two subcategories; first, *lack of practice/preparation*: "Fail to prepare, prepare to fail, right? If you're not (prepared)…you're on the golf course and it might take you a couple of holes to get basically where you should be…it could be gone at that stage" (Jack). Similarly, *rushing preparation* was reported to have a preventative effect, and *physical problems* such as lethargy, illness or fatigue were also reported to prevent flow experience.

Negative state, comprising of *lack of confidence/self-belief, anxiety, negative attitude,* and *fear/worry*, also prevented flow from occurring. This category was summarised by Matt: "If you're worried about failing, or worried about what other people think, or worried about succeeding…whatever you're afraid about, if you let that affect your performance then you're not playing to your full ability."

Lack of, or inappropriate, focus contained the themes *mind drifting*, *not being focused*, and *inappropriate thinking*. Participants mentioned both over-analytical and negative thinking as being able to prevent their flow experiences, illustrated by Nick's quote that:

> (if) your second shot is a 3 iron to a green that has water all the way around it, or a green that has out of bounds right and left and long, and bunkers everywhere, it's very difficult not to think about the trouble.

Non-optimal motivation combined concepts of either a *lack of motivation* or *excessive motivation*. Some golfers discussed that a lack of nerves or challenge prevented their flow experiences, while others talked about 'forcing it' and trying too hard, as Jack discussed: "you're never in the flow when you're forcing it".

Not playing well referred to the players' performance being below the standard required for them to achieve their goals in that event. This suggests that it is difficult or impossible to get into flow while performing badly, which is perhaps unsurprising considering the link between flow and peak performance.

Factors Disrupting Flow Experience

Non-optimal environmental and situational conditions referred to factors external to the golfer that interrupted their experiences, and included concepts such as *inconsistent weather* in terms of wind and rain, and *change in pace of play* (e.g., rushing). Stoppages in play were discussed as being particularly disruptive:

> you're leading a tournament, you're in the zone, you're focused, and all of a sudden...it's called off for a period of time, then your mind starts to go again. You've lost your focus, you've lost your zone. So I think a stoppage in play (is) a nightmare (James).

Furthermore, other golfers noted that coming across a shot or hole that they disliked could affect their focus and disrupt flow, as could *"normal" distractions* (such as sudden noises), *distracting interactions with others*, and *bad luck*. The concepts in this category disrupted flow by distracting the player from the task at hand.

Loss of, or inappropriate, focus also disrupted flow experiences for these golfers, and could occur relatively easily, as Paul described: "your head drifts to a lot of different places because you have so much time." *Becoming aware of the situation* was also a disrupting theme that caused the players to realise how well they were performing and lose focus on the task at hand (e.g. by thinking ahead to outcomes of the performance). Luke also discussed the effects of *negative focus* in terms of seeing the danger on holes: "If you kind of see danger you start focusing on that...and it's harder to focus on the target." This category relates to focusing on variables irrelevant from the task at hand, which could then lead to playing the next shot badly.

Negative state referred to negative thoughts and feelings that could occur during the flow or over a shot, which then disrupted the experience, including the concepts *fear/worry*, *anxiety*, and *loss of self-belief*. This factor could be caused by other disrupting influences (e.g., inappropriate focus) or could be related to the situation that the player is in (e.g., the last hole in a tournament) as Oliver noted: "sometimes we cannot trust. It's the biggest contradiction in golf. Like the 18th, I hit it out of bounds yesterday. The very time you should be standing there trusting yourself, you cannot do it."

Hitting bad shots described the (flawed) process that the golfer goes through in performing the shot, and combined concepts of *feeling uncomfortable about hitting it, not committing to the shot, rushing the shot,* and *getting out of routine.* These processes could then result in negative outcomes for that shot (e.g., finishing in a difficult position such as a bunker), in turn leading to negative emotions (e.g., anger), which the player may struggle to recover from. This can then disrupt flow.

Controllability of Flow

Four of these elite golfers (Oliver, Alex, Rory, Luke) explicitly stated that they perceived flow to be controllable, providing responses such as: "I would think you could help induce it" (Oliver). The other five participants alluded to similar control: James suggested that "I think you can practice and improve it" through exercises designed to increase focus, and motivational talks; Matt believed that "it's definitely possible to intervene"; Paul felt that he would be able to control flow "if I was conditioned from a younger age"; Jack suggested that breathing exercises and effective use of psychology could help; while Nick believed flow could be controlled, "but the only way to do that is by winning." These perceptions were, once again, highly individual.

Negative Flow

Emerging from the data was a concept of "negative flow" opposite to the optimal experience, which two golfers alluded to: Rory noted that "you always get into a rhythm when you're on the golf course, whether it be a bad or a good one"; and Jack reported that "you could start off with 3 bogeys or something and all of a sudden that's the flow you're in then...you're on the back foot straight away" and on certain occasions "people know that "oh this is going to be a struggle"...negative flow starts going, and all of a sudden (the performance) goes the other way."

DISCUSSION

This study aimed to establish a description of how flow occurred within a sample of elite golfers, and suggest whether flow may occur differently in golf than in previously researched sports due to golf's self-paced nature. While explicit comparison is difficult because each previous study has presented and labelled their findings differently, the main concepts found to influence flow in elite sport thus far relate to preparation, mental attitude, focus, motivation, arousal, and environmental and situational conditions (Jackson, 1992, 1995; Young, 2000; Sugiyama and Inomata, 2005; Chavez, 2008). These were also found in the present study, which suggests there are similarities between the occurrence of flow for these elite golfers and the previously researched sports. Similarly, these findings suggest that this sample of golfers perceived flow to be at least potentially controllable, as has been the case with previous research (e.g., Chavez, 2008; Jackson, 1995; Sugiyama and Inomata, 2005).

However, a number of differences were also apparent within this sample. The use of pre-shot or pre-task routines does not appear in extant literature exploring flow in elite sport. These routines helped these golfers achieve an optimal internal state prior to performing each shot, and were perceived by the golfers to be an important facilitator of flow, a suggestion supporting that of Singer (2002). This sample also reported that hitting good shots, playing well and momentum facilitated the occurrence of flow. Due to the period of time between shots, it could be the case that flow occurrence is linked to a build up of momentum in golf. Singer (2002) supports this link by proposing that pre-shot routines are immediately followed by evaluation and feedback, that then leads back into preparation for the next shot, and hence there is a cyclical element within the use of pre-shot routines that could build momentum. Landsberger and Beauchamp (1999) attempted to establish indicators of performance momentum during a competitive round of golf using a system that quantified momentum gains and losses relative to expectations for each stroke and hole. Although they made no link to flow, such a system could be useful for exploring the relationship between flow and momentum in future research.

Situational conditions outside of golf influenced flow occurrence for these athletes, which does not appear to have been reported by existing literature. This finding also differs from Kimiecik and Stein's (1992) Person x Situation Flow Framework which suggested that only situational factors within sport could influence flow. This could be a golf-specific difference in how flow occurs possibly due to the lengthy periods between shots, during which players have time to dwell on these situational conditions (e.g., problems in their personal life). This is less likely to be the case in more reactive, externally paced sports.

The discussion of a "negative flow" by some of these participants also raised questions. Csikszentmihalyi (1990) has discussed *psychic entropy* as an antithesis of flow, "a disorganisation of the self that impairs its effectiveness…(which) can weaken the self to the point that it is no longer able to invest attention and pursue its goals" (p.37). While extensive research has been conducted on negative aspects of experience within sport, such as anxiety, burnout, and stress (Jackson, 1992), it does not appear that any has focused on the most negative states experienced by athletes during performance. Therefore, future studies could begin investigating if, and how, psychic entropy or "negative flow" is experienced in sport, and whether it relates only to golf or other sports as well.

Another suggestion was that of hydration and snacking in order to maintain energy and concentration levels, which has also been identified in previous physiology literature. For example, Smith (2010) discussed that "the onset of mental and physical fatigue through inadequate and/or inappropriate dietary practices will have a significant impact on the player's ability during performance" (p. 643). Therefore it appears to be logical that sufficient energy levels could have an impact on flow states in golf. The use of psychological interventions between shots to help maintain an optimal mental and physiological state was also reported, including self-talk, visualisation, and breathing exercises. These abdominal breathing exercises discussed by the players resonate with centering (e.g., Haddad and Tremayne, 2009), which has been reported to yield physical balance, help the individual to focus prior to a task, and help control physiological arousal (Nideffer, 1994; Nideffer and Sagal, 2006). It seems reasonable that such exercises could be beneficial to golf performance and flow states, and these links should be explored in future. These could all be golf-specific differences due to the time available between shots, which is not the case in the previously researched sports.

Applied Recommendations

Similar to those of Jackson (1992) and Young (2000), applied recommendations for athletes, coaches, and practitioners revolve around putting relevant factors in place to improve the likelihood of flow occurring for golfers. This involves: (i) the promotion of controllable facilitators, (ii) negating controllable preventers and disruptors, and (iii) the practicing of re-focusing strategies to overcome any distractions that may occur.

Setting challenging but achievable goals for an event is one way that the athlete can achieve optimal motivation. These, combined with effective physical and mental preparation, could facilitate challenge-skills balance whereby athletes enter the event believing that they can achieve their goals if they perform at the best of their ability. During the event, the use of psychological skills are encouraged to help the athlete maintain an optimal internal state, particularly between shots; as are snacking and hydration, in order to help the golfer maintain energy and concentration levels throughout the round. Golfers are also advised to employ individualised pre-shot routines. These should foster external focus on the target (Bell and Hardy, 2009), and could use physical cues or triggers, visualisation and self talk, essentially aiming to help golfers feel completely confident and focused before they hit each shot.

Following these recommendations should help minimise controllable preventing and disrupting categories, such as non-optimal preparation and readiness, non-optimal motivation, and ineffective execution of the shot. However, golfers are also advised to develop re-focusing strategies in order to cope with any distractions that do arise prior to or during the event; Orlick's (2007) recommendations for distraction control would be especially useful in this regard. These golf-specific data and recommendations may be useful for golfers, coaches, and psychologists to help prepare in ways that could increase the likelihood of experiencing flow.

This study aimed to introduce the concept of flow to elite golf. Findings suggest that flow may occur slightly differently for this sample of elite golfers than has been the case for previously researched sports. However, it should be noted that these findings are only discussed in relation to this sample and the methods used in the present study, and that they do not suggest causality. If the results of this study do generalise to elite golf in general then future research could conduct similar studies with different samples. For example, all of the participants in this study were male, and further research could explore and compare the flow experiences of female professional golfers. Furthermore, the eight players from this sample who had competed on the European Tour did so only on certain occasions (e.g., via invitation).

This means that although the golfers in the present study were elite, they did not perform regularly at the highest level possible and there could be differences between these professionals and more elite, full-time members of the European Tour. Therefore further research should seek to explore the flow experiences of full-time European Tour players, and could provide insight into flow at the very highest level of the game (e.g., winning European Tour tournaments) and add richer data to that of the present study (e.g., in terms of possible controllability of flow). Similarly, such an exploration could highlight similarities and differences between flow experiences at each level, and could therefore provide applied recommendations relevant for professional or elite-amateur golfers aiming to reach the European Tour.

REFERENCES

Bell, J. J., and Hardy, J. (2009). Effects of attentional focus on skilled performance in golf. *Journal of Applied Sport Psychology, 21*, 163-177.

Canham, M., and Wiley, J. (2003). When time flies: Effects of skilled memory on time transformation in rock climbers. *International Journal of Cognitive Technology, 8*, 26-34.

Catley, D., and Duda, J. (1997). Psychological antecedents of the frequency and intensity of flow in golfers. *International Journal of Sport Psychology, 28*, 309-322.

Chavez, E. J. (2008). Flow in sport: A study of college athletes. *Imagination, Cognition and Personality, 28*, 69-91.

Cohn, P. J. (1991). An exploratory study on peak performance in golf. *TheSport Psychologist, 5*, 1-14.

Creswell, J. W., and Miller, D. L. (2000). Determining validity in qualitative inquiry. *Theory into Practice, 39*, 124-130.

Csikszentmihalyi, M. (1975). *Beyond boredom and anxiety.* San Francisco: Jossey-Bass.

Csikszentmihalyi, M. (1990). *Flow: The psychology of optimal experience.* New York: Harper and Row.

Csikszentmihalyi, M., and Larson, R. (1987). Validity and reliability of the Experience-Sampling Method. *Journal of Youth and Adolescence, 6*, 281-294.

Flick, J., and Waggoner, G. (1997). *On golf: Lessons from America's master teacher.* New York, NY: Villard.

Haddad, K., and Tremayne, P. (2009). The effects of centering on free-throw shooting performance of young athletes. *Sport Psychologist, 23*, 118-136.

Hatfield, B.D., and Hillman, C.H. (2001). The psychophysiology of sport: A mechanistic understanding of the psychology of superior performance. In R. N. Singer, H. A. Hausenblas, and C. M. Janelle (Eds.), *Handbook of sport psychology* (pp. 362-386). New York: Wiley.

Jackson, S. (1992). Athletes in flow: A qualitative investigation of flow states in elite figure skaters. *Journal of Applied Sport Psychology, 4*, 161-180.

Jackson, S. (1995). Factors influencing the occurrence of flow state in elite athletes. *Journal of Applied Sport Psychology, 7*, 138-166.

Jackson, S. (1996). Toward a conceptual understanding of the flow experience in elite athletes. *Research Quarterly for Exercise and Sport, 67*, 76-90.

Jackson, S. A., and Ecklund, R. C. (2004). *The Flow Scales Manual.* Morganstown, WV: Fitness Information Technology.

Jackson, S. A., and Kimiecik, J. (2008). The flow perspective of optimal experience in sport and physical activity. In T. Horn (Ed.), *Advances in sport and exercise psychology* (3rd ed., pp. 377-399). Champaign, IL: Human Kinetics.

Jackson, S., and Roberts, G. (1992). Positive performance state of athletes: Towards a conceptual understanding of peak performance. *Sport Psychologist, 6*, 156-171.

Jackson, S. A., Thomas, P. R., Marsh, H. W., and Smethurst, C. J. (2001). Relationships between flow, self-concept, psychological skills, and performance. *Journal of Applied Sport Psychology, 13*, 201-220.

Kimiecik, J., and Jackson, S.A. (2002). Optimal experience in sport: A flow perspective. In T. Horn (Ed.), *Advances in sport psychology* (2nd ed., pp. 501-527). Champaign, IL: Human Kinetics.

Kimiecik, J. C., and Stein, G. L. (1992). Examining flow experiences in sport contexts: Contextual issues and methodological concerns. *Journal of Applied Sport Psychology, 4*, 144-160.

Landsberger, L. M., and Beauchamp, P. H. (1999). Indicators of performance momentum in competitive golf: An exploratory study. In M.R. Farrally and A.J. Cochran (Eds.), *Science and golf III: Proceedings of the 1998 World Scientific Congress of Golf* (pp. 353-361). Champaign, IL: Human Kinetics.

Lincoln, Y. S., and Guba, E. G. (1985). *Naturalistic inquiry*. Newbury Park: Sage.

Nideffer, R.M. (1994). *Psyched to win*. Champaign, IL: Leisure Press.

Nideffer, R.M., and Sagal, M-S. (2006). Concentration and attention control training. In J. Williams (Ed.), *Applied Psychology: Personal growth to peak performance* (5th ed., pp. 382–403). New York: McGraw-Hill.

Orlick, T. (2007). *In pursuit of excellence* (4th ed.). Champaign, IL: Human Kinetics.

Patton, M. (2002). *Qualitative research and evaluation methods*. Newbury Park: Sage.

Russell, W. D. (2001). An examination of flow state occurrences in college athletes. *Journal of Sport Behaviour, 24*, 83-107.

Silverman, D. (2001). *Interpreting qualitative data: Methods for analysing text, talk and interaction,* (2nd Ed.). London: Sage.

Singer, R. N. (2002). Preperformance state, routines and automaticity: What does it take to realise expertise in self-paced events? *Journal of Sport and Exercise Psychology, 24*, 359-375.

Smith, M. F. (2010). The role of physiology in the development of golf performance. *Sports Medicine, 40*, 635-652.

Stavrou, N. A., Jackson, S.A., Zervas, Y., and Karteroliotis, K. (2007). Flow experience and athletes' performance with reference to the orthogonal model of flow. *The Sport Psychologist, 21*, 438-457.

Strauss, A., and Corbin, J. (1998). *Basics of qualitative research*. London: Sage.

Sugiyama, T., and Inomata, K. (2005). Qualitative examination of flow experience among top Japanese athletes. *Perceptual and Motor Skills, 100*, 969-982.

The European Tour. (n.d.). Retrieved May 17, 2011 from The PGA European Tour website, http://www.europeantour.com.

Young, J. A. (2000). Professional tennis players in the zone. In S. J. Haake, and A. Coe (Eds.), *Tennis science and technology* (pp. 417-422). Malden, MA: Blackwell Science.

In: Athletic Insight's Writings of 2012
Editor: Robert Schinke

ISBN: 978-1-62618-120-5

Chapter 13

CAN ANGER AND TENSION BE HELPFUL? EMOTIONS ASSOCIATED WITH OPTIMAL PERFORMANCE

Andrew M. Lane, Tracey J. Devonport and Chris J. Beedie
University of Wolverhampton, UK

ABSTRACT

Evidence suggests athletes will try to regulate pre-competition emotions to a state that helps goal pursuit (Hanin, 2003) and supposedly unpleasant emotions such as anger and tension have been found to associate with successful performance. The present study focused on emotional states associated with optimal performance. Male athletes (N = 222) were asked to recall an optimal sport performance and then completed the Brunel Mood Scale (Terry, Lane, and Fogarty, 2003) to assess pre-competition emotion. Emotion data were dichotomized into either a depression group (that is whether participants reported a score of 1 or more for either confusion or depression on the BRUMS) or no-symptoms of depression group (a score of zero for confusion and depression, see Lane and Terry, 2000). Results indicated participants in the depression group reported high scores of anger and tension and lower scores of pleasant emotions. Among such participants, happiness inversely related to tension. By contrast, among the no symptoms of unpleasant emotions group, participants reported higher scores of calmness, happiness, and vigor along with lower scores of anger and tension. Among such participants, happiness correlated positively with anger and tension, a finding. Findings lend support to the notion that.

Keywords: Emotions, performance, self-regulation, belief, mood, psychological skills

INTRODUCTION

The importance athletes tend to place in success coupled with the uncertainty of the outcome means athlete's typically experience strong emotions before competition (Lazarus, 2000). Relationships between emotion and performance have been frequently investigated in sport psychology (see Beedie, Terry, and Lane, 2000; Hanin, 2010; Lane, 2007). Studies tend to show that pleasant emotions such as happiness and vigor associate with successful performance, and unpleasant emotions such as anger, anxiety, and depression associate with unsuccessful performance (Lane, 2007; Hanin, 2010). The implication of these findings for practitioners is that interventions should be designed to increase pleasant emotions and reduce unpleasant emotions. However, a growing amount of evidence points to the potentially beneficial effects of unpleasant emotions, particularly high-activation emotions such as anger and anxiety (Beedie et al., 2000; Hanin, 2010). Given that sport psychology practitioners focus a great deal of their efforts in helping athletes prepare for competition, examination of the nature of supposedly unpleasant emotions associated with optimal performance represents a worthwhile line of enquiry. In the present study, we focused on anger and tension and their relationship with other emotions.

In terms of explanations for the switching effect for emotion-performance relationships, Hanin (2010) argued that individuals learn from their emotional experiences and develop meta-beliefs. If a person performed successfully when feeling angry, then a connection is made between high anger and successful performance. Recent research has found that an individual will try to generate supposedly unpleasant emotions[1] if he perceives that these emotions generate appropriate action tendencies (Tamir, Mitchell, and Gross, 2008; Davis, Woodman, and Callow, 2010). Tamir et al. argued that an individual will tolerate experiencing unpleasant emotions in the short-term if he believes that they help attain personally important goals. If an individual wants to perform well in future competition, he will not only accept these feelings as a necessary part of goal pursuit, but is likely to be happy at the fact that he is experiencing them.

Lazarus (2000) argued that it is important to look at the core relational theme related to each emotion when examining its relationship with performance. Anxiety has a core relational theme of "facing uncertain, existential threat" and the theme for anger is 'an offense and me and mine' (p.234). Sports competition is not only inherently uncertain, meaning it can trigger anxiety, but also has numerous factors that could increase anger. For example, an athlete cannot be certain how well he will perform until the competition starts, even if he is highly confident beforehand. Equally, he cannot be certain about the difficulty of a innumerable situational factors including the relatively difficulty of the competition, whether the course/conditions are suitable and so on. There are a multitude of factors that the athlete can plan to control but until competition starts these factors remain as estimate. If an athlete experiences anger and anxiety before competition, these emotions serve to inform the athlete that he needs to attend to factors that might threaten successful performance; in short, the

---

[1] The notion that athletes will seek to increase the intensity of supposedly unpleasant emotions to produce a positive outcome seems to be a contradiction in terms (i.e., something described as unpleasant can also be pleasant). However, if an emotion labeled as unpleasant associates with a positive outcome, such as successful goal attainment, then it is possible that the individual will find experiencing the emotion in that situation can yield a pleasant experience. We argue that the terms "pleasant" and "unpleasant" are preferable to the terms "positive" and "negative" as the former describe feelings, whereas the latter also imply some outcome of those feelings.

above emotions increase arousal and concentration narrows accordingly (Easterbrook, 1959). Therefore, it follows that if feelings anger or anxiety prompt a person to increase effort, and if this response helps goal achievement, the person develops a sense of happiness through anticipatory goal attainment. Lazarus (2000, p.234) proposed that pleasantly toned emotions can accompany stressful events in certain situations.

Lane and Terry (2000) proposed that it is the interaction between emotions that is important for determining whether emotions such as anger and tension are helpful or harmful to performance. Specifically, Lane and Terry suggested that it is the interaction between anger, tension and other unpleasant emotions (such as confusion and depression) that influence whether such emotions are helpful or unhelpful for performance. Lane and Terry contend that anger and tension could associate with motivated behavior when coupled with pleasant emotions such as vigor and moreover, are experienced independently of other unpleasant emotions such as confusion and depression. They argued that anger and tension tend to be associated with poor performance when coupled with anemotion such asdepression (see Lane, Beedie, and Stevens, 2005; Lane, 2007). It is suggested that when experienced independently of depression, anger and tension act as a warning signal to increase effort and mobilize personal resources in order to cope with the demands of the task. By contrast, when experienced with depression, anger and tension are associated with a number of other unpleasant emotions such as increased fatigue and confusion, along with unpleasant cognitions including low self-confidence (Lane, 2001). As Lane and Terry used the Profile of Mood States (POMS: McNair, Lorr, and Droppleman, 1971) which assesses anger, confusion, depression, fatigue tension and vigor, a limitation of their work is that the full range of pleasant emotions has not been investigated. Lane (2007) proposed that future research should look at the role of positive emotions, particularly happiness, when exploring relationships between anger and performance or between tension and performance. It should be noted that Lane and Terry suggested that distinctions between mood and emotion tend to blur when examining psychological states experienced immediately before competition (see Lane et al., 2005). From a measurement perspective, single-adjective checklists where the participant is asked to report how he is feeling right now cannot distinguish mood from emotion (see Lane, 2007).

Given evidence presented above, it is clear that emotions such as anger and anxiety can be helpful for performance. However, the emotional profile experienced by athletes when this effect occurs is less clear. In the present study, we use Lane and Terry's (2000) model that divides participants into either a no-depression or depression group to investigate interactions among discrete emotions. Specifically, we are interested in relationships between high activation emotions (anger and tension) with vigor (pleasantly oriented high activation emotions) and low activation pleasant emotions (happiness and calmness). Consistent with the terminology used by Lane and Terry, we use the term depression and no-depression group. A feature of research that has tested their model is the explanation that the term depression is used to describe an emotional or mood state rather than a clinical condition (see Lane, 2007 for a more detailed explanation).

METHOD

Participants

Participants were 222 volunteer male athletes (Age: $M = 20.24$, $SD = 2.51$) who were heterogeneous in terms of previous sporting experience and the level of competition, with some athletes having competed internationally, others recreationally. The majority of athletes competed at club level. Evidence shows that athletes across the full range of ability experience unpleasant emotions before competition (Terry and Lane, 2000). As studies have shown gender differences in emotions such as anxiety (Perry and Williams, 1998; Pieter and Pieter, 2008), the sample was delimited to male athletes only to control the possible confounding effects of gender.

MEASURES

Brunel Mood Scale-32 (BRUMS-32). Emotions associated with optimal performance was assessed using the Brunel Mood Scale-32 (BRUMS-32) recently developed from two previously validated scales (Matthews, Jones, and Chamberlain, 1990; Terry, Lane, and Fogarty, 2003). The original Brunel Mood Scale (Terry, Lane, Lane, and Keohane, 1999) is a 24-item mood state scale based on the Profile of Mood States (POMS: McNair et al., 1971). The BRUMS assesses the mood states of anger, confusion, depression, fatigue, tension, and vigor. The current 32-item scale was formed by adding items that assess the subscales of happiness and calmness from the University of Wales Institute of Science and Technology (UWIST) Mood Adjective Checklist (Matthews et al., 1990) to the 24-items from the BRUMS. The argument for including a greater number of pleasant states was in response to the frequently cited limitation that the POMS has an excessive focus on unpleasant states. To this end, it has been suggested that positive emotion dimensions, such as happiness and calmness, may also influence performance (Hanin, 2000). With the addition of the two new subscales, the BRUMS-32 is proposed to provide a more balanced assessment of pleasant and unpleasant emotions.

Each of the eight subscales within the BRUMS-32 has four items. Examples of Anger items include 'Annoyed' and 'Bitter'; Confusion items include 'Muddled' and 'Confused'; Depression items include 'Miserable' and 'Unhappy'; Fatigue items include 'Exhausted' and 'Sleepy'; Tension items include 'Nervous' and 'Worried'; and Vigor items include 'Active' and 'Lively'. Calmness items include 'Restful' and 'Composed' and Happiness items include 'Contented' and 'Satisfied'. All items within the BRUMS-32 are rated on a 5-point Likert scale (a response of 0 =not at all and 4 = extremely). Alpha coefficients for each subscale in the present study were over .70.

Depression and No-Depression Groups

To investigate interactions between tension and anger with other unpleasant emotions, data were dichotomized into two groups. Previous research has dichotomized depression mood scores on the BRUMS to produce a depression and no depression group (see Lane and Terry, 2000). The rationale for such a strategy is twofold. The first is based on the notion that self-awareness of experiencing emotion states typically attributed as unhelpful for performance can have a much larger influence on other emotion and cognitive states (Lane et al., 2005). In a series of studies, Lane et al. demonstrated strong associations between a score of one or more on the depressed scale and high scores for anger, tension, fatigue, and confusion. It is argued that athletes will be aware of the emotions they experienced when they performed successfully and try to act in a way commensurate with these feelings, even if they are not truly experiencing them (Totterdell and Holman, 2003); that is, if an athlete believes feeling anxiety and excited is helpful for performance, then he will try to feel those emotions before competing.

A second reason for using this dichotomy is based on evidence that demonstrates that the modal score for athletes before competition is to report zero on the depression scale (Lane and Terry, 2000). Therefore, it is speculated that indicating a score of one or more on the depression scale represents some acknowledgement of the underlying unpleasant emotional state that the athlete might be experiencing. In the present study, we expanded this process to include scores of confusion alongside scores of depressed mood. Evidence shows both emotions associate with poor performance and significantly intercorrelate (Lane and Terry, 2000). Consequently, the depressed group comprised individuals exhibiting scores of one or more for confusion and depression. The no-symptoms of depression group exhibited scores of zero on each scale.

Procedure

Ethical approval was received from the researchers' institutional ethics committee. Participants were recruited from students studying a degree in sport related subjects such as sport and exercise science. Lecturers agreed to allow the researchers to administer questionnaires within lectures. All participants were volunteers and no incentives were offered. Participants were given the BRUMS-32 and invited to participate. Participants completed the BRUMS-32 with reference to how they felt before a performance when they were at their best.

Participants were asked to think carefully about how they felt before this performance with an emphasis on the moments shortly before performance started. This approach to recalling and rating the intensity of emotions before optimal performance mirrors a procedurepreviously used, thereby facilitating meaningful comparisons (Jones and Uphill, 2004; Hanin, 2000). Our measures differed from those of Hanin in that we used a standardized rather than an ideographic scale. Ekman and Davidson (1994) suggest people tend to remember emotionally charged events well, and retrospective measures of emotions have been shown to be reliable up to three months after competition (HaninandSyrja, 1996).

Data Analysis

MANOVA was used to investigate differences in emotions by 'no depression and 'depressed' groups. A correlation matrix was conducted separately for each group.

RESULTS

As shown in Table 1, MANOVA results indicate an overall multivariate significant affect (Wilks' Lambda $_{5,216}$ = 0.56, P< 0.01, Eta^2 = 0.44) for differences in pre-competition emotion by depression groups. As Table 1 indicates, participants that reported no symptoms of depression reported higher scores of calmness, happiness, and vigor along with lower scores of anger and tension.

The correlation matrix for retrospective emotional states associated with optimal performance before competition in the two groups is contained in Table 2.

As Table 2 indicates, there were 5 significant correlations in each group. In the no-symptoms of depression group, all correlations were positive. Happiness correlated positively with anger, tension, calmness and vigor. Finally, tension positively correlated with vigor. In the symptoms of depression group, happiness positively correlated positively with calmness and vigor, but inversely related to tension and anger.

Table 1. Descriptive statistics for differences in emotional states by depression and no-depression groups

	No-symptoms of depression (N = 110)		Depressed emotion (N = 112)				
	M	SD	M	SD	$F_{1,219}$	P	Partial Eta^2
Anger	0.47	0.78	0.57	0.69	5.49	0.02	0.02
Calmness	1.62	0.79	1.19	0.78	11.09	0.00	0.05
Happiness	2.73	0.62	1.97	0.90	54.18	0.00	0.20
Tension	1.34	0.94	1.79	0.87	107.84	0.00	0.33
Vigor	3.31	0.56	2.86	0.73	16.11	0.00	0.07

Table 2. Correlations between emotions in the no-depression and depression groups

	Anger	Calmness	Happiness	Tension
No-symptoms of Depression				
Anger	1.00			
Calmness	-.05	1.00		
Happiness	.27*	.33*	1.00	
Tension	.08	.04	.33*	1.00
Vigor	.16	.15	.53*	.23*
Depression				
Anger	1.00			
Calmness	-.05	1.00		
Happiness	-.26*	.38*	1.00	
Tension	.19	-.28*	-.51*	1.00
Vigor	-.04	.10	.52*	-.02

* P < .05.

DISCUSSION

The aim of the study was to identify emotional states associated with optimal performance. Specifically, we were interested in relationships between high activation unpleasant emotions (anger and tension), pleasant emotions (calmness, happiness, and vigor) and unpleasant emotions (confusion and depression). Results demonstrateda large effect size for differences in emotions between athletes that reported no symptoms of depressionthan athletes that did. Athletes that reported no symptoms depressionalso reported higher scores of calmness, happiness, and vigor coupled with lower scores of anger and tension. Lane and Terry (2005) summarized data from 15 studies that demonstrate athletes that report a score of 1 or more on the depression scale of the BRUMS also report an emotional profile similar to the findings of the present study.

It is argued that relationships between anger and tension with pleasant emotions that offer insight into the nature of the two aforementioned emotions. As Table 2 indicates, correlation results demonstrate a positive correlation between pleasant emotions (calmness, happiness and vigor) and supposedly unpleasant ones(anger and tension) among participants who also did not report experiencing confusion or depression. The implication of this result is that if a participant seeks to increase vigor or happiness, it will be associated with a concurrent increase in anger and tension, or that if tension scores increase, it will be associated with an increase in pleasantly-tone demotions. Positive relationship between anger, tension and happiness might suggest that participants anticipated goal attainment, or were satisfied with their emotional state before competing (Davis et al., 2010; Hanin, 2000; Lazarus, 2000; Tamir et al., 2008). Anger and anxiety are high activation emotions and it should not be surprising that athletes welcome experiencing these emotions before competition.

Hanin (2010) suggested that practitioners should develop individual profiles for emotion performance relationships. Applying findings of the present study to strategies that could be used to regulate emotions before competition, it suggests athletes could use strategies intended to elevate vigor, such as using motivational imagery (Jones, Bray, Mace, MacRae, and Stockbridge, 2002; Mellalieu, Hanton, and Thomas, 2009), positive self-talk (Hardy, Hall, and Alexander, 2001), or listening to energizing music (Bishop, Karageorghis, and Loizou, 2007). Alternatively, athletes could be attempting to increase happiness by using cognitive strategies such as outcome imagery (Taylor and Shaw, 2002) to confirm beliefs that goals will be attained. Equally, the athlete might use somatically focused strategies to generate sensations of tension (Robazza, Pellizzari, and Hanin, 2004) or he might try re-appraising the event (Gross and Thompson, 2007) so that it is perceived as more important (Jones and Uphill, 2004). In order to test this contention, one method that could be employed is the exploration of ideographic emotions used by Robazza and Bortoli (2003) that assesses bodily-somatic descriptors of emotions.

Results show a different pattern of intercorrelations among participants that reported symptoms of depression. As Table 2 indicates, there were positive relationships between happiness and vigor but an inverse relationship between the same emotions with anger and tension. Therefore, this suggests that strategies to increase vigor might lead to an increased sense of happiness along with a reduction in anger and tension. In contrast to Lane and Terry(2007) who proposed that this emotional profile associates with debilitated performance, findings of the present study indicate the above emotional profile can also associate with optimal performance. Research in sport (Hanin, 2010) and other areas of application has found evidence showing that emotions such as depression associate with successful performance (Brinkman and Gendolla, 2008; Dunning and Story, 1991; Stawand Barsade, 1993).

Given the above result it is worth exploring the motivational implications an athlete might experience when feeling depressed. Depression serves to inform the individual that she/he has insufficient resources to cope with the demands of the task and that withdrawal is required. Depression is associated with low-levels of activation and therefore signals to the individual that not doing much is the best course of action to take (i.e., if performance is life threatening). When an athlete feels depressed, the emotion is signalling that at that moment she/he does not have the resources to cope with the demands of the task. However, many athletes attempt to override this emotional state and as a consequence, perform poorly in terms of trying to achieve the goal. However, if a depressed person identifies a reason for the depression and attending to this aspect was seen as sufficiently important, then depression might help performance (Brinkmann and Gendolla, 2008). It is proposed that the search to regulate these emotions will lead to people consider a range of behavioral and cognitive strategies, one of which might be to target factors elicited the emotions initially; that is, by using a problem-focused (Lazarus, 2000) strategy such as increasing effort when performing to cope with the unpleasant emotion, the individual might actually perform better. Alternatively, the "sadder and wiser" (Dunning and Story, 1991) hypothesis suggests people process information more heuristically when feeling depressed and therefore pay closer attention to the details of the challenge presented to them. In contrast, happiness is associated with superficial processing and missing key parts of performance that matter or complacency. Evidence suggests athletes report that pleasant emotions such as happiness and calmness often accompany poor performance, mainly through complacency (Hanin, 2000). Robazza and Bortoli(2003) found that 39% of positive emotions were perceived as dysfunctional for performance and 42.5% of negative emotions were perceived to be functional. Robazza and Bortoli contend that functional perceptions of an emotion may influence an individual's appraisal of the likelihood of experiencing pleasant and unpleasant emotions after competition; that it is the belief that when an athlete experiences an emotion it is useful in terms of goal pursuit.

These findings have implications for practitioners, one of which is the notion that practitioners encourage athletes to increase unpleasant emotions with a view to improve performance. From an instrumental perspective, it could be argued that if an emotional state characterized by feeling depressed and tense helps goal pursuit, then the athlete should be encouraged to regulate her emotions in line with this profile. In agreement with Andersen (2006), we argue a degree of caution should be exercised before such a strategy is considered. Andersen warns on some of the potentially harmful effects of creating scenarios or images in order to increase unpleasant emotions, particularly in the long term. An internal dialogue which an individual could use to increase unpleasant emotions could be undermining self-esteem, and therefore this process could serve to increase the effect of losing on self-worth and the circle of failure is likely to start. Kendler, Hettema, Butera, Gardner, and Prescott (2003) proposed that defeat in major life events such as sports competition can act as the trigger for the onset of clinical conditions. We suggest practitioners explore the narrative and images that an athlete associates with meta-beliefs that an emotional profile of feeling angry, tense and depressed helps performance. If an athlete self-regulates their emotions before performance through the use of negative self-talk, we suggest that exploration of factors related to such beliefs is worthwhile.

It should be noted that a limitation of the present study relates to the assessment of emotion using a retrospective approach. Retrospective measures should not be treated as measures of emotion in real time due to the potential for memory bias. Acknowledging this limitation, retrospective emotion data provides useful information regarding the development of meta-emotional beliefs (Hanin, 2003). The present study assessed memories of emotions associated with successful performance, and according to both Baumeister, Vohs, DeWall, and Zhang (2007) and Tamir et al. (2008), such beliefs can have a strong bearing in the generation of future emotions and cognitions surrounding these emotions. Indeed Baumeister et al. challenged the notion that emotions have a direct association with performance, proposing that their influence is indirect in that individuals engage in behaviors intended to pursue or avoid anticipated emotional outcomes.

In conclusion, findings from the present study show unpleasant emotions can correlate with pleasant emotions before successful performance. It is argued that whilst emotions such as anger and tension are perceived as unpleasant, they are deemed to be necessary due to the corresponding arousal and activation levels associated with increased effort. It is suggested that future research should investigate the type and effectiveness of strategies used to regulate emotions. There is a need for theory-led intervention to examine the efficacy of self-regulation strategies used to change emotions to optimal levels.

REFERENCES

Andersen, M. B. (2006). It's all about sport performance.....and something else. In J. Dosil (Ed.), *The sport psychologist's handbook: A guide for sport-specific performance enhancement* (pp. 687-698). Chichester, UK: John Wiley and Sons.

Baumeister, R. F., Vohs, K. D., DeWall, C. N., and Zhang, L. (2007). How emotion shapes behavior: Feedback, anticipation, and reflection, rather than direct causation. *Personality and Social Psychology Review, 11*, 167-203.

Beedie, C. J., Terry, P. C., and Lane, A. M. (2000). The Profile of Mood States and athletic performance: two meta-analyses. *Journal of Applied Sport Psychology, 12*, 49-68.

Bishop, D. T., Karageorghis, C. I., and Loizou, G. (2007).A grounded theory of young tennis players' use of music to manipulate emotional state.*Journal of Sport and Exercise Psychology, 29*, 584-607.

Brinkmann, K., and Gendolla, G. H. E. (2008). Does depression interfere with effort mobilization? Effects of dysphoria and task difficulty on cardiovascular response. *Journal of Personality and Social Psychology, 94*, 146-157.

Davis, P. A., Woodman, T., and Callow, N. (2010). Better out than in: The influence of anger regulation on physical performance. *Personality and Individual Differences, 49*, 457-460.

Dunning, D., and Story, A. L. (1991). Depression, realism, and the overconfidence effect: Are the sadder wiser when predicting future actions and events? *Journal of Personality and Social Psychology, 61*, 521-532.

Easterbrook, J. A. (1959). The effect of emotion on cue utilization and the organisation of behavior. *Psychological Review, 66*, 183-201.

Ekman, P., and Davidson, R. J. (1994). Afterword: What is the relation between emotion and memory? In P. Ekman and R. J. Davidson (Eds.), *The nature of emotion* (pp. 316-318). Oxford: Oxford University Press.

Gross, J., and Thompson, R. A. (2007). Emotion regulation: Conceptual foundations. In J. Gross (Ed.), *Handbook of emotion regulation* (pp. 3-26). New York: Guilford.

Hanin, Y. L. (2000). Successful and poor performance and emotions. In Y. L. Hanin (Ed.), *Emotions in sport* (pp. 157-187). United States: Human Kinetics.

Hanin, Y. L. (2003). Performance related emotional states in sport: A qualitative analysis [Electronic Version]. *Qualitative Social Research*, 4 retrieved from http://www.qualitative-research.net/fqs-texte/1-03/1-03hanin-e.htm.

Hanin, Y. L. (2010). Coping with Anxiety in Sport. In A. R. Nicholls (Ed.), *Coping in sport: Theory, methods, and related constructs* (pp. 159-175): Nova Science Publishers.

Hanin, Y. L., and Syrjä, P. (1996). Predicted, actual, and recalled affect in Olympic-level soccer players: Idiographic assessment on individualised scales. *Journal of Sport and Exercise Psychology, 18*, 325-335.

Hardy, J., Hall, C. R., and Alexander, M. R. (2001).Exploring self-talk and affective states in sport.*Journal of Sports Sciences, 19*, 469-475.

Jones, M. V., and Uphill, M. (2004).Responses to the Competitive State Anxiety Inventory-2(d) by athletes in anxious and excited scenarios.*Psychology of Sport and Exercise, 5*, 201-212.

Jones, M. V., Bray, S. R., Mace, R. D., MacRae, A. W., and Stockbridge, C. (2002). The Impact of motivational imagery on the emotional state and self-efficacy levels of novice climbers.*Journal of Sport Behavior, 25*, 57.

Kendler, K. S., Hettema, J. M., Butera, F., Gardner, C. O., and Prescott, C. A. (2003).Life event dimensions of loss, humiliation, entrapment, and danger in the prediction of onsets of major depression and generalized anxiety.*Archives of General Psychiatry, 60*, 789.

Lane, A. M. (2001). Relationships between perceptions of performance expectations and mood among distance runners: the moderating effect of depressed mood. *Journal of Science and Medicine in Sport, 4*, 116-128.

Lane, A. M. (2007). The rise and fall of the iceberg: development of a conceptual model of mood-performance relationships. In A. M. Lane (Ed.), *Mood and human performance: Conceptual, measurement, and applied issues* (pp. 1-34.). Hauppauge, NY: Nova Science.

Lane, A. M., and Terry, P. C. (2000). The nature of mood: development of a conceptual model with a focus on depression. *Journal of Applied Sport Psychology, 12* 16-33.

Lane, A. M., and Terry, P. C.(2005). Test of a conceptual model of mood-performance relationships with a focus on depression: A review and synthesis five years on. Paper presented at the International Society of Sport Psychology (ISSP)*11th World Congress of Sport Psychology,* 15-19 August 2005, Sydney Convention and Exhibition Centre, Sydney, Australia.

Lane, A. M., Beedie, C. J., and Stevens, M. J. (2005). Mood matters: A response to Mellalieu. *Journal of Applied Sport Psychology, 17*, 319-325.

Lane, A. M., Devonport, T. J., and Stevens, M. (2010). Relationships between emotional intelligence, pre-race and post-race emotions in 10-mile runners. *Athletic Insight, 2* 205-219.

Lazarus, R. S. (2000). How emotions influence performance in competitive sports. *The Sport Psychologist, 14*, 229-252.

Matthews, G., Jones, D. M., and Chamberlain, A. G. (1990). Refining the measurement of mood: The UWIST Mood Adjective Checklist.*British Journal of Psychology, 81*, 17-42.

McNair, D. M., Lorr, M., and Droppleman, L. F. (1971).*Manual for the Profile of Mood States*. San Diego, CA: Educational and Industrial Testing Services.

Mellalieu, S. D., Hanton, S., and Thomas, O. (2009). The effects of a motivational general-arousal imagery intervention upon preperformance symptoms in male rugby union players.*Psychology of Sport and Exercise, 10*, 175-185.

Perry, J. D., and Williams, J. M. (1998).Relationship of intensity and direction of competitive trait anxiety to skill level and gender in tennis.*The Sport Psychologist, 12*, 169-179.

Pieter, W., and Pieter, M. S. (2008).Mood and performance in aikido athletes. *ActaKinesiologiaeUniversitatisTartuensis, 13*, 107-116.

Robazza, C., and Bortoli, L. (2003). Intensity, idiosyncratic content and functional impact of performance-related emotions in athletes. *Journal of Sports Sciences, 21*, 171-189.

Robazza, C., Pellizzari, M., and Hanin, Y. (2004). Emotion self-regulation and athletic performance: An application of the IZOF model. *Psychology of Sport and Exercise, 5*, 379-404.

Tamir, M., Mitchell, C., and Gross, J. J. (2008). Hedonic and instrumental motives in anger regulation. *Psychological Science, 19*, 324-328.

Taylor, J. A., and Shaw, D. F. (2002). The effects of outcome imagery on golf-putting performance. *Journal of Sports Sciences, 20*(8), 607-613.

Terry, P. C., and Lane, A. M. (2000). Normative values for the Profile of Mood States for use with athletic samples. *Journal of Applied Sport Psychology, 12*, 93-109.

Terry, P. C., Lane, A. M., Lane, H. J., and Keohane, L. (1999). Development and validation of a mood measure for adolescents. *Journal of Sports Sciences, 17*, 861-872.

Terry, P. C., Lane, A. M., and Fogarty, G. J. (2003). Construct validity of the Profile of Mood States - Adolescents for use with adults. *Psychology of Sport and Exercise, 4*, 125-139.

Thayer, R. E., Newman, R., and McClain, T. M. (1994). Self-regulation of mood: strategies for changing a bad mood, raising energy, and reducing tension. *Journal of Personality and Social Psychology, 67*, 910-925.

Thomas, P. R., Murphy, S., and Hardy, L. (1999). Test of Performance Strategies: Development and preliminary validation of a comprehensive measure of athletes' psychological skills. *Journal of Sports Sciences, 17*, 697-711.

Totterdell, P., and Holman, D. (2003). Emotion regulation in customer service roles: Testing a model of emotional labor. *Journal of Occupational Health Psychology, 8*, 55-73.

Revision submitted June 11th 2011

In: Athletic Insight's Writings of 2012
Editor: Robert Schinke
ISBN: 978-1-62618-120-5
© 2013 Nova Science Publishers, Inc.

Chapter 14

DEMOGRAPHIC CHARACTERISTICS AND MOTIVATIONAL PATTERNS OF MASTERS LEVEL COMPETITIVE CYCLISTS

Karen M. Appleby[*], *Kristen Dieffenbach and Teri Peterson*
Idaho State University, West Virginia University, US

ABSTRACT

Masters athletes are a growing and competitive subsection of the athletic population. The purpose of this study was to describe competitive masters level cyclists in relation to: (a) basic demographic characteristics, (b) motivation to compete, and (c) life balance and personal satisfaction issues associated with training and competition. A total of 397 masters cyclists responded to a survey investigating these factors. The results of this study indicate that fun, personal achievement and fitness/health are the main reasons these athletes compete. Further, the majority of participants indicated that their lives, and the life roles they held, were "somewhat balanced". The authors have provided a discussion and application of the findings that may help coaches and sport psychology consultants work more effectively with this population.

INTRODUCTION

Participation in sport among older individuals and masters level sport competition has increased in popularity over the past twenty-five years (Dionigi, 2006; Trappe, 2001). For the purposes of this article, a masters athlete (MA) is defined as an athlete over the age of 30 who competes in age level competition (USA Cycling, 2010a). Specifically, in the sport of cycling, as of March 2006 USA Cycling reported having 22,103 members who identified as MAs. Between the years of 2005-2009 there was a 22% increase in the number of masters level male USA Cycling license holders and a 32% increase in the number of masters level

---

[*] Contact Information: Karen M. Appleby, Ph.D. Idaho State University, Sport Science and Physical Education, Campus Stop 8105, Pocatello, ID 83209-8105; Office: (208) 282-5613; Fax: (208) 282-4654, applkare@isu.edu.

female USA Cycling license holders for (T. Johnson, personal communication, November 7th, 2010). Despite this high participation level in masters level cycling, there is a dearth of empirical literature that identifies important information that could potentially increase the participation and performance of this group.

Research conducted on MAs suggests that these athletes are distinctive in that, while they have much less time to train, they continue to display high levels of commitment in an attempt to reach a very high level of competitive performance (Starkes, Weir, Singh, Hodges, and Kerr, 1999). Furthermore, MAs may also be a unique group in relation to their motivation to continue to train and compete. Previous research has indicated that MAs score very high on measures such as social affiliation and task orientations (Hodge, Allen, and Smellie, 2008). The following section will briefly highlight some of the important issues that distinguish MAs from non-masters athletes (NMA). For the purposes of this study, NMAs were defined as competitive athletes under the age of 30.

SOURCES OF MOTIVATION FOR MASTERS ATHLETES

Several researchers have investigated the motivation to train for and compete in masters level competition (Hodge et al., 2008; Ogles and Masters, 2000). The results of these studies have indicated that MAs have very different motivational reasons to compete in sport than NMAs. For example Ogles and Masters, who studied masters level marathon runners, found that "older runners reported being more motivated by general health orientations, weight concern, life meaning, and affiliation with other runners" (p. 130). Similarly, other research has indicated that competitive performance is deemed less important to MAs than health and wellness benefits that regular training provides (Brodkin and Weiss, 1990; Hastings, 1995). Therefore, it may be that MAs are more inclined to participate and continue sport participation based on factors other than performance enhancement alone.

Motivation to train for and compete in masters level competition may also be explained by the "relative age effect" (Medic, Starkes, Wier, Young, and Grove, 2009; Medic, Starkes, and Young, 2007). The relative age effect, which has been most commonly researched among youth athletes, is defined as the "overall difference in age between individuals within each age group" which may impact performance (Helsen, van Winckel, and Williams, 2005, p. 629). Age category competition has been implemented to reduce the "relative age effect" and to help ensure "fair competition and an equal chance of success for all" (Helsen, et al., 2005, p. 629).

Specifically for MAs, aging may have a noteworthy impact on physical ability which may, in turn, impact the motivation of MAs to compete and participate in masters level competition (Medic et al., 2007). Specific to cycling, "optimal" performance for both males and females, as indicated by 40k time trial times, was achieved between the age ranges of 25-35 (Nessel, 2004). The relative age effect is important to consider in relation to optimal performance because, as Medic et al. (2007) suggest, MAs may be less motivated to train and compete once they reach the upper end of their five-year age bracket. These authors indicate, "considering that…younger masters athletes are much more likely to set a National/World record, it is possible that their intrinsic motivation, perceived competence, and task goal orientation may be higher and their a motivation lower during that period" (p. 1382).

LIFE BALANCE AND TRAINING PATTERNS
AMONG MASTERS ATHLETES

Lifestyle changes that commonly occur around the time of masters level competition, such as new parenthood, may also alter an athlete's athletic lifestyle, training patterns, and motivation to train and compete. A study conducted by Appleby and Fisher (2009) on the impact of motherhood on elite female distance runners suggested that training practices significantly changed for these athletes once they had children. While training continued to be of primary importance, training itself was often modified. The athletes in this study suggested that training was altered in the following ways: (a) total amount of time spent training was decreased, (b) quality of training was emphasized over quantity of training, and (c) creative training strategies were employed in order to lessen the amount of time spent away from children. While the athletes in this study were of MA age, it should be noted that many of them were considered "elite" and, therefore, may have had increased social and financial networks that supported their successful return to competition.

Further, Appleby and Fisher (2009) focused solely on the perceptions of parenthood and athletic participation for female athletes; parenthood is a significant life factor for both female and male athletes. Starkes et al. (1999), for example, reported that male track and field athletes who competed at the masters national level differed from NMAs in relation to time allotted to training due to lifestyle factors such as family responsibilities. Other dimensions noted by these authors that differentiated the training patterns of MAs versus NMAs were work and injury rehabilitation both of which were cited as factors that may undermine the amount of time MAs had to train.

While a number of studies have investigated MAs in the sports of swimming (see Medic et al., 2007; Weir, Kerr, Hodges, McKay, and Starkes, 2002), track and field (see Medic et al., 2009), marathon running (Ogles and Masters, 2000) and triathlon (Baker, Cote, and Deakin, 2006), no study has specifically investigated the life balance negotiations and motivational patterns of masters level cyclists.

Cycling differs from the previously mentioned sports and activities in that (a) it is a team oriented activity and (b) at the highly competitive level, it has higher risk and injury rates associated with participation (Pruit and Carver, 2010). Further, as indicated by the number of Masters level cyclists reported by USA Cycling, the number of MAs who are entering and re-entering the sport of cycling is growing at a rapid rate. While the participation levels of MAs in cycling is very high, there is a lack of information about the athletes who compete at this level and what it means to be a competitive cyclist at this age. Therefore, the purpose of this research study was to investigate competitive masters level cyclists in relation to: (a) basic demographic characteristics, (b) motivation to compete, and (c) life balance and personal satisfaction issues associated with training and competition. This is an important study because, while participation levels of this group are very high, those who provide support for these athletes, such as coaches and sport psychology consultants (SPC), may know very little about the unique demographic and motivational factors that influence this group.

METHODOLOGY

Upon human subjects approval, a pilot study was conducted. This pilot study consisted of 12 masters level cyclists who took the online survey and provided feedback on both the survey questions and the online process. Changes were made to the survey based on the pilot participants' feedback. The online survey was provided through a secure web-link (surveymonkey.com) that did not connect names or IP addresses to the survey data.

Participant Recruitment and Procedures

Participant recruitment for the main study began by contacting coaches at several of the premiere cycling coaching groups in the nation. These coaches were asked if they would be willing to direct their current masters level athletes to the online survey related to this study. Once this contact was made, a snowballing technique (Patton, 1990) was used in which participants were asked to pass the survey onto other competitive masters cyclists they knew. A request for participation was also listed on a race registration website that housed registration for several Masters level competitions. On this webpage, a brief description of the study was provided and access to the online survey was supplied. Due to the small number of participants ($N=3$) over 65 who answered the survey, we were unable to include cyclists over this age in the data analysis. Since there were 24 participants in the age range of 55-59 and 13 in the age range of 60-64 these two categories were combined. We felt these age ranges were physiologically similar and, therefore, would be a valid representation of participants in this age range. With only three individuals in the oldest group, the researchers were concerned that the sample size was too small to accurately represent this age group. In addition, the researchers did not believe that putting a 93 year old in with a 55 year participant would be a valid representation across that age group due to large physiological differences. Therefore, 397 masters cyclists between the ages of 30 and 65 ($n_{males} = 335$, $n_{females} = 62$) were included in this study.

Instrument

A survey (see Appendix) was constructed to gather information on the following major categories of questions: (a) demographic information and racing history, (b) motivational factors related to riding and competing, and (c) perceptions of life balance and satisfaction in relation to training for and competing in cycling. To ensure face validity of this survey, members of the cycling profession (i.e., professional coaches) who work with MAs were asked to provide input and feedback on the survey questions. A pilot study (described above) was also conducted as another measure of face validity.

Data Analysis

Descriptive statistics were reported on (a) demographic information, (b) motivational factors related to training and competing, (c) perceptions of life balance and satisfaction in relation to training for and competing in cycling. For nominal or categorical variables, frequencies were reported as percentages. For continuous variables, the means and standard deviations are reported. Since this study had respondents of both genders, motivation and life balance variables were compared between males and females. To compare genders on binary (yes/no) responses a Fisher's exact test for proportions was used. To compare genders on ordinal responses a Mann-Whitney U test was calculated. Observed significance levels (p-values) are reported, as well as to whether or not the test achieved the level of accepted statistical significance ($\alpha = .05$).

RESULTS AND DISCUSSION

The questions related to demographic information included information such as age[1], gender, race/ethnicity, marital status, and highest educational level (see Table 1). This sample consisted of 84.4% male and 15.6% female respondents. Of those who reported their gender 346 were male and 62 were female.

Table 1. Demographic Characteristics of Masters Level Cyclists

Age		Gender	Race/Ethnicity	Marital Status	Highest Education Level
30-34:	13.6%	Male: 84.4%	White: 91.6%	Married: 77.9%	High School: 3.0%
34-39:	25.2%	Female: 15.6%	Hispanic: 2.6%	Single: 11.9%	Some College: 13.1%
40-44:	22.2%		As/Pac. Islander: 2.0%	Divorced: 9.9%	Associates: 6.3%
45-49:	16.1%		Am. Indian: 1.3%	Widowed: 0.3%	Bachelors: 24.9%
50-54:	13.9%		Black: . 05%%		Some Grad. Work: 10.6%
55-65:	9.1%		Other: 2.0%		Graduate Degree: 27.5%
					Doctoral Degree: 14.6%

This difference in sample size is not important when using an independent sample t-test unless there are significant differences in the variances. Therefore, when calculating an independent sample t-test the assumption of equal variances was first checked using a Levene's test. If this assumption was violated, a nonparametric equivalent test would have been run. In addition, when comparing proportions between these two groups a Fisher's Exact test was used. This test does not rely on asymptotic assumptions, rather in an observational study it is equivalent to a permutation test and is appropriate regardless of sample size (Ramsey and Schafer, 2002).

---

[1] Age was categorized in relation to the following USA Cycling Masters category groupings: (a) 30-34, (b) 35-39, (c) 40-44, (d) 45-49, and (e) 50-54. The age category 55-65 represents two USA Cycling Masters categories, but was grouped together due to low sample size numbers in each category.

The average age of study participants was 43.1 years with a standard deviation of 7.9 years. Additionally, 60.7% reported having children and 88.6% reported working full time. Questions related to racing history investigated issues such as previous bike racing experience at the junior (under age 18), espoir (ages 18-23), and collegiate levels. Overall, 19.5% of participants indicated that they had competed at the junior level, 30.6% had competed at the espoir level, and 16.0% had competed at the collegiate level.

The average age at which the cyclists in this sample began competing was 28.3 years old with a standard deviation of 10.9 years. The average number of years the participants have been competing is 11.6 years with a standard deviation of 7.8 years. Although the participants reported training anywhere from 2.5 hours per week to 30 hours per week, the average was 12.5 hours with a standard deviation of 4.2 hours. Only 26.7% of participants reported competing in 10 or fewer events per year while 25% reported participating in 26 or more events per year. Fifty percent of the participants in this study reported competing in 11 to 30 events per year.

Motivational Factors Related to Training and Competing

Motivation to compete. Motivation to compete is an important aspect to consider when attempting to understand the competitive habits of MAs (see Table 2). Participants were given a list of twelve motivations to compete plus an option to indicate an unlisted motivation. Participants were asked to choose all applicable motivations. Approximately eight percent (8.1%) of participants did not respond to this question.

Table 2. Motivation to Compete

Motivational Source	% of Participants who indicated this was a reason why they competed
Fun	87.9
Personal Achievement	86.8
Fitness/Health	85.8
To Compete	77.3
Teammates	53.4
Thrill Factor/Need for Speed	48.2
Stress Relief	47.4
Travel	18.4
Private Time	15.1
Set/Break Records	11.8
Prizes	6.8
Swag/Freebies	3.0

Therefore, the percentages reported here are for the 365 total participants who responded to this question. The top three motivational sources to compete for the participants in this study were Fun (87.9%), Personal Achievement (86.8%), and for Fitness/Health (85.8%). Other motivational factors to compete were ranked as follows: to Compete (77.3%),

Teammates (53.4%), to achieve Thrill/Speed (48.2%), Stress Relief (47.4%), to Travel (18.4%), Private Time (15.1%), and to Set/Break Records (11.8%).

Data were also analyzed using a Fisher's Exact Test in relation to gender and motivation to compete. Fisher's Exact Test tests for a difference between two proportions. As stated earlier, this test is appropriate regardless of sample sizes. The results indicated that there was not a significant difference in relation to gender and motivation to compete in the following categories: (a) Stress Relief ($p = .237$), (b) Fun ($p = .253$), (c) Fitness/Health ($p = .671$), (d) Teammates ($p = .552$), (e) Private Time ($p = .143$), (f) to Compete ($p = .725$), (g) to Travel ($p = .850$), (h) to Set/Break Records ($p = .652$), and (i) Thrill/Need for Speed ($p = .659$). A significant difference was found in relation to Personal Achievement and Gender ($p = .027$). In relation to this finding, 85.3% of males indicated that they chose to compete due to personal achievement, while 96.2% of females indicated that personal achievement was a reason they chose to compete.

Perceptions of Life Balance and Satisfaction

Perceptions of overall life balance and life satisfaction were also examined. Survey questions explored concepts such as various life roles, perceptions of how training for and competing in cycling enriched perceptions of overall life balance, how training for and competing in cycling interfered with life roles, and how training and competition in cycling impacted overall stress and life satisfaction.

Life roles. When investigating perceptions of balance and satisfaction, understanding how many roles and responsibilities these athletes held was critical (see Table 3). The number of roles the participants in this study indicated they held ranged from 0-10. Two people (0.5%) indicated they had no life roles. For data analysis purposes we assumed they skipped this question, and thus, reported data "missing" relative to the roles question.

The mean number of roles participants suggested they held was 4.3 (see Table 3). The top life role (91.3%) that participants consistently reported was the role of "athlete". The next three life roles reportedly held by participants in this study were: (a) Spouse/Significant Other (82.8%), (b) Employee (73.7%), and (c) Parent (57.0%). Secondary to these life roles were: (a) Employers (31.4%), (b) Coach (26.1%), (c) Team Manager/Director (19.7%), (d) Community Service Volunteer (16.2%), (e) Second Job Employee (6.8%), (f) Church Leader (6.6%), (g) Caretaker for an elderly family member (5.3%), and 11.9% suggested they held other roles not listed on the survey. These included roles such as grandparent, student, business owner, and race promoter.

Gender and life roles. The data were also analyzed in relation to gender and life roles. An independent t-test was performed to assess if there was a difference in the average number of roles indicated by males and females. Since this analysis would be sensitive to heteroscedasticity if the sample sizes were different a Levene's test was calculated. There was no significant difference in the variances of males and females (F-0.252, $p=.616$). The results of the t-test indicated that there was no significant difference in the number of life roles that males and females held ($t=0.55$, $df=393$, $p=.582$). A Fishers Exact Test was used to analyze the differences in the proportion of males and females who indicated they held specific life roles.

Table 3. Life Roles

Life Role Category	%of Participants who indicated holding this life role
Athlete	91.4%
Spouse/Significant Other	82.8%
Employee	73.7%
Parent	57.0%
Employer	31.4%
Coach	26.1%
Team Manager/Director	19.7%
Community Service Volunteer	16.2%
Other	11.9%
2nd Job Employee	6.8%
Church Leader	6.6%
Caretaker for and elderly family member	5.3%

As stated earlier, this test is appropriate regardless of sample size. There was no significant difference between males and females on the following life roles: (a) Spouse/significant other ($p=.095$) (b) Athlete ($p=.451$), (c) Employer ($p=.452$), (d) Employee ($p=1.000$), (e) Coach ($p=.750$), (f) Team Manager/Director ($p=.482$), (g) Church Leader ($p=.398$), (h) 2nd Job Employee ($p=.582$), and (i) Caretaker for an elderly family member ($p=.110$).

There were, however, significant differences found between genders in the proportion who indicated the life roles of being a parent ($p<.001$), a community service volunteer ($p=.022$), and other life roles not listed on the survey ($p=.008$). Males (84.2%) in this study suggested that being a spouse/significant other was a major life role more frequently than females (72.6%). Similarly, it was found that 61.5% of males and 31.7% of females consider parenting a major life role. This is consistent with a significant difference in self-reported parenthood between the two genders ($p<.001$). Of males, 64.6% reported having children, while only 34.4% of females reported having children. Further, the results of this analysis suggested that 26.7% of women versus 14.3% of men consider volunteering for community service a major life role. Finally, 23.3% of females versus 9.9% of men had indicated other life roles that were not included on this survey.

Enrichment of life balance and family relationships. We also investigated information related to participants' perceptions of how training for and competing in cycling enhanced overall life balance. On a scale of 1 to 5 with 1 indicating their lives were "not at all balanced" and 5 indicating their lives were "very balanced," the average response was 3.5. Only 4% responded that their lives were "not at all" balanced, while 89.6% responded that their lives ranged from "somewhat balanced" to "very balanced." To analyze gender differences on the ordinal response scales, a Mann-Whitney U test was performed. According to Ramsey and Schafer (2002) this test is appropriate unless one sample is less than 5. This was not the case for this data. Results of this analysis suggest there was not a significant difference between males and females ($p=.607$) in relation to how balanced these athletes perceived their lives were. With respect to the number of hours participants trained per week a Spearman's rank correlation coefficient was calculated. There was no relationship between amount of training and perceived overall life balance ($r_s = 0.044$, $p=.388$).

In relation to how frequently training for and competing in cycling enriched one's perceived ability to parent (1=never, 5=frequently), 82.9% indicated this enrichment occasionally or more frequently with an average response of 3.6. There was suggestive but inconclusive evidence of a difference between males and females ($p=.082$). The mean for males on this question was 3.6 while the mean for females on this question was 3.9. There was no significant relationship between hours of training and perceived enrichment in parenting ($r_s = -0.018$, $p=.790$).

In terms of how frequently cycling enriched or improved their relationship with their significant other/family, 82.8% indicated occasionally or more frequently with an average response of 3.7. Again, suggestive but inconclusive evidence of a significant difference ($p=.059$) was found on this variable with respect to gender. The mean for males on this question was 3.7 while the mean for females on this question was 4.0 suggesting that the females in this study felt that cycling enriched their relationship with their significant other more frequently than males. There was suggestive but inconclusive evidence of a weak positive relationship between hours of training and perceived enrichment in relationship with their significant other/family ($r_s = 0.099$, $p=.059$). In this case, the more time spent training the more the participant felt their familial relationships were improved.

Reduction of life balance and family relationships. Another topic related to life balance that was investigated was how often training for and competing in cycling caused a conflict with work responsibilities and family relationships. In relation to how often cycling interfered with parenting responsibilities (1=never, 5=frequently) the average response was 2.9, with 40.9% indicating that such a conflict occurred either never or rarely. A Mann-Whitney U test was performed to compare genders on these ordinal responses. It was found that there was no significant difference in relation to gender ($p=.325$). The mean for males on this question was 2.9 while the mean for females was 3.2. There was no significant relationship between hours of training and how often cycling interfered with parenting ($r_s = -0.012$, $p=.860$). There was, however, suggestive but inconclusive evidence of a difference between males and females ($p=.062$) when reporting how often parenting responsibilities derail cycling plans (1=never, 5=frequently). The mean for males on this question was 3.6 while the mean for females was 3.2. The males in this study felt that parenting derailed their cycling plans more often than females. There was a weak but significant negative relationship between the number of hours the participant trained per week and how frequently they felt parenting responsibilities derailed cycling plans ($r_s = -0.177$, $p=.003$). Thus, the more participants trained per week, the less frequently they felt parenting responsibilities derailed their cycling plans.

Another important aspect of perceptions of life balance and satisfaction are work related issues. In relation to how often cycling caused a conflict with work or work relationships (1=never, 5=frequently) the average response was 2.6, with 52.7% indicating that such a conflict occurred either never or rarely. In asking how often work derailed cycling plans (1=never, 5=frequently) the average response was 3.4, with only 25.5% indicating that such a conflict occurred either never or rarely. No significant differences were found between males and female in terms of how often cycling caused conflict with work ($p=.408$). Males reported a mean of 2.6 and females reported a mean of 2.7 in relation to this question. Further, there were no significant gender differences ($p=.397$) reported in relation to how often work causes one to shorten cycling training or plans. The mean for males on the question was 3.4 and the mean for females on this question was 3.5. There was no significant relationship between hours of training and frequency of cycling causing a conflict with work ($r_s = -0.022$, $p=.670$). There was suggestive but inconclusive evidence of a positive relationship between hours of training and how frequently work derailed cycling plans ($r_s = 0.097$, $p=.060$). In this case the more time spent training the more frequently the participant felt work derailed cycling plans. This, however, was a weak relationship.

Cycling and perceived stress. Relative to how often training contributed to life stress (1=never, 5=frequently) the average response was 2.9 with 49.0% reporting never or rarely. In terms of how often cycling competition contributed to overall stress levels (1=never, 5=frequently) the average response was 3.0 with 41.6% reporting never or rarely. There was a difference in gender in relation to how often training for cycling contributed to overall life stress ($p=.020$) and how often competing in cycling contributed to overall life stress ($p<.000$). Males reported a mean of 2.8 and females reported a mean of 3.1 on the question of how often training contributed to life stress (1=never, 5=frequently). The female participants in this study indicated feeling that cycling training contributed to overall life stress more often.

In terms of how often competing in cycling contributed to life stress (1=never, 5=frequently), the mean for males was 2.9 and the mean for females was 3.6. Again, the female participants in this study felt that competing in cycling contributed to life stress more often. There was no significant relationship between the amount of time spent training each week and the frequency with which training ($r_s = 0.007$, $p=.886$) or cycling competition ($r_s = 0.037$, $p=.465$) contributed to overall stress.

DISCUSSION

Demographics

The demographic profile of masters level cyclists is an important aspect to consider in order to understand the motivational and life balance issues of athletes who compete at this level. This information has the potential to positively impact marketing efforts for USA Cycling and help in the development and creation of events and competitions that would suit this group based on motivation to compete and participate. Further, the information on motivation and life balance is an important aspect to consider for those who work as coaches and SPCs for athletes at this level of competition.

Gender. The gender breakdown of the participants in this study mirror the gender classification of current license holders in the organization. According to the results of the USA Cycling membership demographics from 2009-2010 (USA Cycling, 2010b), 87% of all cyclists in this organization (counting all ages) were male while 12% were female. This is similar to the gender separation of participants in this study which were 84.4% male and 15.6% female. This would indicate that, not only was the sample surveyed in this study representative of the population in general, but that there are a higher number of females racing and competing at a masters level than at other ages of competitive cycling.

Age. The age breakdown of the participants in this study also mirror that of age classifications in the USA Cycling organization. USA Cycling (2010b) reports that the highest percentage of license holders in the organization are in the age categories of 35-44 (32%), 45-54 (22%), and 25-34 (20%). Accordingly, the participants in this study followed the same pattern. The participants in this study were in the age categories of 35+ (50.3%), 45+ (32%), and 30+ (31.2%). Again, not only does this point toward the representative sample of the population in this study (average age of 43.1), but that there are specific age groups (i.e., that of 35-50) that could be heavily marketed for masters level competitions and events and for training and sport psychology consulting.

It is also interesting to note in relation to age that, on average, participants reported that they started competing in cycling at age of 28.3 years. Only 19.5% reported competing at a Junior (under 18 years of age) level, 30.6% reported competing at the Espoir (18-23 years of age) level, and 16% reported competing at the collegiate level. This suggests that the majority of the participants in this study started their cycling training and competing in their late 20's. This is consistent with previous research conducted by Baker et al. (2006) on masters level triathletes. These researchers found that, specifically among non-elite triathletes, competitive sport involvement decreased for participants in their early 20's and then resurged after age 26.

Time spent training and competing. Overall, the participants in this study described a high investment in training and competing. They reported having competed for an average of 11.6 years and 75% respondents stated that they competed in 11 or more competitions per year. Another interesting and important aspect discovered about this group was that, on average, these athletes reported training 12.5 hours per week. This amount of exercise is considerably higher than the national recommended average for general health requirements. These requirements suggest adults should engage in 150 minutes of exercise a week (U.S. Department of Health and Human Services, 2010). This correlates to 21 minutes of physical activity a day. On average, the participants in this study reported engaging in training approximately 107 minutes on average per day.

Motivation to Train and Compete

The participants in this study reported engaging in numerous life roles (see Table 3). Indeed, and unsurprisingly, this is a busy group of competitive athletes. The participants in this study often reported modifying training patterns and time devoted to cycling in relation to work and family responsibilities. This is consistent with the findings of other researchers who have found that training decreases due to other life roles such as work (Weir et al. 2002). As suggested by Starkes et al. (1999) MAs "...have far greater family and work responsibilities than younger athletes, and less access to coaches and facilities, yet they continue to devote large amounts of personal time and effort to training and maintaining high sport commitment levels" (p. 296). The negotiation of training and competition with life roles is a critical aspect for coaches and SPCs to consider when working with this group of athletes.

The number one reported life role by participants in this study was that of "athlete." This, perhaps, indicates that athletic identity is extremely high for this group of individuals. Athletic identity complex and has been linked to motivation, self-concept, and adherence to sport and exercise settings (Anderson, et al, 2011; Anderson, 2004). The concept of athletic identity is a multifaceted personal construction for each individual athlete. However, some distinguished aspects of athletic identity are pertinent to the discussion of athletic identity as it relates to the findings of this study. For example, Anderson (2004) suggested that athletic identity is a "multidimensional" construct that includes factors such as appearance, importance, competence, and encouragement (p. 40). While more research is warranted in the area of athletic identity and MAs, this finding may suggest that these athletes are motivated to participate because they feel as if their identities are associated with their ability to sustain training and performance and that they have appropriate indicators of social support in the cycling community. Further, the results of this study suggest that the MAs in this study had high levels of intrinsic motivation. These athletes did not indicate receiving external rewards such as money for competing. In fact, garnering external rewards such as "swag/freebies" was reported lowest among reasons to compete for the athletes in this study. Again, this is consistent with research conducted by Baker et al. (2006) which suggests that masters level triathletes are an intrinsically motivated group.

Other important concepts to consider when investigating motivation of masters athletes include previous athletic or physical activity experience participants have had prior to their initiation into masters level competition (Baker et al. 2006). In a study on masters level triathletes conducted by Baker et al. it was found that these athletes had "considerable involvement in sport and physical activity" before beginning their competitive lives as masters triathletes (p. 404). The positive correlation between previous physical activity and masters level participation was explained by these researchers, in part, due to increased intrinsic motivation for sport and physical activity types of activities and enhanced motor skill development perhaps making masters level triathletes more confident in their abilities.

Other research has suggested that MAs are motivated to compete due to health, personal achievement, and social reasons (Hodge et al. 2008; Ogles and Masters, 2000) more than performance alone. The findings of this study are consistent with these reports in that the concepts of "personal achievement" and "fitness and health" were reported among the top reasons why participants in this study were motivated to compete. The next category of motivation indicated by the MAs in this study was "Teammates." This motivational aspect is much different from previous studies on the MA population, which have investigated individual sports. As noted earlier, cycling is a "team" oriented sport. A large motivating factor for the participants in this study was related to having a social network of fellow team members with whom to compete. It is assumed that the positive influence of "Teammates" on motivation to train and compete for the participants in this study stems from having a social support network. According to Cutrona and Russell (as cited in Rees and Hardy, 2007) social support, which can stem from emotional, tangible, esteem, and informational aspects has been cited as having a positive influence on life quality (Wrisberg and Johnson, 2002) and performance (Rees, Hardy, and Freeman, 2007). However, it should also be noted that social support, as reported by Rees and Hardy (2007), can be detrimental if provided by "unskilled" or unknowledgeable sources (p. 344). Therefore, it can be assumed that teammates (such as those indicated as motivating to the participants in this study) can provide valuable aspects of support because they understand the commitments, requirements, and sacrifices that are often associated with high level performance in cycling.

However, it is also very interesting to note that having "fun" was the number one reason why the participants in this study chose to compete. This is consistent with patterns of involvement related to youth athletes. Other researchers have found that the number one reason children begin their participation in sport is to have fun (Lockwood and Perlman, 2008; Meisterjahn and Dieffenbach, 2008). Further, it has also been suggested that there is a dip in participation for youth level athletes after the age of 12 (Gould and Petlichkoff, 1988). This occurs in relation to a number of factors including de-selection, injury, age, and choice to engage in other activities. The findings of this study mirror these same patterns of involvement in that that highest number of athletes who compete at this level start at age 28 and there was a significant drop in participation after age 55. It is possible that this drop is related to the same factors of de-selection, injury, age, and choice to engage in other activities. Future researchers should note that a limitation of the current study is that the authors did not investigate why participation dropped after this age and investigate this pattern of discontinuation.

Life Balance

Finally, it is important to consider the concept of life balance and how this impacts training and competition for competitive MAs. The findings of this study suggest that overall, 89.6% of the participants in this study consider their overall lives to be "somewhat" to "very" balanced (only 4% reported "not at all"). Further, participants reported that training and competing for cycling often enriched both their parenting and relationship with significant others. These findings could, perhaps, point to the notion that these athletes often train and travel to competition with family members (i.e., significant others and children) therefore enriching these relationships. Further research should investigate the commonalities of parents cycling with their children and the prevalence of partners who train and travel to competitions together.

As indicated by previous research (Starkes et al., 1999) work and job related responsibilities often impact MAs and their abilities to train and compete. The results of this study are consistent with these findings. When asked if work derailed training for and competing in cycling it was found that the more one trained, the more likely one was to suggest that work commonly disrupted cycling plans (either training or competition). This finding is not surprising considering 73.7% of the participants in this study considered "employee" a major life role. This is an important life balance factor for coaches and sport psychology consultants (SPCs) who work with the masters athlete population to consider,

There was one gender difference reported in the life balance category and that was the concept of how cycling contributed to the overall stress of one's life. Women in this study were more likely to suggest that cycling, specifically competing in cycling events, attributed to their overall life stress. One reason may be the social perceptions of parenthood for women. It has been commonly reported that female athletes who are also mothers may experience stress in relation to their feelings of life responsibilities (Appleby and Fisher, 2009). Being an athlete may make parenthood and athleticism seem even more incompatible because, in accordance with social conventions, female athletes may have to balance childrearing and training more often than male athletes. However, as was reported by Appleby and Fisher, elite female distance runners who had returned to competition after pregnancy were often able to successfully continue their quest for performance. These runners recognized that maintaining their "athletic identity…served to strengthen the balance they were seeking in their lives while at the same time they modeled healthy behaviors for their children" (p. 14). However, it should be noted that there are a number of reasons why this finding may have occurred, however, due to the limitations of this study, not all of the reasons can be accurately identified.

Applications

The findings of this study are applicable in a number of ways. First, understanding the demographic variables of a population is very important in order to create events that are competitive and successful and to market through the appropriate format. The demographic findings of this study suggest that the majority of the MAs in this study are highly educated, willing to travel to race, married, and have children. Therefore, the organizing bodies that sponsor races would be well-suited to choose locations for races and events that are family friendly and are in destination locations. Further, it may be a salient suggestion to provide youth races at events in order to promote cycling and family related activities at such events. Finally, from a psychological perspective, adding these types of activities may help decrease life stress reported by female athletes in this study who often feel that competing in cycling often increased life stress. While a limitation of this study was that we did not specifically ask what life factors precipitated this stress, one factor may be choosing between parenting and athletic responsibilities. By making races and events more family oriented, and creating activities in which all family members can engage, female athletes may experience less stress in relation to this responsibility.

The findings of this study also have rich potential for those who work directly with masters athletes such as coaches and SPCs. Knowing the life roles that athletes of this level hold is a very important concept when considering training for these athletes. Further, understanding the motivational patterns of enjoyment, social networking, and personal achievement, is important for coaches and SPCs of these athletes to understand. Masters level athletes may not be as motivated solely to win championships but, due to their high level of intrinsic motivation, they are motivated to perform well relative to their own previously set performance standards.

FUTURE RESEARCH DIRECTIONS

The findings of this study provide a platform for further research in the area of MAs in competitive environments. For example, this study provided a preliminary glimpse into athletic identity and how it relates to MAs in the sport of cycling. This would be a very interesting area to investigate further as it could possibly provide insight into how constructs such as self-concept, motivation, social support, and confidence lend to adherence to athletic competition later in life.

Another potential area of study would be to look more specifically at how training and competing impact other life roles and the perception of life balance. While the quantitative data gathered in this study give us a baseline of information on how high level MAs balance life, work, family and athletic participation, it would be interesting to investigate this from a qualitative perspective. Gathering in-depth descriptions of how life balance is negotiated and achieved could provide rich insight into why some athletes are successful at pursuing their athletic endeavors later in life.

APPENDIX. SURVEY OF DEMOGRAPHIC AND MOTIVATIONAL PATTERNS OF MASTERS CYCLISTS

Current age: _____

Gender: M   F

Ethnicity: *(check one)*

____ Black   ____ Hispanic

____ American Indian   ____ White, non Hispanic

____ Asian/ Pacific Islander   ____ Other

Highest education level: *(check one)*

____ High school diploma   ____ Some college

____ 2 year associates degree ____ 4 year undergraduate degree (BS/BA)

____ Graduate degree (MBA/MA/MS/etc.)   ____Doctoral degree

(PhD/PsyD/MD/DDS/etc.)

Occupation: _____

Employment Status: *(check one)* ___ Full time ____ Part time____Retired____ Other

Marital status: *(check one)*

____ Single/ Never married   ____ Married or long term committed relationship

____ Divorced   ____ Widowed

Do you have children? Yes   No

If yes, how many _____ and age _____

How old were you when you started cycling competitively? ____

Did you ever race bicycles competitively as a junior (under 18)? Yes No

Did you ever race bicycles competitively as an espoir (18-23)? Yes No

Did you ever participate in competitive collegiate cycling? Yes No

Did you ever race bicycles competitively as a senior rider before you qualified to race as

a masters level athlete? Yes   No

Including this year, total number of years you have competed in competitive cycling
events?_____

Average number of cycling competitions a year *(check one)*

<5   16-20   >30

6-10   21-25

11-15   26-30

If you race in masters'/age categories which age groups do you typically race in for road
      events? *(check all that apply)* 30+   45+   60+   Other _____

                                          35+   55+   70+

If you race in masters'/age categories which age groups do you typically race in for
mountain bike events?

      (check all that apply)   30+   45+   60+   Other _____

                                          35+   55+   70+

If you race in masters'/age categories which age groups do you typically race in for track
      events *(check all that apply)* 30+   45+   60+   Other _____

                                          35+   55+   70+

On average, how many days a week do you train/ride?

      2 or less   3   4   5   6   7

Do you train year round? Yes No

      If no, how many months a year do you typically train? ____

Average training per week (all training activities) during the off season? ____ hours

Average training per week (all training activities) during the season? _____ hours

Average number of cycling events (organized tours and charity rides) a year *(check one)*

      <5   16-20   >30

      6-10   21-25

      11-15   26-30

Average number of cycling competitions a year *(check one)*

      <5   16-20   >30

      6-10   21-25

      11-15   26-30

Why do you ride? *(rank those that apply with 1 being most important)*

      Stress relief   Fun   Personal achievement

      Fitness/health   Teammates   Private time

      To compete   To travel   Thrill factor/ need for speed

      Other: _____

Why do you compete? *(rank those that apply with 1 being most important)*

      Stress relief   Fun   Personal achievement

      Fitness/health   Teammates   To travel

Swag/ Freebees   Prizes   Records/ prizes

Thrill factor/ Need for speed   Other: _____

Please check all of the roles and responsibilities that apply to you:

___ Spouse/significant other   ___ Parent   ___ Athlete

___ Employer   ___ Employee   ___ Coach

___ Team manager/director   ___ Church leader   ___ 2nd job/employee

___ Community Service volunteer   ___ Caretaker for disabled/elderly family member

___ Other: _____

How balanced do you currently feel your life is?

1	2	3	4	5

Very   Somewhat   Not at all

Are you satisfied with your current life balance? Yes No

If not satisfied, why?

How often does cycling enrich or improve your relationship with your significant other?

1	2	3	4	5	
Frequently	Sometimes	Occasionally	Rarely	Never	N/A

How often does cycling cause a conflict with your significant other?

1	2	3	4	5	
Frequently	Sometimes	Occasionally	Rarely	Never	N/A

How often does cycling enrich or improve your ability to parent and your parent child relationships?

1	2	3	4	5	
Frequently	Sometimes	Occasionally	Rarely	Never	N/A

How often does cycling cause a conflict with or interfere with parenting duties and parent child relationships?

1	2	3	4	5	
Frequently	Sometimes	Occasionally	Rarely	Never	N/A

How often do parenting duties/family duties derail or cause you to alter or shorten your

training plans?

1	2	3	4	5	
Frequently	Sometimes	Occasionally	Rarely	Never	N/A

How often does cycling enrich or improve your ability to work and relationships at work?

1	2	3	4	5	
Frequently	Sometimes	Occasionally	Rarely	Never	N/A

How often does cycling cause a conflict with work?

1	2	3	4	5	
Frequently	Sometimes	Occasionally	Rarely	Never	N/A

How often does work derail or cause you to alter or shorten training plans?

1	2	3	4	5	
Frequently	Sometimes	Occasionally	Rarely	Never	N/A

In general, how often does training reduce your overall stress level?

1	2	3	4	5
Frequently	Sometimes	Occasionally	Rarely	Never

In general, how often does cycling competition reduce your overall stress level?

1	2	3	4	5
Frequently	Sometimes	Occasionally	Rarely	Never

In general, how often does training contribute to your overall stress level?

1	2	3	4	5
Frequently	Sometimes	Occasionally	Rarely	Never

In general, how often does cycling competition contribute to your overall stress level?

1	2	3	4	5
Frequently	Sometimes	Occasionally	Rarely	Never

REFERENCES

Appleby, K. M., and Fisher, L. A. (2009). "Running in and out of Motherhood": The experience of returning to competition after pregnancy for elite female distance runners. *Women in Sport and Physical Activity Journal, 18*, 3-17.

Anderson, C. B., Masse, L. C., Hong, Z., Coleman, K., and Shine, C. (2011). Ethnic, gender, and BMI differences in athletic identity and children and adolescents. Journal *of Physical Activity and Health, 8*, 200-209.

Anderson, C. B. (2004). Athletic identity and its relation to exercise behavior: Scale development and initial validation. *Journal of Sport and Exercise Psychology, 26*, 39-56.

Baker, J., Cote, J., and Deakin, J. (2006). Patterns of early involvement in expert and nonexpert masters triathletes. *Research Quarterly for Exercise and Sport, 77*, 401-407.

Brodkin, P., and Weiss, M. R. (1990). Developmental differences in motivation for participating in competitive swimming. *Journal of Sport and Exercise Psychology, 12*, 248-263.

Dionigi, R. (2006). Competitive sport and aging: The need for qualitative sociological research. *Journal of Aging and Physical Activity, 14*, 365-379.

Gould, D., and Petlichkoff, L. (1988). Participation motivation and attrition in young athletes. In F. L. Smoll, R. A. Magill, and M. J. Ash (Eds.), *Children in sport (3rd ed.).* (pp.161-178). Champaign IL: Human Kinetics.

Hastings, D. W. (1995). Reasons for participating in a serious leisure career: Comparison of Canadian and U.S. masters swimmers. *International Review for the Sociology of Sport, 30*, 101-122.

Helsen, W. F., van Winckel, J., and Williams, M. (2005). The relative age effect in youth soccer across Europe. *Journal of Sport Sciences, 23*, 629-636.

Hodge, K., Allen, J. B., and Smellie, L., (2008). Motivation in masters sport: Achievement and social goals. *Psychology of Sport and Exercise, 9*, 157-176.

Lockwood, P, and Perlman, D. J. (2008). Enhancing the youth sport experience: A re-examination of methods, coaching style, and motivational climate. *Journal of Youth Sports, 4*, 30-34.

Medic, N., Starkes, J. L., and Young, B. W. (2007). Examining relative age effects on performance achievement and participation rates in Masters athletes. *Journal of Sport Sciences, 25*, 1377-1389.

Medic, N., Starkes, J. L., Weir, P., Young, B. W., and Grove, R. (2009). Relative age effect in masters sports: Replication and extension. *Research Quarterly for Exercise and Sport, 80*, 669-675.

Meisterjahn, R., and Dieffenbach, K. (2008). Winning vs. participation in youth sports: Kids' values and their perception of their parents' attitudes. *Journal of Youth Sports, 4*, 4-7.

Nessel, E. H. (2004). The physiology of aging as it relates to sports. *Journal of the American Medical Athletic Association, 17*, 12-17.

Ogles, B. M., and Masters, K. S. (2000). Older vs. younger adult male marathon runners: Participative motives and training habits. *Journal of Sport Behavior, 23*, 130 143.

Patton, M. (1990). *Qualitative evaluation and research methods.* Newbury Park, CA: Sage Publications.

Pruit, A., and Carver, T. M. (2010). Cycling. In D. J. Caine, P. Harmer, and M. Schiff (Eds.), *Epidemiology of injury in Olympic sports* (pp. 107-113). Hoboken, NJ: Wiley-Blackwell.

Ramsey, F. L., and Schafer, D. W. (2002). *The statistical sleuth: A course in methods of data analysis.* Pacific Grove, CA: Duxbury.

Rees, T., and Hardy, L. (2000). An investigation of the social support experiences of high-level sports performers. *The Sport Psychologist, 14*, 327-347.

Starkes, J. L., Weir, P. L., Singh, P., Hodges, N., and Kerr, T. (1999). Aging and the retention of sport expertise. *International Journal of Sport Psychology, 30*, 283 301.

U.S. Department of Health and Human Services (2010). Surgeon General's vision for a healthy fit nation-2010. Retrieved from http://www.surgeongeneral.gov/library/ obesityvision/obesityvision2010.pdf.

Trappe, S. (2001). Master athletes. *International Journal of Sport Nutrition and Exercise Metabolism, 11*(Suppl.), S196-S207.

Vealey, R. S., Hayashi, S. W., Garner-Holman, M., and Giacobbi, P. (1998). Sources of sport confidence: Conceptualization and instrument development. *Journal of Sport and Exercise Psychology, 20*, 54-80.

Weir, P. L., Kerr, T., Hodges, N. J., McKay, S. M., and Starkes, J. L. (2002). Master swimmers: How are they different from younger elite swimmers? An examination of practice and performance patterns. *Journal of Aging and Physical Activity, 10*, 41-63.

Wilson, R. C., Sullivan, P. J., Myers, N. D., and Feltz, D. L. (2004). Sources of sport confidence of master athletes. *Journal of Sport and Exercise Psychology, 26*, 369-384.

USA Cycling (2010a). USA cycling rulebook. Retrieved from http://www.usacycling.org /news/user/story.php?id=4220.

USA Cycling (2010b). Member demographics: Summary of current license holders. Retrieved from http://www.usacycling.org/corp/demographicslastyr.php?PRINT=1US.

Wrisberg, C., and Johnson, M. (2002). Quality of life. In M. Kellmann (Ed.), *Enhancingrecovery: Preventing underperformance in athletes* (pp. 253-267). Champaign, IL: Human Kinetics.

Date of Re-submission: July 29th, 2011

In: Athletic Insight's Writings of 2012
Editor: Robert Schinke

ISBN: 978-1-62618-120-5
© 2013 Nova Science Publishers, Inc.

Chapter 15

SUBJECTIVE BELIEFS AMONG COACHES ABOUT HOW RELATIONAL FACTORS AFFECT INTRINSIC MOTIVATION, RESPONSIBILITY AND DEVELOPMENT IN SPORT

Frode Moen [*]

Department of Education,
Norwegian University of Science and Technology, Norway

ABSTRACT

This article studies subjective beliefs about relational issues between coaches and athletes in sport, and how they affect the achievement process seen from the coaches' point of view. Relationship dimensions such as dependency, independency and mutuality are discussed from the viewpoint of how they affect intrinsic motivation, the ability for athletes to take responsibility in the achievement process and achieve better performances. A concourse of 36 different opinions on how relational issues affect motivation, responsibility and development was presented to 18 different Norwegian coaches who are working with talented Norwegian athletes at the late junior and early senior age. The analysis show that the coaches have congruence views about what they believe are the most ideal relationship between them self and their athletes in sport. The dominant view was that the relationship between the coach and the athlete should be built on mutuality. The author will discuss this one factor that emerged from their analysis and behavioural consequences for coaches.

Keywords: Relational issues, sport, coach, development

---

[*] Contact Information: Norwegian Institute of Science and Technology; Idrettssenteret*A314, Dragvoll, Loholtallé 81; Telephone: 47 73598226; E-mail: frmoe@online.no.

INTRODUCTION

The coach-athlete relationship is found to be an important issue in sport (Jowett and Cockerill, 2002). Research shows that the coach is an important factor in order to develop successful athletes (Blom, Watson II, and Spadaro, 2010; Jowett and Cockerill, 2003). Thus, it seems to be the interactions between the coach and the athletes which generates successful performances and results (Jones, Armour and Potrac, 2004). Research in sport has therefore been occupied with studying what is effective coaching (Abraham, Collins and Martindale, 2006; Chelladurai, 2007; Côté and Gilbert, 2009; Horn, 2002; Myers, Chase, Beauchamp and Jackson, 2010; Myers, Feltz, Maier, Wolfe and Reckase, 2006; Myers, Wolfe, Maier, Feltz and Reckase, 2006). Both coaches and athletes have been the subject of considerable research. However, little attention has jet been paid to the nature of the relationship between them (Jones, et al., 2004; Taylor and Wilson, 2005).

Relationship issues between the coach and the athlete seem to have been an ignored area in sport psychology and research: *"Research in sport psychology concerning athletes and relationship issues with the coach has been almost non-existent"* (Lavoi, 2002, p. 4). Relationship issues should therefore be an area for further investigations.

An interesting issue in sport psychology is therefore to investigate what coaches in sport think about relational issues between themselves and their athletes. Therefore, the question to be addressed in this study is: *What are the subjective beliefs among coaches about how relational issues affect intrinsic motivation, responsibility and development for athletes in sport?*

THEORETICAL BACKGROUND

Many factors seem to be important in order to achieve successful performances (Ericsson, Charness, Feltovich and Hoffman, 2006; Moen, 2009; Tanenbaum and Eklund, 2007; Weinberg and Gould, 2007). The extensive evidence from research studying expert performers, both in sport and in other areas in life, claim that deliberate practice makes the difference between expert performers and normal performers (Ericsson, Krampe and Tesch-Römer, 1993; Starkes and Ericsson, 2003). Thus, one of the differences between expert performers and normal performers reflect a life-long period of deliberate effort to improve performances in specific domains (the ten-year rule).

To be committed to the achievement process for such a long period (the ten year rule), intrinsic motivation must be high. Thus, the value and importance of intrinsic motivation in the achievement process cannot be overstated (Jowett, 2003; Deci and Ryan, 2002, 1985; Olympou, Jowett and Duda, 2008). Further, in order to be deliberate over time, the athlete must be aware of what he or she needs to prioritize to perform better and take responsibility in the achievement process.

Awareness is therefore a necessity in order to take responsibility (Howell, 1982; Moen, 2009; Whitmore, 2002). Responsibility in the achievement process is one other important difference between expert performers and normal performers (Ericsson, et al., 1993; Weiner, 1995).

Taking responsibility upon the causes which lead to success or failure is important in order to develop peoples performances. (Bandura, 1997; Skaalvik, 1990, 1994; Weiner, 1995;

Withley and Frieze, 1985). Thus, of the two factors which seem to be of great importance in order to pursue growth and development over time, intrinsic motivation (effort over a long period) and responsibility in the learning process (deliberate practice) turn out to be two important factors. Therefore, successful coach-athlete relationships should affect these factors.

Coach-Athlete Relationship

Helping relationships have one common goal in the way that they are aimed at helping the person who seeks help to achieve growth and development (Kvalsund, 2006; Moen, 2009). Carl Rogers (1967, p.40), defines a helping relationship as *"(...) one of the participants intends that there should come about, in one or both parties, more appreciation of, more expression of, more functional use of the latent inner resources of the individual"*. He claims that this applies for all relationships that facilitate growth and learning. A successful helping relationship between the coach and the athlete in sport should therefore stimulate the athlete to grow and develop his or her talent (Jowett and Poczwardowski, 2007; Weinberg and Gould, 2007).

Interestingly, the coach–athlete relationship in sport is considered to be particularly crucial in terms of positive outcome or not (Jowett and Cockerill, 2002; Lyle, 1999). Up to recently, researchers within sport have claimed more attention to coach-athlete relationship issues (Jones, et al., 2004; Jowett, 2003; Lavoi, 2002; Taylor and Wilson, 2005). While numerous of studies have investigated how leadership behaviours manifested by coaches have affected athletes satisfaction, performances, self-esteem, confidence and anxiety, studies investigating the interpersonal dynamics between the coach and the athlete have received less attention (Olympou, et al., 2008).

The studies which have investigated relationship issues within sport claim that effective relationships include basic ingredients such as empathic understanding, honesty, support, liking, acceptance, responsiveness, friendliness, cooperation, caring, respect and positive regard (Jowett and Cockerill, 2003; Jowett and Meek, 2000). Ineffective relationships are found to be undermined by lack of interest and emotion, remoteness, even antagonism, deceit, exploitation and physical or sexual abuse (Balague,1999; Brackenridge, 2001; Jowett, 2003). Interestingly, these findings are in accordance with research within clinical therapy, which emphasize the importance of empathic understanding, honesty, respect and positive regard with the client in order to achieve positive progress in therapeutic consultations (Vaglum, 2008). The coach–athlete relationship in sport is defined by mutual and causal interdependence between coaches' and athletes' feelings, thoughts and behaviours (Jowett, 2008; Jowett and Cockerill, 2002; Jowett, Paull, and Pensgaard, 2005). Therefore, to systematically study the coach-athlete relationship researchers developed an operationalised model through the constructs of the three Cs: *Closeness, Commitment* and *Complementarity* (Jowett and Cockerill, 2002; Jowett and Ntoumanis, 2004). Closeness describes the depth of the coach-athlete emotional attachment in the relationship. Studies have found that without first establishing the emotional attachment in the relationship, the coach-athlete relationship is at a dead end (Trzashoma- Bicsérdy, Bognár, Révész, and Géczi, 2001; Vargas-Tonsing, and Guan, 2007). Commitment reflects coaches and athletes' intention or desire to maintain their relationship over time. Complementarity defines to what degree the relationship is perceived as cooperative and effective (Jowett and Cockerill, 2002). Optimal coach-athlete relationships are therefore described by high degree of these 3 Cs. In similarity, Macmurray (1999) claims that it is only in personal relationships with others people can achieve personal growth and development. Thus, there must exist a degree of closeness, commitment and complementary to establish personal relationships with others. Kvalsund (2005) and Mcmurray (1999) both describe relationships within three major categories: (1) dependent relationships, (2) independent relationships, and (3) relationships based on mutuality (Allgood and Kvalsund, 2003; Kvalsund, 1998, 2005; Mcmurray, 1999; Moen, 2009).

Dependency. Dependent relationships are characterized by the reliance on another person, such as a parent or a teacher. Such relationships are most relevant in the early phases of life, when it is necessary to receive help because of the lack of experience and competence. In sport dependent relationships are claimed to be optimal when athletes are in their younger years (below 15 years old) (Hogg, 1995). Dependent relationships can be either positive or negative. They are positive when the person who seeks help thinks or feels the assistance is necessary and desirable, however, they can also become negative if either the person who seeks help or the helper thinks that it is no longer necessary. Thus, positive dependent relationships acknowledge the dependence of a helper and his or her experience or competence in order to do what the person who seeks help wants to do. There is a gap in experience and competence between the person giving help and the person receiving help.

Independency. Independent relationships are characterized by the acceptance that there is no need or dependency of a helper to support and help the independent person in order to do what the independent person wants to do. Self-support from the independent person is enough, and the person is fully capable of managing him- or herself in order to do what he or she wants. In sport, such relationships seem to be preferred for senior athletes (Hogg, 1995). Independent relationships can also be either positive or negative. A positive independent relationship occurs when a person acknowledges his or her independence and the other person in the relationship also acknowledges that there is no need for him or her any more. Positive independent relationships are characterized by a mutual acknowledgment of the independence of the other person. If one part in such relationships does not acknowledge the independence of the other person, the relationship will become negative. In sport then, it should be interesting to investigate if experienced athletes seek independency or not in their achievement process.

Mutuality. Relationships based on mutuality are relationships which aim to encourage the independence of both parts in the relationship without provoking dependence. Mutuality occurs when the helper in the relationship is active to stimulate the person who seeks help to discovery and new reflections based on his or her own experience and knowledge. Thus, it is not the helper's experience and knowledge which is the origin in such relationships. In sport, where the superior goal is to obtain extraordinary performances, there must be a recognition that there exists some dependency between the coach and the athlete. This acknowledgment however is reciprocal, given the fact that both sides of the relationship play different, independent and complimentary roles. Mutuality throughout the interaction between the coach and the athlete should therefore be described as the normal attitude, in which the endeavour is directed at improvement. Both sides are in a helping relationship in which the interaction between them will change both of them. As the coach becomes affirmed and empowered through the interaction with the athlete, the athlete will be in a positive, growth enhancing relationship with the coach. Both of them end up benefiting from the relationship which is created. In sport, such relationships are claimed to be for athletes between 15 and 18 years old (Hogg, 1995).

According to research within sport studying the coach-athlete relationship, mutuality and independence seem to describe the optimal relationship between coaches and their athletes (Jowett and Cockerill, 2003; Jowett and Meek, 2000; Olympou, et al., 2008), and research argues that the relationship between the coach and the athlete is an integrated part of coach behaviour (Lyle, 2002; Rieke, Hammermeister and Chase, 2008). Thus, coach behaviour affects the relationship which develops between him- or herself and the athlete. As a consequence coach behaviour should be directed towards building relationships which are optimal in order to achieve growth and development. In order to do so, the optimal relationship between the coach and the athlete must be properly defined. The question to be addressed in this study is focusing on the coaches' views related to relational issues between themselves and their athletes and how this affect intrinsic motivation, responsibility and development. Therefore, the question to be addressed in this study is: *What are the subjective beliefs among coaches about how relational issues affect intrinsic motivation, responsibility and development in sport?*

METHODOLOGY

Q methodology provides a basis for a systematic study of subjectivity, which recommends it to researchers interested in qualitative aspects of human behaviour. Thus, Q methodology is rooted in the qualitative research tradition and subjectivity is revealed by a systematic categorizing of people's thoughts, feelings, values and experiences related to the current research issue (Brown, 1996). The process of studying coaches subjective beliefs related to the current issue is in this study completed through a series of five steps: 1) Definition of the concourse, 2) Development of Q sample, 3) The selection of P sample, 4) Q sorting, and 5) Analysis and interpretations.

Definition of the Concourse

The first step in Q methodology is to establish a "concourse," originally called a "trait universe" (Stephenson, 1950), which is a collection of thoughts, feelings, values and experiences related to a specific topic (Stephenson, 1986).

The concourse in this study was established through an analysis of discussions and interviews with coaches and athletes within sport related to this research issue, and a review of relevant literature within the field. Then the statements from this process were systematically organized, analyzed and presented as the concourse. In principle, the concourse contains all possible ways of communicating about the actual topic within a specific culture (Kvalsund, 1998).

Development of Q Sample

The Q sample is then drawn from the concourse of statements. The Q sample is a comprehensive selection of the views within the concourse (Kvalsund, 1998). The concourse can consist of an infinite number of subjective statements. Although it is impossible to grasp the entire (infinite) concourse, the researcher seeks to get hold of a wide range of statements related to the research topic. The size of a Q sample is dependent upon how many statements it takes to do that.

It is important to grasp as much breadth as possible so that the viewpoints from the concourse are represented. During this phase it is important to organize all the sub themes emerging from the concourse. In the present study, two main themes (what Stephenson calls effects (1950)) emerged in the concourse; relationship and benefit/achievement. Within the theme "relationship" three subthemes (what Stephenson calls levels (1950)) seemed to be relevant; dependency, independency and mutuality. Within the theme "benefit/achievement" three other subthemes or effects seemed to be relevant; intrinsic motivation, responsibility, and achievement. In this study, it is important to differentiate whether coaches in sport believe the most effective relationship related to benefit/achievement is based on dependency, independency or mutuality, or a combination of some of the three. As a result, the design for the statements was created as shown in Table 1.

Table 1. The design of the statements based on cultural effects

Effects	Levels			No.
relationship	a. dependency	b. independency	c. mutuality	3
benefit	d. motivation	e. responsibility	f. achievement	3

Each combination of independent effects and levels becomes a categorical cell. Based on this, we must look to the levels to see all possible combinations of cells, since they are the multiplication of levels by all three effects. Using the design in Table 1, nine combinations of statements are obtained, as shown in Table 2.

Table 2. The combination of levels in the design

Effects	Levels								
relationship	a	a	a	b	b	b	c	c	c
benefit	d	e	f	d	e	f	d	e	f
Statement No.	1, 10, 19, 28	2, 11, 20, 29	3, 12, 21, 30	4, 13, 22, 31	5, 14, 23, 32	6, 15, 24, 33	7, 16, 25, 34	8, 17, 26, 35	9, 18, 27, 36

In principle, there are 3x3 cells. Each cell consists of statements that are interrelated but are somewhat different. In this study, four statements were developed to represent each og the 9 cells, which resulted in 36 statements (Appendix). To make it impossible for the sorter to see the structure in the sample, statements were randomly allocated a number from 1 to 36.

The Selection of P Sample

The data was collected from eighteen coaches who participated at an up-grading course arranged by the Norwegian Olympic committee together with the Norwegian school of sport sciences (NIH) (P sample).

The coaches were evaluating the statements based on their experiences as coaches for talented athletes at the late junior age and/or early senior age. The coaches were from different sports such as cross country skiing, motor cross, biathlon, athletics, tae kwondo, football, bicycling and handball. Their ages were from twenty one to thirty five. Out of the eighteen coaches five of them were women. Importantly, Q methodology uses much smaller populations than what is common in quantitative research (Brown, 1980).

THE Q SORTING

First, the coaches were requested to take their time to read all the statements in the Q-sample considering an instructed specific condition: "*Consider the following statements that are about relational issues between coaches and athletes. Which of the statements describe the most optimal relationship between a coach and an athlete in your opinion. Consider the statements concerning how they affect motivation, responsibility and achievement seen from the athletes' point of view.*" It was further emphasized that they should rank the statements with regards to what they think their athletes believe are ideal. Each statement had to be evaluated from the extreme positive to the extreme negative end of a continuum. Zero indicates a neutral viewpoint or no meaning. This is an operation referred to as "Q sorting" (McKeown and Thomas, 1988). The scores range from a score of +5 for "most strongly agree" to a score of -5 for "most strongly disagree" under the so-called forced quasi-normal distribution of the statements, as shown Figure 1 below (Brown, 1980, p. 197-198).

The coach is free, however, to place an item anywhere within the distribution. While performing the Q sort, the athletes draw distinctions on the basis of psychological significance.

most strongly disagree	very strongly disagree	strongly disagree	disagree	disagree	neutral	agree	agree	strongly agree	very strongly agree	Most Strongly agree
-5	-4	-3	-2	-1	0	+1	+2	+3	+4	+5

Figure 1. The scoreboard for the Q sorting.

The statements placed in the middle area (-1, 0, +1) raise no emotional feelings for the coaches. These statements are psychologically insignificant. At each end of the scale, are statements that the athletes relate more strongly to. These are the statements that are psychologically significant to them (Brown, 1980). The coaches continued their Q sorting until all the statements were distributed into the scoreboard. It took approximately one hour for the coaches to distribute the 36 statements. Each scoreboard was signed by the coaches so that the researchers had the opportunity to make interviews with them during analysis and interpretations of their Q sortings.

Analysis and Interpretations

The different Q sorts arranged by the athletes were then entered into the computer program PQMethod (Schmolck, 2002), which is a statistical program tailored for Q studies. For any *n* Q sorts, the correlations produce a matrix of size *n x n,* or in this case 18 x 18 cells in the overall matrix. If the correlation coefficient is high this indicates that two coaches sorted the Q sample statements in a similar manner. The 18 X 18 correlation matrix was then subjected to a Centroid factor analysis, initially with the default value of seven factors extracted. The coaches who sorted the statements approximately similar, produced this factor solution (McKeown and Thomas, 1988). Thus, the factor represents natural categories of subjectivity that can be discovered by the researcher (Brown, 2002). Stephenson points out that Q data and Q methodology is abductive in its approach, and its interest is in causes and laws, and not on a search for facts by testing hypotheses (Stephenson, 1950). This implies that the researcher must work to understand the Q sorters mind through gaining insight regarding the subjectivity that is disclosed (Stephenson, 1986, p.53). After the first analysis and interpretations of the factors, each Q sorter was interviewed by the researcher in order to check whether or not the factors did represent the common conversational modes for the individuals on the factors. Q analysis has therefore their centre point in each case, the view from the individual's perspective, whereas quantitative methods tend to view the same events from an external perspective. Thus, the analysis are mapping the coaches subjective beliefs based on the concourse that represents all possible beliefs regarding this research issue. Q-methodology therefore refers to factors as operant factors, and uses different criteria's in their analysis compared to what is seen in traditional quantitative methods (Brown, 1980).

RESULTS

Table 3 shows the rotated factors and their loadings. It is important to decide how high a factor loading should be if that sort is to be regarded as an important contributor to a factor (Pett, Lackey, and Sullivan, 2003, p.208). In this study .45 was selected to be the minimum factor loading (Comrey and Lee, 1992, p.243) for defining Q sorts (Q sorts marked by an X in Table 3). The Centroid factor analysis resulted in one factor with an Eigen value of 9.3, counting for 52 % of the variance. Two other factors also had an Eigen value just above 1, but after experimenting with various alternatives by rotation by hand, the author decided to consider a varimax rotation with a one-factor solution as shown in Table 3.

As shown in the factor matrix in Table 3, Factor A has 17 pure cases (sorts that load only on one factor), which were marked "X" after each factor loading. This is a really strong factor, counting for 52 percent of the variance; it is also the only prominent factor from the factor analysis. Thus, all the coaches share congruence views about what they believe is the most ideal relationship between themselves and their athletes in sport. The remainder of this study focuses on analysis of this factor reflected in their sortings. The statements on the extreme sides in Figure 1, with rank scores of +5, +4, +3, -3, -4, and -5, reflect the intense feelings and attitudes of each a coach and characterize the factor, so analysis were mainly focused on the interpretation of those statements (Brown, 1980).

Factor A: A Relationship based on Mutuality

Factor A agreed most strongly (+5) with statement No. 7—"For me as an athlete it is of great importance that someone listens to me and confirms me both as an athlete and as a person. This stimulates me to work harder." This factor agreed very strongly (+4) with statement No. 9—"My best performances are a result from effective interaction between me and my coach." and statement No. 17—"When my coach asks questions which make me reflect upon my learning process and how to realize more of my potential, I feel I manage to take responsibility in the process." All statements emphasize mutuality as central in the relationship between the coach and the athlete (category c Table 1). Interestingly, the three statements together cover all three possible benefits from the three different relationship categories; motivation, responsibility and achievement.

Table 3. The matrix of rotated factors and their loadings

| Q-SORT | Factors | | |
	A	undefined	undefined
1	**0.85 X**	-0.23	0.28
2	**0.72 X**	0.32	-0.29
3	**0.78 X**	0.07	0.21
4	**0.75 X**	0.21	-0.14
5	**0.81 X**	0.29	-0.12
6	**0.52 X**	0.04	-0.46
7	**0.80 X**	-0.08	-0.18
8	**0.49 X**	-0.45	-0.41
9	**0.90 X**	-0.19	0.24
10	0.42	-0.40	0.34
11	**0.89 X**	-0.07	0.22
12	**0.83 X**	-0.28	0.00
13	**0.73 X**	-0.12	-0.30
14	**0.57 X**	-0.20	-0.16
15	**0.72 X**	-0.08	0.40
16	**0.50 X**	0.33	0.28
17	**0.68 X**	0.39	0.05
18	**0.73 X**	0.49	0.03
Eiegen values	*9.31*	*1.34*	*1.22*
% expl. Var.	52	7	7

Further, this factor also agreed (+3) with statement No. 18—"To perform at my best, my coach and I are mutually dependent on each other. He/ She needs to understand me and I have to understand him/ her."; statement No. 8—"When my coach and I are capable of using each other's competence in the learning process it is easier for me to take responsibility."; and statement No. 33—"I wouldn't perform as well if I didn't have the help and quality assurance from my coach in the learning process." Again the statements emphasize the importance of mutuality (No. 18 and 8) in order to perform and take responsibility. Statement no.33 shows that the coaches also believe that the athletes acknowledge that contact with another person (a coach) is necessary in order to perform at their best level. Thus, the dependency in mutuality is emphasized too. Five out of the six most agreed upon statements emphasize mutuality. This view was further strengthened and confirmed through the analysis of the statements Factor A disagreed with.

Factor A disagreed most strongly (-5) with statement no. 13—"I need no help from others than myself in my learning process." Thus, again the coaches believe that the athletes need to acknowledge that contact with a coach is important in order to develop their talent. This acknowledgement is also emphasized in the next statement this factor disagreed very strongly (-4) with: statement no. 6—"My best achievements are solely a result from my independence practice with no interference from others." The next statement the factor disagreed very strongly with is statement no. 3—"My best performances are solely a result of the decisions made by my coach." This statement shows that the coaches believe that dependency is clearly not preferred by the athletes; they believe that the athletes want to be involved in their learning process and to take part in decisions concerning their performance pursuit.

The statements this factor disagreed with strongly (-3) were statement no. 35—"Too much involvement of me in my learning process makes it difficult for me to take responsibility."; and statement No. 5—"I am more capable of taking responsibility when I have to exercise on my own without help from my coach." These two statements strengthen the view discussed above; coaches believe that involvement is wanted from athletes in order to be capable of taking responsibility in their own achievement process. Independency does not stimulate responsibility (5). Further, the last statement this factor disagreed strongly with is also strengthening this view; Statement no. 1—"My motivation increases when my coach makes decisions concerning my training." Thus, lack of involvement does not stimulate motivation either.

When studying the statements that the coaches disagreed with it is clear that contact with a helper is necessary and that the helper must involve the athlete in the process. Both dependency and independency is clearly not wanted.

DISCUSSION AND CONCLUSION

The results show that all psychological significant statements in this study, except for two (No. 35, 1), are clearly rooted in the fact that the coaches believe that contact with a helper is a necessity to achieve optimal performances, stimulate intrinsic motivation and affect the athletes' abilities to take responsibility in the achievement process (No. 3, 5, 6, 7, 8, 9, 13, 17, 18, 33). The obvious need for contact shows that relationships based on independency are clearly not wanted. This is also confirmed directly (No. 6, 13). It is however important to notice that the results show that the coaches believe that there are no contradiction between the need for contact with someone and the aim to develop the athletes' independence (No. 5, 8, 17). On the contrary, the coaches believe that contact with a helper seems to be necessary in order to stimulate independency (being more capable of taking responsibility). Thus, the obvious need for contact with a helper does not seem to equal a relationship based on dependency. It is also clear that the coaches believe that both parts in the relationship must have a mutual understanding of their responsibility to stimulate independency (No. 8, 17). It seems to be the coaches' abilities to invite their athletes into deeper reflections through powerful questions, so that the athletes discover how to realize more of their potential resources, which give athletes the opportunity to act independently. The results give reason to believe that it seems to be the quality of this significant interaction between the coaches and their athletes that stimulates awareness about a focused case. Raised awareness about a focused case seems to be important for the athletes' possibilities to take responsibility in their achievement process and being able to act independently. Thus, questions asked by coaches which stimulate their athletes to reflections and awareness seem to make their athletes more capable of taking responsibility (No. 17). The results give reason to believe that coaches abilities to ask powerful questions (No. 17) and empower their athletes through active listening, (No. 7) are important to develop optimal coach-athlete relationships. Therefore, mutuality seems to be the best way to describe the optimal relationships between the coaches and their athletes in this study.

These findings are in accordance with earlier findings which claim that mutuality is optimal coach-athlete relationships in the athletes' late junior years as discussed introductorily (Hogg, 1995; Jowett and Cockerill, 2003; Jowett and Meek, 2000; Olympiou, et al., 2008). Most athletes who are coached by coaches in this study were in their late junior age. However, some were also in their early senior years, and optimal relationships for senior athletes are claimed to be independent coach-athlete relationships (Hogg, 1995). It is therefore a bit interesting that neither of the coaches believed that independent coach-athlete relationships were better in order to achieve optimal performances, stimulate intrinsic motivation and affect the athletes' abilities to take responsibility in the achievement process.

The findings in this study also confirm the construct of the operationalised model discussed introductorily (the three Cs), used to study coach-athlete relationships through closeness, commitment and complementarity (Jowett and Cockerill, 2002; Jowett and Ntoumanis, 2004). Closeness emphasizes emphatic understanding as one important factor in effective coach-athlete relationships (Jowett and Cockerill, 2003, 2002; Jowett and Ntoumanis, 2004). The results in this study confirm this: Coaches abilities to listen to their athletes (No. 7), confirm their athletes (No. 7), and understand their athletes (No. 18) are believed to be very important among the coaches. Closeness is therefore confirmed as an important relational construct also in study (Jowett and Cockerill, 2002). Complementarity coach-athlete relationships are perceived as cooperative and effective (Jowett and Cockerill, 2002). The results in this study also confirm this construct: Coaches believe that coach-athlete relationships should be based on effective interactions (No. 9), coaches and athletes are supposed to be mutually dependent on each other (No. 18), and they are supposed to be using each other's competence in the achievement process (No. 8). Thus, the results indicate that the coaches in this study believe that they need to meet their athletes with a respectful attitude so that their athletes really experience that they are learning and performing together and using each other's competence and experience in the process. Complementary is therefore confirmed as an important relational construct in this study (Jowett and Cockerill, 2002). As discussed introductorily, commitment reflects coaches and athletes' intention or desire to maintain their relationship over time. This relational issue was not represented in the statements in the Q sample in this study. Therefore, the data in this study cannot draw conclusions regarding the construct commitment. However, the obvious claim for contact gives reason to believe that the coaches believe that there must be a strong commitment in the relationship between coaches and their athletes in this study.

As discussed introductorily, research argues that coach-athlete relationships are integrated parts of coaches' behaviours (Lyle, 2002; Rieke, et al., 2008). When analysing and interpreting the most psychological significant statements among the coaches in this study, there seem to be a need of a mixture of attending- and influencing behaviour from the coaches. The results indicate that to build coach-athlete relationships on mutuality, coaches first of all need to be aware of and give attention to their athletes'. Therefore, attending behaviour seems to be a necessity. Thus, the coaches believe that it is of great importance that the athletes are truly heard and understood in order to achieve optimal performances, stimulate intrinsic motivation and affect the athletes' abilities to take responsibility in the achievement process (No. 1, 3, 5, 6, 7, 8, 9, 13, 17, 18, 35). However, the results also show that the coaches' abilities to influence their athletes are emphasized (No. 5, 6, 13, 17, 33). Attending skills and influencing skills are important communication skills (Ivey and Ivey, 2006). As a consequence: Coaches communication skills seem to be of importance. These results indicate that the coaches in this study believe that they must be flexible and act with a paradoxical mixture of humility in one situation, and determined in another. Thus, in one situation attending skills seem to be important and in another influencing skills seem to be preferred. Future research should investigate these different situational demands and how different situations seem to claim different skills from coaches.

APPENDIX

Normalized factor scores of the factor

Statements	Normalized Factor Scores (Z-scores) F1	Q-sort values
My motivation increases when my coach makes decisions concerning my training.	-1.16	-3
It is easier for me to take responsibility for my training when my coach is in charge of what I do.	-0.67	-1
My best performances are solely a result of the decisions made by my coach.	-1.61	-4
My motivation increases when I can practice my sport on my own without interference from others than myself.	-0.95	-2
I am more capable of taking responsibility when I have to exercise on my own without help from my coach.	-1.05	-3
My best achievements are solely a result from my independence practice with no interference from others.	-1.73	-4
For me as an athlete it is of great importance that someone listens to me and confirms me both as an athlete and as a person. This stimulates me to work harder.	1.80	5
When my coach and I are capable of using each other's competence in the learning process it is easier for me to take responsibility.	1.24	3

Statements	Normalized Factor Scores (Z-scores)	Q-sort values
My best performances are a result from effective interaction between me and my coach.	1.68	4
I experience that dependency between me and my coach is motivating.	-0.69	-1
My coach's competence and experience is of vital importance for me to take responsibility in my learning process.	0.54	1
I am solely dependent on my coach's competence and experience to perform at my best on the tasks I am facing.	-0.89	-2
I need no help from others than myself in my learning process.	-2.14	-5
My ability to take responsibility in my learning process is the result from a lot of practice on my own with no particular help from others.	0.18	0
When I am in charge of my learning process with no interference from others, I achieve the tasks I am facing.	-0.49	-1
It is vital for my motivation that both my coach and I strive to understand each other in the learning process.	1.12	2
When my coach asks questions which make me reflect upon my learning process and how to realize more of my potential, I feel I manage to take responsibility in the process.	1.62	4
To perform at my best, my coach and I are mutually dependent on each other. He/She needs to understand me and I have to understand him/her.	1.42	3
Being dependent on my coach reduces my motivation.	-0.31	-1
Without my coach's competence and experience it would be difficult to take responsibility in the learning process.	0.43	1
If my coach in general is condescending towards me, I lose my interest for the learning process and achieve less.	0.32	1
When I solely have to practice on my own I totally lose my motivation.	0.54	2
I find it difficult to take control and responsibility for the learning process if I have no help from others.	0.08	0
When I in general have to practice on my own I achieve less than I would do if I had help from others.	0.63	2
My motivation declines when my coach leaves me too much responsibility and requires too much independence in the learning process.	-0.79	-2
It is difficult for me to take responsibility in the learning process when my coach and I are mutual dependent on each other.	-0.77	-2
I perform poorly if my coach doesn't understand me and I don't understand him or her.	0.54	1
With no coach to tell me what is right and wrong in the learning process I will lose my motivation.	-0.02	0
With no coach to tell me what is right and wrong in the learning process it would be difficult for me to take responsibility.	0.18	0
Without my coach's experience and competence I would not be able to perform at my best.	0.73	2
Without help from others in the learning process I completely lose my motivation.	0.11	0
My inability to take responsibility in the learning process is because I haven't been encouraged to train on my own.	-0.11	0
I wouldn't perform as well if I didn't have the help and quality assurance from my coach in the learning process.	1.23	3
I lose motivation when my coach involves me too much and doesn't tell me what I should do.	-0.30	-1
Too much involvement of me in my learning process makes it difficult for me to take responsibility.	-0.96	-3
If I feel small and incompetent in my relationship with my coach I normally don't perform at my best.	0.27	1

* Translated from Norwegian to English by the authors.

Another important conclusion after examining the results in this study is that the coaches and their athletes have to spend considerable time together in order to create coach-athlete relationships based on mutuality. Considerable time together seems to be a necessity in order to establish the thrust and knowledge about each other which is needed to establish an open and respectful dialogue between them in different situations. Coach behaviour which meet these demands should stimulate coach-athlete relationships towards mutuality.

The data from this study cannot draw conclusions regarding causal predominance between relational issues and intrinsic motivation, responsibility and development. However, these issues should be investigated in future research. Also, the problem addressed in this study should be investigated further among athletes (both younger and older) and coaches in sport. Since research both among athletes and coaches indicate that mutuality is the relationship which is preferred, survey investigations should be conducted to investigate if this is the case in practical settings.

REFERENCES

Abraham, A., Collins, D., and Martindale, R. (2006) The coaching schematic: Validation through expert coach consensus. *Journal of Sport Sciences 24*, 549-564.

Allgood, E., and Kvalsund, R. (2003). *Personhood, professionalism and the helping relation: Dialogues and reflections.* Trondheim: Tapir AkademiskForlag.

Balague, G. (1999). Understanding identity, value, and meaning when working with elite athletes. *The Sport Psychologist, 13*, 89 - 98.

Bandura, A. (1997). *Self-efficacy: The exercise of control.* New York: Freeman.

Blom, L. C., Watson II, J. C., and Spadaro, N. (2010). The impact of a coaching intervention on the coach-athlete dyad and athlete sport experience. *Athletic Insight- The Online Journal of Sport Psychology*, 12. Retrieved from http://www.athleticinsight.com/Vol12Iss3/Feature.htm.

Brackenridge, C. H. (2001). *Spoilsports: Understanding and preventing sexual exploitation in sport.* London: Routledge.

Brown, S. R. (2002). Subjective behaviour analysis.*Operant Subjectivity 25*, 145-163.

Brown, S. R. (1996). Q methodology and qualitative research.*Qualitative Health Research, 6*, 561-567.

Brown, S. R. (1980). *Political subjectivity, applications of Q methodology in political science.*Yale University.

Chelladurai, P. (2007). Leadership in sports. In G. Tenenbaum., and R.C. Eklund (Eds.), *The handbook of sport psychology* (3rd edition, pp. 113-135). New York: Wiley.

Comrey, A. L., and Lee, H. B. (1992). *A first course in factor analysis.* Lawrence Erlbaum.2nd edition.

Côté, J., and Gilbert, W. (2009). An integrative definition of coaching effectiveness and expertise. *International Journal of Sport Science and Coaching, 4*, 307-232.

Deci, E. L., and Ryan, R. M. (1985). *Intrinsic motivation and self-determination in human behaviour.* New York: Plenum.

Deci, E. L., and Ryan, R. M. (2002). *Handbook of self-determination research.* Rochester, New York: University of Rochester Press.

Ericsson, K. A., Krampe, R. T., and Tesch-Römer, C. (1993). The role of deliberate practice in the acquisition of expert performance. *Psychological Review, 100*, 363-406.

Ericsson, K. A., Charness, N., Feltovich, P. J., and Hoffman, R. R. (2006). *The Cambrigde handbook of expertise and expert performance.* Cambridge University Press.

Hogg, J. M. (1995). *Mental skills for swim coaches: A coaching text on the psychological aspects of competitive swimming.* Edmonton, Alberta, Canada: Sport Excel Publishing.

Horn, T. S. (2002). Coaching effectiveness in the sports domain. In T. S. Horn (Ed.) *Advances in sport psychology* (2nd edition, pp. 309-354). Champaign, IL: Human Kinetics.

Howell, W.S. (1982). *The empathic communicator.* University of Minnesota: Wadsworth Publishing Company.

Ivey, A. E., and Ivey, M. B. (2006). *Intentional interviewing and counselling. Facilitating client development in a multicultural society.* Emeryville, CA: Wadsworth. 6th edition.

Jones, R., Armour, K., and Potrac, P. (2004). *Sportscoaching cultures: From practice to theory.* Routledge: Taylor and Francis Group, London.

Jowett, S. (2003). When the "Honeymoon" is over: A case study of a coach-athlete dyad in crisis. *The Sport Psychologist, 17*, 444-460.

Jowett, S. (2008). Moderators and mediators of the association between the coach-athlete relationship and physical self-concept. *International Journal of Coaching Science, 2*, 43–62.

Jowett, S. and Cockerill, I.M. (2002). Incompatibility in the coach–athleterelationship. In I.M. Cockerill (Ed.), *Solutions in sport psychology* (pp.16–31). London: Thomson Learning.

Jowett, S., and Cockerill, I. M. (2003). Olympic medalists' perspective of the athlete-coach relationship. *Psychology of Sport and Exercise, 4*, 313-331.

Jowett, S, and Meek, G. (2000). Coach-athlete relationships in married couples: An exploratory content analysis. *The Sport Psychologist, 14*, 157-175.

Jowett, S., and Ntoumanis, N. (2004). The coach-athlete relationship questionnaire (CART – Q): Development and initial validation. *Scandinavian Journal of Medicine and Science in Sports, 14*, 245–257.

Jowett, S., and Poczwardowski, A. (2007). Understanding the coach-athlete relationship. In S. Jowett., and D. Lavallee (Eds.), *Social psychology in sport* (pp. 3–14). Champaign, IL: Human Kinetics.

Jowett, S., Paull, G., and Pensgaard, A. M. (2005). Coach-athlete relationship. In J. Taylor and G. S. Wilson (Eds.), *Applying sport psychology: Four perspectives* (pp. 153-170). Champaign, IL: Human Kinetics.

Kvalsund, R. (1998). *A theory of the person.* Department of Education Faculty of Social Science and Technology Management. The Norwegian University Of Science And Technology Trondheim.

Kvalsund, R. (2005). *Coaching, metode: Prosess: Relasjon.* Norway: Synergy Publishing.

Kvalsund, R. (2006). *Oppmerksomhetogpåvirkningihjelperelasjoner.* Norway: Tapir AkademiskeForlag.

Lavoi, N. M. (2002). Examining relationships in sport context. Disseration abstracts International: Section B: *The Sciences and Engeneering. 63* (6-B).

Lyle, J. (1999). Coaching philosophy and coaching behaviour. In N. Cross, and J. Lyle (Eds.), *The coaching process: Principles and practice for sport* (pp. 25–46). Oxford: Butterworth-Heineman.

Lyle, J. (2002). *Sports coaching concepts – a framework for coaches' behaviour.* Routledge, London.

McKeown, B., and Thomas, D. (1988).*Q Methodology.* London: Sage.

Macmurray, J. (1999). *Persons in relation.* London: Humanities Press International.

Moen, F., and Kvalsund, R. (2008). What communications or relational factors characterize the method, skills and techniques of executive coaching? *The International Journal of Coaching in Organizations,* 102-123.

Moen, F., and Skaalvik, E. (2009). Coaching and the effects on performance psychology. *International Journal of Evidence based Coaching and Mentoring, 7,* 31-49.

Moen, F. (2009). *Coaching and performance psychology.* Department of Education, Norwegian University of Science and Technology, NTNU, Doctoral dissertation.

Myers, N. D., Chase, M. A., Beauchamp, M. R., and Jackson, B. (2010). The coaching competency scale II – High School Teams. *Educational and Psychological Measurement, 70,* 477-494.

Myers, N. D., Feltz, D. L., Maier, K. S., Wolfe, E. W., and Reckase, M. D. (2006). Athletes' evaluations of their head coach's coaching competency. *Research Quarterly for Exercise and Sport, 77,* 111-121.

Myers, N. D., Wolfe, E. W., Maier, K. S., Feltz, D. L., and Reckase, M. D. (2006). Extending validity evidence for multidimensional measures of coaching competency. *Research Quarterly for Exercise and Sport, 77,* 451-463.

Olympiou, A., Jowett, S., and Duda, J. L. (2008). The psychological interface between the coach-created motivational climate and the coach-athlete relationship in team sports. *The Sport Psychologist, 22,* 423-438

Pett, M. A., Lackey, N. R., and Sullivan, J. J. (2003). *Making sense of factor analysis: The use of factor analysis for instrument development in health care research.* Thousand Oaks, CA: Sage.

Rieke, M., Hammermeister, J. and Chase M. (2008). Servant leadership in sport: a new paradigm for effective coach behaviour. *International Journal of Sport Science and Coaching 3,* 227-239.

Rogers, C. R. (1967). *On becoming a person: A therapist's view of psychotherapy.* London: Constable.

Schmolck, P. (2002). PQMethod download mirror retrieved from http://www.qmethod.org/Tutorials/pqmethod.htm

Skaalvik, E. M. (1990). Gender differences in general academic self-concept and success expectations on defined academic problems.*Journal of Educational Psychology,* 82, 591-598.

Skaalvik, E. M. (1994). Attribution of perceived achievement in school in general and in maths and verbal areas: Relations with academic self-concept and self-esteem. *British Journal of Educational Psychology,* 64, 133-143.

Starkes, J. L., and Ericsson, K. A. (2003).*Expert performance in sports: Advances in research on sport expertise.* Champaign, IL: Human Kinetics.

Stephenson, W. (1950). A statistical approach to typology: The study of trait universes. *Journal of Clinical Psychology.* 6, 26-38.

Stephenson, W. (1986). Protoconcurcus: The concourse theory of communication. *Operant Subjectivity,* 9, 37-58, 73-96.

Tanenbaum, G., and Eklund, R. C. (2007). *Handbook of sport psychology*. New Jersey: John Wiley and Sons, Inc.

Taylor, J., and Wilson, W. (2005). *Applying sport psychology: Four perspectives*. Human Kinetics Publishers.

Trzashoma- Bicsérdy, G., Bognár, G, Révész, L., and Géczi, G. (2001). The coach-athlete relationship in successful Hungarian individual sports. *International Journal of Sport Science and Coaching, 2*, 485- 495 .

Vaglum, P. (2008). Måvialltidbryossomrelasjoneneipsykiatriskarbeid? In B, Thorsen (Ed.), *Oss imellom: Om relasjonenesbetydning for mental helse*. Norway: Hertervik Akademisk.

Vargas-Tonsing, T. M., and Guan, J. M. (2007). Athletes' preferences for informational and emotional pre-game speech content. *International Journal of Sport Science and Coaching, 2*, 171-180.

Weinberg, R. S., and Gould, D. (2007). *Foundations of sport and exercise psychology*. Human Kinetics Publishers; 4th edition.

Weiner, B. (1995). *Judgement of responsibility: A foundation for a theory of social conduct*. New York: Guilford.

Whitmore, J. (2002). *Coaching for performance: Growing people, performance and purpose*. London: Nicholas Brealey Publishing.

Withley, B. E., and Frieze, I. H. (1985). Children's causal attribution for success and failure in achievement settings: A meta-analysis. *Journal of Educational Psychology, 5*, 608-616.

In: Athletic Insight's Writings of 2012
Editor: Robert Schinke

ISBN: 978-1-62618-120-5
© 2013 Nova Science Publishers, Inc.

Chapter 16

ASSESSMENT OF ESTIMATED VERSUS ACTUAL CALORIC EXPENDITURE[*]

Kylee J. Heston[#], Daniel D. Houlihan and Kendra J. Homan

University of North Dakota, Grand Forks, ND, US
Minnesota State University, Mankato, MN, US
Utah State University, Logan, UT, US

ABSTRACT

Obesity in our nation has reached epidemic levels. Contributing to the problem is people's inaccuracies when accounting for caloric expenditure. For the purpose of this article, the researchers used the planning fallacy to explain why people may misestimate caloric expenditure. Nine men and women ages 17-34 participated in this study. Actual caloric expenditure was assessed through the use of the bodybugg™ armband apparatus. It was hypothesized that individuals would underestimate calories burned in an entire day, while overestimating caloric expenditure during exercise. Results indicated that individuals underestimated caloric expenditure both throughout the entire day and during exercise. With the proper tools and education, including an accurate perception of caloric expenditure and the ability to engage in a weight loss and/or healthy living program, healthy and maintainable results are possible.

Keywords: Exercise, caloric expenditure, weight loss, planning fallacy, bodybugg™ apparatus

---

[*] The information in the article has not been published elsewhere nor has it been submitted for publication elsewhere.

[#] Correspondence concerning this article should be addressed to Kylee J. Heston, Department of Psychology, University of North Dakota, Grand Forks, ND 58207. E-mail: kylee.j.heston@und.edu.

INTRODUCTION

With obesity levels in our nation reaching epidemic levels, the weight loss industry is booming. Unfortunately, even with a plethora of weight loss options available, the National Center for Health Statistics, Centers for Disease Control and Prevention continue to report obesity as a growing concern (Flegal, Carroll, Ogden, and Curtin, 2010). Obesity and being overweight are met with a variety of potentially fatal consequences including diabetes, high blood pressure, and congestive heart failure (National Institute of Health, 1998), making the reversal of this problem increasingly important. Even without the achievement of significant weight loss, creating additional caloric expenditure through exercise and increased involvement in daily physical behavior along with healthy nutrition consumption may be met with health improvement benefits (Bacon and Aphramor, 2011; Borer, 2008; Rosenkranz, Townsend, Steffens, and Harms, 2010). Failing to account for actual daily energy expenditure when making recommendations for nutritional caloric restriction may be leading to the inability to achieve and maintain healthy weight loss and healthy living goals.

Additionally, estimating caloric expenditure is important when working with athletes and sports teams. Athletic performance is not only about encompassing technical skill. An athlete must also be physically and mentally prepared for practice and competition. In order to perform to the best of one's ability, both physically and mentally, one must give their body the proper nutrition that one needs. Misestimating caloric expenditure, and consequently caloric intake, can inhibit one's mental and physical performance. As a result, having the ability to accurately estimate caloric expenditure can greatly enhance an athlete's performance.

Research has demonstrated that obesity and weight loss are each sustained by the surplus or deficit in the balance between energy intake and energy expenditure (Celi et al., 2010). One step toward maintaining weight loss is creating the appropriate deficit between energy intake and energy expenditure. Safe weight loss is advised at no more than one to two pounds per week, equaling a daily deficit of 500 to 1,000 calories (Carels et al., 2008). The problem with many weight loss programs is that the allotted daily caloric intake is set at such a low level that most individuals who are following the diets are actually starving themselves. Typical restrictions are 1,200 calories daily intake for women and 1,400 calories for men. Such restrictions have the potential to cause physical and psychological consequences of starvation, and the individual may be unable to maintain the diet (Applebaum, 2008).

Applebaum (2008) demonstrated the negative potential of such caloric restriction by comparing the numbers to past instances of intentional torture and murder of victims by starvation. One such example is Russian and British prisoners of war in Tost, Germany during World War II who were allotted 1,611 calories per day as a means of torture. Evidence that these caloric numbers were extreme was noted in an early publication by Keys (1946). The men in this study were initially fed an average diet of 3,150 calories per day to maintain their weight, an amount that was much more than the recommendations described above. During the starvation period of the study, calories were restricted to 1,760 per day and resulted in depression, fatigue, anemia, weakness, edema, and bradycardia (Keys, 1946).

Many researchers indicate that individuals are inaccurate in their estimates of daily caloric expenditure and of calories burned during an exercise session (Church et al., 2009; Donnelly and Smith, 2005; King et al., 2008; Slotterback, Leeman, and Oakes, 2006). In a few studies, results indicate that study participants who engaged in regular exercise tended to lose less weight than what would be expected compared to those did not engage in regular exercise in a given week. It is thought that this is due to individuals who engage in regular exercise giving themselves credit for more calories burned than their actual expenditure and then over-indulging (Church et al., 2009; Donnelly and Smith, 2005; King et al., 2008).

Slotterback et al. (2006) also suggested that individuals are frequently wrong in their estimations of caloric expenditure. It was found that more intense, shorter lasting activities (e.g., intentional physical exercise) were estimated as burning more calories than longer, less intense activities (e.g., lawn mowing, child care, cleaning), even though both types of activities were matched up according to the amount of calories burned. The planning fallacy may provide a probable explanation as to why this occurs.

The planning fallacy is described as the inclination to misestimate task completion times despite having knowledge of past similar experiences (Buehler, Griffin, and Ross, 1994). The planning fallacy has frequently been studied in the realm of task completion time and the theory behind it may be useful in understanding misestimation of caloric expenditure. Results of this research indicated that individuals tend to underestimate predictions of task completion times for longer and more familiar tasks, while tending to overestimate prediction times for shorter and newer tasks (Roy, Mitten, and Christenfeld, 2008). For the purpose of our paper, misestimation will be based on the length and novelty of exercise and daily behavior leading to caloric expenditure.

Caloric expenditure during exercise may be overestimated because it is not a common occurrence throughout the day. Daily chores, on the other hand, are engaged in more frequently and, thus, may lead to underestimation. When people underestimate the amount of calories burned in daily tasks, they are more likely to underestimate calories burned for the entire day.

With this underestimation in mind, people may give themselves permission to severely restrict their daily caloric intake. Whether the individual is overeating after an exercise session or under-eating for the entire day, each scenario has the potential for negative outcome. The study of the caloric expenditure in relation to exercise and daily behavior is virtually nonexistent in the non-laboratory research, as there has been no reliable way, outside of the clinical setting, to measure the true amount of exercise or caloric expenditure an individual has engaged in.

While caloric expenditure is often measured through various methods such as the heart rate monitor, studies show that these tools are not highly accurate in assessment of caloric expenditure. Spierer, Hagins, Rundle, and Pappas (2011) compared the heart rate monitor to indirect calorimetry, the gold standard in laboratory assessment of energy expenditure, and found that the heart rate monitor significantly underestimated and at times substantially underestimated the amount of calories burned during various physical activity tasks.

The advent of the bodybugg™ (www.bodybugg.com), which uses SenseWear™ Armband (SWA) technology, has allowed for the study of caloric expenditure in relation to exercise and daily behavior outside of the clinical setting. The SWA technology has found to be a valid and reliable tool for assessing caloric expenditure when tested against indirect calorimetry (Fruin and Walberg-Rankin, 2004). Fruin and Walberg-Rankin (2004) assessed the reliability and validity of the SWA technology via comparison with indirect calorimetry during cycling, treadmill walking, and periods of rest. The authors concluded that the device is especially valid and reliable at detecting energy expenditure at rest. No significant differences were found between the SWA and indirect calorimetry during cycling; yet walking energy expenditure was significantly overestimated without incline and underestimated with incline.

Drenowatz and Eisenmann (2011) assessed reliability and validity against indirect calorimetry and found that the SWA provides accurate results for energy expenditure during low and moderate intensity activity, yet is less accurate during high intensity activity. Overall, both studies found the SWA to be a reliable and valid tool for use outside of the laboratory setting, while indirect calorimetry continues to provide the most accurate assessment tool for laboratory based studies. For the purpose of this study, the bodybugg™ was used to determine accuracy of individual estimation of caloric expenditure.

In accordance with the planning fallacy, it was hypothesized that individuals would underestimate their overall caloric expenditure for the entire day and would overestimate calories burned for each exercise session.

METHOD

Participants

A total of 9 individuals participated in the study. Participants were both men ($N = 5$) and women ($N = 4$) and ranged in age from 17 to 34 years ($M=28.22$, $SD=6.04$). All participants identified themselves as Caucasian, non-Hispanic. Participants were recruited via flyer from establishments in the Twin Cities area of Minnesota, including a business office, a fitness facility, and a restaurant. Participation is this study was voluntary and all procedures were in accordance with state and federal guideline for the protection of human participants. This study was approved by the Internal Review Board at Minnesota State University at Mankato before data collection commenced. Requirements for participation were that the individual was currently engaging in some type of exercise regimen and was over 16 years of age. No specifications were set for intensity, frequency, or type of exercise regimen engaged in. Individuals who were less than 18 years of age were required to obtain parental consent. Because there were no age restrictions for adults, and individuals were recruited throughout the community, ages varied. Additionally, the participant had to be willing to wear the bodybugg™ device throughout the entire 14 days of the study.

Materials

Data for the experiment was collected through the bodybugg™ and data collection sheets on which participants recorded how many calories they estimated having burned for the entire day along with any exercise they completed that day. They were also directed to list the type of exercise, the duration, the intensity, and the estimated caloric expenditure for each exercise. The bodybugg™ was worn by the participants for the duration of the study in order to measure the actual caloric expenditure of the participant throughout the day, including that of each exercise session. The bodybugg™ uses "sensor fusion" to interpret caloric expenditure by collecting a variety of body data using multiple physiological sensors; whereas, previous devices, such as the heart rate monitor, use only one sensor. The sensors included an accelerometer that measured motion and sensors for heat flux, galvanic skin response, and skin temperature (Andre et al., 2006).

These, along with data entered manually including age, gender, height, and weight are what add to the accuracy of this device in assessing energy expenditure over other devices on the market (Fruin and Walberg-Rankin, 2004).

Procedure

Participants were required to wear the bodybugg™ during all waking hours for 14 consecutive days. During this time they were instructed to go about their daily activities as usual and to follow their current exercise regime. Upon exercising, participants were instructed to complete the data collection sheets logging the type of exercise, the duration, the intensity, and the estimated caloric expenditure. Participants were instructed to complete daily estimates of caloric expenditure every evening. All of the data recorded by the participant was returned to the experimenter at the end of the study. The data being recorded by the bodybugg™ was stored within its memory system for the entire 14 day period and obtained by the experimenter at the end of that period. Participants merely had to wear the device for the data to be recorded; no other action on their part was required. Participants wore the bodybugg™ apparatus 92% of the time (116 of 126 combined days). Participant estimations of caloric expenditure for the entire day and for each exercise session engaged in were compared to actual caloric expenditure collected via the bodybugg™. Data from the bodybugg™ apparatus was obtained by the researcher at the end of the 14 day period via a web program at http://my.apexfitness.com/. Upon downloading the bodybugg™ data onto the website, the experimenter was able to see the times the participant wore the device, their activity level throughout use, how many calories they burned per minute in a six minute average, and their total caloric expenditure for the entire day. Exercise times were delineated by participants on the data collection sheets, and clear differences in average expenditure for exercise start and end times could be viewed through bar graph assessment provided on a six-minute average by the bodybugg™ web program. Actual caloric expenditure was collected in this way and compared to individual estimations using the statistical software analysis package SPSS 16.0. Actual and estimated data for the entire day and during exercise sessions can be viewed in Tables 1 and 2. For daily results in Table 1, no data is entered in the table when the participant did not wear the bodybugg™ apparatus for the entire day. Because individuals did not exercise every day, in Table 2 no data is placed during periods where exercise was not engaged in, while multiple numbers indicate more than one exercise session that day. As the data was calculated using overall combined actual and estimated daily and exercise energy expenditure for all participants combined, the impact of number of exercise sessions and days exercised did not affect results. Due to wide variability of exercise type both within and between participants (basketball, running, biking, mountain biking, volleyball, walking, badminton, tennis, indoor cycling, aerobics, strength training, etc.) and the limited number of each type of exercise session, analysis assessing the variability in caloric assessment based on exercise type was not conducted.

Table 1. Participant's estimated and actual calories burned for the entire day

		Participant 1	Participant 2	Participant 3	Participant 4	Participant 5	Participant 6	Participant 7	Participant 8	Participant 9
Day 1	Estimate	3,500	520	2,400	2,370	2,000	1,600	2,000	2,000	2,000
	Actual	2,605	2,015	2,926	3,744	2,611	2,431	2,465	2,562	1,900
Day 2	Estimate	3,500	-----	2,500	2,400	2,300	1,550	2,010	1,800	2,250
	Actual	2,489	-----	3,250	3,359	2,900	2,763	3,031	2,435	2,184
Day 3	Estimate	3,600	600	3,000	2,600	1,800	1,300	2,114	1,800	2,050
	Actual	1,963	1,859	3,335	4,342	2,676	2,340	2,901	2,363	2,359
Day 4	Estimate	3,400	500	2,000	2,050	2,100	1,400	1,800	1,700	2,100
	Actual	1,940	1,827	2,685	3,036	2,610	2,460	2,470	2,376	2,041
Day 5	Estimate	3,000	-----	2,400	2,050	2,100	1,250	2,012	1,900	2,300
	Actual	1,913	-----	2,906	2,730	2,241	1,901	3,020	2,795	2,202
Day 6	Estimate	3,300	430	4,500	2,250	2,300	1,100	1,700	1,700	2,000
	Actual	2,144	1,880	4,760	2,879	2,352	2,120	3,315	2,484	1,836
Day 7	Estimate	3,000	400	5,000	2,500	2,200	1,100	1,800	1,750	2,300
	Actual	2,300	1,782	4,834	4,368	2,337	1,902	2,844	2,560	2,099
Day 8	Estimate	3,600	550	3,000	2,300	2,100	1,550	1,400	1,800	2,150
	Actual	1,975	1,749	3,475	3,250	2,199	2,185	2,413	2,426	2,254
Day 9	Estimate	3,000	400	2,500	2,300	2,400	1,500	1,500	1,950	2,250
	Actual	2,300	1,781	2,808	3,157	2,914	2,591	2,796	2,468	2,105
Day 10	Estimate	3,400	500	3,400	2,620	2,300	1,450	1,900	2,000	1,950
	Actual	2,046	2,010	3,294	3,669	2,784	2,450	3,444	2,474	2,103
Day 11	Estimate	3,000	-----	2,600	2,050	2,300	1,200	1,900	2,000	2,200
	Actual	1,869	-----	2,695	2,678	2,643	2,368	2,911	2,222	2,448

		Participant 1	Participant 2	Participant 3	Participant 4	Participant 5	Participant 6	Participant 7	Participant 8	Participant 9
Day 12	Estimate	3,000	-----	2,000	2,050	2,000	1,400	-----	1,500	2,000
	Actual	1,927	-----	2,497	2,711	2,242	2,518	-----	2,067	2,202
Day 13	Estimate	-----	-----	2,300	2,050	2,200	-----	2,000	1,750	2,150
	Actual	-----	-----	2,694	2,807	2,341	-----	2,769	2,301	2,098
Day 14	Estimate	-----	-----	2,000	2,630	2,200	1,100	1,500	2,050	2,100
	Actual	-----	-----	2,621	3,717	2,136	1,916	2,686	2,547	1,983

Table 2. Participant's estimated and actual calories burned for each exercise session

		Participant 1	Participant 2	Participant 3	Participant 4	Participant 5	Participant 6	Participant 7	Participant 8	Participant 9
Day 1	Estimate	500	120	200	320	300	400	-----	400	-----
	Actual	358	274	114	586	375	431	-----	381	-----
Day 2	Estimate	500	-----	-----	350	350	450	150/40	150	200
	Actual	351	-----	-----	445	295	571	146/28	177	299
Day 3	Estimate	-----	200	600/400	550	-----	-----	250	200	-----
	Actual	-----	77	412/407	1,038	-----	-----	256	242	-----
Day 4	Estimate	400	-----	-----	-----	310	-----	-----	-----	-----
	Actual	86	-----	-----	-----	311	-----	-----	-----	-----
Day 5	Estimate	-----	-----	-----	-----	-----	-----	430	-----	300
	Actual	-----	-----	-----	-----	-----	-----	823	-----	321
Day 6	Estimate	300	30	2,500	200	-----	-----	300	-----	-----
	Actual	46	53	2,963	175	-----	-----	290	-----	-----
Day 7	Estimate	-----	-----	3,000	450	-----	-----	50	-----	250
	Actual	-----	-----	3,731	800	-----	-----	31	-----	302

Table 2. (Continued)

		Participant 1	Participant 2	Participant 3	Participant 4	Participant 5	Participant 6	Participant 7	Participant 8	Participant 9
Day 8	Estimate	-----	-----	1,000	250	-----	-----	-----	-----	175
	Actual	-----	-----	1,602	436	-----	-----	-----	-----	177
Day 9	Estimate	-----	-----	500	250	300	350	-----	350	300
	Actual	-----	-----	331	539	421	420	-----	348	308
Day 10	Estimate	400	100123	600/400/400	570	-----	150	55/150	200/100	-----
	Actual	194		373/410/271	1,170	-----	388	39/229	367/248	-----
Day 11	Estimate	-----	-----	600	-----	-----	-----	50	250	150
	Actual	-----	-----	426	-----	-----	-----	124	285	138
Day 12	Estimate	-----	-----	-----	-----	-----	300	-----	-----	-----
	Actual	-----	-----	-----	-----	-----	334	-----	-----	-----
Day 13	Estimate	-----	-----	300	-----	-----	-----	60/50	100	100
	Actual	-----	-----	749	-----	-----	-----	335/135	198	238
Day 14	Estimate	-----	-----	-----	580	-----	-----	258	300	100
	Actual	-----	-----	-----	1,199	-----	-----	258	370	237

RESULTS

The Wilcoxon signed-rank test was used in the data analysis due to the small subject size and the data not meeting the assumptions necessary to conduct a paired-samples t-test, including high skew due to the large range in data. The analysis revealed that actual calories burned for the entire day (*Median* = 2,465.00) were significantly higher than the estimates provided by the participants (*Median* = 2,031.00), $T = 50.42$, $p < .001$, $r = -.40$. This indicates that individuals underestimated their overall caloric expenditure for the entire day (see Table 1 for participants' estimated and actual calories burned for the entire day). Additionally, the analysis revealed that actual calories burned for exercise sessions (*Median* = 326.70) were significantly higher than participant estimated caloric expenditure (*Median* = 300.00), $T = 32.19$, $p < .01$, $r = -.26$. This indicates that individuals underestimated their caloric expenditure for exercise sessions (see Table 2 for participants' estimated and actual calories burned for the each exercise session).

In order to determine if there were gender differences in the estimation of calories burned for the entire day and for exercise sessions, the Wilcoxon signed-rank test was performed on the data. Through the analyses, the researchers confirmed that both men ($T = 37.70$, $p < .01$, $r = -.27$; *Median* = 2,621) and women ($T = 5.67$, $p < .001$, $r = -.57$; *Median* = 2,428.5) significantly underestimated their caloric expenditure for the entire day. For exercise sessions, however, women's recordings (*Median* = 285) were significantly underestimated, $T = 7.29$, $p < .001$, $r = -.50$; while men's recordings (*Median* = 407.4) were underestimated as well, but their estimations were not significant, $T = 16.71$, $r = -.16$. This indicates that both men and women significantly underestimate the number of calories they are burning in an entire day; yet for exercise sessions, men are slightly more accurate than women in estimations of caloric expenditure.

DISCUSSION

The researchers demonstrated that individuals significantly underestimated caloric expenditure both for the entire day and the exercise session. It is not surprising that caloric expenditure was underestimated for the entire day. This finding supports the researchers' hypothesis and follows along with the results of the Slotterback et al. (2006) study in which participants underestimated the amount of calories they burned during daily activities.

More surprising was the finding that individuals significantly underestimated their caloric expenditure for the exercise session. The results of past research indicate that people overestimate caloric expenditure during their exercise sessions (Church et al., 2009; Donnelly and Smith, 2005; King et al., 2008); however, to the knowledge of these researchers, this was the first study which empirically tested participant estimations against their actual caloric expenditure. According to the planning fallacy, individuals overestimate task completion time for less familiar and shorter tasks (Roy et al., 2008). As exercise sessions are engaged in less frequently than repetitive daily activities, it was hypothesized that individuals would overestimate caloric expenditure during exercise sessions. The frequency of engagement in the same types of exercise on a daily basis was overlooked for this hypothesis. Repetitive exercise sessions may be just as mundane as the daily activities, making underestimation more plausible. It would be beneficial to test this idea in future studies by having people note when they are engaging in a novel activity and to compare the estimates based on newer activities against their regular exercise routines.

Inaccuracies in the participant's estimates regarding both their caloric burn during exercise and throughout the day can be seen by looking at the current data. Estimations of caloric expenditure for the entire day ranged from 400-5,000 calories (*Median* = 2,031), while the actual range was from 1,749-4,834 (*Median* = 2,465). Estimations for exercise sessions ranged from 30 to 3,000 (*Median* = 300) with the actual ranging from 31.60 to 3,731.60 (*Median* = 326.7). See Tables 1 and 2 for side-by-side comparisons of the data which demonstrates the amount of misestimation that occurred throughout the study.

It is important to create a healthy deficit between caloric expenditure and intake. Individuals cannot simply cut 500-1,000 calories from their current nutritional consumption or restrict their caloric intake to extreme levels in an attempt at weight loss. Knowledge of actual energy expenditure is important in deciding on the caloric intake appropriate for healthy, sustainable weight loss. Decisions toward caloric reduction should be made only by accounting for actual caloric expenditure. If individuals create too severe a deficit and give up on their weight loss goals, the health benefits associated with weight loss and increased caloric expenditure may be missed.

Many individuals need not restrict their calories anywhere near the 1,200-1,400 calorie range to lose two pounds per week. Only 30% of the daily actual caloric expenditures in the current study were less than 2,200, with the lower 6.8% being inaccurate due to the bodybugg™ apparatus not being worn. One participant burned an average of 3,528 calories per day (4,834 calories in one day) resulting in the individual being able to consume 2,528 calories per day and still lose two pounds per week. The participant had the ability to consume much more on the days he burned over 4,000 calories. Caloric intake lower than 2,528 calories for this individual has the potential to result in ill physical and psychological effects and may be difficult to maintain.

Future studies utilizing the bodybugg™ will be able to provide more accurate estimations of caloric expenditure during various tasks, including both exercise and daily behavior. More detailed analysis into the accuracy of the bodybugg™ system will further enable such study. Obtaining more accurate estimations may allow for weight loss programs to be tailored more specifically to each individual based on their actual caloric expenditure. Even without the use of the bodybugg™, such estimations will provide an anchor for assessment of safe caloric intake toward weight loss. Over time, such estimations may be tailored to each individual based on their actual weight loss. Currently, many individuals hoping to achieve weight loss or the health benefits associated with increases in caloric expenditure may be unaware of the amount of caloric expenditure associated with exercise and daily physical behavior making creating a healthy exercise program difficult.

Additionally, data comparison between Tables 1 and 2 provides evidence that even without exercise individuals have the potential for significant daily energy expenditure. Individuals unaware of the benefits of increased physical activity throughout the day, even without exercise, may be more inclined to restrict caloric intake on days when specific exercise sessions are not engaged in. Providing knowledge to the public regarding more accurate caloric expenditure associated with physical activity in general, along with information on safe and effective weight loss and the health benefits of increased physical activity, may give individuals the opportunity to create a safe and healthy weight loss program.

Several potential limitations of our study need to be noted. An initial concern lies in the small sample size of participants for the study and the consequential inability for the results to be generalized to the general population. It should be pointed out, however, that estimations were made for each day ($n = 118$) and each exercise session ($n = 68$), thus, the analyses were based on a rather large number of data points for each participant. This study provides a good stepping stone toward future research, and it will be useful to replicate the study with a larger, more representative sample of the population. A second limitation involves the compliance problems of the participants. Unfortunately, the researchers came across situations in which participants did not follow the protocol for wearing the bodybugg™ during all waking hours for 14 consecutive days, resulting in some missing data. This problem could be avoided in the future if a daily reminder was used to prompt the participant to wear the device. Finally, the while the bodybugg™ tool has been found to be valid and reliable for certain activities and intensity levels, activity type and intensity level were not taken into consideration with these results. Future studies using the bodybugg™ may benefit from tailoring activities and intensity levels to those that have been found most reliable in comparisons of energy expenditure to indirect calorimetry. The field will also benefit from more extensive study of the reliability and validity of the bodybugg™ apparatus for various exercise activities as well as daily physical behaviors.

Future researchers should examine if individuals underestimate their caloric expenditure in exercises that are novel as compared to exercises that are routine. Findings confirming underestimation would support the application of the planning fallacy to novel exercise programs. The literature would also benefit from a study assessing the accuracy of estimations of caloric expenditure in everyday tasks such as household chores, shopping, yard work, etc. While studies have shown misestimations in guessing caloric expenditure from a list of regular activities, a better assessment may result when the individuals are actually engaging in the behaviors. Differences in intensity levels, length of time, etc. for each daily task could then be taken into account. It is likely that individuals would underestimate caloric expenditure, as they did with both daily expenditure and exercise in this study. This would provide further evidence of the necessity to empower people with the knowledge of caloric expenditure for daily tasks as well as exercise. The bodybugg™ apparatus may also be beneficial for use in studies assessing the benefits of caloric expenditure aside from weight loss by assessing the reinforcement potential of having immediate feedback regarding caloric expenditure and step counts on the additional wristband apparatus (which can be purchased along with the bodybugg™ apparatus). Increases in caloric expenditure could then be compared to any associated health benefits.

In conclusion, this report demonstrated that individuals tend to significantly underestimate the calories they expend during the entire day and during each exercise session. This information can be beneficial to individuals who are trying to lose weight as well as to coaches and athletes who are trying to reach optimal performance in their athletic endeavors. It is important to create a healthy deficit between caloric expenditure and intake if one is trying to lose or maintain weight or trying to reach optimal athletic performance. Being able to accurately estimate caloric expenditure during various tasks may allow for weight loss and training programs to be tailored more specifically to each individual based on their actual caloric expenditure.

DISCLOSURE

This research was supported in part by a small research grant from the Graduate School at Minnesota State University at Mankato. None of the researchers were involved with either BodyMedia, Inc. or Apex Fitness Group, the manufacturer and distributor of the bodybugg™, before, during, or after the study.

REFERENCES

Applebaum, M. (2008). Why diets fail: Expert diet advice as a cause of diet failure. *American Psychologist, 63*, 200-202.

Andre, D., Pelletier, R., Farringdon, J., Safier, S., Talbott, W., Stone, R., et al. (2006). Thedevelopment of the SenseWear® armband, a revolutionary energy assessment device to assessphysical activity and lifestyle.*BodyMedia, Inc.* Retrieved from http://www. bodybugg.com/pdf/wp_accuracy_ee.pdf.

Bacon, L., and Aphramor, L. (2011). Weight science: Evaluating the evidence for a paradigm shift. *Nutrition Journal, 10*, 1-13.

Borer, K. T. (2008). How effective is exercise in producing fat loss? *Kinesiology, 40*, 126-137.

Buehler, R., Griffin, D., and Ross, M. (1994).Exploring the "planning fallacy": Why people underestimate their task completion times. *Journal of Personality and Social Psychology, 67*, 366-381.

Carels, R. A., Young, K. M., Coit, C., Clayton, A. M., Spencer, A., and Hobbs, M. (2008). Can following the caloric restriction recommendations from the dietary guidelines for Americans help individuals lose weight?*Eating Behaviors, 9*, 328-335.

Celi, F. S., Brychta, R. J., Linderman, J. D., Butler, P. W., Alberobello, A. T., Smith, S., et al. (2010). Minimal changes in environmental temperature result in a significant increase in energy expenditure and changes in the hormonal homeostasis in healthy adults. *European Journal of Endocrinology, 163*, 863-872.

Church, T. S., Martin, C. K., Thompson, A. M., Earnest, C. P., Mikus, C. R., and Blair, S. N. (2009). Changes in weight, waist circumference and compensatory responses with different doses of exercise among sedentary, overweight postmenopausal women. *PLoS ONE, 4*, e4515.

Donnelly, J. E., and Smith, B. K. (2005). Is exercise effective for weight loss with ad libitum diet? Energy balance, compensation, and gender differences. *Exercise Sport Science Review, 33*, 169-174.

Drenowatz, C. and Eisenmann, J. (2011). Validation of the SenseWear Armband at high intensity exercise. *European Journal of Applied Physiology, 111*, 883-887.

Flegal, K. M., Carroll, M. D., Ogden, C. L., and Curtin, L. R. (2010). Prevalence and trends in obesity among US adults, 1999-2008. *Journal of the American Medical Association, 303*, 235-241.

Fruin, M. L., and Walberg-Rankin, J. (2004). Validity of a multi-sensor armband in estimating rest and exercise energy expenditure. *Medicine and Science in Sports and Exercise, 36*, 1063-1069.

Keys, A. (1946). Human starvation and its consequences. *Journal of the American Dietetic Association, 22*, 582-587.

King, N. A., Hopkins, M., Caudwell, P., Stubbs, R. J., and Blundell, J. E. (2008). Individual variability following 12 weeks of supervised exercise: Identification and characterization of compensation for exercise-induced weight loss. *International Journal of Obesity, 32*, 177-184.

National Institute of Health: National Heart, Lung, and Blood Institute (1998). Clinical guidelines on the identification, evaluation, and treatment of overweight and obesity in adults: The evidence report. Bethesda, MD: Author.

Rosenkranz, S. K., Townsend, D. K., Steffens, S. E., and Harms, C. A. (2010). Effects of a high-fat meal on pulmonary function in healthy subjects. *European Journal of Applied Physiology, 109*, 499-506.

Roy, M. M., Mitten, S. T., and Christenfeld, N. J. S. (2008). Correcting memory improves accuracy of predicted task duration. *Journal of Experimental Psychology: Applied, 14*, 266-275.

Slotterback, C. S., Leeman, H., and Oakes, M. E. (2006). No pain, no gain: Perceptionsof calorie expenditures of exercise and daily activities. *Current Psychology: Developmental, Learning, Personality, and Social, 25*,28-41.

Spierer, D., Hagins, M., Rundle, A., and Pappas, E. (2011). A comparison of energy expenditure estimates from the Actiheart and Actical physical activity monitors during low intensity activities, walking, and jogging. *European Journal of Applied Physiology, 111*, 659-667.

In: Athletic Insight's Writings of 2012
Editor: Robert Schinke

ISBN: 978-1-62618-120-5
© 2013 Nova Science Publishers, Inc.

Chapter 17

COACHING BEHAVIORS IN CANADIAN YOUTH SPORTS

*Kaitlyn LaForge[1], Philip J. Sullivan[*1] and Gordon A. Bloom[2]*

[1]Brock University, Ontario, Canada
[2]McGill University, Quebec, Canada

ABSTRACT

The purpose of the study was to examine coaching behaviors based on youth sport context and coaching certification. Sixty-three coaches, equally divided among three coaching contexts in Canada, and with varying degrees of certification, each completed the Revised Leadership Scale for Sport (Zhang, Jensen, and Mann, 1997). Results showed no significant interactions or main effects for context or possession of certification, which suggested that Canadian youth sport coaches exhibited similar perceived coaching behaviors regardless of context. These perceived behaviors were mostly positive, with high occurrences of training and instruction, positive feedback, and consideration behaviors. The perceived focus on positive and supportive coaching behaviors, regardless of the contextual stream or formal coaching educationmay help create environments that foster positive psychosocial development of youth sport athletes in Canada.

Keywords: Coaching Behaviors, Youth Sport, Canadian Contexts

INTRODUCTION

Coaches influence the youth sport experience through their goals, values, attitudes, and behaviors (Fraser-Thomas and Côté, 2009; Newin, Bloom, and Loughead, 2008; Smith and

* Address Correspondence to: Philip J. Sullivan, Ph.D. Department of Kinesiology; Brock University; 500 Glenridge Avenue; St. Catharines, Ontario; L2S 3A1 CANADA; Phone: 905-688-5550 ext. 4787; Fax: 905-688-8364; Email: psullivan@brocku.ca.

Smoll, 2002). The degree of enjoyment experienced by youth and their desire to continue involvement in sport has largely been influenced by their coach (e.g., Fraser-Thomas, Côté, and Deakin, 2005; Smoll, Smith, Barnett, and Everett, 1993; Weiss and Williams, 2004). Appropriate coaching behaviors have been linked to higher self-esteem, higher competence, and longer involvement in sport (Amorose and Anderson-Butcher, 2007; Conroy and Coatsworth, 2006; Smith, Zane, Smoll, and Coppel, 1983). Coaching behavior has also been linked to several negative outcomes in youth sport, particularly athlete withdrawal (Weiss and Williams, 2004). In fact, as many as one-third of youth athletes do not participate in sport the following year (Weiss and Ferrer-Caja, 2002). Several reasons have been cited for sport withdrawal including disliking the coach (Hedstrom and Gould, 2004). Clearly, coaching in youth sport is a highly influential role, and can have a profound effect on the states and attributes of the participants, and subsequently, the individual and social benefits of sport. Given its importance, it is surprising that most coaches have limited awareness of their own coaching behaviors (Fraser-Thomas and Côté, 2009; Smith, Smoll, Curtis, and Hunt, 1978; Williams et al., 2003).

Various models have attempted to describe coaching behavior and its effects on athlete development, including the Mediational Model of Leadership (Smoll and Smith, 1989), the Multidimensional Model of Leadership (Chelladurai, 1990), the Coaching Model (Côté, Salmela, Trudel, Baria, and Russell, 1995), the Model of Great Coaching (Becker, 2009), and Horn's Model of Coaching Effectiveness (Horn, 2008). Though each model is unique, common themes include the impact of coaches' personal characteristics and contextual factors on coaching behavior. Personal characteristics include age, gender, psychological traits, and years of experience. Contextual factors include level of competition (i.e., recreational vs. competitive), practice or game settings, type of sport, and previous win/loss record. Horn suggested that personal characteristics interact with contextual factors and organizational climate to influence and form coaching behaviors.

The personal characteristics of coaches have been shown to affect coaching behaviors, including previous experience. For example, research has indicated that previous experience affected coaches' self-efficacy (i.e., coaching efficacy), which influenced coaches' behaviors (Feltz, Chase, Moritz, and Sullivan, 1999; Sullivan and Kent, 2003).

Gilbert and Trudel (2001) also examined the impact of experience on youth sport coach development and found that experiential learning was important to developing knowledge and behaviors as a coach. Although previous experience is only one example of a coaches' personal attributes, it appears to be an important characteristic that impacts coaching behaviors.

In addition to coaching characteristics, contextual factors, including culture, have also influenced coaches' behavior(e.g., Chelladurai, Imamura, Yamaguchi, Oinmua, and Miyauchi, 1988; Duchesne, Bloom, and Sabiston, 2011; Ryska, Yin, Cooley, and Ginn, 1999; Solomon and Lobinger, 2011; Weinberg, Grove, and Jackson, 1992). More specifically, Weinberg et al. revealed differences between American and Australian coaches in their application and perceived efficiency of self-efficacy building strategies.

American coaches found that using difficult training situations and emphasizing anxiety as a sign of readiness to be more effective in building athletes' self-efficacy compared to Australian coaches. In a similar manner, Ryskaet al. found differences in coaching strategies between Australian and American coaches. American coaches focused on strategies that facilitated task-related cohesion (e.g., increased attentiveness of each athlete's team responsibilities and cooperative team training), whereas Australian coaches focused on strategies that facilitated social cohesion (e.g., recognizing personal differences among athletes and gaining understanding of individuals). These studies suggest that culture is a contextual variable that affects coaching behaviors.

Coaching behaviors of the Multidimensional Model of Leadership are typically measured using the Revised Leadership Scale for Sport (RLSS; Zhang Jensen, and Mann, 1997). The model contends that antecedent factors (situational, member, and leader characteristics) influence three types of leadership behaviors: actual, preferred, and required behaviors (i.e., behaviors dictated by goals, structure, and norms of an organization).

The performance and satisfaction of members depend on the degree of congruence of the three aspects of leadership behaviors (Chelladurai, 1990). These behaviors include social support (i.e., the extent to which the coach satisfies the athletes' interpersonal needs), situation consideration (i.e., behaviors that consider factors such as time, individual, and environment), positive feedback (i.e., behaviors that express appreciation and contribution of the athletes' performances), and training and instruction (i.e., behaviors that help improve athletic performance).

Further, coaches' decision making is measured by two factors: democratic behaviors (i.e., the extent to which a coach permits athletes to participate in decision-making processes), and autocratic behaviors (i.e., the extent to which the coach stress his/her authority; Zhang et al., 1997).

In Canada, coach education is governed by the Canadian Association of Coaching (CAC) whose mission is to deliver the skills, knowledge, and attitudes needed to provide effective coaching (Bloom, 2011). The CAC created the National Coaching Certification Program (NCCP) in 1974 to train and certify coaches in over 60 sports. Previously, coaches were certified based on five levels of training, each with three courses. Theoretical courses involved general coaching principles applicable to all sports.

Technical courses involved specific techniques and strategies for each individual sport. Practical courses involved structured coaching placements before registration at the given level. Recently, the NCCP has been re-developed from a knowledge- and course-based approach to a competency-based program which focuses on the environment or context in which the coach is coaching (Bloom, 2011).

There are three youth sport coaching contexts in Canada: community, instructional, and competitive (Coaching Association of Canada, 2008). Community coaches focus on broad-based participation including both initiation and on-going participation in sport. These coaches are involved with athletes of varying ages ranging from children to adults. Instructional coaches work with athletes to develop skill proficiency in non-competitive environments in a variety of situations (i.e., beginner, intermediate, and advanced athletic contexts). Competitive coaches work with athletes to develop skills for use in regional, national, or international competitions in long-term situations (e.g., introductory, developmental, and high performance environments). Although youth sport has been repeatedly noted as a distinct context that may influence coaching behavior (Horn, 2008; Smoll and Smith, 1989), each Canadian youth sport coaching context (i.e., community, competitive, or instructional) may be a distinctive or separate contextual variable (Sullivan, Paquette, Holt, and Bloom, 2012).

Specifically, as each youth sport context receives different information in terms of level of competition and NCCP education, subsequent coaching knowledge should result in coaching behavioral differences. For example, community coaches receive information that teaches them how to create a fun, safe, and developmentally appropriate environment, instructional coaches receive information regarding the development of tactical and technical skills, and competitive coaches receive information regarding long-term athlete development and advanced knowledge regarding tactical, technical, physical, and psychological domains which should lead to performance excellence (Coaching Association of Canada, 2008).

This distinction is consistent with coaching research that distinguishes different aspects of coaching. For example, Lyle (1999) discussed coaching for participation compared to coaching for performance, and Chelladurai (2007) commented on coaching for participants' enjoyments as opposed to coaching to foster their excellence.

In terms of coach development, national coach education programs have been shown to be an important source of coaching knowledge. Lemyre, Trudel, and Durand-Bush (2007) examined coaching certification in Canada and found that first year youth sport head coaches sought out formal coaching education programs (i.e., NCCP in Canada).

Other national coaching education programs include the National Coaching Accreditation Scheme (NCAS) in Australia, the National Coaching Certificate (NCC) in the UK, and the American Sport Education Program (ASEP) in the United States. Many coaches found these programs helpful in developing their coaching knowledge.

Additional studies have revealed that coaching education programs in both Canada and the United States provided coaches of all levels of experience with important sources of coaching information (Vargas-Tonsing, 2007; Wiersma and Sherman, 2005; Wright, Trudel, and Culver, 2007). Although formal education programs are not the only source of coaching knowledge, these programs ensure the unified acquisition of coaching information (Lemyre et al., 2007). Although some research has found that coaches acquired information and knowledge through coach education courses, there is currently little research on the impact of coach education programs on coaching behaviors, and particularly on youth sport coaching behaviors. Studies have shown that national coaching education programs like the NCCP facilitated positive changes in coaches' beliefs in terms of coaching efficacy (Campbell and Sullivan, 2005; Lee, Malete, and Feltz, 2002; Malete and Feltz, 2000), and coaches' behaviors in terms of imagery use (Hall, Jedlic, Munroe-Chandler, and Hall, 2007), although none focused specifically on youth sport coaches.

Furthermore, participation in smaller-scale training programs (Cassidy, Potrac, and McKenzie, 2006; Newin et al., 2008) and university-based programs (Jones and Turner, 2006; Knowles, Gilbourne, Borrie, and Nevill, 2001) also positively influenced coaches' understanding and behaviors. The results of these studies revealed coaching education / training programs have positively affected coaching behaviors in terms of applying theoretical knowledge, communication skills, and reflective teaching practices. However, to the best of our knowledge, no studies have directly addressed the influence of a national coaching education program (i.e., the NCCP) on behaviors of youth sport coaches in Canada or elsewhere.

The present study was designed to investigate the differences in behaviors among community, instructional, and competitive youth sport coaches in Canada. The study also examined differences in coaching behaviors based on coaching certification. It was hypothesized that coaching behaviors would differ based on the specific youth sport context in which the coach was involved (Chelladurai, 2007; Côté et al., 1995; Gilbert, Gallimore, and Trudel, 2009; Horn, 2008). However, as coaching behaviors are considered bi-directional, there were no specific hypotheses a priori (c.f., Horn). It was further hypothesized that coaching behaviors would differ based on possession of coaching certification (i.e., NCCP; Hall et al., 2007). Since certified coaches should have previously acquired knowledge compared to coaches who did not complete formal coaching education programs, it was hypothesized that coaching behaviors would differ although again, due to the small amount of research in the field, no specific hypotheses were made a priori.

METHODOLOGY

Participants

The sample consisted of 63 participants, with 21 coaches equally represented in each context (community, competitive, and instructional). Participants were currently coaching athletes who ranged in age from 8-18 and were playing a variety of team sports. Coaches self-reported their context. Demographic data (e.g., sex, age, and experience of the coach) were taken from the descriptive data questionnaire given at the beginning of the survey. This sample comprised 47 males and 16 females, ranging in age from 16 to 70 years ($M = 43.2$ years, $SD = 11.8$) and ranging in experience from 1 to 45 years ($M = 17.13$ years, $SD = 11.04$). Forty-six coaches were certified (15 instructional, 19 community, 12 competitive) and 17 were not (6 instructional, 2 community, 9 competitive); 12 participants completed NCCP Level 1, 13 completed NCCP Level 2, nine completed NCCP Level 3, nine completed certification other than the NCCP, and two failed to indicate their highest level of certification. One coach failed to indicate whether he/she possessed any coaching certification.

Previous research on coaching certification on a similar construct (i.e., coaching efficacy) has shown an effect size of .78 (Sullivan and Gee, 2008). Based on this effect size, with a p of .05 a sample size of 21 gives the present design acceptable power ($\beta = .75$; Cohen, 1987)

Instruments

Coaching behaviors were measured by Zhang et al.'s (1997) RLSS, through six subscales consisting of 60 items. All items were assessed on a 5-point Likert-type scale ranging from 1 (always) to 5 (never), and all items were preceded by the phrase, "In coaching, I". The training and instruction subscale was measured by 10 items (e.g., use a variety of drills for a practice). The autocratic behavior subscale was represented through 8 items (e.g., disregard athletes' fears and dissatisfactions).

The democratic behavior subscale was assessed by 12 items (e.g., ask for the opinion of the athletes on important matters before going ahead). The social support subscale was denoted by 8 items (e.g., remain sensitive to the needs of the athletes). The positive feedback subscale was measured through 12 items (e.g., encourages an athlete when the athlete makes mistakes). The situation consideration subscale was represented by 10 items (e.g., set goals that are compatible with the athletes' ability).

This version of the RLSS measured the coaches' self-perceptions of their behaviors, not actual coaching behaviors. Horn (2008) noted that measuring both actual and perceived coaching behaviors were valid forms of assessment which comprised distinct, but equally important constructs in the coaching process.

The RLSS has previously been used to study perceived coaching behaviors(e.g., Magnusen, 2010; Sullivan and Kent, 2003). The RLSS was used in the current study as it has provides subscales (i.e., situational consideration) which may be important to youth sport. The RLSS has been supported in terms of construct and face validity, internal consistency, and factor structure (see Table 1; Zhang et al., 1997).

Procedure

Following the approval of a university research ethics board, the RLSS was formatted for the online survey provider SurveyMonkey.com. The presidents of various youth sport organizations from two Canadian provinces were contacted with information about the present study. The presidents emailed an invitation to their coaches and those who responded favorably were contacted by the researchers and provided a link to the survey website. Participants provided consent via the internet site provider and were asked to first complete a demographic data questionnaire followed by the survey. Participation in the study was strictly voluntary.

Design

The present study consisted of a 3 x 2 between-subjects design. The independent variables were coaching context (community, instructional, and competitive) and coaching certification (certified vs. non-certified) and the dependent variables were the six factors of the RLSS(i.e., democratic behaviors, positive feedback, training and instruction, situation consideration, social support, autocratic behaviors).

Results

The assumptions required for multivariate analysis were checked for all six factors of the RLSS. The means, standard deviations, skewness, and kurtosis for each subscale are presented in Table 1.

The positive feedback subscale showed moderate skewness and kurtosis, though transformation of data was not required. Multivariate outliers were checked using Malhalanobis distance calculations and no outliers were found at $p< .001$. Cronbach's alphas were calculated to check for internal consistency, with most variables showing alphas greater than Nunally's (1970) criteria of .70. Autocratic behavior was the only variable with a calculated alpha of less than .70 (.52), and was removed from subsequent analyses.

Table 2 shows the correlation matrix for the factors of the RLSS. No issues of multicollinearity were found as all factor correlations were below .80 as suggested by Tabachnick and Fidell (2007). Years of coaching experience was not significantly correlated with any of the coaching behavior factors and was not subsequently calculated as a covariate.

Table 1. Descriptive Statistics for Coaching Behavior Subscales

Descriptive Statistic Measurement					
Subscale	Mean	Standard	Skewness	Kurtosis	Chronbach's
		Deviation			α
Positive Feedback	1.47	.47	1.56	2.79	.87
Training and Instruction	1.60	.66	.86	1.16	.85
Situation Consideration	1.79	.44	.53	.94	.77
Social Support	2.47	.62	.36	-.37	.75
Democratic Behavior	2.73	.66	.86	1.16	.87
Autocratic Behavior	3.35	.48	-.64	.60	.52

Table 2. Correlation Matrix for Coaching Behavior Subscales

Subscales	1	2	3	4	5	6	7
1. Democratic Behavior	-.	10	.01	.15	.42**	.18	-.17
2. Positive Feedback	-		.45**	.55**	.16	-.23	-.15
3. Training and Instruction			-	.73**	.31*	-.02	-.23
4. Situation Consideration				-	.30*	-.43	-.22
5. Social Support					-	.19	-.24
6. Autocratic Behavior						-	-.05
7. Coaching Experience							-

Note: *p < .05. **p< .01.

The results for the 3 (community, instructional, and competitive coaching contexts) x 2 (certified or not certified) factorial MANOVA, with coaching behaviors as the dependent variables, showed that Box's test of equality of covariance matrices was non-significant, revealing that coaching behavior variables were equal across groups. No significant interactions were found, $F (10, 106) = .38$. Furthermore, no significant main effects were found for coaching context, $F (10, 108) = 1.87$, or possession of certification, $F (5, 53) = .64$. These results revealed that perceived coaching behaviors were consistent despite the context of the sport or the possession of coaching certification for Canadian youth sport coaches.

DISCUSSION

The current study investigated the differences in coaching behaviors among the three new Canadian coaching contexts (competitive, instructional, and community) and between certified and non-certified youth sport coaches. The hypotheses that coaching behaviors would vary as a result of contextual differences orpossession of coaching certification werenot supported. It was found that perceived coaching behaviors did not significantly differ among youth sport coaches regardless of the situational context or certification. Despite this, both theoretical and practical recommendations can be drawn from the current results.

Our results allude to a unique contextual element when conceptualizing youth sport (i.e., Becker, 2009; Chelladurai, 1990; Côté et al., 1995; Horn, 2008; Smoll and Smith, 1989). The previous theories all contend that differences in coaching behaviors should arise based on cultural environments, team settings, or level of competition. However, our results showed that the situational and contextual characteristics of competitive, instructional, and community coaching contexts in Canada had no effect on coaches' perceived behaviors in youth sport. It is possible that these three contexts of youth sport were not separate but actually comprised one youth sport coaching context. This conclusion would be consistent with previous suggestions that youth sport be grouped under a unique sport context (Horn, 2008; Smoll and Smith 1989). Rather than rebuke existing coaching theories, this suggests that Canadian youth sport contexts may been compassed within a distinct context of youth sport. Further research is needed to examine this suggestion.

In terms of coaching certification, previous research has shown that the attendance of formal coaching education programs resulted in changes in coaching behaviors (e.g., Hall et al., 2007) and attitudes (Campbell and Sullivan, 2005; Lee et al., 2002; MaleteandFeltz, 2000). However, the current findings suggested that perceptions of coaching behaviors did not significantly differ based on NCCP certification. One possible explanation was that alternative sources of coaching knowledge (e.g., previous playing experience, mentoring, and internet research) may be more influential on coaching behaviors than formal coaching education programs. Previous research has suggested that the impact of formal education programs may be limited when compared to knowledge gained from informal learning sessions (Gilbert and Trudel, 2001; Jones, Armour, and Potrac, 2003; Lemyre et al., 2007; Wilson, Bloom, and Harvey, 2010). Specifically, coaching behaviors acquired through unmediated (e.g., observing other youth sport coaches) and internal (e.g., reflecting on coaching experiences) sources have been shown to be more influential than coaching behaviors acquired in mediated or formal learning environments (Werthner and Trudel, 2006). On average, the participants in our sample had coached for 17 years and their perceived coaching behaviors may have been influenced more by informal learning sources.

The results of the present study also suggested that both certified and non-certified coaches, in all contexts, used higher levels of supportive behaviors. Compared to other measured behaviors in the study, coaches perceived themselves as most often employing positive feedback, training and instruction, and situational consideration behaviors. In short, the youth sport coaches in the present study perceived themselves as using behaviors that focused on teaching proper athletic techniques, praising good performance, and considering individual circumstances. As a result, the use of positive reinforcement and encouragement behaviors has been found to create positive, sporting environments (Fraser-Thomas and Côté, 2006; Fraser-Thomas et al., 2005; Gould and Carson, 2011). Although the current study examined only the coaches' perceived behaviors, these perceptions offer distinct concepts that suggest important information for youth sport coaching (Horn, 2008). In sum, the results suggested that these coaches perceived themselves as employing supportive behaviors in youth sport despite context and certification.

One additional possibility to explain our results may be the recent reorganization of the CAC from a knowledge-based to a competency-based coach education program. The new NCCP model centers coaching education and training on specific contextual streams (i.e., community, instructional, and competitive). The NCCP has been transitioning to its new model over the past 10 years and there may not be have been enough time to affect changes in coaching behaviors as a result of the new program. Perhaps if this study is replicated in the future, the effects of the new NCCP model would be evident and the differences in coaching behavior based on contextual coaching streams would result.

The findings of the present study offer some interesting practical implications for coaching youth sport. First, in spite of pragmatic restrictions (such as geographical isolation or financial reasons) or simply awaiting formal certification, youth sport coaches can develop higher levels of positive feedback, training and instruction, and situational consideration behaviors through informal or unmediated means. In addition, these behaviors occurred despite the context in which the youth athlete was enrolled, and helped create positive sport environments which can transfer into various life domains such as academics and occupation (Coatsworth and Conroy, 2009). Second, youth sport coaches may be not transferring knowledge from formal certification programs into behavioral practices.

As previously suggested, this could be a reflection of the previous knowledge-based NCCP programs. However, these results may indicate that coaches, who are exposed to the same material by the same instructor, will vary in the application of knowledge acquired in formal learning situations (Trudel, Gilbert, and Werthner, in press). Future studies should continue examine coaching behaviors as a result of formal and informal learning situations in various contextual environments.

Although the present study improved our understanding of coaching behaviors in Canadian youth sport contexts, with both certified and non-certified coaches, there are several limitations that need to be addressed. First, the present study included a small sample size, which was a result of the difficulty in finding purely instructional coaches. Second, coaches self-reported their contexts and it is possible that they did not fully understand the differences among the three contexts. Future studies should address this limitation by ensuring that the coaches understand the differences among community, competitive, and instructional contexts. Lastly, the present study focused solely on the coaches' self-perceptions of their behaviors. Various theories have noted that the impact of the coaching process on athlete outcomes was mediated by the athletes' interpretations of the coaches' behaviors (Horn, 2008; Smith and Smoll, 2002). Future studies should also examine the athletes' perceptions of their certified and non-certified coaches' behaviors in the separate Canadian youth sport contexts.

In conclusion, the results of the present study showed that regardless of coaching context or certification, Canadian youth sport coaches exhibited similar perceived behaviors, with higher occurrences of positive feedback, training and instruction, and situational consideration behaviors. In other words, both certified and non-certified coaches perceived themselves as focused on developing positive and supportive youth sport environments regardless of whether the youth were enrolled in competitive or recreational contexts. As coaches in the present study perceived the use of positive and supportive behaviors, this focus may continue to aid the positive psychosocial development and growth of youth sport athletes regardless of the contextual stream they are enrolled in or the formal education level of their coaches. Despite these similarities, youth sport coaches are encouraged to attend formal education programs to gain knowledge of the athletes and to train specifically within their contextual stream.

REFERENCES

Amorose, A. J., and Anderson-Butcher, D. (2007). Autonomy-supportive coaching and self-determined motivation in high school and college athletes: A test of self-determination theory. *Psychology of Sport and Exercise, 8,* 654-670.

Becker, A. (2009). It's not what they do, it's how they do it: Athlete experiences of great coaching. *International Journal of Sport Sciences and Coaching, 4,* 93-119.

Bloom, G. A. (2011). Coaching psychology. In P. R. E. Crocker (Ed.), *Sport and exercise psychology: A Canadian perspective* (2nd ed., pp. 278-305). Toronto: Pearson.

Campbell, T., and Sullivan, P. J. (2005). The effect of a standardized coaching education program on the efficacy of novice coaches. *Avante, 11,* 38-45.

Cassidy, T., Potrac, P., and McKenzie, A. (2006). Evaluating and reflecting upon a coach education initiative: The CoDe of rugby. *The Sport Psychologist, 20,* 145-161.

Chelladurai, P. (1990). Leadership in sports: A review. *International Journal of Sport Psychology, 21,* 328-354.

Chelladurai, P. (2007). Leadership in sports. In G. Tenenbaum and R. C. Eklund (Eds.), *Handbook of sport psychology* (pp. 113-135). New York: Wiley.

Chelladurai, P., Imamura, H., Yamaguchi, Y., Oinmua, Y., and Miyauchi, T. (1988). Sport leadership in a cross-national setting: The case of Japanese and Canadian university athletes. *Journal of Sport and Exercise Psychology, 10,* 374-389.

Chelladurai, P., and Saleh, S. (1980). Dimensions of leader behavior in sports: Development of a leadership style. *Journal of Sport Psychology, 2,* 34-45.

Coatsworth, D. J., and Conroy, D. E. (2009). The effects of autonomy-supportive coaching, need-satisfaction, and self-perceptions on initiative and identity in youth swimmers. *Developmental Psychology, 45,* 320-328.

Coaching Association of Canada (2008). *The NCCP model.* Retrieved from http://www.coach.ca/eng/certification/nccp_for_coaches/nccp_model.cfm.

Cohen, J. (1987). *Statistical power analysis for the behavioral sciences.* Hillside, NJ: Lawrence Erlbaum Associates.

Conroy, D. E., and Coatsworth, D. J. (2006). Coach training as a strategy for promoting youth social development. *The Sport Psychologist, 20,* 128-144.

Côté, J., Salmela, J. H., Trudel, P., Baria, A., and Russell, S. J. (1995). The coaching model: A grounded assessment of expert gymnastic coaches' knowledge. *Journal of Sport and ExercisePsychology, 17,* 1-17.

Duchesne, C., Bloom, G.A., and Sabiston, C. M. (2011). Intercollegiate coaches' experiences with elite international athletes in an American sport context. *International Journal of Coaching Science, 5,* 49-68.

Feltz, D. L., Chase, M. A., Moritz, S. E., and Sullivan, P. J. (1999). A conceptual model of coaching efficacy: Preliminary investigation and instrumentdevelopment. *Journal of Educational Psychology, 91,* 765-776.

Fraser-Thomas, J., and Côté J. (2006). Youth sports: Implementing findings and moving forward with research. *Athletic Insight: The Online Journal of Sport Psychology, 8,* 12-27.

Fraser-Thomas, J., and Côté J. (2009). Understanding adolescents' positive and negative development experiences in sport. *The Sport Psychologist, 23,* 3-23.

Fraser-Thomas, J., Côté J., and Deakin, J. (2005). Youth sport programs: An avenue to foster positive youth development. *Physical Education and Sport Pedagogy, 10,* 19–40.

Gilbert, W., Gallimore, R., and Trudel, P. (2009). A learning community approach to coach development in youth sport. *Journal of Coaching Education, 2,* 1-21.

Gilbert W. D., and Trudel, P.(2001). Learning to coach through experience: Reflection in model youth sport coaches. *Journal of Teaching in Physical Education, 21,* 16-34.

Gould, D., and Carson, S. (2011). Youth athletes' perceptions of the relationship between coaching behaviors and developmental experiences. *International Journal of Coaching Science, 5,* 3-29.

Hall, N., Jedlic, B., Munroe-Chandler, K., and Hall, C. (2007). The effects of an education program on coaches' encouragement of imagery use. *International Journal of Coaching Science, 1,* 79-86.

Hedstrom, R., and Gould, D. (2004). *Research in youth sports: Critical issues status.* East Lansing, MI: Institute for the Study of Youth Sports.

Horn, T. S. (2008). Coaching effectiveness in the sport domain. In T. S. Horn (Ed.), *Advances in sport psychology* (pp. 239-267). Champaign, IL: Human Kinetics.

Jones, R. L., Armour, K. M., and Potrac, P. (2003). Constructing expert knowledge: A case study of a top-level professional soccer coach. *Sport, Education, and Society, 8,* 213-229.

Jones, R. L., and Turner, P. (2006). Teaching coaches to coach holistically: Can problem-based learning (PBL) help? *Physical Education and Sport Pedagogy, 11,* 181-202.

Knowles, Z., Gilbourne, D., Borrie, A., and Nevill, A. (2001). Developing the reflective sports coach: A study exploring the processes of reflective practice within a higher education coaching programme. *Reflective Practice, 2,*185-207.

Lee, K. S., Malete, L., and Feltz, D. L. (2002). The strength of coaching efficacy between certified and non-certified Singapore coaches. *International Journal of Applied Sport Sciences, 14,* 55-67.

Lemyre, F., Trudel, P., and Durand-Bush, N. (2007). How youth-sport coaches learn to coach. *The Sport Psychologist, 21,* 191-209.

Lyle, J. (1999). Coaches' decision making. In N. Cross and J. Lyle (Eds.), *The coaching process: Principles and practice for sport,* (pp. 210-232). Oxford: Butterworth Heinemann.

Magnusen, M. J. (2010). Differences in strength and conditioning coach self-perception of leadership style behaviors at the National Basketball Association, Division I-A, and Division II levels. *Journal of Strength and Conditioning Research, 24,* 1440-1450.

Malete, L., and Feltz, D. L. (2000). The effect of a coaching education program on coaching efficacy. *The Sport Psychologist, 14,* 410-417.

Newin, J., Bloom, G. A., and Loughead, T. M. (2008). Youth ice hockey coaches' perceptions of a team-building intervention program. *The Sport Psychologist, 22,* 54-72.

Nunally, J. C. (1970). *Introduction to psychological measurement.* New York: McGraw-Hill.

Ryska, A., Yin, Z., Cooley, D., and Ginn, R. (1999). Developing team cohesion: A comparison of cognitive-behavioral strategies of U. S. and Australian sport coaches. *The Journal ofPsychology, 133*, 523-539.

Smith, R. E., and Smoll, F. L. (2002). Youth sports as a behavior setting for psychosocial interventions. In J. Van Raalte and B. W. Brewer (Eds.), *Exploring sport and exercise psychology* (2nd ed., pp. 341-371). Washington, DC: American Psychological Association.

Smith, R. E., Smoll, F. L., and Barnett, N. P. (1995). Reduction of children's sport anxiety through social support and stress-reduction training for coaches. *Journal of Applied Developmental Psychology, 16,* 125-142.

Smith, R. E., Smoll, F. L., Curtis, B., and Hunt, E. (1978). Toward a mediational model of coach-player relationships. *ResearchQuarterly, 49*, 528-541.

Smith R. E., Zane N. W., Smoll F. L., and Coppel, D. B. (1983). Behavioral assessment in youth sports: Coaching behaviors and children's attitudes. *Medicine and Science in Sports and Exercise, 15*, 208-214.

Smoll, F. L., and Smith, R. E. (1989). Leadership behaviors in sport: A theoretical model and research paradigm. *Journal of Applied Social Psychology, 19*, 1522-1551.

Smoll, F. L., Smith, R. E., Barnett, N. P., and Everett, J. J. (1993). Enhancement of children's self-esteem through social support training for youth sport coaches. *Journal of Applied Psychology, 78,* 602-610.

Solomon, G. B., and Lobinger, B. H. (2011). Sources of expectancy information among coaches: A cross-cultural investigation. *Theories and Applications the International Edition, 1,* 46-57.

Sullivan, P. J., and Gee, C. (2008). The effects of different coaching education content on the efficacy of coaches. *International Journal of Coaching Science, 2*, 59-66.

Sullivan, P. J., and Kent, A. (2003). Coaching efficacy as a predictor of leadership style in intercollegiate athletics. *Journal of Applied Sport Psychology, 15*, 1-11.

Sullivan, P. J., Paquette, K., Holt, N., and Bloom, G. A. (2012). The impact of sport context on the efficacy and leadership styles of youth sport coaches. *The Sport Psychologist, 26,* 122-134..

Tabachnick B. G., and Fidell, L. S. (2007). *Using multivariate statistics* (5th ed.). Boston: Allyn and Bacon.

Trudel, P., Gilbert, W., and Werthner, P. (in press). Coach education effectiveness. In J. Lyle and C. Cushion (Eds.), *Sports coaching*. London: Elsvier.

Vargas-Tonsing, T. M. (2007). Coaches' preferences for continuing coaching education. *International Journal of Sports Science and Coaching, 2*, 25-35.

Weinberg, R., Grove, R., and Jackson, A. (1992). Strategies for building self-efficacy in tennis players: A comparative analysis of Australian and American coaches. *The Sport Psychologist, 6,* 3-13.

Weiss, M. R., and Ferrer-Caja, E. (2002). Motivation orientations and sport behavior. In T. S. Horn's (Ed.), *Advances in sport psychology* (2nd ed., pp. 101-183). Champaign, IL: Human Kinetics.

Weiss, M. R., and Williams, L. (2004). The why of youth sport involvement: A developmental perspective on motivational processes. In M.R. Weiss (Ed.), *Developmental sport and exercise psychology: A lifespan perspective* (pp. 223-268). Morgantown, WV: Fitness Information Technology.

Werthner, P., and Trudel, P. (2006).A new theoretical perspective for understanding how coaches learn to coach. *The Sport Psychologist, 20,* 198-212.

Wiersma, L. D., and Sherman, C. P. (2005). Volunteer youth sport coaches' perspectives of coaching education/certification and parental codes of conduct. *Research Quarterly for Exercise and Sport, 76,* 324-338.

Wilson, L. M., Bloom, G. A., and Harvey, W. J. (2010). Sources of knowledge acquisition: Perspectives of the high school teacher/coach. *Physical Education and Sport Pedagogy, 15,* 383-399.

Williams, J. M., Jerome, G. J., Kenow, L. J., Rogers, T., Sartain, T. A., and Darland, G. (2003). Factor structure of Coaching Behavior Questionnaire and its relationship to athlete variables. *The Sport Psychologist, 17,* 16-34.

Wright, T., Trudel, P., and Culver, D. M. (2007). Learning how to coach: The different learning situations reported by youth ice hockey coaches. *Physical Education and Sport Pedagogy, 12,* 127-144.

Zhang, J., Jensen, B. E., and Mann, B. L. (1997). Modification and revision of the LeadershipScale for Sport. *Journal of Sport Behavior, 20,* 105-122.

In: Athletic Insight's Writings of 2012
Editor: Robert Schinke

ISBN: 978-1-62618-120-5
© 2013 Nova Science Publishers, Inc.

Chapter 18

HIGH-PRESSURE MATCHES DO NOT INFLUENCE HOME-FIELD ADVANTAGE: A 30-YEAR RETROSPECTIVE ANALYSIS OF ENGLISH PROFESSIONAL FOOTBALL

Murray Griffin[*], *Adrian Whatling and Dominic Micklewright*

Centre for Sports and Exercise Science, Department of Biological Sciences,
University of Essex, Colchester, UK

ABSTRACT

This analysis reevaluated the existence of home advantage (HA) within English professional soccer using a point-based calculation that included drawn matches. The analysis also examined whether the magnitude of HA is influenced by the crowd size or the relative importance of the match.

Thirty seasons of archival data (1978/79-2007/08) regarding home results, away results and corresponding crowd attendance was gathered for every club in the top four English professional football leagues. HA was calculated as the number of home points gained throughout the season expressed as a percentage of all points gained whether home and away.

Therefore a HA value of greater than 50% would indicate a more points gained at home whereas a HA value of less than 50% would indicate more points gained away. HA was confirmed for all four divisions (mean 61.7, $s=0.3\%$) but there was no difference between the divisions in the magnitude of HA ($F_{3,116}=0.3$, $P>0.05$) despite differences in crowd size ($F_{3,87}=226$, $P<0.0001$). The magnitude of HA was no different between high-stake large-crowd play-offs matches and corresponding league fixtures ($t_{21}=-0.3$, $P>0.05$).

Home advantage is evident in English professional soccer but the apparently complex underlying causes are not very well understood. The magnitude of HA does not appear to be influenced by crowd size or match importance.

---

[*] Corresponding Author: Dr Murray Griffin, PhD, CPsychol. School of Biological Sciences, University of Essex, Wivenhoe Park, Colchester, Essex, UK. CO4 3SQ. Tel: +44 (0) 1206 873336; Fax: +44(0)1206 872592 e-mail: mgriffin@essex.ac.uk.

Keywords: Team sport, team advantage, team performance, confidence, crowd size

INTRODUCTION

Home-field advantage (HA) has been defined as teams winning over 50% of matches played under a balanced home and away schedule (Courneya and Carron, 1992). A variation in HA of between 51 to 81% has been reported for a range of sports including American football, baseball and hockey (Schwartz and Barsky, 1977), basketball (Silva and Andrew, 1987) and football (Nevill et al., 1996; Pollard, 1986; Pollard and Pollard 2005a; Poulter, 2009). Courneya and Carron (1992) concluded that the magnitude of HA within sports is consistent and remains stable over time but, more recently, Pollard and Pollard (2005a) reported wide regional variation in HA throughout the European domestic football leagues. Schwartz and Barsky (1977) suggested that HA may be influenced by crowd density after finding HA to be only 48% in relatively empty stadia (less than 20%) compared to a HA of 57% when crowd density increased to greater than 40% stadia capacity. Furthermore, no HA was found for the Scottish 3rd Division or Vauxhall Conference football divisions, where crowds were relatively small (Nevill et al., 1996). Another investigation calculated the HA of the four English professional football divisions to be 64% but also concluded that the HA was less prevalent among non-professional leagues where crowd density was less of a factor (Pollard, 1986). Collectively these findings suggest that HA is a complex social phenomenon that is probably influenced by a range of factors, the most commonly reported of which relates to crowd characteristics.

British professional football clubs usually allocate 5–10% of their stadium capacity for away fans meaning the majority of the crowd will be supporting the home team. Schwartz and Barsky (1977) were amongst the first to examine the effect of crowd size and found that, among the four most common North American sports, the winning percentage of home teams increased in proportion to the absolute size of the crowd. An association has also been found between absolute crowd size and HA within English and Scottish football, noting that when crowd sizes were small HA was almost absent (Nevill et al., 1996). Commercial decisions for sports teams to move to bigger stadia, do not always consider such pitfalls. A greater HA was found among clubs with special facilities such as artificial pitches and varying pitch sizes (Clarke and Norman, 1995), and among teams playing on artificial pitches prior to them being discontinued (Barnett and Hilditch, 1993). Bray and Widmeyer (2000) explained that it is players' perceptions of home crowd support and familiarity with the home environment that has the greatest influence upon their team's performance.

Most accounts of HA have focused on the facilitative effect that a supporting crowd and familiar environment has upon the home team but what might be more important is the inhibitive effects that such circumstances have on the visiting team. This was referred to by Silva and Andrew (1987) as the 'away disadvantage' because their archival analysis of over 400 collegiate basketball games revealed that the greater success of home teams could not be attributed to a supportive audience but to the inferior performance from the visiting team. Nevill et al. (1996) suggested that some of the circumstances associated with playing away perhaps provoked away players into more reckless behaviour, such as committing fouls. In fact, one analysis of American collegiate basketball teams found that spectator booing conferred a slight advantage to home teams since visiting teams were found to commit more fouls (Greer, 1983). One interesting endocrinology study found elevated levels of salivary testosterone among football players when they played at home which the authors speculated might account for the associated increases in territoriality and competitive encounters (Neave and Wolfson, 2003). Although, home teams have been found to outperform their opponents in terms of functionally aggressive behaviour (Varca, 1980), it was concluded in a relatively recent study of the English premiership that the loss of a player due to a red card may have less impact on the defensive tactics of an away team (Carmichael and Thomas, 2005).

There have been different views on whether HA in English professional Football has remained constant over time (Courneya and Carron, 1992) or has gradually diminished (Nevill and Holder, 1999; Pollard, 1986; Schwartz and Barsky, 1977). Baumeister (1984) suggested that patterns in team performance reflect the dramatic changes to the sports scene in the United States of America. Similarly, there have been significant changes within English professional football leagues during the last 30 years that could have a diminishing effect on the HA effect. For instance, improvements to travel, accommodation, away team stadium facilities, crowd marshaling and the professionalization of referees and linesman are but some of the factors that could have eased the level of away team discomfort in more recent years.

An interesting proposition is that HA is significantly diminished during high-stakes matches. Baseball and basketball home teams have been found to 'choke' during high-pressure, end-of-series championship games (Baumeister and Steinhilber, 1984). In complete contrast to the assumption that supportive audiences facilitate team performance, it has been proposed that during high-pressure games such audiences can be detrimental to performance due to increased pressure, ramifications of failure, increased self-focus and self-protecting strategies (Butler and Baumeister, 1998). It has also been suggested that choking at home might be attributable to increased attention to well-learned processes that lead to decrements in skillful execution (Beilock and Carr, 2001; Beilock et al., 2004). Pollard (1986) reported a suppressed HA (50.5%) effect between 1960 and 1984 during the quarter finals of the Football Association Cup which is the last stage to be played at home before neutral ground semi-finals. Unfortunately, their findings are confounded by the fact that often teams of quite different standards encounter each other in the quarter finals of the Football Association Cup. However, since the Pollard paper, a play-off system was introduced to English professional football involving one home and one away match between two teams at comparably similar standards. These play-off results present a unique opportunity to examine home-field advantage within critical end-of-season matches yet, to our knowledge, there has been no published analysis of this kind.

Some European football HA studies have omitted drawn matches (Boyko, Boyko and Boyko, 2007; Carmichael and Thomas, 2005; Clarke and Norman, 1995; Johnston, 2008; Nevill et al., 1996; Page and Page, 2007; Pollard, 1986). One disadvantage of this method is that it does not capture the perceived success and satisfaction that away teams experience when securing a draw, particularly when the opponent home side is considered to be of a better or at least equal standard. However some studies have included drawn matches (Pollard and Pollard, 2005b; Thomas, Reeves and Davies, 2004) in HA calculations which is perhaps a useful alternative to including only won and lost matches especially in the context of points-based league systems where drawn matches attract a point.

This study used a points based HA calculation incorporating drawn matches to evaluate whether the magnitude of HA in English professional football has i) differed during high pressure play-off matches ii) diminished over the long term and iii) been influenced by crowd size and team ability. It was hypothesized that the inclusion of drawn matches would show a diminished effect of high pressure matches, crowd size and team ability. It was also hypothesized that over the last 30 years the HA effect in English professional football will have diminished as away team conditions have improved.

METHOD

Design and Data Sampling

This analysis, which was approved by [removed for blind review] ethics committee, involved the collection and analysis of publically available archival data from the Football Association (FA), the Football League (FL), the Press Association, the official British professional football Sky Sports Yearbooks and the Rothmans Football Yearbooks. A total of thirty seasons (1978–1979 to 2007–2008) of team results were compiled for all four major professional English football divisions. The names of these divisions have changed during the capture period of this analysis but at the time of writing the names of the four leagues were the Premiership, the Championship, League One and League Two. The sample used in this analysis is consistent with the criteria specified by Bray (1999) for examining the home and away percentage differential in that it includes an equal number of home and away contests, a large number of teams ($N = 92$) and many seasons of competition with accurate archival data for a large number of matches ($N = 115000$).

Home-Field Advantage Calculations for League Matches

For the league matches a relatively simple method of calculating HA was possible since an equal number of home and away matches are played by each of the English professional football teams. The HA calculation method used in this analysis deliberately incorporated drawn matches as well as won and lost matches. The league match HA was calculated as the number of home points gained throughout the season expressed as a percentage of all points gained whether home and away. Therefore a HA value of greater than 50% would indicate a more points gained at home whereas a HA value of less than 50% would indicate more points gained away. The higher the HA value above 50% the greater the points home advantage.

Home-Field Advantage Calculations for Play-Off Matches

The football league play-off results provide an ideal source of archival data for evaluating HA in critical end-of-season contests. The play-offs involve teams positioned 3rd to 6th in the second and third divisions, and the teams positioned 4th to 7th in the fourth division because teams positioned higher are automatically promoted into the next division. Consequently, the standard of teams opposing each other is usually very similar, something which does not always occur in normal league matches. During the initial play-off round, each team plays once at home and once away against the same opponent team. Since the play-off finals are played at a neutral ground these results were excluded from our analysis. Twelve matches for twenty two seasons were included in this analysis ($N = 264$). Each set of twelve play-off matches meant there was a total number of 36 points available. The HA was measured by calculating the number of points won at home as a percentage of all point won. League match HA were also calculated for the twelve corresponding play-off teams in each season so that, by comparing league against play-off HA, it was possible to ascertain whether HA is diminished or not during the crucial high-stakes matches. Attendance figures were recorded for each of the play-offs matches and league matches for the corresponding teams.

Data Analysis

Paired samples t-tests were used to compare play-off matches (high pressure) against league matches of corresponding teams (normal league pressure). Chi square (x^2) tests were performed to determine if any statistically significant differences existed between the final league placing of the teams involved in the play-offs (i.e. 3rd, 4th, 5th etc..) and the eventual play-off champion.

The effect of team ability was analyzed by comparing HA between leagues using a one-way between-subjects ANOVA. A Pearson's Product Moment correlation test was used to measure the relationship between HA and attendance numbers. Long term changes in home advantage were evaluated by comparing decade-by-decade HA for each of the leagues using a one-way between-subjects ANOVA with post hoc paired samples t-tests.

Unless otherwise stated, an alpha level of 0.05 was used to indicate statistical significance and values are presented mean ± one standard deviation. Effect sizes for significant results are reported as either eta-squared (η^2) or partial eta-squared (η_p^2).

RESULTS

Long Term Changes in Home Advantage and Team Ability Effects

Home advantage during the 30 seasons between 1978-79 and 2007-08 was found across all four divisions (mean 61.7, $s=0.3\%$) as well as separately for the top tier division (mean 61.8, $s=2.9\%$), the second tier division (mean 61.9, $s=2.2\%$), the third tier division (mean 61.8, $s=2.6\%$) and the fourth tier division (mean 61.3, $s=3.5\%$). A one-way between-subjects ANOVA showed no difference in HA between the four divisions ($F_{3,116}=0.3$, $P>0.05$). Season-by-season HA scores are presented in Table 1.

Further analysis of HA revealed a decade-by-decade reduction in HA for the top tier division, ($F_{2,18}=4.7$, $P<0.05$, $\eta_p^2=0.345$), the 2nd tier division ($F_{2,18}=13.0$, $P<0.0005$, $\eta_p^2=0.590$), the 3rd tier division, ($F_{2,18}=12.7$, $P<0.0005$, $\eta_p^2=0.586$) and the 4th tier division ($F_{2,18}=4.1$, $P<0.05$, $\eta_p^2=0.313$). Decade-by-decade changes in HA with post-hoc paired samples t-test outcomes are illustrated in Figure 1.

Crowd Effects on Home Advantage

A one-way between-subjects ANOVA showed a difference between the divisions in average crowd attendance ($F_{3,87}=226$, $P<0.0001$, $\eta_p^2=0.99$). Average crowd attendance was mean 27984, $s=6039$ for the top tier division, mean 13404, $s=2799$ for the second tier division, mean 6302, $s+1117$ for the third tier division and mean 3800, $s=557$ for the fourth tier division. Pearson's Product Moment Correlation tests indicated no relationship between absolute crowd size and HA for the top tier division ($r=-0.086$, $P>0.05$) or the fourth tier division ($r=-0.245$, $P>0.05$). A negative relationship was found between absolute crowd size and HA in the second tier division ($r=-0.704$, $P<0.001$) and the third tier division ($r=-0.473$, $P<0.05$). Season-by-season crowd attendance values for each division are presented in Table 2.

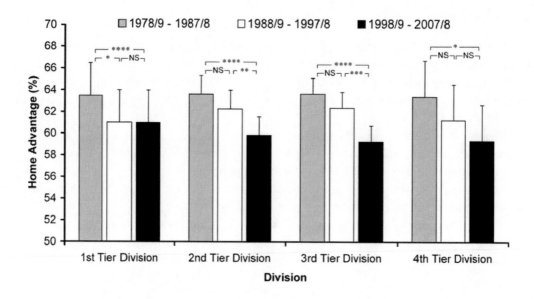

Figure 1.

Table 1. Season by season home advantage outcomes for each division

Soccer League Season	Total Games Played	Top Tier Division HA (%)	2nd Tier Division HA (%)	3rd Tier Division HA (%)	4th Tier Division HA (%)	Season Average HA (%)
1978-79	2028	60.8	62.8	64.0	63.7	62.8
1979-80	2028	63.9	63.1	65.2	63.1	63.8
1980-81	2028	65.4	62.6	62.7	63.8	63.6
1981-82	2028	60.3	64.9	62.0	60.8	62.0
1982-83	2028	68.7	64.9	67.7	65.5	66.7
1983-84	2028	62.8	64.5	66.1	66.7	65.0
1984-85	2028	64.0	61.7	63.0	64.6	63.3
1985-86	2028	62.5	65.3	62.4	63.6	63.5
1986-87	2028 *	66.3	64.2	62.3	62.6	63.9
1987-88	2030 *	60.1	62.2	61.1	59.6	60.8
1988-89	2036	56.7	63.4	63.0	64.3	61.9
1989-90	2036	62.3	61.8	61.6	60.4	61.5
1990-91	2036 *	67.4	61.8	61.0	66.6	64.2
1991-92	2028	60.7	61.1	63.7	62.2	61.9
1992-93	2028	61.2	62.0	61.1	57.9	60.6
1993-94	2028	57.7	64.3	61.9	55.8	59.9

Soccer League Season	Total Games Played	Top Tier Division HA (%)	2nd Tier Division HA (%)	3rd Tier Division HA (%)	4th Tier Division HA (%)	Season Average HA (%)
1994-95	2028 *	59.8	65.3	60.1	59.1	61.1
1995-96	2036	63.0	59.2	64.7	60.4	61.8
1996-97	2036	59.4	62.2	63.1	60.8	61.4
1997-98	2036	61.9	61.7	63.5	64.8	63.0
1998-99	2036	60.7	61.2	57.9	60.0	60.0
1999-00	2036	62.0	62.7	57.2	58.5	60.1
2000-01	2036	62.8	59.4	58.3	65.5	61.5
2001-02	2036	57.4	60.9	62.2	62.5	60.8
2002-03	2036	65.4	58.4	57.0	57.9	59.7
2003-04	2036	59.0	58.6	61.7	60.7	60.0
2004-05	2036	61.7	58.4	58.9	61.3	60.1
2005-06	2036	58.6	59.0	59.0	57.1	58.4
2006-07	2036	61.8	61.1	58.8	58.7	60.1
2007-08	2036	60.4	58.7	61.5	51.1	57.9
Mean	2032.3	61.8	61.9	61.8	61.3	61.7
SD	4.0	2.9	2.2	2.6	3.5	2.0
Mode	2036.0	65.4	64.9	63.0	60.8	60.8
Median	2036.0	61.8	61.9	62.0	61.1	61.5
Max	2036.0	68.7	65.3	67.7	66.7	66.7
Min	2028.0	56.7	58.4	57.0	51.1	57.9

* Note: Periodic changes to the English Soccer Leagues has resulted in slight changes in the total number of league games played in each season. However, throughout this time-span the total number of professional teams has remained a constant (N = 92).

Table 2. Season by season crowd attendance for each division

Soccer League Season	Top Tier Division Average Attendance (n)	2nd Tier Division AverageAttendance (n))	3rd Tier Division AverageAttendance (n)	4th Tier Division Average Attendance (n)	Season Average Attendance (n)
1986-87	19794	7551	4259	3713	8829.3
1987-88	19273	10557	4984	3211	9506.3
1988-89	20553	11636	5499	3245	10233.3
1989-90	20745	12441	5079	3426	10422.8
1990-91	22681	11386	5137	3204	10602.0
1991-92	21622	10525	5423	3404	10243.5
1992-93	21125	10641	6310	3334	10352.5
1993-94	23083	11752	5385	3418	10909.5
1994-95	24294	10882	5511	3384	11017.8

Table 2. (Continued)

Soccer League Season	Top Tier Division Average Attendance (n)	2nd Tier Division Average Attendance (n))	3rd Tier Division Average Attendance (n)	4th Tier Division Average Attendance (n)	Season Average Attendance (n)
2001-02	34450	15250	7210	4380	15322.5
1995-96	27570	11855	5122	3557	12026.0
1996-97	28463	12514	5768	3350	12523.8
1997-98	29141	14133	7168	3447	13472.3
1998-99	30586	13665	7510	3813	13893.5
1999-00	30757	14155	6704	3916	13883.0
2000-01	32906	14335	6340	3915	14374.0
2002-03	35462	15436	7045	4459	15600.5
2003-04	35020	15894	7505	5390	15952.3
2004-05	33890	17410	7740	4500	15885.0
2005-06	33875	17615	7460	4060	15752.5
2006-07	34361	18222	7485	4134	16050.5
2007-08	35989	17023	7991	4335	16334.5
Mean	27984	13404	6302	3800	12872.1
SD	6039	2799	1117	557	2528.5
Mode	N/A	N/A	N/A	N/A	N/A
Median	28802	13090	6325	3635	12998.0
Range	16716	10671	3732	2186	7505.3
Max	35989	18222	7991	5390	16334.5
Min	19273	7551	4259	3204	8829.3

The Effects of High-Pressure Play-Off Matches on Home Advantage

A home advantage was found for the play-off matches (mean 62.3, $s=17.0\%$) and for the league matches between the corresponding teams (mean 64.0, $s=12.1\%$). However, there was no difference in HA between the play-off matches and league matches for the corresponding teams ($t_{21}=-0.3$, $P>0.05$).

Three HA outliers were identified through stem and leaf plot analysis in the seasons 1998/99, 2005/06 and 2007/08 which were removed. Subsequent analysis still showed no difference in HA between the play-off matches (63.3, $s=14.5\%$) and league matches (63.5, $s=9.0\%$) for the corresponding teams ($t_{18}=-0.5$, $P>0.05$).

Average crowd attendance was higher for play-off matches compared to corresponding league fixtures (mean 14553, s=1856 vs. mean 10429, s=2190, t_{21}=22.1, P<0.0001, η^2=0.96). Pearson's Product Moment Correlation tests found that there was no relationship between crowd attendance and HA for the play-off matches (r=-0.336, P>0.05) or for the corresponding league fixtures (r=-0.150, P>0.05).

Season by season HA scores and average crowd attendance figures for the play-off matches and corresponding league fixtures are provided in Table 3.

Play-off Success and Final League Placing

A Chi square test indicated a difference in the frequency of promotion via winning the play-off finals according to final league placement (x^2=22, P< 0.005). The frequency of promotion according to final league placement for each division is presented in Table 4.

Table 3. Season by season home advantage and average attendance levels for play-off matches and league fixtures for the corresponding teams

Season	Play-Off Matches		Same-Team League Matches	
	HA (%)	Average Attendance	HA (%)	Average Attendance
1986-87	63.6	15098	64.3	11427
1987-88	55.6	13825	44.4	8570
1988-89	72.7	11686	59.4	6236
1989-90	50.0	13583	68.8	9997
1990-91	78.1	12889	72.7	7642
1991-92	78.1	12642	78.1	8822
1992-93	81.8	14198	68.8	8006
1993-94	63.6	12509	68.8	8326
1994-95	60.0	12435	72.7	9168
1995-96	50.0	12628	59.4	8111
1996-97	68.8	13646	54.5	9586
1997-98	80.0	12569	72.7	10302
1998-99	87.5	15726	36.4	12099
1999-00	56.3	14452	64.5	10428
2000-01	81.8	15777	54.5	11088
2001-02	45.2	15784	70.0	11204
2002-03	68.8	17229	50.0	13490
2003-04	50.0	17807	54.5	13872
2004-05	68.8	16898	58.8	13472
2005-06	21.9	15954	75.0	12866
2006-07	28.6	17449	68.8	13466
2007-08	58.8	15374	90.9	11250
Mean	62.3	14553	64.0	10429
SD	17.0	1856	12.1	2190
Mode	50.0	N/A	68.8	N/A
Median	63.6	14325	66.6	10365
Max	87.5	17807	90.9	13872
Min	21.9	11686	36.4	6236

Note: The play-off system was introduced in 1986-87 season rendering 22 seasons of data suitable for analysis.

Table 4. Frequency of promotion according to final league placement for each division

Final League Placement	Frequency of Promotion after Play-off Matches		
	2nd Tier Division	3rd Tier Division	4th Tier Division
3rd	8	9	Automatically Promoted*
4th	4	3	12
Final League Placement	Frequency of Promotion after Play-off Matches		
	2nd Tier Division	3rd Tier Division	4th Tier Division
5th	5	5	2
6th	4	5	5
7th	Outside Play-off Zone*	Outside Play-off Zone*	2
Total	21**	22	21***

* In the 2nd and 3rd tier divisions the top two placed teams are automatically promoted and play-off matches are conducted for the next four placed teams between 3rd and 6th position. In the 4th tier division the top three placed teams are automatically promoted and play-off matches are conducted for the next four teams placed between 4th and 7th position.

** The inaugural 2nd Tier play-off victor in 1986-87 actually finished 19th in Division 1 and is not included in the analysis resulting in a total of 21. The play-off format changed in season 1988-89.

*** In 1994-95 the top two teams only, were automatically promoted from the 4th Tier. The play-off victor finished 3rd and is not included in the analysis resulting in a total of 21.

DISCUSSION

The results of this study show that, even when drawn matches are taken into account, a HA has occurred in all English professional football leagues since 1978-79 which is consistent with others' previous findings (Nevill et al., 1996; Pollard and Pollard, 2005a; Poulter, 2009; Schwartz and Barsky, 1977; Silva and Andrew, 1987). However, contrary to Nevill et al. (1996) no difference was found in the magnitude of HA between the different professional football leagues and the similarity in HA between the four divisions occurred despite vastly different average crowd attendances. On the basis of our findings we must therefore conclude that, while the presence of a crowd might be a factor in HA the absolute size of the crowd does not appear to influence the magnitude of the HA effect. Perhaps the size of the crowd compared to team norms is important and certainly worthy of more investigation. For instance, a large crowd might have more of a HA impact on a team usually accustomed to smaller crowds whereas a small crowd might suppress the HA effect among teams who usually experience high crowd numbers. In other words, large fluctuations in the level of home support for a particular team could potentially influence their HA. It has also been proposed that HA is related to crowd density rather than crowd volume (Agnew and Carron, 1994). This is an interesting argument because, for example, 10000 supporting spectators distributed around a 60000 capacity stadium clearly will not have the same presence than when occupying a smaller capacity stadium.

We hypothesized a diminished HA effect over the long term as conditions for away teams have improved in English professional football. Our data, illustrated in Figure 1, showing a decade-by-decade reduction in HA, supports this hypothesis and is consistent with previous similar findings (Nevill and Holder, 1999; Pollard, 1986; Schwartz and Barsky, 1977). The decade-by-decade reductions in HA across all the English professional football leagues does appear to mirror changes to the organization and governance within the sport or other factors which have perhaps attenuated the level of disruption experienced by teams playing at away venues. Interestingly, Figure 1 shows a sharp reduction in HA effect from the 1990's in the top division but a more gradual decade-by-decade reduction in the other leagues. Anecdotally, this perhaps reflects the increased speed with which the top league clubs have improved away team conditions. Such explanations are of course extremely difficult to find evidence for, yet they do highlight the complexity surrounding the causes of HA and certainly warrant more detailed investigation. Since the magnitude of HA was found to be less among the big four sports of the United States of America compared to English football (Pollard and Pollard, 2005a), perhaps one way of investigating influences on HA would be to attempt to identify differences in potential factors between these sports.

Our results show that the average crowd size was greater during vital play-off matches compared to league fixtures between the corresponding teams. It would be reasonable to assume that a large home crowd during an important match might be advantageous but it has also been suggested that such circumstances just exacerbate the consequences of failure and can engender excessive performance pressure and self-attention (Butler and Baumeister, 1998). Certainly, the potential costs of failure in English football play-offs today have never been greater. In financial terms alone, promotion to the Premiership is worth approximately thirty million pounds instantaneously, without factoring in ticket sales, merchandising, media contracts and substantial balloon payments should immediate relegation follow.

Several studies have suggested that HA increases as a function of crowd density (Agnew and Carron, 1994) and crowd size (Nevill and Holder, 1999) but our results do not support these claims. Despite variation in crowd size, Contrary to Jamieson (2010) we found no difference between the HA during important play-off matches and league matches with corresponding teams indicating that the higher pressure associated with some matches has little effect on the HA. Although some evidence of 'home choke' was demonstrated for baseball and basketball (Baumeister and Steinhilber, 1984), the results of our analysis revealed no such effect in English professional football. In fact, subsequent analyses of baseball and basketball found no evidence to support the 'home-choke' hypothesis (Schlenker et al., 1995; Tauer et al., 2009). Perhaps the differences between sports in HA and choke are attributable to the social and organizational that were described by Pollard and Pollard (2005a) or perhaps, as Leith (1988) speculates, it is the mere consideration of 'choking' among certain teams that ultimately becomes a self-fulfilling prophecy. Perhaps it is the perception of the away disadvantage by certain teams that predisposes them to choking, something that could be further examined perhaps using qualitative rather than quantitative archival methods. Regardless of the explanation, the home choke phenomenon does not appear to prevail within English professional football and the evidence for its existence in the major North American sports is inconclusive.

Anecdotally, a commonly held view among supporters has long decreed that the worst position to finish in the league is the play-off position immediately below those who have automatically qualified for promotion (i.e. 3rd in the second tier and third tier divisions and 4[th]in the fourth tier division). The myth contests that the psychological 'blow' of just missing out on automatic promotion, often manifests itself in reduced self-confidence, increased self-focus and changes in expectancies, leading to sub-standard performance in the subsequent play-offs and swift elimination. Baumeister (1995) attests to this notion by suggesting that increased focus on past negative performance outcomes in itself is likely to provoke further poor performance. But our results have found that of all the teams who qualify for play-off matches, the team positioned highest in the league is the one who most often successful and eventually promoted (Table 4). Therefore, our results suggest that missing automatic promotion but being the highest ranked team in the pool of play-off teams is, if anything, advantageous with respect to the likeliness of success in subsequent play-off matches.

The issue of HA probably has very little direct influence on the applied practice of managing teams. Nevertheless, the prospect of away matches is our view a source of anxiety and unsettling to teams. What our findings shows is that HA is not really effected by high-stake high-pressure matches. Any additional (cognitive) anxiety experienced by players and teams in the build up to such matches is therefore to some extent irrational. Any applied attempt to alleviate anxiety prior to an important match, whatever method used, could use the type of factual outcomes presented in our paper.

CONCLUSIONS

The results of this analysis provide strong support for HA within English professional football even when drawn matches are taken into consideration. Despite large variations in terms of audience size and contrary to previous studies, the HA effect appears to be largely unaffected. The slight decline in HA over the past 30 years may be a reflection of changing social, organizational and governance factors within English football that has perhaps eased the conditions for visiting teams. Due to their apparent complexity, uncovering the precise underling causes of HA represents a significant challenge. Nevertheless, we can conclude that HA also does not appear to be affected by high pressure matches. Compelling evidence exists for a home field advantage in football but the challenge for researchers is to explain the causes of such effects.

AUTHOR NOTE

This study was not funded by any organization outside of the University of Essex and none of the authors of this manuscript have any conflict of interest.

REFERENCES

Agnew, G. A., and Carron, A. V. (1994). Crowd effects and the home advantage. *International Journal of Sport Psychology*, *25*, 53-62.

Barnett, V., and Hilditch, S. (1993) The effect of an artificial pitch surface on home team performance in football. *Journal of the Royal Statistical Society*, *156*, 39-50.

Baumeister, R. F. (1995). Disputing the effects of championship pressures and home audiences. *Journal of Personality and Social Psychology*, *68*, 644-648.

Baumeister, R. F. (1984). Choking under pressure: Self-consciousness and paradoxical effects of incentives on skilled performance. *Journal of Personality and Social Psychology*, *46*, 610-620.

Baumeister, R. F., and Steinhilber, A. (1984). Paradoxical effects of supportive audiences on performance under pressure: The home field disadvantage in sports championships. *Journal of Personality and Social Psychology*, *47*, 85-93.

Beilock, S. L., and Carr, T. H. (2001). On the fragility of skilled performance: What governs choking under pressure? *Journal of Experimental Psychology: General*, *130*, 701-725.

Beilock, S. L., Kulp, C. A., Holt, L. E., and Carr, T. H. (2004). More on the fragility of performance: Choking under pressure in mathematical problem solving. *Journal of Experimental Psychology: General*, *133*, 584-600.

Boyko, R. H., Boyko, R. A., and Boyko, M. G. (2007). Referee bias contributes to home advantage in English Premiership football. *Journal of Sports Sciences*, 25, 1185-1194.

Bray, S. R. (1999). The home advantage from an individual team perspective. *Journal of Applied Sport Psychology*, *11*, 116-125.

Bray, S. R., and Widmeyer, N. W. (2000). Athletes' perceptions of the home advantage: An investigation of perceived causal factors. *Journal Sport Behaviour*, *23*, 1-10.

Butler, J. L., and Baumeister, R. F. (1998). The trouble with friendly faces: Skilled performance with a supportive audience. *Journal of Personality and Social Psychology*, *75*, 1213-1230.

Carmichael, F., and Thomas, D. (2005). Home-Field Effect and Team Performance. *Journal of Sports Economics*, *6*, 264-281.

Clarke, S. R., and Norman, J. M. (1995). Home ground advantage of individual clubs in English soccer. *The Statistician*,*44*, 509-521.

Courneya, K. S., and Carron, A. V. (1992). The home advantage in sport competitions: A literature review. *Journal of Sport and Exercise Psychology*, *14*, 28-39.

Greer, D. L. (1983). Spectator booing and the home advantage: A study of social influence in the basketball arena. *Social Psychology Quarterly*, *46*, 252-261.

Jamieson, J. P. (2010)The Home Field Advantage in Athletics: A Meta-Analysis. *Journal of Applied Social Psychology*, *40*, 1579–1848.

Johnston, R. (2008). On referee bias, crowd size, and home advantage in the English soccer Premiership. *Journal of Sports Sciences*, *26*, 563-568.

Leith, L. M. (1988). Choking in sports: Are we our own worst enemies. *International Journal of Sport Psychology*, *19*, 59-64.

Neave, N., and Wolfson, S. (2003). Testosterone, territoriality, and the "home advantage". *Physiology and Behavior*, *78*, 269-275.

Nevill, A. M., and Holder, R. L. (1999). Home advantage in sport: An overview of studies on the advantage of playing at home. *Sports Medicine*, *28*, 221-236.

Nevill, A. M., Newell, S. M., and Gale, S. (1996). Factors associated with home advantage in English and Scottish football matches. *Journal of Sports Sciences*, *14*, 181-186.

Page, L., and Page, K. (2007). The second leg home advantage: Evidence from European football cup competitions. *Journal of Sports Sciences*, *25*, 1547-1556.

Pollard, R. (1986). Home advantage in soccer: A retrospective analysis. *Journal of Sports Sciences*,*4*, 237-248.

Pollard, R., and Pollard, G. (2005a). Home advantage in football: A review of its existence and causes *International Journal of Football Science*, *3*, 28-38.

Pollard, R., and Pollard, G. (2005b). Long-term trends in home advantage in professional team sports in North America and England (1876-2003). *Journal of Sports Sciences*, *23*, 337-350.

Poulter, D. R. (2009). Home advantage and player nationality in international club football. *Journal of Sports Sciences*, *27*, 797-805.

Schlenker, B. R., Phillips, S. T., Boniecki, K. A., and Schlenker, B. R. (1995). Where is the home choke. *Journal of Personality and Social Psychology*, *68*, 649-652.

Schwartz, B., and Barsky, S. F. (1977). The home advantage. *Social Forces*, 55, 641-661.

Silva, J. M., and Andrew, A. (1987). An analysis of game location and basketball performance in the Atlantic Coast Conference. *International Journal of Sport Psychology*, *18*, 188-204.

Tauer, J. M., Guenther, C. L., and Rozek, C. (2009). Is there a home choke in decisive playoff basketball games? *Journal of Applied Sport Psychology*, *21*, 148-162.

Thomas, S., Reeves, C., and Davies, S. (2004). An analysis of home advantage in the English football premiership. *Perceptual and Motor Skills*, *99*, 1212-1216.

Varca, P. E. (1980). An analysis of home and away game performance of male college basketball teams. *Journal of Sport and Exercise Psychology*, *2*, 149-165.

In: Athletic Insight's Writings of 2012
Editor: Robert Schinke

ISBN: 978-1-62618-120-5
© 2013 Nova Science Publishers, Inc.

Chapter 19

PSYCHOLOGICAL PREPARATION IN FREE-THROW SHOTS IN BASKETBALL – A REVIEW

Ronnie Lidor[1,2] and Gal Ziv[1,2]*

[1]The Zinman College of Physical Education and Sport Sciences, Wingate Institute, Israel
[2]Faculty of Education, University of Haifa, Israel

ABSTRACT

The purpose of this article was to review a series of studies ($n = 34$) on psychological preparation in free-throw (FT) shots in basketball. The main finding of this review was that FT performances can be enhanced by the use of psychological techniques, such as quite eye (QE), focusing attention, pre-performance routines, verbal feedback, and modeling. However, prior to the implementation of these interventions, sport psychology consultants (SPCs) should be aware of a number of research limitations and methodological concerns associated with the reviewed studies, among them the lack of data on the effectiveness of interventional techniques in achieving FT success in actual games, the lack of authentic practice, and the lack of qualitative data on psychological profiles of FT shooters. In addition, a number of practical implications for SPCs aimed at preparing basketball players for the FT are given.

Keywords: Basketball, free-throw shots, psychological preparation, psychological interventions

A free-throw (FT) shot is commonly awarded to a basketball player after a foul is made against him or her while in the act of shooting, or when another rule infraction is committed by one of the players of the opposing team (International Basketball Federation, 2010). If the foul made on the player causes him or her to miss the shot, the player receives either two or three FTs, depending on whether the shot was taken in front of or behind the three-point line.

---

* Please send all correspondence to: Dr. Ronnie Lidor, Professor, The Zinman College of Physical Education and Sport Sciences, Wingate Institute, Netanya 42902, Israel. Fax: +972-9-8650960, E-mail: lidor@wincol.ac.il.

If, despite the foul, the player still makes the attempted shot, the number of FTs is reduced to one, and the basket counts. Each successful FT shot is worth one point.

Recent studies on set shots (i.e., lower and upper limb shooting motions during which the feet do not leave the floor) in basketball have shown that highly trained players were more accurate in performing FTs (as one class of set shots) than performing set shots from other distances and angles (Keetch, Lee, and Schmidt, 2008; Keetch, Schmidt, Lee, and Young, 2005). The authors of these studies classified a FT in basketball as an *especial skill,* namely a skill that "as a result of massive amounts of practice, has a special status within a generalizable class of motor skills and that is distinguished by its enhanced performance capability relative to the other members of the same class" (Keetch et al., 2005, p. 976). However, in spite of the advantages associated with shooting FTs, among them the short distance of the shot and the absence of defense, players still have difficulty excelling in shooting from the FT line. For example, it was reported that the successful FT shooting percentage of male college players is only about 70-75% (Krause and Hayes, 1994). Similar findings were found for elite European players (Lidor et al., 2010). FT shooting percentages of players in the NBA were reported as slightly higher than 75% (National Basketball Association, 2011).

To plan sport psychology programs aimed at helping basketball players improve their FT performances, those professionals who work with these players should obtain relevant information on psychological interventions that can be used to enhance FT shooting. This knowledge can be implemented in the effective planning of psychological preparation of basketball players for the FT act, and can also be integrated into the general sport psychology program aimed at preparing the players for practices and games.

The purpose of this article was to review a series of studies ($n = 34$) on sport psychology interventions used to facilitate FT performances in basketball. A literature search for peer-reviewed papers in the English language was conducted using two databases (PubMed and SPORTDiscus). Search terms included *free throw* and *basketball.* The inclusion criterion was that the studies included psychological aspects of FT performance. Articles were excluded if psychological interventions in FTs were not examined in the study. In addition, a manual search of the reference lists in the relevant studies found in the computerized search was performed. Both quantitative and qualitative studies were included. The search yielded 34 studies, and these are included in our review.

PSYCHOLOGICAL INTERVENTIONS

Coping with Anxiety and Choking Under Pressure

Choking under pressure refers to a decrease in performance under stressful or high-pressure situations. Six studies examined the relationship between self-consciousness and choking. In one study, the relationship between self-consciousness and choking was observed in 38 male and 43 female Australian competitive basketball players (Dandy, Brewer, and Tottman, 2001). FT percentages were observed during training (30 FT shots in sets of five), and were compared to the FT percentage in competitive games. FT percentage was lower in competition when compared to training in both male (63.0 ± 10.7% vs. 75.8 ± 11.3%, respectively) and female (60.5 ± 13.6% vs. 75.1 ± 9.6%, respectively) players. These differences may suggest that choking was a factor in the lower percentages during game play. However, other factors may have led to the reduced shooting percentages during actual game play, among them the number of FT shots thrown in a row (five during practice versus usually one, two, or three during game play), fatigue, and external distractors. A correlation between self-consciousness and choking was found in males ($r = .34$) but not in females ($r = .05$). The authors suggested that the gender difference could have been due to the timing of the testing. The male players were tested during a time when they were in contention for the playoffs, whereas the female players were tested after the playoff selections were already made.

Another study of 66 undergraduate college players examined whether self-consciousness and trait anxiety can predict choking (Wang, Marchant, and Gibbs, 2004). The players performed 20 FTs under a low-pressure condition (performing the throws with only a research assistant present) and under a high-pressure condition (performing the throws in front of peers while a video camera recorded the throws, and with monetary compensation for each shot made). Data showed decreased FT performance in the high-pressure condition. This difference in performance was negatively correlated with individual self-consciousness ($r = -.49$), social anxiety ($r = -.27$), and somatic trait anxiety ($r = -.30$). These findings also suggest that players with high self-consciousness were more likely to choke under pressure. Individual self-consciousness was found to be the strongest predictor of choking ($R^2 = .24$).

A somewhat different aspect of self-consciousness was examined in 80 male undergraduate students (Leith, 1988). In this study, an attempt was made to determine whether the mere mention of the word *choke* can lead to reduced performance. The students were assigned to four experimental groups: (a) pre-test, an experimental condition, post-test; (b) pre-test, post-test; (c) an experimental condition, post-test; and (d) post-test only. The experimental conditions included giving the participants a short paragraph to read that presented the notion that research had shown that individuals tend to choke at the FT line, and that the cause of this was not known. The results showed reduced FT performance in the two groups that read the paragraph compared to the two groups that performed FTs without reading it. This study suggested that coaches might avoid the frequent use of the term *choke,* and avoid mentioning the possibility that the players would choke in game situations.

In another study(Otten, 2009), college undergraduate students with basketball experience were divided into an experimental group ($n = 201$, 15 FT shots under a low-pressure condition and 15 shots under a high-pressure condition) and a control group ($n = 42$, two sets of 15 FT shots each under the low-pressure condition). The high-pressure condition was established by telling the participants that they were being taped and that their performances would be viewed in psychology classes to examine how players perform under pressure. Participants were given questionnaires dealing with implicit knowledge of the skill, sport confidence, competitive state anxiety, self-consciousness, and the concept of *reinvestment,* which was defined as "purposefully endeavoring to run the skill with explicitly available knowledge of it" (Masters, Polman, and Hammond, 1993, p. 655). The results showed that FT performance improved slightly from Set 1 to Set 2 in both the experimental and control groups. In the experimental group, 128 participants showed improved performance in the high-pressure condition, 13 showed no change in performance, and 60 showed reduced performance. The best predictor of performance under pressure was the perceived control factor. In addition, a high "reinvestment" score predicted higher cognitive and somatic anxiety under the high-pressure condition. Based on these data, sport psychology consultants

(SPCs) are encouraged to avoid reinvesting attention to the task in order to reduce anxiety, and to train players to exhibit more perceived control and feelings of confidence.

Similar individual differences were found in a study of 66 undergraduate college basketball players (Wang, Marchant, and Morris, 2004). The players performed 20 FTs under a low-pressure condition (performing the throws with only a research assistant present) and under a high-pressure condition (performing the throws in front of peers while a video camera recorded all throws, and with monetary compensation for each shot made). The findings showed decreased performance in the high-pressure (12.53 ± 3.94 successful shots) compared to the low-pressure (13.56 ± 2.51 successful shots) condition, representing a low to moderate effect size. Of the 66 participants, 36 suffered reduced performance in the high-pressure condition, six had no changes in performance, and 24 actually showed improved performance in the high-pressure condition. The results suggest that some athletes choke under pressure while others thrive under it.

Lastly, since choking is usually detrimental to performance, it is important to understand how to alleviate it. In one study (Mesagno, Marchant, and Morris, 2009), a single-subject design was used in which three "choking-susceptible" players were selected out of 41 competitive players. The selected players performed six sets of 10 FTs under each of the following conditions: (a) low pressure, (b) high pressure – audience presence, videotaping, and financial incentive, and (c) high pressure with music playing in the background. Based on both quantitative and qualitative analyses, it appeared that public self-awareness led to decreased performance in the high-pressure condition. This pressure was reduced during the high pressure with music condition, leading to improved FT performance. Since this music intervention is not feasible in actual games, more practical strategies such as performing a pre-performance routine should be examined.

Attention and Gaze Control

The use of focusing attention instructions in shooting FTs was examined in a number of studies (see Wulf, 2007 for an extensive review of the use of internal and external focusing attention instructions in motor skill acquisition). One study examined the effects of attentional focus on FT performance, movement accuracy, and electromyography (EMG) activity (Zachry, Wulf, Mercer, and Bezodis, 2005). The participants were asked to perform two sets of 10 FTs under two conditions: (a) external focus (focusing on the center of the rear of the rim) and (b) internal focus (focusing on the motion of the wrist during the follow-through of the throw). Performance was found to be better under the external focus condition than under the internal focus condition. An EMG showed less activation in the biceps and triceps under the external focus condition compared to the internal focus condition.

The influence of distractions on attention during FT shooting was examined using a dual-task paradigm in 30 players with at least two years of basketball experience (Price, Gill, Etnier, and Kornatz, 2009). The primary task was FT shooting and the secondary task was responding to auditory stimuli. The auditory probes were presented during the phases of the preparation, the pre-shot (first upward motion of ball), the shot (the remaining motion of the ball until it leaves the hands), and the flight. No significant differences were found in the FT percentages between the four phases in which the auditory probes were presented. Reaction time to the auditory stimuli increased in the phases of preparation and pre-shot. In addition, experienced players performed better than less experienced players. The slower reaction times during the phases of preparation and pre-shot suggest that focusing-attention strategies that can turn the player's attention away from crowd noise or reduce negative self-talk could be useful.

In recent years, gaze data have been used to assess where athletes look when performing various types of motor skills. Specifically, the term *Quiet Eye* (QE) has been defined as the final fixation or tracking gaze located on a specific location for more than 100 msec and within 3° of visual angle (Vickers, 2007). The QE onset begins prior to the final movement of the task and ends when the gaze deviates from the object it was fixated upon. QE has been found to be a characteristic of elite performers in sports that require high accuracy(e.g., Harle and Vickers, 2001; Vickers, 1992).

In one study (Vickers, 1996), gaze data of expert (≥ 75%) and near expert (< 65%) FT shooters were compared. The players threw consecutive FTs until at least 10 hits and 10 misses were reached. The preparation phase for the FTs was longer by 500 msec in the experts when compared to the near experts. QE duration in experts was longer in hits (972 msec) than in misses (806 msec), and in near experts it was less than 400 msec in both hits and misses. The offset of the fixation from the ball occurred earlier in the experts (when hands moved into shooting action and entered the visual field) compared to the near experts, who maintained the fixation for longer durations. This distinct pattern of longer fixation on the rim prior to shooting and early fixation offset when shooting action occurs was found in players averaging over 75% of FT shooting. This finding offers one possible explanation of the reasons behind the success of elite FT shooters.

Differencesbetween a low style and a high style of shooting were examined in a study of six experienced players (de Oliveira, Oudejans, and Beek, 2008). Players shot 10 FTs and 10 jump shots while gaze data were recorded. The difference in styles led to a situation in which, during the low-style shooting, the hands blocked the gaze of the shooters as they were raised to throw the ball. This did not occur in the high style of shooting. The results showed that fixation on a target was longer before the hands reached the line of sight of the players in the low style of shooting compared to the high style of shooting. However, after the hands reached the line of sight, fixation was longer in the high-style of shooting.

The influence of anxiety on gaze control and performance was examined in a group of 10 university players (Wilson, Vine, and Wood, 2009). The players shot FTs under two counterbalanced conditions: control and high-pressure (e.g., performance comparison to other players, financial rewards to the best three players, telling participants that they are doing poorly compared to teammates). FTs were shot in blocks of 10, consisting of two shots in five sets in order to simulate game situations. FT percentages were higher under the control condition (68.6%) compared to the high-pressure condition (50.5%). QE was longer in the control condition and in hits when compared to the high-pressure conditions and misses, respectively. In addition, players made more fixations during the high-pressure condition, but each fixation was shorter in duration compared to those in the control condition. These results suggest that under stressful conditions gaze control is impaired, and can be related to poor performance. Therefore, if gaze control and QE can be taught, it might be possible to reduce the detrimental effects of stressful conditions on FT performance.

Indeed, one study examined whether QE can be trained (Harle and Vickers, 2001). FT performances of three female basketball teams were compared over two competitive seasons. One team underwent 3-step QE training in both seasons. In the first step, participants were told to hold their head up and direct their gaze at the hoop, bounce the ball three times, and repeat the phrase "nothing but net". In the second step, participants were told to hold the ball and maintain QE on a single location on the hoop for 1.5 sec, while saying the words "sight, focus". In the third step, participants were instructed to shoot the ball using a quick and fluid action, with the ball moving up through the center of the visual field and masking the target. During that step, participants were told that it was not necessary to maintain their gaze at the hoop while they were shooting the ball. During Season 1, the team undergoing QE training improved during the experimental trials but not in competitive games. In fact, this team had the lowest game FT percentage (54.14%) compared to the two other teams (67.67% and 61.34%). However, by the end of Season 2 the team undergoing QE training improved by 22.62% to 76.66%, while team two declined from 67.67% to 66.18% and team three improved from 61.34% to 74.05%.

Lastly, studies that measure gaze can help us improve learning strategies. For example, an attempt was made in a study of 16 males with little or no experience in basketball to examine whether being given different verbal instructions could lead to different search strategies when watching an instructional video, as well as to different results in FT shooting (Al-Abood, Bennett, Hernandez, Ashford, and Davids, 2002). Participants performed a pre-test of five FTs and were divided into a movement effects group and a movement dynamics group. The movement effects group was instructed to look at how a model scored a basket, and the movement dynamics group was instructed to focus on the model's movements. The video was shown once on a small screen and once on a large screen, while gaze data was recorded. This was followed by a post-test of five FTs. Only the movement effects group improved shooting performances from pre-test to post-test. Gaze data showed that the movement effects group made more and longer fixations on the model than the movement dynamics group. In addition, the movement effects group spent proportionally more time looking at areas outside the model's body compared to the movement dynamics group.

Pre-performance Routines

A *pre-performance routine* has been defined as a set of physical and psychological behaviors that is used prior to the performance of self-paced events (Lidor, 2010). This is typically composed of motor, cognitive, and emotional behaviors that are regularly performed immediately before the execution of self-paced tasks. The FT shot is considered to be a *self-paced task* since the shooter is able to determine when to initiate the shooting act. Players who stand on the line and prepare themselves for the FT know in advance how much time is available to them, and therefore they can release the ball when they feel comfortable and ready to do so within that time.

In one study of 16 male and female NCAA Division I players, pre-performance routines were examined during five male and five female intercollegiate games (Czech, Ploszay, and Burke, 2004). No statistically significant differences in FT accuracy were found between players who maintained the routine more than 90% of the time and those who maintained the routine less than 30% of the time (74% and 68%, respectively). However, shot percentages increased from 65% in the first shot to 83% in the second shot in the players who performed the pre-performance routine consistently. In contrast, shot percentage was reduced from 70% in the first shot to 65% in the second shot in the group that did not perform the routine consistently. No statistically significant data were reported for this finding. In addition, no effect sizes were reported in this study.

The relationship between the pre-shot interval – the duration of time prior to the throw – and the FT percentage was examined in male and female NCAA Division I players and male intramural players (Wrisberg and Pein, 1992). A low to moderate correlation was found between the standard deviation (SD) of the pre-shot interval and the FT percentage ($r = -.28$), suggesting that a more consistent pre-shot interval is somewhat related to a better FT performance. No correlations were found between FT percentage and the actual mean pre-shot interval. Differences between skill levels were also indicated: NCAA players had better FT percentages, longer mean pre-shot intervals, and lower SDs of the pre-shot interval than intramural players.

In another study, the temporal and behavioral consistency of pre-performance routines of 15 NBA players was observed in 14 NBA playoff games (Lonsdale and Tam, 2008). The mean pre-performance routine duration was 6.05 ± 2.09 sec. The researchers designated routines as either regular, brief (< -1 SD), or long (> 1 SD). No differences in FT percentage were found among the three temporal conditions (81.81%, 81.59%, and 78.38% for the regular, brief, and long durations, respectively). All players followed a dominant routine, but deviated from that routine in 56 out of 284 shot attempts, collectively. When the routine was followed, the FT percentage was higher than when the routine was not followed (83.77 vs. 71.43%, respectively). This 12% difference, while observational in nature, is noteworthy and may be of importance to game outcome.

The effects of altering the patterns of behavior and duration of a pre-performance routine were examined in a study of 17 male NCAA Division I players (Mack, 2001). The players' routines were observed during games, and based on these observations it was found that the players performed 20 FTs under each of the following conditions: (a) normal routine, normal duration (exactly like the usual routine of the players as observed in actual games), (b) normal routine, altered duration (same behavior but double the usual duration of the routine), (c) altered routine, normal duration (a specific new routine given by the researcher during the normal duration for each player), and (d) altered routine, altered duration (a specific new routine in double the normal duration for each player). The results showed that altering the behavior during the routine reduced FT performance, but lengthening the duration of that routine did not affect performance. These findings suggest that it is more important to maintain the same routine than to maintain a similar routine duration.

Different results were obtained in a study of 10 female college players who performed 10 FTs under each of two conditions: ritual and non-ritual (Southard, Miracle, and Landwer, 1989). Under the ritual condition, players performed the FT exactly as they would have performed it in a game situation. In the non-ritual condition, players were not allowed to perform their ritual and were instructed to shoot the ball without making any movements other than the ones necessary for shooting the ball. The total time of the ritual was 4.94 ± 1.16 seconds, and 11.0 ± 1.6 patterns of behavior were recorded during that time. In the non-ritual condition, the total time was $2.46 \pm .53$ seconds, and only three patterns of behavior were recorded. No differences in FT performances were found between the two conditions.

It was suggested by Southard and colleagues (Southard et al., 1989) that it is not the number of movements performed by the shooter throughout the routine, the sequence of the movements, or the total time of the routine that account for the FT success, since these variables changed between the ritual and non-ritual conditions. Rather, it could have been the average duration of the behaviors that influenced the outcome of shooting, due to the fact that the shooting success was similar between the two conditions. However, this observation should be taken with caution. The fact that only one variable was similar between the two conditions does not mean that this was the reason for the lack of difference between them. Several other factors could have influenced the results, among them the low number of FTs performed (only 10 in each condition) and the fact that the ritual and the non-ritual conditions were not counter-balanced.

In a follow-up study (Southard and Miracle, 1993), eight female college players were asked to perform 15 FTs in each of the following conditions: (a) standard routine, (b) half-time routine (same routine but half the normal duration of routine), (c) double-time routine (same routine but double the duration of the routine), and (d) variable time routine (duration of routine changed from shot to shot). The total time of the standard routine condition was 4.87 ± .81 sec. The relative time to complete the routine behaviors remained constant, even when the total time was either doubled or reduced in half. Performance was negatively affected only in the variable time condition. These findings suggest that it is more important to maintain the consistency of the routine rather than the total time of the routine. However, in this study the sample size was small and the effect sizes were not reported. Despite the small sample size, the difference between the successful shots in the double-time condition (11.0 ± 1.6) and the standard condition (9.87 ± 2.1) had an effect size of .54. This moderate effect size may suggest that doubling the time of the pre-performance routine can lead to improved performance.

A different approach of studying pre-performance routines was taken in a study of 30 male players (Predebon and Docker, 1992). In this study, after obtaining baseline FT performances, players were divided into three groups: (a) no routine, (b) physical routine, and (3) imagery and physical routine. In the last group, players were asked to first imagine the shot sequence without the ball, and then to continue with their usual physical routine. Each player performed 20 shots in three sessions that took place over six weeks. The results showed that forcing players to use a no-routine protocol led to a reduction in performance from a baseline mean of 14.1 ± 1.86 successful shots to 10.1 ± 3.65 successful shots during Session 1, and 11.9 ± 2.36 successful shots after Session 3 (after 6 weeks). It should be noted that neither of the pre-performance routine groups improved their FT performance compared to baseline. This could be due to the fact that these players had already used a pre-performance routine during practices and games.

The contribution of pre-performance routines to achievement in FTs in pressure situationswas examined in a study of 25 male high-school basketball players (Gayton, Cielinski, Rancis-Keniston, and Hearns, 1989). The players were asked to perform 50 FTs in five sets of 10 trials. The first 10 shots were used as warm up shots. The remaining 40 shots were performed while alternating between using the routine and not using it. Pressure was provoked by having the players shoot in front of their peers and by recording their achievements on a large board placed alongside the FT line. FT performance was better under the pre-performance conditions (13.52 ± 2.55 successful shots out of 20) when compared to the no pre-performance routine (11.00 ± 2.84 successful shots out of 20). However, it is possible that the stressful situations evoked in the study were not authentic enough to actually induce pressure or stress in the FT shooters.

Arousal

One study examined whether training under different arousal conditions influenced FT performance (Movahedi, Sheikh, Bagherzadeh, Hemayattalab, and Ashayeri, 2007). Thirty-seven male physical education students were divided into two experimental groups: low arousal and high arousal (i.e., using motivational techniques such as pep talk and goal-setting). Both groups took part in FT training sessions three times per week for six weeks. FT performance was tested before and after the training program. The post-test was conducted under the same arousal conditions as those introduced in training, as well as under different conditions: the group that practiced under high-arousal performed the post-test under low-arousal and vice versa. A 15-FT retention test was also conducted 10 days after the last practice session. Shooting performances decreased significantly in the post-test, which was conducted under the two different arousal conditions. Similar findings were observed in the retention test, which also was conducted under both low- and high-arousal conditions. As the authors suggested, the findings of this study provide support for the concept of specificity in training. If players are required to perform under high-arousal conditions, their training should simulate these conditions.

Goal Setting and Self-Regulation

One study of 12 female intercollegiate players examined the effectiveness of goal setting in FT performances (Shoenfelt, 1996). The players underwent a pre-season training program that included behavioral modeling, relaxation, mental rehearsal, and goal setting. After midseason, players were divided into a treatment group and a control group: the treatment group was instructed to set goals for their FT performances and received feedback about their performance and technique. In order to control for the *Hawthorne effect*, the control group received the same treatment, but for their field-goal performance. The results showed improved FT performance in the treatment group and a decline in performance in the control group. Quite expectedly, the field-goal performance of the control group improved, while that of the intervention group did not. Unfortunately, it is impossible to say whether it was the goal setting or the provision of feedback that led to the observed improvements in this study.

In another study (Miller and McAuley, 1987), a group of 18 undergraduate students was randomly assigned to a goal-setting group or a control group. In a 5-week training program, the goal-setting group was instructed on how to set goals for their FT performances. The goal-setting group met together for 10 minutes each week. The control group had similar weekly meetings in which techniques of FTs were taught. Each team performed 20 FTs each week. The results of this study showed that while FT self-efficacy significantly increased in the goal-setting group and not in the control group, there were no statistically significant differences in the actual FT performances between the groups. However, in four weeks out of the 5-week training program, the goal-setting group performed better than the control group. The authors also suggested that the goal-setting group showed more stable performances throughout the 5-week program compared to the control group. Therefore, while this study did not fully support the importance of goal-setting in improving FT performances, it revealed a trend in that direction. The effectiveness of three psychological techniques used in different phases of the FT act – goal setting and strategic planning prior to the execution, self-regulation during the performance, and self-reflection after the execution – were examined in another study (Cleary, Zimmerman, and Keating, 2006). Fifty physical education students were divided into five groups: three experimental groups (three-phase self-regulation, two-phase self-regulation, and one-phase self-regulation) and two control groups (practice only and no practice). The three-phase self-regulation group was instructed to set goals, to record and monitor their performance, and to adjust their performance accordingly. The two-phase group only set goals and recorded their performance. The one-phase group only set goals. Each of the five groups completed 12 minutes of FT practice and also completed a post-test. Shooting performance was higher in the three-phase and two-phase groups than in the one-phase group and the control groups. These results suggested that, at least in novices, self-regulation techniques can improve FT performance. The data that emerged from the studies on goal setting and self-regulation are inconclusive. There is some evidence that, at least in novices, goal-setting can be a useful strategy for increasing FT performances. However, this cannot be said for more experienced players. Additional research using large sample sizes of experienced players is needed.

Imagery and Relaxation

In one study (Onestak, 1997), 48 male university athletes were divided into three experimental groups: (a) visuo-motor behavior rehearsal, (b) videotaped modeling, and (c) a combination of the two. Each participant threw 25 FTs each day for three days as a pre-test phase. This was followed by specific training for each group: the visuo-motor rehearsal group underwent 30-min sessions in which relaxation and imaging techniques were taught. The videotaped modeling group included watching two videotapes of elite players. At the end of eight days of training, the participants performed 25 FT shots every day for three days as a post-test phase. The results showed similar improvements in FT performance in all groups. As a control group was not included in this study, it is not clear whether the improved performance in all groups was due to the treatment or to a testing effect. In a study of 18 NCAA Division III female players, the contribution of imagery and relaxation techniques to FT performance was examined (Lamir and and Rainey, 1994). The players were divided into an imagery group and a relaxation group. Each group participated in two FT training sessions per week for two weeks. The imagery group was instructed to focus on kinesthetic, visual, and auditory stimuli, and the relaxation group was directed to perform a diaphragmatic breathing technique. Compared to baseline performance, the imagery group failed to improve (71% and 70% success, respectively), while the relaxation group improved their FT percentage (65% and 74%, respectively), but no statistical significance was indicated for this improvement. The authors acknowledged several limitations in this study, among them the small sample size of the players, which could have led to the lack of statistical significance. It is also possible that a *ceiling effect* prevented a more distinct difference. Three studies used a single-subject design to assess the effects of imagery and relaxation on FT performance. In one study (Kearns and Crossman, 1992) three male varsity players completed four sessions of imagery in the laboratory, and continued performing what they had learned in practices as well as at home. During practice, FT percentage improved by 5-6% in all three participants. During games, FT percentage improved by 14% and 15% for two participants, but decreased by 3% for the third participant. It should be noted that the third participant threw only 16 FTs in game situations during the intervention phase. As indicated by the authors, it was possible that the results of the third participant could have been better if a greater number of FTs had been performed. While the results are in favor of the use of imagery, control participants were not included, and therefore it is unclear whether the improvement was due to other factors as well, such as a *testing effect*. In a second study, three male Division II players were trained in relaxation and imagery so that they would be able to identify negative self-statements and replace them with positive self-statements (Hamilton and Fremouw, 1985). Players met individually with the researchers for 3-4 hours during the first week, 2-3 hours during the second week, and .5-1 hour for the remainder of the 11-week study. After the intervention, positive self-statements significantly increased and negative self-statements significantly decreased. Game FT percentages increased in all three participants: from 36% to 68% in the first participant, from 37.5% to 67% in the second, and from 50% to 75% in the third. In a third single-subject design study (Carboni, Burke, Joyner, Hardy, and Blom, 2002), the effectiveness of imagery was examined in six NCAA Division I players. Five players underwent the intervention while one player served as a control. The players were introduced to an imagery technique that was based on reaching a relaxed state and imagining themselves successfully shooting 10 FTs in a correct form. They performed two weekly sessions of 50 FTs each for six weeks. While all of the players felt that imagery had helped them to improve, the FT-percentage results observed in this study were inconsistent: two players out of the five who underwent the imagery training exhibited an improvement in FT percentage, while two demonstrated no improvement when compared to their previous season's average. The control player did improve his FT percentages when compared to his previous season average. In essence, the subjective feelings of the players did not match the actual quantitative results. The individual differences between players (two were former players), the short time period of the intervention, and the comparison to the previous year's average rather than to baseline results make the results difficult to interpret.

VERBAL FEEDBACK, MODELING, AND BIOFEEDBACK TRAINING

The influence of three types of feedback on FT performances were examined in 24 adolescent basketball players with little or no experience in one-hand FT shooting (Luk, Cruz, and Lin, 2009). The players were divided into four groups: (a) verbal feedback, (b) verbal cues with videotaped modeling, (c) verbal cues with video replay, and (d) control. Each player performed 120 FTs over two days, followed by a retention test of 20 FTs. The verbal feedback group received verbal cues on their performance errors at the end of each set. The videotaped modeling group observed an expert perform FTs, and was given verbal cues after each set. The video replay group watched a replay of their performances in addition to receiving the verbal cues after each set. FT performances improved significantly in the video modeling and video replay groups, while no differences were observed in the control group and the verbal cues group. Shooting technique improved significantly in all three experimental groups, but not in the control group. The results of this study suggest that the use of feedback provided by video, either modeling or replay, can be useful in improving FT performances in novice players. While only verbal cues failed to lead to improvement in FT performances in the previous study (Luk et al., 2009), a study using a single-subject design suggested otherwise (Kladopoulos and McComas, 2001). In this study, three NCAA Division

II female players were instructed on the correct technique of performing FTs. The players took part in three or four training sessions per week for a total of 25 sessions, in which 10 FTs were performed in each. During baseline, the session ended after these 10 FTs were performed. During training sessions, after the 10 shots were performed players were instructed how to properly shoot the FT. This was followed by 10 more shots, in which positive verbal feedback was provided to the players. The results showed that by Session 3 of the training program the proper shooting technique was achieved by all three players. In addition, FT performances improved from approximately 60% in baseline to over 72% at the end of the training sessions. Thus, it was shown that positive verbal feedback associated with correct shooting technique can improve FT performances. Lastly, the effectiveness of a cognitive strategy incorporating biofeedback in FT performances was examined in 36 college graduate students (Kavussanu, Crews, and Gill, 1998). Participants were divided into three groups: (a) EMG, electroencephalogram, and heart rate biofeedback, (b) EMG biofeedback only, and (c) control (a no-biofeedback condition). Participants completed six sessions of biofeedback training after a FT pre-test and prior to a FT post-test. During these sessions, participants were asked to think about the way they perform the FT. No differences in FT performances were observed between any of the groups. However, the best responders to the biofeedback training improved their performance from pre- to post-test, while the worst responders failed to do so. It is unclear from this study whether biofeedback can be useful in improving FT performances.

WHAT CAN WE LEARN FROM THE STUDIES ON THE USE OF PSYCHOLOGICAL INTERVENTIONS IN FTS?

Based on the studies discussed in our review, a number of observations can be made, as follows:

QE

Gaze data were collected in five FT studies. Two observations can be made on the use of QE (i.e., the final tracking gaze located on a specific location for more than 100 msec and within 3° of visual angle) in FTs in basketball: longer QE durations have been found to be associated with improved FT performances, and QE can be taught. Longer fixations on the rim prior to shooting and early fixation offset when shooting actions occurred were observed in skilled FT shooters (> 75% of shooting success). In addition, FTs shooters improved their shooting accuracy after being exposed to QE training.

Pre-Performance Routines

Eight studies examining the effectiveness of pre-performance routines in FTs were reported. It was observed that FT shooters who were taught a routine, or applied their own routines, prior to the FT act improved their shooting performances. It was also observed that it was beneficial for the shooters to maintain a fixed set of patterns of motor behaviors before they shoot the ball. In order to achieve success they could alter the time they devoted to preparation, but not the regular order of acts they selected to use. Additional research on the use of pre-performance routines in FTs is needed so that the specific aspects of the selected routines which are helpful (e.g., the motor, psychological, or emotional aspects) can be better understood.

Imagery and Relaxation

Five studies were reported on the use of imagery and relaxation in FT performances. Inconsistencies were found regarding the effects of relaxation and imagery techniques on FT performances. A number of methodological limitations hinder our ability to conclude that imagery and relaxation can serve as useful techniques. Among these limitations were the small sample sizes and the lack of control conditions.

Verbal Feedback and Modeling

Verbal feedback and modeling can improve FT performances. The provision of feedback and the use of modeling have been found to be effective instructional strategies in motor skill acquisition (see Schmidt and Wrisberg, 2008), and both strategies can also help FT shooters to enhance their shooting accuracy. Probably, a combination of the two strategies would result in a better shooting performance.

Individual Differences

From the reviewed studies in which FTs were performed under simulated pressure conditions, it was observed that some of the shooters choked under pressure conditions, while other thrived under such conditions. Since the shooters reacted differently under pressure conditions, an individualized approach should be adopted when preparing basketball players for the FT act, namely each player should be provided with those psychological interventions that most fit his or her psychological needs.

RESEARCH LIMITATIONS AND METHODOLOGICAL CONCERNS

The Lack of Data on the Effectiveness of Interventional Techniques in Achieving FT Success in Actual Games

In a typical FT study, players are taught a psychological intervention and then asked to perform a number of blocks of FT shots in order to assess the contribution of the learned intervention to the shooting performance. In essence, the FT shots were performed in artificial experimental settings in order to avoid distracted conditions that might hinder performance. Rarely has a follow-up phase on FT performances demonstrated in actual games been used by researchers. Indeed, there are a number of difficulties in the implementation of a follow-up phase in FT studies, among them the low number of FT shots taken by each player during the game. However, additional research is needed to elucidate the relationship between psychological preparation and FT success in actual games.

The Lack of Authentic Practice

In most studies on FTs, the participants were provided with a number of shooting blocks, typically two to four blocks of 10 to 25 FTs each. In none of the studies did the participants perform cycles of two to three shots followed by a rest period, as required during actual game situations. Focusing and re-focusing is one of the psychological demands of sport tasks such as the FT (Moran, 2005). It is assumed that it would be more beneficial for the basketball player to apply the learned psychological techniques in conditions that authentically reflect what is required for him or her to do during actual games. Therefore, it is assumed that performing blocks of two to three shots instead of 10 to 25 consecutive shots would enable the shooter to apply his or her psychological preparation in a more effective way.

The Lack of Qualitative Data on Psychological Profiles of FT Shooters

To develop effective sport psychology programs aimed at improving shooting ability of basketball players, qualitative data on the psychological profile of the players should be collected, not only at the beginning of the program but also throughout the program. Data on the feelings, perceptions, and thoughts of basketball players associated with their FT performances should be continuously gathered. This information, typically obtained by observation, in-depth interviews, and written materials (e.g., a player's journal), has rarely been obtained in studies on FTs. By collecting qualitative data, it is assumed that (SPCs and basketball coaches can better understand the specific needs of the individual player, and subsequently plan better psychological interventions.

The Lack of Data on Beginning Shooters

Most of the participants who took part in the FT studies discussed in our review were adult college and university players. The effectiveness of interventional techniques on FT performances in beginning basketball players has not yet been studied. It is assumed that sport psychology interventions should be taught to beginners in the early stages of learning a motor skill (e.g., a FT in basketball), so that they may benefit from them as do performers who are already skilled in their use (see Sinclair and Sinclair, 1994). It can also be assumed that beginners will benefit from the use of certain techniques, but not from others. For example, beginning volleyball players who were taught a motor-emphasized pre-performance routine when learning to serve in volleyball achieved better than those who were guided to apply a cognitive-emphasized pre-performance routine (Lidor and Mayan, 2005). For advanced performers who have gained experience in practicing sports skills such as serving in volleyball and FTs in basketball, cognitive-oriented routines would probably be more beneficial.

CONCLUSION

A typical basketball season is composed of three phases – preparation, competition, and transition. SPCs should teach their players how to prepare themselves for performing FTs effectively during the entire season, that is, in each phase of the season. Specific psychological preparation for the FT shots should be synthesized with the general psychological preparation given to the players throughout the season. Information obtained on the use of the task-pertinent psychological interventions discussed in our review can help the SPC better develop specific psychological preparations aimed at improving FT performance. It is suggested that the SPC obtain information on the psychological needs of the FT shooter prior to the selection of the intervention, in order to optimally match the actual needs of the shooter with the selected psychological preparation.

REFERENCES

Al-Abood, S. A., Bennett, S. J., Hernandez, F. M., Ashford, D., and Davids, K. (2002). Effect of verbal instructions and image size on visual search strategies in basketball free throw shooting. *Journal of Sports Sciences, 20*, 271-278.

Carboni, J., Burke, K. L., Joyner, A. B., Hardy, C. J., and Blom, L. C. (2002). The effects of brief imagery on free throw shooting performance and concentrational style of intercollegiate basketball players: a single-subject design. *International Sports Journal, 6*, 60-67.

Cleary, T. J., Zimmerman, B. J., and Keating, T. (2006). Training physical education students to self-regulate during basketball free throw practice. *Research Quarterly for Exercise and Sport, 77*, 251-262.

Czech, D. R., Ploszay, A. J., and Burke, K. L. (2004). An examination of the maintenance of preshot routines in basketball free throw shooting. *Journal of Sport Behavior, 27*, 323-329.

Dandy, J., Brewer, N., and Tottman, R. (2001). Self-consciousness and performance decrements within a sporting context. *Journal of Social Psychology, 141*, 150-152.

de Oliveira, R. F., Oudejans, R. R. D., and Beek, P. J. (2008). Gaze behavior in basketball shooting: Further evidence for online visual control. *Research Quarterly for Exercise and Sport, 79*, 399-404.

Gayton, W. F., Cielinski, K. L., Rancis-Keniston, W. J., and Hearns, J. F. (1989). Effects of preshot routine on free-throw shooting. *Perceptual and Motor Skills, 68*, 317-318.

Hamilton, S. A., and Fremouw, W. J. (1985). Cognitive-behavioral training for college basketball free-throw performance. *Cognitive Therapy and Research, 9*, 479-583.

Harle, S. K., and Vickers, J. N. (2001). Training quiet eye improves accuracy in the basketball free throw. *The Sport Psychologist, 15*, 289-305.

International Basketball Federation. (2010). Official Basketball Rules 2010. p. 46. Retrieved January 9, 2011 from http://www.fiba.com/downloads/Rules/2010/OfficialBasketballRules2010.pdf

Kavussanu, M., Crews, D., and Gill, D. (1998). The effects of single versus multiple measures of biofeedback on basketball free throw shooting performance. *International Journal of Sport Psychology, 29*, 132-144.

Kearns, D. W., and Crossman, J. (1992). Effects of a cognitive intervention package on the free throw performance of varsity basketball players during practice and competition. *Perceptual and Motor Skills, 75*, 1243-1253.

Keetch, K. M., Lee, T. D., and Schmidt, R. A. (2008). Especial skills: Specificity embedded within generality. *Journal of Sport and Exercise Psychology, 30*, 723-736.

Keetch, K. M., Schmidt, R. A., Lee, T. D., and Young, D. E. (2005). Especial skills: Their emergence with massive amounts of practice. *Journal of Experimental Psychology: Human Perception and Performance, 31*, 970-978.

Kladopoulos, C. N., and McComas, J. J. (2001). The effects of form training on foul-shooting performance in members of a women's college basketball team. *Journal of Applied Behavior Analysis, 34*, 329-332.

Krause, J., and Hayes, D. (1994). Score on the throw. In J. Krause (Ed.), *Coaching basketball* (pp. 138-141). Indianapolis, IN: Master Press.

Lamirand, M., and Rainey, D. (1994). Mental imagery, relaxation, and accuracy of basketball foul shooting. *Perceptual and Motor Skills, 78*, 1229-1230.

Leith, L. M. (1988). Choking in sports. Are we our own worst enemies? *International Journal of Sport Psychology, 19*, 59-64.

Lidor, R. (2010). Pre-performance routines. In S. J. Hanrahan and M. B. Andersen (Eds.), *Routledge handbook of applied sport psychology* (pp. 537-546). London, UK: Routledge.

Lidor, R., and Mayan, Z. (2005). Can beginning learners benefit from preperformance routines when serving in volleyball? *The Sport Psychologist, 19*, 343-363.

Lonsdale, C., and Tam, J. T. M. (2008). On the temporal and behavioural consistency of pre-performance routines: An intra-individual analysis of elite basketball players' free throw shooting accuracy. *Journal of Sports Sciences, 26*, 259-266.

Luk, K. M., Cruz, A., and Lin, V. F. P. (2009). The effects of video feedback with verbal cues on performance of basketball free throw shooting by female junior basketball beginners. *Asian Journal of Physical Education and Recreation, 15*, 43-51.

Mack, M. G. (2001). Effects of time and movements of the preshot routine on free throw shooting. *Perceptual and Motor Skills, 93*, 567-573.

Masters, R. S. W., Polman, R. C. J., and Hammond, N. V. (1993). 'Reinvestment': A dimension of personality implicated in skill breakdown under pressure. *Personality and Individual Differences, 14*, 655-666.

Mesagno, C., Marchant, D., and Morris, T. (2009). Alleviating choking: The sounds of distraction. *Journal of Applied Sport Psychology, 21*, 131-147.

Miller, J. T., and McAuley, E. (1987). Effects of a goal-setting training program on basketball free-throw self-efficacy and performance. *The Sport Psychologist, 1*, 103-113.

Moran, A. P. (2005). Training attention and concentration skills in athletes. In D. Hackfort, J. L. Duda and R. Lidor (Eds.), *Handbook of research in applied sport and exercise psychology: International perspectives* (pp. 61-73). Morgantown, WV: Fitness Information Technology.

Movahedi, A., Sheikh, M., Bagherzadeh, F., Hemayattalab, R., and Ashayeri, H. (2007). A practice-specificity-based model of arousal for achieving peak performance. *Journal of Motor Behavior, 39*, 457-462.

National Basketball Association. (2011). *Statistics*. Retrieved January 3, 2011, from www.nba.com/statistics

Onestak, D. M. (1997). The effect of visuo-motor behavior rehearsal (VMBR) and videotaped modeling (VM) on the free throw performance of intercollegiate athletes. *Journal of Sport Behavior, 20*, 185-198.

Otten, M. (2009). Choking vs. clutch performance: A study of sport performance under pressure. *Journal of Sport and Exercise Psychology, 31*, 583-601.

Predebon, J., and Docker, S. B. (1992). Free-throw shooting performance as a function of preshot routines. *Perceptual and Motor Skills, 75*, 167-171.

Price, J., Gill, D. L., Etnier, J., and Kornatz, K. (2009). Free-throw shooting during dual-task performance: Implications for attentional demand and performance. *Research Quarterly for Exercise and Sport, 80*, 718-726.

Schmidt, R. A., and Wrisberg, C. A. (2008). *Motor learning and performance: A problem-based learning approach* (4th ed.). Champaign, IL: Human Kinetics.

Shoenfelt, E. L. (1996). Goal setting and feedback as a posttraining strategy to increase the transfer of training. *Perceptual and Motor Skills, 83*, 176-178.

Sinclair, G. D., and Sinclair, D. A. (1994). Developing reflective performers by integrating mental management skills with the learning process. *The Sport Psychologist, 8*, 13-27.

Southard, D., and Miracle, A. (1993). Rhythmicity, ritual, and motor performance: A study of free throw shooting in basketball. *Research Quarterly for Exercise and Sport, 64*, 284-290.

Southard, D., Miracle, A., and Landwer, G. (1989). Ritual and free-throw shooting in basketball. *Journal of Sports Sciences, 7*, 163-173.

Vickers, J. N. (1992). Gaze control in putting. *Perception, 21*, 117-132.

Vickers, J. N. (1996). Control of visual attention during the basketball free throw. *American Journal of Sports Medicine, 24*, S93-s97.

Vickers, J. N. (2007). *Perception, cognition, and decision training*. Champaign, IL: Human Kinetics.

Wang, J., Marchant, D., and Gibbs, P. (2004). Self-consciousness and trait anxiety as predictors of choking in sport. *Journal of Science and Medicine in Sport, 7*, 174-185.

Wang, J., Marchant, D., and Morris, T. (2004). Coping style and susceptibility to choking. *Journal of Sport Behavior, 27*, 75-92.

Wilson, M. R., Vine, S. J., and Wood, G. (2009). The influence of anxiety on visual attentional control in basketball free throw shooting. *Journal of Sport and Exercise Psychology, 31*, 152-168.

Wrisberg, C. A., and Pein, R. L. (1992). The preshot interval and free throw shooting accuracy: An exploratory investigation. *The Sport Psychologist, 6*, 14-23.

Wulf, G. (2007). Attentional focus and motor learning: A review of 10 years of research. *Bewegung und Training, 1*, 4-14.

Zachry, T., Wulf, G., Mercer, J., and Bezodis, N. (2005). Increased movement accuracy and reduced EMG activity as the result of adopting an external focus of attention. *Brain Research Bulletin, 67*, 304-309.

In: Athletic Insight's Writings of 2012
Editor: Robert Schinke

ISBN: 978-1-62618-120-5
© 2013 Nova Science Publishers, Inc.

Chapter 20

EXERCISE TO THE EXTREME? IDENTIFYING AND ADDRESSING UNHEALTHY EXERCISE BEHAVIORS

Justine J. Reel,[1] and Dana Voelker[2#]*
[1]Department of Health Promotion and Education, University of Utah,
Salt Lake City, UT, US
[2]Department of Kinesiology, Sports, Studies, and Physical Education,
the College at Brockport, State, University of New York, Brockport, NY, US

ABSTRACT

Physical activity has been associated with numerous physical and psychological benefits and exercise has been considered a "medicine" for helping depression and anxiety, and managing stress (Hausenblas, Cook, and Chittester, 2008). However, exercise taken to the extreme can have deleterious effects and can resemble an addiction. Various terms have been used to label this over exercise behavior, including exercise dependence, exercise addiction, and dysfunctional exercise (Calogero and Pedrotty-Stump, 2010). This chapter will focus on identifying unhealthy exercise patterns and symptoms as well as how to address over exercise behaviors. The importance of a mindful and intuitive approach to exercise is covered with an emphasis on promoting diverse activities for enjoyment motives.

Associated with numerous physical and psychological benefits physical activity and exercise are usually viewed in a positive light (Hays, 2002). Physical activity interventions have been used to reduce depression and anxiety, improve mood, and prevent disease (Hausenblas, Cook, and Chittester, 2008). Physical activity has also been found to improve muscular strength, endurance, and coordination (Kruger, Ham, and Prohaska, 2009). Related to the global obesity epidemic, exercise has been viewed as a necessary "medicine" to treat overweight and obese individuals. By increasing physical activity and reducing excess body

---

[*] Department of Health Promotion and Education, 1901 E. South Campus Drive, #2142, University of Utah, Salt Lake City, UT 84112. Telephone: (801) 581-3481, Email: Justine.Reel@hsc.utah.edu.
[#] Email: voelkerd@gmail.com.

weight, medical conditions such as type 2 diabetes, heart disease, and cancers can be prevented (Kruger et al., 2009). Unfortunately, too much exercise is also cause for concern.

In the 1970s, the term "runner's high" was used to describe the euphoric effect of exercise. Despite the positive benefits of physical activity, too much exercise was identified as unhealthy for certain populations. For example, the addictive potential of exercise (i.e., "running addiction") was examined in a 1979 study conducted with twelve adult male runners aged 23 to 48 years old (Sachs and Pargman, 1979), and medical doctors in the late 1800s observed hyperactive behaviors among clients with anorexia nervosa which they was characterized as both excessive and obsessive (Beumont, Arthur, Russell, and Touyz, 1994). More recently, the negative effects of over-exercise have also been identified in athletes (i.e., overtraining), which may result in performance decrements and fatigue (Pereira et al., 2012). This chapter will explore the terms used to describe over-exercise, the frequency of over-exercise behaviors among both the general population and athletes, as well as important identification, referral, and treatment processes for those who are symptomatic.

TERMS TO DESCRIBE UNHEALTHY EXERCISE

Disagreement exists as to what unhealthy exercise should be called (Adkins and Keel, 2005). Terms for over-exercise behaviors have included, but are not limited to, exercise addiction, excessive exercise, exercise dependence, exercise abuse, compulsive exercise, "activity anorexia," and obligatory exercise (Calogero and Pedrotty-Stump, 2010). Generally excessive exercise has been defined as having an "excessive" quantity of movement relative to frequency, intensity and duration that can result in increased risk of physical injury (Davis and Fox, 1993). By contrast, the term "compulsive exercise" captures the quality of movement patterns in which exercise can appear obligatory, obsessive, or compensatory in nature (i.e., exercise to purge food or change body weight/shape) (Meyer and Taranis, 2011). Although both the quantity and quality of movement patterns are important, many researchers and clinicians argue that dysfunctional exercise is largely tied to the client's mindset (quality) rather than the actual amount of movement (e.g., Calegoro and Pedrotty-Stump, 2010; Seigel and Hetta, 2001). For example, a recent study showed no correlation between the quantity of exercise and the level of disordered eating (Taranis and Meyer, 2011). This finding suggests that the compulsive and compensatory features of exercise that resemble addiction are more salient than the quantity of exercise alone.

The addictive-like mindset of feeling compelled to move was labeled as "exercise dependence" by de Coverley Veale in 1987. Similar to compulsive exercise, the term "exercise dependence" captured the potentially compulsive nature of movement and described a negative mood state experienced in the absence of physical activity (Reel, 2012). Interestingly, exercise dependence could occur in the absence of an eating disorder (i.e., primary exercise dependence) or represent a purging behavior symptomatic of an eating disorder (i.e., secondary exercise dependence) (de Coverley Veale, 1987). Thus, the presence of an eating disorder may be an important but not always a clear indicator of over-exercise. Although definitions in the literature are varied, all point to a range of concerning health risks. The term "over-exercise" will be used in the remainder of this chapter to describe any exercise behaviors that pose risk for physical and psychological consequences among athletes and exercisers.

FREQUENCY OF OVER-EXERCISE

Estimations of the frequency of over-exercise are inconsistent due to methodological variations across studies, including how over-exercise is defined (e.g., dependence, addiction, obligatory exercise), the instruments used, the population studied, and the sample sizes obtained. Such inconsistencies in the literature have led some researchers to conclude that the frequency of exercise addiction is high (e.g., McNamara and McCabe, 2012; Smith, Wright, and Winrow, 2010), while others suggest that true exercise addiction is quite rare (e.g., Bamber, Cokerill, and Carroll, 2000; Szabó, 2010). Berczik et al. (2012) discuss specific concerns over how researchers have defined and measured exercise addiction. For example, reporting symptoms of exercise addiction through a self-report measure does not necessarily have diagnostic value, thus leading to the possibility of over-estimating the phenomenon in some studies (Berczik et al., 2012). Still, the notion that over-exercise is an extant and important concern is consistent across the literature.

Traditionally, the frequency of exercise addiction has been estimated to be approximately 3% in the general population (Sussman, Lisha, and Griffiths, 2011). For example, about 2.5% of American university sport and fitness course participants (Hausenblas and Downs, 2002b), 3% of British adult exercisers (Griffiths, Szabó, and Terry, 2005), and 3.6% of British adult gym attendees were at risk for exercise addiction (Szabó and Griffiths, 2007). More recent data from a national prevalence survey suggests that between .3 and .5% of the general population and between 1.9% and 3.2% of exercisers are at risk for exercise dependence (Mónok et al., 2012).

Interestingly, other studies have shown that a greater proportion of college-aged students are at risk for exercise addiction as compared to the general population. For example, across five studies with physically active American undergraduate students, Hausenblas and Downs (2002a) found prevalence rates between 3.1% and 13.4%. Szabó and Griffiths (2007) categorized 6.9% of British undergraduate sport science students as symptomatic. These results may reflect a greater propensity towards physical activity in some college-aged populations, especially among those in sport, exercise, health, or physical education-related disciplines.

It has been similarly suggested that exercise addiction may be greater among exercise sub-groups where physical activity is a critical part of identity formation (Brewer, Van Raalte, and Linder, 1993; Hall, Hill, Appleton, Kozub, 2009; Smith, Hale, and Collins, 1998). For example, exercise addiction and dependence have been found among a considerable proportion of runners, triathletes, bodybuilders, and dancers. Slay, Hayaki, Napolitano, and Brownell (1998) identified 26.2% of male and 25% of female runners as obligatory exercisers. In another investigation, 45% of male and 65% of female middle distance runners were classified as exercise dependent (Hall, Hill, Appleton, and Kozub, 2009). Smith, Wright, and Winrow (2010) found that over a third of their sample of male and female competitive runners (n=91) were at risk of exercise dependence while only a small proportion of both competitive and non-competitive runners (n=184) were completely symptom-free.

In a study with triathletes, Blaydon and Lindner (2002) found that 31.5% of male and 25% of females in their sample were symptomatic of primary exercise dependence while an additional 19.8% of male and 28% of females were symptomatic of secondary exercise dependence. Among weightlifters, 15.1% were at risk for exercise dependence with 17 being body builders and 5 being power lifters (Hale, Roth, DeLong, and Briggs, 2010). When compared to existing normative data, Pierce and Daleng (2002) identified elevated levels of exercise dependence in elite female dancers. Finally, among a sample of elite Australian athletes representing 25 sports, approximately 35% were categorized as exercise dependent (McNamara and McCabe, 2012). While more research is clearly needed, preliminary evidence suggests that over-exercise may be a special concern among specific sub-groups of athletes.

When examining the full body of literature related to unhealthy exercise behaviors, researchers warn that results on the frequency of over-exercise should be interpreted with caution. Specifically, the critical reader should consider how over-exercise was defined, the instruments used to assess over-exercise, as well as both the sample size and sampling method employed. Taken together, the abovementioned findings suggest that the prevalence of true exercise addiction (i.e., clinical cases) is relatively rare. However, even a small proportion of the population may reflect large numbers of affected individuals. Finally, special attention may be paid towards specific sub-groups where physical activity is a highly valued and important aspect of personal and professional identity. Given the associated health risks, prevention and intervention mechanisms are therefore warranted.

OVER-EXERCISE IN SPORT

As previously mentioned, various forms of over-exercise have been identified in specific sub-groups of athletes. Most research on over-exercise in the sport context has focused on runners, triathletes, bodybuilders, weight-lifters, and dancers. Some studies indicate that over-exercise may differ between athletes of varying sport types. For example, Pierce, Daleng, and McGowan (1993) found that female ballet and modern dancers were significantly more likely to report symptoms of exercise dependence than female endurance (runners) and non-endurance athletes (field hockey players). Elevated exercise dependence in dancers may reflect a strong desire for technical proficiency as well as a drive to maintain the aesthetic standards of their dance form. Pierce and Morris (1998) found that mean exercise dependence among competitive power lifters was greater than previous reports by endurance athletes. Hale, Roth, DeLong, and Briggs (2010) found that body builders and power lifters demonstrated greater exercise dependence than fitness lifters. Similar to dancers, elevated scores of exercise dependence may be associated with a drive to achieve the musculature necessary to succeed in these activities.

Other research suggests that over-exercise may vary as a function of competitive status. For example, competitive bodybuilders and runners have been found to be significantly more symptomatic of exercise dependence than their non-competitive counterparts (Smith and Hale, 2004; Smith, Wright, and Winrow, 2010). Interestingly, sex differences in exercise dependence among the bodybuilders and runners in these studies were not identified (Smith and Hale, 2004; Smith, Wright, and Winrow, 2010) suggesting that male and female athletes may be equally vulnerable to unhealthy exercise behaviors.

More recently, researchers have examined the correlates and predictors of over-exercise among athlete populations, including a range of social and psychological processes. For example, Hall, Hill, Appleton, and Kozub (2009) found that both self-oriented (e.g., setting high standards for oneself) and socially-prescribed perfectionism (e.g., desiring to achieve high standards set by others) significantly predicted exercise dependence among middle distance runners. Their findings also suggest that those with a tendency to experience frequent fluctuations in self-esteem as well as those who exercise to validate their sense of self may be particularly at risk for exercise-dependent behaviors. Slay et al. (1998) found that obligatory runners were increasingly motivated by negative factors (e.g., experiencing depression, anxiety, and irritability if they stop running) as compared to non-obligatory runners. Among elite Australian athletes, McNamara and McCabe (2012) similarly found that those classified as exercise-dependent reported more maladaptive beliefs relative to exercise as compared to their non-dependent counterparts. Specifically, these athletes more often endorsed the notion that failing to train would result in severe physical, psychological, or social consequences. Maladaptive exercise beliefs of this nature accounted for 62% of the variance in exercise-dependent symptoms, which make belief systems an important factor in predicting over-exercise in athletes.

In addition to complex psychological processes, exercise dependence in athletes may be associated with a range of environmental influences. For example, McNamara and McCabe (2012) found that elite exercise-dependent athletes reported higher levels of pressure from coaches and teammates and lower levels of social support than their non-dependent counterparts.

These researchers concluded that pressure from important others to train harder or alter weight, shape, and body size to achieve performance success may promote exercise-dependent behaviors among elite-level athletes. Additionally, those athletes with poor social support may be more likely to depend on exercise as an alternative method of coping with stress. Interestingly, other findings suggest that high levels of social support in the sport environment may also promote exercise dependence.

For example, Hurst, Hale, Smith, and Collins (2000) found that experienced bodybuilders were more exercise dependent and perceived higher levels of social support than inexperienced bodybuilders. Thus, a strong social network within bodybuilding may strengthen identification with and reinforce dependence on that activity. Together, these findings suggest a dynamic and complex interplay between psychological and social forces in predicting exercise dependence in athletes and may be important points of intervention for practicing professionals.

With the number of athletes who may be affected by over-exercise and the severity of the health consequences, attention to these groups is clearly warranted. Interestingly, other literature suggests that "addiction" to exercise may not always be negative. Given that exercise is a natural and important component of any sport, some researchers have attempted to make a distinction between positive and negative addiction to exercise in athletic contexts. For example, Leedy (2000) found that the most highly addicted runners reported lower levels of depression and anxiety traits than their recreational counterparts.

These results suggest that a high commitment to running may not always be associated with negative consequences and might actually provide a productive outlet for managing negative mood states. A high commitment to running, then, may be most appropriately defined as a "negative addiction" only when the individual continues to run despite physical, psychological, and/or social impairments (Leedy, 2000). When over-exercise is recognized as unhealthy rather than merely a commitment to sport or exercise, treatment is warranted.

IDENTIFYING AND ASSESSING FOR OVER-EXERCISE

Hausenblas and Downs (2002a) paralleled over-exercise behaviors (i.e., exercise dependence) with features of substance dependence in which exercise was defined as the "substance" of choice. For example, individuals with an unhealthy relationship with exercise are likely to experience increased tolerance for movement (i.e., a need to increase exercise frequency to avoid guilt), withdrawal effects (i.e., experiencing symptoms such as anxiety and fatigue when unable to exercise), intention effects (i.e., exercising longer and more often than was planned), lack of control (i.e., a persistent desire or unsuccessful effort to decrease or control exercise), time (i.e., spending a great amount of time exercising), reductions in other activities (i.e., prioritizing exercise over social, occupational, or recreational activities), and continuance (i.e., exercising despite injury and illness). Furthermore, individuals who exhibit exercise dependence feel unable to incorporate rest days into their workout routines. Unhealthy exercise is often characterized by rigid routines that tend to burn more calories (e.g., running). Additional psychological features of unhealthy exercise have included rapid mood swings, irritability, fatigue, anxiety, impaired concentration, and sleep disturbances (Hausenblas and Downs, 2002b).

Understanding both an individual's psychological mindset and reasons for exercise is critical when determining whether an individual's exercise behaviors are unhealthy. Although numerous questionnaires (e.g., Commitment to Running Scale; Carmack and Martens, 1979, Obligatory Exercise Scale; Pasman and Thompson, 1988) have been used in research to evaluate excessive exercise, these self-report measures are limited in scope and do not include a comprehensive definition for unhealthy exercise (Hausenblas and Downs, 2002a). In response, the Exercise Dependence Scale (EDS; Hausenblas and Downs, 2002a) was developed based on the DSM-IV-TR (*Diagnostic and Statistical Manual of Mental Disorders*) criteria for substance dependence (APA, 2000) and modified for exercise. The EDS, a 29-item measure for dysfunctional exercise, covers the following criteria for exercise dependence:

1) narrow, stereotyped patterns of regular exercise once or more daily;
2) increased priority of exercise routines over other activities;
3) increased tolerance to the amount of exercise performed over the years;
4) presence of withdrawal symptoms (e.g., depressed mood) when not exercising ;
5) relief or avoidance of withdrawal symptoms by further exercise;
6) subjective awareness of feeling compelled to exercise; and
7) rapid reinstatement of the previous pattern of exercise and withdrawal symptoms after a period of abstinence (Hausenblas and Downs, 2002a).

Being rooted in clear diagnostic criteria, the EDS has been more useful in assessing clinical forms of exercise dependence than some other self-report measures.

In addition to self-report measures, clinical interviews are also useful in assessing unhealthy exercise. Specifically, clinical interviewers should question individuals about both the quantity and quality of their exercise behaviors. While it is important to understand the frequency, intensity, and duration of exercise sessions, interviews should probe to understand the meaning of exercise. For example, to understand the compelling nature of exercise, the interviewer might ask: "What motivates you to exercise?" and "Do you ever feel obligated to exercise?" These questions open up dialogue for understanding how exercise can be an unhealthy aspect of one's life (Mond and Calogero, 2009: Reel, 2012). In addition to exploring the feelings surrounding exercise, gathering specifics as to what "counts" as exercise is also important. Clients who report a narrow and rigid definition of acceptable movements should be further evaluated for other symptoms. For example, in assessing exercise tolerance (i.e., increased amounts of exercise needed to get the same effect), clinicians should ask how much exercise routines have increased and whether negative feelings ensue when they are unable to exercise. Finally, it is important to understand whether individuals can be flexible enough to exercise with other people to experience varying exercise intensity levels or to try different types of activities (Reel, 2012). It is possible to use objective measures to assess physical activity levels (e.g., pedometers, accelerometers), but a clinical interview and/or questionnaire is usually adequate. Importantly, motion devices as an exercise assessment tool should be used with caution, as pedometers and/or accelerometers may serve as an additional reinforcement for obsessive thoughts and compulsive exercise behaviors (Carter, Reel, Miyairi, O'Melia, Stotz, 2010).

ADDRESSING OVER-EXERCISE IN TREATMENT SETTINGS

Generally treating over-exercise should focus on changing the mindset from feeling compelled to exercise to engaging in more mindful movement and intuitive exercise. Mindful movement has been defined as being more aware of how the body feels while exercising and recognizing pain as it occurs. Those who engage in mindful movement (e.g., meditative walk) can incorporate multiple senses to see, hear and smell their surrounding environment. The term, "intuitive exercise" has been used in clinical settings (Reel, 2012) and involves listening to the body for whether exercise is healthy or obligatory. Similarly to intuitive eating approaches which promote the concept of no good and bad foods, intuitive exercise philosophy suggests that all types of movement, regardless of the type or intensity, count as exercise (Reel, 2013).

Although exercise is a necessary part of healthy living, incorporating exercise into treatment for those struggling with over-exercise has been controversial. Historically, exercise was avoided for fear that any movement would contribute to an individual's distorted thinking around exercise. In fact, this concern that high frequency exercise behaviors would further damage exercise-related cognitions and undermine weight restoration for those suffering with secondary exercise dependence led many early treatment providers to prescribe bed rest for their clients (Cox and Orford, 2004; Waldron and Hatch, 2009). However, incorporating exercise into treatment for individuals with secondary exercise dependence was shown to decrease anxiety around meals, improve treatment compliance, increase healthy weight gain, and prevent relapse (Thien, Thomas, Markin and Birmingham, 2000; Touyz, Lennerts, Arthur, and Beumont, 1993). Although results related to weight gain as a positive outcome of exercise therapy have been equivocal, Szabó and Green (2002) discovered that resistance training during eating disorder treatment was useful for both improving psychological well-being and increasing body composition.

In order to address exercise issues within a treatment setting, it has been recommended that clients who are medically cleared to exercise should engage in movement that is prescribed, supervised (to the extent possible within one's level of care) and individualized to the client's needs and preferences (Calogero and Pedrotty, 2004). Education about healthy, mindful exercise with the opportunity to discuss conflicting motivations related to exercise should be integrated into comprehensive treatment efforts (Calogero and Pedrotty-Stump, 2010; Reel and Estes, 2004). Clients who have the opportunity to practice exercise within a treatment setting (e.g., yoga class as part of a residential program) should be afforded the opportunity to process feelings following exercise session to maximize progress in changing their exercise mindset (Calogero and Pedrotty, 2004).

At the same time, exercise is not safe or appropriate for all individuals in treatment and should be restricted to those clients who are medically cleared by a physician to participate in an exercise program (Beumont, et al., 1994). Exercise that is provided within a supervised setting should be deliberately prescribed with specific functions (Tokumura, Yoshiba, Tanaka, Nanri and Watanabe, 2003). For example, stretching can be helpful for clients who have spent much time sitting and may experience back pain. Light lifting or resistance training can be useful in providing impact to improve bone health. Exercise (e.g., yoga) that promotes mindfulness, relaxation and enjoyment while being modified to fit the desired intensity can be introduced into an exercise program (Boudette, 2006; Dittman and Freedman, 2009). Running generally should be avoided during initial stages of treatment due to high caloric demands and potential for injury and stress fractures. Also, running often involves moving despite feeling pain which is the opposite of "mindful exercise" (i.e., listening to one's body and adapting exercise to what feels good). As a general rule, it is recommended that a treatment program expose individuals to a wide variety of movement patterns and types of exercise to deliver the message that many forms of activities "count" as exercise. Thien et al. (2000) introduced a graded exercise protocol (i.e., 7 levels) for follow-up outpatient clients with anorexia nervosa. The first 2 levels allowed for only stretching, sitting and lying for clients who were at 75% of ideal body weight (IBW). Beginning in the third level some low impact cardiovascular movement was added for clients at 80% IBW. Resistance training to build strength was recommended at level 5 when clients reached 90% IBW. The final level prescribed stretching, resistance strength training and low impact cardiovascular exercise three times a week for clients at 100% IBW (Thein, Thomas, Markin, and Birmingham, 2000).

Outpatient settings afford individuals more independence related to executing meal and exercise plans on their own. To prescribe and support exercise in an outpatient setting it has been recommended that the treatment team include an exercise specialist who is knowledgeable about the specific needs and challenges associated with the eating disorder population (Reel and Estes, 2004). This specialist should work with the physician on the treatment team to prescribe an exercise routine that emphasizes quality over quantity (Reel, 2013). The client should be encouraged to begin exercise gradually and introduce a variety of movement types. Yoga classes, resistance training and other forms of stretching have been recommended to encourage mindful, intuitive movement with motivations beyond appearance and calorie burning (Douglass, 2009; Reel, 2012; 2013).

Supervising physical activity is much manageable in a residential or in-patient setting. Nonetheless all activity should be monitored throughout the day. It has been recommended that all exercise and movement be structured (planned) and supervised by staff with exercise qualifications who can gauge intensity of exercise (Beumont, Arthur, Russell and Touyz, 1994). During exercise classes, the instructor can observe facial expressions to determine whether any clients are "abusing" exercise or becoming overly intense during the session. Some yoga postures may need to be modified to avoid competition within the group. Generally, mirrors have been discouraged in a treatment setting but, if used, mirrors should only be a guide for technique rather than a way for clients to monitor weight changes and appearance.

Although an exercise specialist can observe an exercise session or simulate movement within an outpatient session, it is likely that most exercise will be unsupervised. However, family members and supportive others can help support exercise plan so that individuals with over-exercise behaviors are not engaging in additional activities that lead to excessive energy expenditure. Family members and friends may need to be educated on how exercise is actually a helpful treatment tool. Some personal trainers can help monitor exercise routines for outpatient clients, but few have received training in eating disorder population needs. An individual may be encouraged to exercise with a friend who can help set a moderate, less intense pace. Finally, it is recommended that the treatment team consider whether the client is able to continue organized sports and other activities that may have contributed to exercise abuse prior to admission to treatment.

In addition to being supervised and prescribed, exercise incorporated into treatment should be individualized for each client (Carter, Reel, Miyairi, O'Melia, and Stotz, 2010). For example, there may be exercise differences for individuals with bulimia nervosa and binge eating disorder who may be able to engage in aerobic exercise sooner than individuals with anorexia nervosa who are still working towards weight restoration. Additionally, client preferences may allow for certain modifications in the types of activities performed. Some individuals may feel triggered (i.e., experience negative body image) by participating in yoga and may choose Nia or Zumba instead. Although individualizing exercise plans may be less feasible due to staffing needs within a residential setting, each client should be provided with a personalized exercise plan as she or he is transitioning to an outpatient setting (Carter, et al., 2010). A case study about over-exercise is presented in the next section.

CASE STUDY OF OVER-EXERCISE

When it comes to detecting unhealthy exercise behaviors, parents, coaches, athletic trainers, fitness professionals, performance consultants, and other practitioners are often the "first-responders." Understanding risk factors, signs and symptoms, and referral processes for exercise addiction is therefore critical for those who work closely with athletes and exercisers. The following is a case scenario to illustrate these key points.

Mark is a cross-country runner for his high school team. In addition to running an average of 65 miles per week for training, he is a self-proclaimed "avid exerciser" and hits the gym an additional 4 to 5 times per week to get some extra cardio. When you have expressed concern, Mark says that running helps him escape his stressful home life. Mark notes that he prides himself on being so active because most others are "disgustingly" obese and unhealthy and suggests that he never wants to be like "those people."

Mark appears to maintain his weight, but is very thin. He has experienced several stress fractures over the course of his high school career already, but continues to run in spite of obvious physical pain. Mark is terrified at the thought of cutting back on his training for the sake of rehab and claims that taking time off "is not an option." Mark does not have many friends, and running alone further isolates him. You are concerned with his reasons for exercise as well as his health. While Mark argues that he has to get a track scholarship that will help him pay for college, you are worried that he will not make it that far physically and mentally.

Mark is demonstrating key signs and symptoms of exercise addiction. The volume of training, negative motivations for exercise, continuation of exercise despite physical and psychological consequences, and the developing health risks are all relevant concerns. As someone who works closely with Mark, it is imperative that the issue be immediately addressed rather than ignored. The process outlined by Reel and Voelker (2012) for addressing disordered eating is also useful for addressing unhealthy exercise behaviors. For example, a coach may strategically employ caring confrontation techniques to broach the subject with Mark. These include meeting him in private to communicate specific concerns using a non-judgmental, sensitive but direct, and empathic approach that emphasizes the importance of health over performance (e.g., *I noticed you are running in spite of what appears to be physical pain, such as limping and grimacing as you train. This behavior is concerning because, as your coach, I truly care about your health and I want to help you*). Referring Mark to a licensed healthcare professional with expertise in exercise addiction (e.g., physician, mental health professional) is of utmost importance and a part of ethical practice. If met with resistance, this coach may consider suspending Mark's sport participation until proper treatment recommendations are followed. While seemingly harsh, this approach is in line with a health-first focus. Remaining supportive throughout the treatment process is an important step in promoting recovery.

CONCLUSION

Exercise clearly has numerous benefits, but it is important to recognize that unhealthy exercise exists. Specifically, over-exercise behaviors, which have been defined ina variety of ways in the literature (e.g., exercise addiction, exercise dependence), should be identified when certain symptoms (e.g., exercise tolerance, mood swings, isolation) are observed. Furthermore, the importance of assessing for quality and quantity of exercise behaviors using questionnaires and clinical interviews has been noted. Certain groups, such as athletes, may be more at risk for developing over-exercise behaviors which may be inherent in the sport environment. Treatment for over-exercise should include education about healthy exercise with a prescription for a more moderate, mindful approach to movement.

REFERENCES

Adkins, E. C., and Keel, P. K. (2005). Does "excessive" or "compulsive" best describe exercise as a symptom of bulimia nervosa? *International Journal of Eating Disorders, 38,* 24-29.

American Psychiatric Association (2000). *Diagnostic and statistical manual of mental disorders* (4th ed., text revision). Washington, DC: Author.

Bamber, D. J., Cockerill, I. M., and Carroll, D. (2000). The pathological status of exercise dependence. *British Journal of Sports Medicine, 34,* 125–132, doi: 10.1136/bjsm.34.2.125.

Berczik, K., Szabó, A., Griffiths, M. D., Kurimay, T., Kun, B., Urbán, R., and Demetrovics, Z. (2012). Exercise addiction: Symptoms, diagnosis, epidemiology, and etiology. *Substance Use and Misuse, 47,* 403-417. doi: 10.3109/10826084.2011.639120.

Beumont, P. J. V., Arthur, B., Russell, J. D., and Touyz, S. W. (1994). Excessive physical activity in dieting disorder patients: Proposals for a supervised exercise program. *International Journal of Eating Disorders, 15,* 21-36. doi: 10.1002/1098-108X(199401)15:1<21::AID-EAT2260150104>3.0.CO;2-K.

Blaydon, M.J., and Lindner, K.J. (2002). Eating disorders and exercise dependence in triathletes. *Eating Disorders, 10,* 49–60. doi: 10.1080/106402602753573559.

Boudette, R. (2006). How can the practice of yoga be helpful in recovery from an eating disorder? *Eating Disorders, 14,* 167-170. doi: 10.1080/10640260500536334.

Brewer, B. W., Van Raalte, J. L., and Linder, D. E. (1993). Athletic identity: Hercules' muscles or achilles' heel? *International Journal of Sport Psychology, 25,* 237–254.

Calogero, R. M., and Pedrotty, K. N. (2004). The practice and process of healthy exercise: An investigation of the treatment of exercise abuse in women with eating disorders. *Eating Disorders, 12,* 273-291. Doi: 10.1080/10640260490521352.

Calogero, R. M., and Pedrotty-Stump, K. N. (2010). Incorporating exercise into eating disorder treatment and recovery. In M. Maine, B. H. McGilley, and D. Bunnell (Eds.), *Treatment of eating disorders: Bridging the research to practice gap* (pp. 425-443). London, UK: Elsevier.

Carmack, M. A., and Martens, R. (1979). Measuring commitment to running: A survey of runners' attitudes and mental states. *Journal of Sport Psychology, 1,* 25-42.

Carter, J., Reel, J.J., Miyairi, M., O'Melia, A., and Stotz, S. (2010). Moving toward health: Exercise and eating disorders. Symposium presented at the American Psychological Association Convention. San Diego, CA.

Cox, R., and Orford, J. (2004). A qualitative study of the meaning of exercise for people who could be labelled as 'addicted' to exercise – can 'addiction' be applied to high frequency exercising? *Addiction Research and Theory, 12,* 167-188. doi: 10.1080/16066353100001634537.

Davis, C., and Fox, J. (1993). Excessive exercise and weight preoccupation in women. *Addicitve Behaviors, 18,* 201-211.

de Coverley Veale, D. M. V. (1987). Exercise dependence. *Addiction, 82,* 735-740.

Dittman, K. A., and Freedman, M. R. (2009). Body awareness, eating attitudes, and spiritual beliefs of women practicing yoga. *Eating Disorders, 17,* 273-292. doi: 1080/10640260902991111.

Douglass, L. (2009). Yoga as an intervention in the treatment of eating disorders: Does it help? *Eating Disorders, 17,* 126-139.

Griffiths, M. D., Szabó, A., and Terry, A. (2005). The exercise addiction inventory: A quick and easy screening tool for health practitioners. *British Journal of Sports Medicine, 39,* e30. doi: 10.1136/bjsm.2004.017020.

Hale, B. D., Roth, A. D., DeLong, R. E., and Briggs, M. S. (2010). Exercise dependence and the drive for muscularity in male bodybuilders, power lifters, and fitness lifters. *Body Image, 7,* 234-239. doi:10.1016/j.bodyim.2010.02.001.

Hall, H. K., Hill, A. P., Appleton, P. R., and Kozub, S. A. (2009). The mediating influence of unconditional self-acceptance and labile self-esteem on the relationship between multidimensional perfectionism and exercise dependence. *Psychology of Sport and Exercise, 10,* 35-44. doi:10.1016/j.psychsport.2008.05.003.

Hausenblas, H. A., Cook, B. J., and Chittester, N. I. (2008). Can exercise treat eating disorders? *Exercise and Sport Sciences Reviews, 36,* 43-47.

Hausenblas, H. A., and Downs, S. D. (2002a). How much is too much? The development and validation of the exercise dependence scale. *Psychology and Health, 17,* 387-404. doi: 10.1080/0887044022000004894

Hausenblas, H. A., and Downs, D. S. (2002b). Relationship among sex, imagery, and exercise dependence symptoms. *Psychology of Addictive Behaviors, 16,* 169–172. doi: 10.1037//0893-164X.16.2.169

Hays, K. F. (2002). *Move Your Body, Tone Your Mood.* Oakland, CA: New Harbinger.

Hurst, R. Hale, B. Smith, D., and Collins, D. (2000). Exercise dependence, social physique anxiety, and social support in experienced and inexperienced bodybuilders and weightlifters. *British Journal of Sports Medicine, 34,* 431-435.

Kruger, J., Ham, S. A., and Prohaska, T. R. (2009). Behavioral risk factors associated with overweight and obesity among older adults: The 2005 national health interview survey. *Preventing Chronic Disease: Public Health Research, Practice, and Policy, 6,* 1-17. http:www.cdc.gov/pcd/issues/2009/jan/07_0183.htm. Accessed October 25, 2012.

Leedy, M. G. (2000). Commitment to distance running: Coping mechanism or addiction? *Journal of Sport Behavior, 23,* 255 – 270.

McNamara, J. and McCabe, M. P. (2012). Striving for success or addiction? Exercise dependence among elite Australian athletes. *Journal of Sports Sciences, 30,* 755-766. doi: 10.1080/02640414.2012.667879.

Meyer, C., and Taranis, L. (2011). Exercise in the eating disorders: Terms and definitions. *European Eating Disorders Review, 19,* 169-173.

Mond, J. M., and Calogero, R. M. (2009). Excessive exercise in eating disorder patients and in healthy women. *Australian and New Zealand Journal of Psychiatry, 43,* 227-234.

Mónok, K., Berczik, K., Urbán, R., Szabo, A., Griffiths, M. D., Farkas, J., Magi, A., Eisinger, A., Kurimay, T., Kökönyei, G., Kun, B., Paksi, B., and Demetrovics, Z. (2012). Psychometric properties and concurrent validity of two exercise addiction measures: A population wide study. *Psychology of Sport and Exercise, 13,* 739 – 746. Doi: 10.1016/j.psychsport.2012.06.003.

Pasman, L., and Thompson, J. K. (1988). Body image and eating disturbance in obligatory runners, obligatory weightlifters and sedentary individuals. *International Journal of Eating Disorders, 7,* 759-769.

Pereira, B. C., Filho, L. A., Alves, G. F., Pauli, J. R., Ropelle, E. R., Souza, C. T., et al. (2012). A new overtraining protocol for mice based on downhill running sessions. *Clinical and Experimental Pharmacology and Physiology, 39,* 793-798. doi: 10.1111/j.1440-1681.2012.05728x

Pierce, E. F., and Daleng, M. L. (2002). Exercise dependence in elite female dancers. *Journal of Dance Medicine and Science, 6,* 4-6.

Pierce, E. F., Daleng, M. L., and McGowan, R. W. (1993). Scores on exercise dependence among dancers. *Perceptual and Motor Skills, 76,* 521-535.

Pierce, E. F. and Morris, J. T. (1998). Exercise dependence among competitive power lifters. *Perceptual and Motor Skills, 86,* 1097-1098.

Reel, J. J., Ed. (2013). *Eating disorders: An encyclopedia of causes, treatment and prevention.* Santa Barbara, CA: ABC-CLIO Greenwood.

Reel, J. J. (2012). Promoting "intuitive exercise": Exercise education and eating disorder treatment. Presented at the Rosewood Institute. Wickenburg, AZ.

Reel, J. J., and Estes, H. (2004). Treatment considerations for athletes with eating disorders. In K. Beal (Ed.) *Disordered eating in athletes: A comprehensive guide for health professionals* (pp. 131-146). Champaign, IL: Human Kinetics.

Reel, J. J., and Voelker, D. K. (2012). "Sculpted to perfection": Addressing and managing body image concerns and disordered eating among athletes. In R. J. Schinke (Ed.) *Athletic insight's writings in sport psychology* (pp. 301-316). Hauppage, NY: Nova Science.

Sachs, M. L., and Pargman, D. (1979). Running addiction: A depth interview examination. *Journal of Sport Behavior, 2,* 143-155.

Seigel, K., and Hetta, J. (2001). Exercise and eating disorder symptoms among young females. *Eating and Weight Disorders, 6,* 32-39.

Slay, H. A., Hayaki, J., Napolitano, M. A., and Brownell, K. D. (1998). Motivations for running and eating attitudes in obligatory versus nonobligatory runners. *International Journal of Eating Disorders, 23,* 267–275.

Smith, D. K., and Hale, B. D. (2004). Validity and factor structure of the bodybuilding dependence scale. *British Journal of Sports Medicine, 38,* 177-181. doi: 10.1136/bjsm.2002.003269

Smith, D. K., Hale, B. D., and Collins, D. (1998). Measurement of exercise dependence in bodybuilders. *Journal of Sports Medicine and Physical Fitness, 38,* 66–74.

Smith, D., Wright, C., and Winrow, D. (2010). Exercise dependence and social physique anxiety in competitive and noncompetitive runners. *International Journal of Sport and Exercise Psychology, 8,* 61–69.

Sussman, S., Lisha, N., and Griffiths, M. D. (2011). Prevalence of the addictions: A problem of the majority or the minority? *Evaluation and the Health Professions, 34,* 3–56. doi: 10.1177/0163278710380124

Szabó, A. (2010). Addiction to exercise: A symptom or a disorder? New York, NY: Nova Science.

Szabó, C. P. and Green, K. (2002). Hospitalized anorexics and resistance training: Impact on body composition and psychological well-being. A preliminary study. *Eating Weight Disorders, 7,* 293-297.

Szabó, A., and Griffiths, M. D. (2007). Exercise addiction in British sport science students. *International Journal of Mental Health and Addiction, 5,* 25–28. doi: 10.1007/s11469-006-9050-8

Taranis, L., and Meyer, C. (2011). Associations between specific components of compulsive exercise and eating-disordered cognitions and behaviors among young women. *International Journal of Eating Disorders, 44,* 452-456.

Thien, V., Thomas, A., Markin, D. and Birmingham, C. L. (2000). Pilot study of a graded exercise program for the treatment of anorexia nervosa. *International Journal of Eating Disorders, 28,* 101-106.

Tokumura, M., Yoshiba, S., Tanaka, T., Nanri, S., and Watanabe, H. (2003). Prescribed exercise training improves exercise capacity of convalescent children and adolescents with anorexia nervosa. *European Journal of Pediatrics, 162,* 430-431. doi: 10.1007/s00431-003-1203-1.

Touyz, S. W., Lennerts, W., Arthur, B., and Beumont, P. J. V. (1993). Anaerobic exercise as an adjunct to refeeding patients with anorexia nervosa: Does it compromise weight gain? *European Eating Disorders Review, 1,* 177-181.

Waldron, J. J., and Hatch, S. J. (2009). "I have to exercise to eat!" Body image and eating disorders in exercisers. In J. J Reel and K. A. Beals (Eds.), *The hidden faces of eating disorders and body image* (pp. 159-176). Reston, VA: AAHPERD/NAGWS.

In: Athletic Insight's Writings of 2012
Editor: Robert Schinke

ISBN: 978-1-62618-120-5
© 2013 Nova Science Publishers, Inc.

Chapter 21

ASIAN PROFESSIONAL TENNIS PLAYERS' STRESS SOURCES AND COPING STRATEGIES: A QUALITATIVE INVESTIGATION

Sunghee Park
Assistant professor at Kookmin University, Korea

ABSTRACT

The purpose of this study was to identify Asian professional tennis players' stress sources and coping strategies to understand its influences on their performance and subjective well-being during the training and competition periods. A qualitative research method was employed, and data were analyzed by thematic analysis. The results indicated that Asian professional tennis players perceived psychological, physiological, social, and environmental stress sources and employed psychological skills, active coping, searching for social support, and avoidance to deal with those stress sources. The findings also revealed influences of culture and sport-specific contexts in athletes' perceived stressors and coping styles.

Over the past few decades, researchers (e.g., Anshel and Kassidis, 1997; Gould, Dieffenbach, and Moffett, 2002) have examined athletes' stress sources and coping strategies in the context of attempting to identify negative influences on athletes' performance enhancement (stressors) and attempting to define the psychological profiles of successful athletes (coping skills). Researchers (e.g., Anshel and Wells, 2000; Cohn, 1990) have identified a number of potential stressors for athletes (e.g., physical, mental, and social stressors) and the findings (e.g., Haney and Long, 1995; Klint and Weiss, 1986; Smith, Ptacek, and Smoll, 1992) have indicated that the ability to cope with those stressors is closely related to athletes' performance, increases in the probability of injury, and withdrawal from sport.

Those earlier findings have helped scholars understand athletes' stress sources and identify frequently used coping strategies related to their performance issues (Polman, 2012), whereas more recent studies have focused on examining specific stress sources which are related to the specific type of sport, differences between the training period and the competition period, and the influences of the cultural- and sport-specific context (e.g., Hodya and Anshel, 2003; Nicholls, Jones, Polman, and Borkoles, 2009; Nicholls, Levy, Grice, and Polman, 2009). As it has been the case in other areas of sport psychology (e.g., Kamphoff, Gill, Araki, and Hammond, 2010), however, stress and coping study area has not yet been the subject of a sufficient body of research into the cultural- or sport-specific contextual issues. Several researchers (e.g., Anshel, Williams, and Hodge, 1997; Hodya and Anshel, 2003) have emphasized the potential influence of cultural aspects and sport-specific contexts (e.g., organizational culture, the athletic system) on athletes' perceived stress sources and coping styles. Findings from cross-cultural studies in other areas of sports psychology have also indicated that Asian and Western athletes exhibit differences in their use of coping strategies and in how they develop their sense of self (Anshel et al., 1997; Bhalla and Weiss, 2010). Since the majority of studies in this area have considered Western samples, there is little evidence related to the cultural influences and sport-specific contexts in relation to athletes' perceived stress sources and coping styles. In addition, professional tennis players have unique lifestyles, in that they travel the world to participate in professional tennis tournaments from a young age. They typically participate in 20 to 25 tournaments per year, with each tournament lasting 1 to 2 weeks; most players travel 6 to 8 months per year, and once they depart for their first destination abroad, they are typically abroad for a continuous period ranging from 4 to 8 weeks.

Examining Asian professional tennis players' stress sources and coping strategies therefore might help us to reveal the influences of cultural background and sport-specific lifestyles on athletes' perceived stressors and to identify effective coping strategies. The purpose of this study was to identify Asian professional tennis players' stress sources and coping strategies, so that it might provide better understanding of their influences on the athletes' performance and subjective well-being during the training and competition periods, respectively. The findings might also help identify athletes' frequently used coping strategies and effectiveness of those strategies for dealing with their stressors.

METHOD

A qualitative research method was employed to achieve the research goal of understanding Asian professional tennis players' stress sources and coping strategies. Data were collected through interviews conducted either face-to-face or by telephone. As Patton (2002) has previously highlighted, the qualitative method allows researchers to collect a rich body of information from a small number of homogenous informants who are able to provide detailed stories related to the research questions; using this method helped the researcher better understand participants' in-depth accounts and experiences.

Participants

All study participants were current professional tennis players from four different Asian nations (India, Japan, South Korea, and Taiwan), including three male and seven female players. The mean age of the participants was 25.5 years, and they have been on the professional tennis tour for an average of 5 years, participating in an average of 22 international tournaments per year, and remaining abroad for an average of 7 months per year.

Procedure

In order to ensure the selection of information rich-cases, the current study employed purposeful sampling. Participants were recruited during an international tournament held in Korea. I acquired the contact details of several potential participants from a Korean professional tennis coach and invited 12 athletes to participate in the study. All agreed to take part; two athletes had to depart from the Korean tournament before data collection began, however, and attempts to reach them again were unsuccessful.

A semi-structured interview guide was developed which had been informed by the existing literature related to athletes' stress and coping strategies (e.g., Anshel and Wells, 2000; Crocker, 1992) and which was greatly informed by Patton's (2002) interview question guidelines. The interview guide included demographic questions (e.g., age, sex), experiential and behavioral questions (e.g., as a professional tennis player, have you experienced distress?), solicitations of opinion and assessments of value (e.g., how does stress influence your performance?), and feeling questions (e.g., how do you feel when you experience distress?). Prior to collecting the data, all participants were read information about the current study and signed a consent form. The interview location and date for each participant were selected and scheduled for the participants' convenience; interviews with three athletes were conducted via telephone due to geographic limitations and scheduling conflicts.

Analysis

Audio recordings were made of the interviews, and the conversations were transcribed verbatim. The average duration of an interview was 55.3 minutes and ranged between 49 and 65 minutes.

Thematic analysis was used to analyze the raw data, and I followed Patton's (2002) three-step thematic analysis guide. The first step involved reading and re-reading the interview transcripts while listening to the audio recordings to ensure a fuller understanding of the participants' accounts and the precise meanings of their chosen language. In the second step, I sorted the raw data into meaning units and classified those data into categories by identifying and labeling the patterns inherent to the data. The third step involved developing low-order themes based on previously categorized patterns and then organizing these lower-order themes into higher-order themes. I used the extant literature pertinent to the study area (e.g., Carver, Scheier, and Weintraub, 1989; Lazarus and Folkman, 1984) to better understand and interpret the raw data.

To enhance the credibility of the research, I used member checking, analyst triangulation, and audit trial (Patton, 2002). To perform member checking, prior to engaging in any analysis, the transcripts were sent to the participants, who were provided an opportunity to review our dialogue; eight participants responded to the researcher with their feedback. After the analysis, the categorized themes were disseminated to the respondents; the researcher received confirmation from seven participants that the results were based on their original discussions. Three other sports psychology PhD students were involved in the analytical process, discussing patterns, categories, and low- and high-order themes with the researcher until agreement had been reached on all themes. In the final stage of the analysis, one expert completed an audit trial, which involved: (a) assessing the rigidness of the data analysis, and (b) confirming that the final themes reflected the original data (Patton, 2002).

RESULTS

In the process of performing the analysis, I identified 131 meaning units, 61 codes, 9 lower-order themes, and four higher-order themes related to participants' stress sources, including psychological, physiological, social, and environmental factors. Regarding coping strategies, I identified 99 meaning units, 27 codes, six lower-order themes, and four higher-order themes, including using psychological skills, active coping, social support, and other strategies.

All participants reported having experienced various kinds of stress sources and experiencing the most stress before and during the competition, which they related to fear of failure and the nature of their competitiveness. Eight participants responded that their perceived stress influenced their performance; five perceived that their stress had both positive and negative impacts on their athletic lives. The results indicated that the athletes identified various on-court and off-court stressors and that the stress sources were closely related to their performance accomplishment whether they were in a training session or participating in a competition. To identify athletes' stress sources and coping strategies during the two respective periods, the findings are reported based on the training and competition periods.

Stress Sources and Coping Strategies during the Training Period

The findings indicated that the athletes perceived psychological, physiological, and social stressors during the training period. To reduce those stressors, athletes employed psychological skills, active coping, social support, and other coping strategies.

Stress Sources during the Training Period
Although athletes did not compete or travel during the training period, their perceived stress sources were closely related to performance issues. Psychological stress sources during the training period were discussed from five athletes who reported worries such as experiencing a drop in their world ranking or their ranking points. One participant said, "[I] [am] almost always concerned about dropping my world ranking and ranking point". They also showed a tendency toward identity foreclosure, in terms of a high commitment to their sport and an absence of other activities or interests outside of their sport. Other psychological stressors included competitive pressure, self-expectations, and loss of self-confidence.

All participants discussed physiological stress, reporting concerns over physical injuries and their strength and conditioning. Since the athletes participate in over 20 tournaments per year—competing and traveling abroad for over 20 weeks—they often reported experiencing restlessness and feelings of overtiredness. Maintaining their physical condition during their training periods was therefore closely related to their upcoming competitions and in order to achieve their goals, they had to be very conscious of their physical strength and overall health. One participant said, "I always have to think about my physical condition. I have to take care of myself even outside the tennis court". Avoiding injuries and recovering from existing injuries were also discussed as stressful processes during training periods. Another player mentioned her worries and concerns about her injuries, saying, "Having treatment and recovering from injury are very stressful...I think injury is one of the worst thing can happen to you. It makes you feel very depressed".

Respondents identified their inter-personal issues as another potential stress source, including their relationships with coaches and teammates, the high expectations of their "close others" (i.e., family members, coaches, and sponsors), the lack of time they had available to spend with their close others, and their generally narrow social networks. As is the case in other sports, building a strong coach-athlete relationship was mentioned as an important ingredient for athletic success by the participants, who saw the importance of their coaches' roles in their skill development and in the amount of time they spent together, whether at home or abroad. One athlete discussed this issue in greater depth, saying;

> ...since I was young, I have spent so much time with my coach...we usually have a good relationship. But if things go wrong and when we have conflict it is really hard for me. I don't know what to do".

Three Korean participants perceived a conflict with their teammates as a source of stress. In most cases, Korean professional tennis players live at the team's dormitory, with teammates. Four athletes from other nations did not mention teammate issues as a stress source. Three participants reported that the high performance expectations of their close others represented a stress source even during the training period.

Athletes were aware of their high level of commitment to their sport, yet still perceived themselves as not having a high degree of control over a number of issues, such as their lack of a well-developed social network and the lack of sufficient time to pursue off-court activities because of training and competition requirements. Half the participants therefore discussed their lack of a social network and the lack of time they had available to spend with their close others as stress sources. One participant said,

> I can't have time even if I want to do something else. I want to see my friends and talk to them but I can't. I also can't spend holidays with my families or friend because I usually have to train or compete.

Coping Strategies during the Training Period
The athletes used various coping strategies to overcome those stressful events or stressors. For psychological issues, participants tended to use several different psychological skills, many of which they also used on the tennis court. Those psychological skills included positive self-talk, meditation, relaxation techniques, and maintaining their focus on positive events. One Indian athlete said, "I try to be positive even if I have got an injury. It helps me to take care of myself and I believe it is a better way to deal with the situation".

Participants seemed to employ active coping in dealing with their inter-personal issues and with concerns over their physical strength and conditioning. Athletes' active coping was based on problem-focused coping. Athletes who experienced conflict with their coaches or teammates, for instance, tried to engage them in conversation, while athletes who had concerns about their physical strength or skills employed imagery or spent more time on physical strength training. One athlete said, "When I have trouble with my coach, I try to talk". Another athlete also described their use of active coping, saying, "I try to put more time into my physical strength training if I have worries and concerns about [physical] conditioning". Searching for other activities outside of their sport was also reported as part of their active coping strategies meant to allow them to release stress. Seven respondents reported having searched for other activities and having engaged in those activities with the goal of forgetting or releasing their stress. Those activities included reading, listening to music, writing, visiting nice places, and playing other sports. One Japanese tennis player said, "When I get too stressed I just go out and do whatever I want, rather than worrying about tennis. Go to the cinema and watch a film or drive to nice places that I like... Actually, it really helps".

Searching for social support was a strategy reported by seven athletes, and social support was one of the most effective coping strategies for them to release their stress during the training period. Athletes' social support networks included family, friends, coaches, and teammates. During the training season—as opposed to the competition period—professional tennis players are typically able to stay in their own countries, and most tried to spend more time with their friends and families as compared to what they were able to do during the competition periods. One participant said;

> I like to see my friends and talk to them about stressful events, whether it is related to tennis or inter-personal issues. When I talk to them, usually they listen to me and show me empathy so it makes me feel better.

Participants also reported other coping strategies, such as avoidance and crying. Korean professional tennis players reported avoidance more often than did participants from other nations, especially when they perceived themselves to have a low degree of control over the stress sources (e.g., other people's expectations). One Japanese player mentioned crying when she was under too much stress from training or due to the competitive nature of her sport.

Stress Sources and Coping Strategies during the Competitive Period

The results indicated that participants experienced their most stressful feelings before and during competition. All respondents discussed psychological, physiological, social, and environmental stress sources before, during, and after their competition. Similar to what the athletes reported during the training period, athletes used psychological skills, active coping, social support, and other coping strategies to deal with their stress sources during the competition period.

Stress Sources during the Competition Period

During competition, psychological stressors, such as competition anxiety, feeling pressure to win, worrying about dropping in the rankings, meeting other people's high expectations, and over competitiveness were reported more than any other theme. One Korean participant said, "I am worrying about dropping my world ranking and my win-loss record. Thinking about losing my match really becomes a big stress for me". Another participant, from Taiwan, said, "Most of all, pressure about my game results is the biggest concern for me". Some respondents also noted having been exposed to negative influences as a result of those pre- and during-competition stressors, including being distracted from preparing for their competition, being them physically weakened, and seeing their performance as being hindered. One participant said, "When I started to worry about my match, I could not even sleep the day before the competition. This is really bad. My physical condition gets worse and you know...I usually can't perform well if that happens". Participants discussed dissatisfaction with their match (N=9) and having lost their match (N=8) as the biggest stress sources after the competition. One participant said, "When I could not win and I did not play well, I feel so bad". According to participants, the expectations both of their close others and of people related to the sport (e.g., people from the sport's institute, media, and audiences) also caused them competition-related stress, especially during big tournaments.

All participants discussed having been exposed to some negative influences as a result of those stressors; five participants, however, also perceived that experiencing stress could be helpful in getting them to perform well by helping them to regulate their arousal, increase their motivation, and develop cognitive and coping strategies. One participant said, "Stress is a form of pressure that gets a person to perform efficiently...I actually perform better when there is a certain degree of pressure".

Athletes' physical stress sources included concerns over being injured during the competition, a lack of physical preparation, and being generally dissatisfied with their tennis skills. One participant who had a chronic back injury spoke about her physical concerns before and during the competition, saying, "I really have to be very careful warming up because of my back. I do not want to get injured again on the court so I have to prepare physically almost perfectly, but this is not very easy".

Social issues included coaches' behavior and interactions with their opponents. Five respondents mentioned their coaches' behavior (i.e., giving too much advice, repeating talks about preparation and strategy, and showing negative body language during the match) as potential stress sources. One participant said, "My coach says the same thing so many times before I go on the court. Sometimes I almost lose my concentration. It really irritates me". Regarding coaches' behavior, another player said;

> I hope my coach can be supportive all the time when I am on the court...but I know when I see my coach's face or body language...something is not right I can tell...if I see this, my performance becomes even worse.

Unlike during the training period, most competitions are held outside the players' hometowns. During the competition period, the competitive environments were also perceived to be stress sources for athletes. Participants discussed various environmental issues such as difficulties adjusting to the court surface, food, weather, equipment, bad calls by the referee, and difficulties communicating in English. One participant mentioned feeling unpleasant because of the various environmental issues, saying, "I feel very stressed when the umpire has a bad call...I am very sensitive on the court. So if I lose my concentration, everything could be a problem, like balls, the court surface, and even my racket". Five participants from non-English speaking nations reported a lack of communication skills in English as one of their stressors. English communication was discussed as a post-match stressor in particular because, as professional tennis players, they have an obligation to deal with media. As one Korean player said;

> I feel stressful when I have to do interviews or speak after [the match]... I did not have this stress when I was playing just small tournaments but at the big tournaments, if you beat some good players, you have to talk to media... Because I do not speak good English that is so stressful.

Coping Strategies during the Competition Period

The participants' most-frequently used coping strategies during the competition period were psychological skills and emotion-focused coping, in efforts to reduce their competition anxiety and adopt a more positive mindset before and during the competition. This is because, as professional tennis players, participants' perceived stress sources were closely related to competition pressure or anxiety; the athletes had their own psychological skills, which helped them to regulate their arousal and anxiety levels during the competition period. More specifically, the athletes employed relaxation techniques, such as controlling their breathing, meditation, imagery, positive self-talk, and focusing on routine. One participant, for example, said, "I try to put the pressure aside and encourage myself by positive wording". Another said, "I usually try to have time to relax before the match, to have peace of mind and to be positive". To cope with the post-match stress, athletes tried to build positive emotions by having fun with friends or close others and by organizing their thoughts via writing diaries.

Participants also employed active coping, including putting more effort into overcoming their difficulties, taking care of their equipment, and preparing for the competition before the actual competition. One athlete said, "I usually put a pretty long time into warming myself up for the match. I take longer than other people but I like this because it makes me feel that I am ready to go". To deal with the post-match stress, six participants reported searching for other activities unrelated to sport, such as going out shopping, learning new things, and playing computer games. One participant said, "When I have a bad match, I really don't want to think about it. I just go out shopping and do something else...anything to help me not to think of tennis".

Only three participants mentioned social support as a coping strategy during the competition period. Compared to the training period ($N=7$), far fewer respondents employed social support as a coping strategy; this might be reflective of their travel requirements. Since they have to be way from home to participate in international tournaments, the travel causes them to be away from their social support networks except for coaches and peers. Athletes' social support networks during the competition period are therefore far narrower as compared to their networks during the training period. During the competition period, athletes reported trying to talk to their coaches and peers regarding their competition stressors and making new plans for future competitions. One participant said;

I try to talk to my coach. When I talk to my coach about the match, I can see where did it go wrong and what I could have done better. Also, it helps me to learn from what I have done. So, I think it is good for me.

Avoidance, turning to religion, and acceptance were also reported as coping strategies during the competition period. Athletes tried to avoid facing their actual stress sources, especially when they were related to the expectations of other people or to bad calls made by the referees. Those participants who were observantly religious said that they sometimes would listen to their Sunday services after losing a match or when they were feeling competition-related stress. One participant discussed the usefulness of acceptance, in terms of moving on to the next tournament. He said, "I know it was bad but there are so many tournaments out there. You have to accept what has happened and move on to the next one".

DISCUSSION

The present study identified Asian professional tennis players' stress sources and copings strategies. The results indicate that athletes' perceived stress sources were closely related to their competition or performance issues whether during the training period or the competition period. The results also showed that athletes employed various coping strategies and that, as professional tennis players, participants used psychological skills more than any other coping strategies in dealing with competition-related stressors.

As it was reported in previous research (e.g., Giacobbi, Lynn, Wetherington, Bodendorf, and Langley, 2004; Woodman and Hardy, 2001), athletes' stress sources are categorized into four different themes: psychological, physiological, social, and environmental factors. As it was mentioned earlier, the major concerns of the participants in the current study were closely related to their performance outcomes and competition anxiety, which parallels the findings presented in previous studies (e.g., Anshel and Wells, 2000; Nicholls and Polman, 2007). In addition, the current findings also revealed that professional tennis players also experience physical responses as stress reactions, such as being injured, a lack of or inability to sleep, and increased levels of arousal; this is in line with previous findings (e.g., Hellriegel and Woodman, 1992). Regardless of the type of sport or the cultural background, athletes seem able to perceive competition anxiety and performance-related stressors, and have various responses to those stresses.

The current results, however, have also revealed different stress sources as compared with those presented previously, which could be related to the participants' culture and sport-specific contexts. These findings include anxiety over communication, food, and peer conflict. Since professional tennis players have to travel around the world and are obligated to conduct interviews and give public statements in English, more than half of the participants from non-English speaking nations (Korea and Japan) discussed those interviews and statements as potential sources of stress. One respondent even confided that he could not concentrate on his match when he knew he had to do interviews. The results indicated that "learning and communicating in another language" could be a challenge for young athletes who want to be professional tennis players because most processes and events at international tennis tournaments are conducted in English. Since previous studies conducted with professional tennis players (Alison and Meyer, 1988; Young, Pearce, Kane, and Pain, 2006) investigated athletes from English-speaking nations, communicating in English was not considered to be a potential stress source. This language-related stress source therefore can be considered as a culture-related factor, and could be expected to differ among athletes from different nations.

Among Korean participants, conflict with peers was also reported as an inter-personal stress source, especially during the training period. The results might relate to the unique, sport-specific context in Korea; even though tennis is an individual sport, professional players are supported by companies (sponsors), train with the same coaches hired by those sponsors, and live with other players supported by the same sponsors.

Another unique finding related to athletes' stress sources was financial-related issues. Unlike previous studies (e.g., Fletcher and Hanton, 2003; Scanlan, Stein, and Ravizza, 1989), the current respondents did not mention any financial-related issues as stress sources. The results could be related again to the sport-specific context and, in particular, to the sponsorship system now in place for professional tennis players. The participants were all top players in their nations and had companies who supported their travel and living expenses, coaches' fees, and expenses for their equipment (e.g., rackets, strings, clothes, and shoes). Financial issues therefore did not seem to be a primary concern for the current participants.

Nicholls, Jones, et al. (2009) found that international cross-country runners perceived fatigue and the environment as stress sources during their training period, whereas ability and outcome were more frequently reported as stressors during match days. The current participants, however, did not mention environmental issues as stressors during the training period but did discuss several environmental factors as stress sources during the competition period. The results paralleled those reported by Nichllos, Levy et al. (2009), which investigated attitudes among rugby players and found that they perceived bad calls by officials and the presence of the crowd as stress sources. This could be related to athletes' appraisals of their own situations and to sport-specific factors. Professional tennis players, for example, typically train in their hometown or some other familiar environment, but competitions often require them to travel abroad, meaning they must then adjust to a new environment (e.g., court surface, balls, food).

Participants employed a number of coping strategies in attempting to deal with their stressors, including: psychological skills, active coping, searching for social support, and avoidance. This approach paralleled Crocker's (1992) finding, that athletes' coping strategies span a number of categories. As professional tennis players, the participants were aware of the effectiveness of psychological skills and used those skills to reduce their stressors during both the training period and the competition period. Psychological skills were frequently used when athletes had to deal with performance-related issues such as competition anxiety, concerns over performance outcomes, and competition pressure. Participants also sought out more social support and employed active coping methods to deal with stressors during the training period, whereas during the competition period, they tended to deal with their stressors on their own, rather than looking for support from their close others. The results could be explained as relating to the sport-specific context. Tennis is an individual sport and, in most cases, players are expected to deal with their own difficulties and issues once they are on the court; as such, it is perhaps to be expected that these professional athletes would attempt to cope with their stressors individually during the competition period.

As was reported in previous findings by Roth and Cohen (1986), athletes' perceived control influenced which coping styles they chose to adopt. When athletes perceived themselves as having some measure of control over the situation or the stress sources, they attempted to approach those issues via problem-focused coping; when they perceived themselves as having a low degree of control over the situation, however, they tended to use avoidance as a means of reducing their stress. When they were in conflict with their coaches and teammates, for example, they would try to engage in conversation with them; in way of contrast, in scenarios in which they had a low degree of control over the situation (e.g., a bad call by the referee, or in dealing with other people's expectations) they showed avoidance in dealing with those stressors.

During the training period, athletes sought out social support from their close others and perceived having someone to talk to as helping them deal with their stressors. Social support was not widely reported as a coping strategy, however, during the competition period. The players tended to be away from their social support network when participating in international tournaments, which could explain their perceptions of having lost social support during the competition period.

The current findings carried with them practical implications. As was mentioned above, since athletes' culture- and sport-specific contexts are potential influencers of their stress sources, practitioners need to understand athletes' cultural backgrounds, sport-specific contexts, and sport-specific, stress-related events. If a young athlete wants to be a professional tennis player, for example, practitioners can advise the youth on the nature of professional tennis culture, such as having to be interviewed in English after the match, and suggest to them that they prepare and hone the off-court skills they will need in order to deal with the obligations which go along with being a professional tennis player. As athletes' cognitive appraisal of, and perceived control over, the situation was seen to have influenced not only their stress levels but also their coping strategies, identifying athletes' cognitive appraisal methodologies may help athletes develop coping skills and strategies tailored to certain stressors. Finally, as athletes tend to be away from their social support networks during competition periods, practitioners and close others should seek to open non-traditional communication channels (e.g., instant chat, e-mail) with athletes while they are travelling, which would better enable them to provide support to the athletes when necessary.

The current study was the first, to the author's knowledge, to have examined Asian professional tennis players' stress sources and coping strategies during both the training and the competition periods. The findings identify some of the specific influences an athlete's culture and sport-specific context might have on their perceived stress sources and selection of coping strategies. Out of 10 participants, nine were from non-English speaking nations; more than half of these individuals (N=5), discussed having to communicate in English as a major stress sources of being a professional tennis player. In addition, because of the financial support system for professional players, the respondents did not report any financial concerns or worries. Those findings indicated that more research is needed to identify the influences the athletes' environments and culture-related issues exert on their perceived stress sources. Moreover, every sport has its own league system. Understanding the sport-specific stressors will allow practitioners to better assist athletes' in assessing their subjective well-being and in affecting performance enhancement. The way in which athletes recognize and cope with stress has been a topic of interest for many years, and findings have frequently shown that athletes utilize a diverse range of coping strategies (e.g., Roth and Cohen, 1986; Woodman and Hardy, 2001). The effectiveness of various coping strategies in dealing with specific types of stressors, however, has not yet received much attention in scholarly studies. The current study revealed that athletes' perceived psychological skills and the extent and strength of their social support network were helpful to them in dealing with competition stressors, and other stress sources encountered during the training period; the effectiveness of other types of coping strategies, however, was not assessed. Understanding which coping strategies are effective for specific situations could help athletes deal with those specific events; to do so, more research is needed.

There are several limitations to the current study. Since the data were collected from a small number of participants, the findings of the present study could not be generalized as quantitative research findings. The current results did provide an in-depth understanding of Asian professional tennis players' experiences, however, and those findings could help other athletes who are in a situation similar to that of the current participants. Data collection for the current study was carried out while athletes were engaged in their competition period. For this reason, athletes' responses related to the stress sources they experience during the training period relied on their memories and previous experiences, and the results might have been influenced by participants' recall bias and memory decays.

CONCLUSION

The results from the current study reveal that Asian professional tennis players' perceived a range of psychological, physiological, social, and environmental stress sources, and that they employed psychological skills, active coping, searching for social support, and avoidance to deal with those stress sources. The findings also revealed differences and similarities in stress sources and coping styles between the athletes included in the current study and those interviewed as part of previous studies, and provided some evidence that the culture- and sport-specific contexts exert some influence on athletes' perceived stress sources.

REFERENCES

Allison, M. T., and Meyer, C. (1988). Career problems and retirement among elite athletes: The female tennis professional. *Sociology of Sport Journal, 5*, 212-222.

Anshel, M. H., and Kassidis, S. N. (1997). Copings styles and situational appraisals predictors of coping strategies following stressful events in sport as a function of gender and skill level. *British Journal of Sport Psychology, 88*, 263-276.

Anshel, M. H., and Wells, B. (2000). Sources of acute stress and coping styles in competitive sport. *Anxiety, Stress, and Coping, 13*, 1-26.

Anshel, M. H., Williams, L. R. T., and Horge, K. (1997). Cross-cultural and gender differnces o coping style in sport. *International Journal of Sport Psychology, 28*, 141-156.

Bhalla, J. A., and Weiss, M. R. (2010). A cross-cultural perspective of parental influence on female adolescents' achievement beliefs and behaviors in sport and school domains. *Research Quarterly for Exercise and Sport, 81*, 494-505.

Carver, C. S., Scheier, M. F., and Weintraub, J. W. (1989). Assessing coping strategies: A theatrically based approach. *Journal of Personality and Social Psychology, 56,* 267-283.

Cohn, P. J. (1990). An exploratory study on sources of stress and athlete burnout in young golf. *The Sport Psychologists, 4,* 95-106.

Croker, P. R. E. (1992). Managing stress by competitive athletes, way of coping. *International Journal of Sport Psychology, 23,* 161-175.

Fletcher, D., and Hanton, S. (2003). Sources of organizational stress in elite sport performers. *The Sport Psychologists, 17,* 175-195.

Giacobbi, P., Lynn, T. K., Wetherington, J., Bodendorf, J., and Langley, B. (2004). Stress and coping during the transition to university for first-year female athletes. *The Sport Psychologists, 18,* 1-20.

Gould, D., Diffenbach, K., and Moffett, A. (2002). Psychological characteristics and their development in Olympic champions. *Journal of Applied Sport Psychology, 14,* 172-204.

Haney, C. J., and Long, B. C. (1995). Coping effectiveness: a path analysis of self-efficacy, control, coping, and performance in sport competitors. *Journal of Applied Social Psychology, 25,* 1726-1746.

Hellriegel, D. J. W. and Woodman, R. W. (1992). *Organizational behaviour (6th ed).* St. Paul, MN; West Publishing Company.

Hodaya, D. and Anshel, M. H. (2003). Sources of stress and coping among Australian and Indonesian athletes. *Australian Journal of Psychology, 55,* 159-165.

Kamphoff, C., Gill, D. G., Araki, K., and Hammond, C. C. (2010). A Content Analysis of Cultural Diversity in the Association for Applied Sport Psychology's Conference Programs. *Journal of Applied Sport Psychology, 22,* 231-245.

Kint, K. A., and Weiss, M. R. (1986). Dropping in and dropping out: participation motives of current and former youth athletes. *Canadian Journal of Applied Sport Sciences, 11,* 106-114.

Lazarus, R. S., and Folkman, S. (1984). *Stress, appraisal, and coping.* New York: Springer.

Nicholls, A. R., and Polman, R. C. (2007). Coping in sport: a systematic review. *Journal of Sport Science, 25,* 11-31.

Nicholls, A. R., Jones, R., Polman, R. C. J., and Borkoles, E. (2009). Acute sport-related stressors, coping, and emotions among professional rugby union players. *The Sport Psychologist, 20,* 314-329.

Nicholls, A. R., Levy, A. R., Grice, A and Polman, R. C. J. (2009). Stress, appraisals, training, and competition. *European Journal of Spot Science, 9,* 285-293.

Patton, M. Q. (2002). *Qualitative research and evaluation methods* (3rd ed). California: Sage Publications, Inc.

Polman, R. (2012). Elite athletes' experiences of coping with stress. In J. Thatcher, M. Jones, and D. Lavallee (Eds.) *Coping and emotion in sport* (pp. 284-301). Routledge: New York.

Roth, S., and Cohen, L. J. (1986). Approach, avoidance, and coping with stress. *American Psychologist, 7,* 813-819.

Scalnan, T. K., Stein, G. L., and Ravizza, K. (1989). An in-depth study of former elite figure skaters: III. Sources of stress. *Journal of Sport and Exercise Psychology, 11*, 54-64.

Smith, R. E., Ptacek, J. T., and Smoll, F. L. (1992). Sensation seeking, stress, and adolescent injuries: a test of stress-buffering, risk-taking, and coping skills hypothesis. *Journal of Personality and Social Psychology, 62*, 1016-1024.

Woodman, T., and Hardy, L. (2001). A case study of organizational stress in elite sport. *Journal of Applied Sport Psychology, 13,* 207-238.

Young, J. A., Pearce, A. J., Kane, R., and Pain, M. (2006). Leaving the professional tennis circuit: Exploratory study of experiences and reactions from elite female athletes. *British Journal of Sport Medicine, 40*, 477-483.

INDEX

F

S